A59-5022

12-8-59

A HISTORY OF GHANA

A HISTORY OF GHANA

BY

W. E. F. WARD

Ruskin House

GEORGE ALLEN AND UNWIN LTD

MUSEUM STREET LONDON

FIRST PUBLISHED IN 1948
SECOND IMPRESSION 1952
REVISED SECOND EDITION (THIRD IMPRESSION) 1958

*Previously published under the title of
'A History of The Gold Coast'*

PRINTED IN GREAT BRITAIN
in 11 on 12 point Georgian type
BY THE BLACKFRIARS PRESS LTD
LEICESTER

PREFACE TO THE FIRST EDITION

EVERY one who writes on Gold Coast history should begin, after the fashion of the country, by pouring a libation and sacrificing a sheep in honour of Dr. Claridge, whose monumental *History of the Gold Coast and Ashanti* is not likely to be superseded. Though I have gone direct to many of the sources which Dr. Claridge used, I have based great parts of my narrative on his, particularly when describing diplomatic negotiations and wars between the British and the Ashanti.

There can be no question of superseding Claridge's great work; but I have tried to supplement it. Claridge's book was published in 1915. Since then much has happened in the Gold Coast which should be recorded, and much has been added to our understanding of African thought and custom, notably by the researches of Captain Rattray, Dr. Fortes and Dr. Field. I have tried to bring the narrative up to date, and to take advantage of the new light thrown by this modern research not only upon anthropology but upon history.

Secondly, as I have hinted above, Claridge is fullest and most interesting when dealing with military operations and with the negotiations between rival Governments. I have compressed the story of military and diplomatic affairs to leave more room for social and economic history.

Thirdly, although this book is based only to a slight degree on original research among European archives, it does incorporate the results of my own research among African traditional history. Rattray has published some Ashanti tribal histories in his *Ashanti Law and Constitution*. I have done similar work in other Ashanti States, and in Akim, Akwapim, Adansi and Akwamu; and, as footnotes will show, I have made considerable use of these traditions.

The European reader may wonder what these tribal memories are worth. Of course, they vary considerably in fullness and in length. As a general rule, Akan village traditions go back at least to the time of Napoleon, and any important town will have traditions going back a hundred years earlier. The traditions of the paramount chief of a big State will usually take us back to the

5

time of Cromwell; and in a few cases we can get isolated facts which must date from Queen Elizabeth's reign.

The question of their reliability cannot be answered briefly. The first thing to bear in mind is that to the Gold Coast African, with his ancestor-worship and intense reverence for the past, the dividing line between past and present is not nearly as clear as to the Englishman. The relationship between the present Asantehene and Osei Tutu is quite different from that between Mr. Churchill and the first Duke of Marlborough. Mr. Churchill will feel admiration for his great ancestor, pride in being of his family, and determination to be worthy of him. But the Asantehene will feel himself in constant contact with Osei Tutu; Osei Tutu is present at his side guiding him; it is hardly too much to say that on occasion he *is* Osei Tutu.

To the African, therefore, history is living in a way it cannot be to the European. The recital of history goes right to the roots of the African's emotions. An elder once gave me the story of a gallant feat of arms performed by an ancestor of his seventy years ago. He told me the story in a voice restrained into monotony; but when he had ended, he broke down, got up hastily and left the circle, and walked up and down outside for twenty minutes striving to recover his self-control. When he came back, he apologized: "A man's tears," he said, "come from his own head, not from other people's; I can talk about the general history of the tribe without weeping, but when my own family is concerned the tears have to come."

It can be imagined that the African is not disposed to reveal such sacred matters lightly, either to a stranger or to one of his own tribe whom he thinks likely to fail in respect. I have often spent a whole month in a village before the chief and his elders could make up their minds to trust me. And it is a common complaint among the older people that the young folk of today are not interested in tradition, and therefore cannot be told it. In one village which I visited there lived one of my own students, who was born and bred in the place. After I had stayed there a month the elders agreed to tell me their history; but they would not allow the student to be present. I had explained most carefully that my reason for wanting to learn their history was that I wanted to teach it to African students, and some day perhaps print it in a book. They were adamant. "Yes," they said, "that is all right; we will tell you, and you can tell other people. But it is not the custom for us to talk of these matters before young people, and we are not going to do it. He must stay outside." The sad result of this is that the traditional history is vanishing from the national memory; for those who know it die without passing on their knowledge.

I need not emphasize how grateful I am for the unforgettable hospitality I have had from these old men and women, who have entrusted me with their traditional knowledge, which they could not always bring themselves to impart to their own children, and which they have recalled only at the cost of great emotional suffering.

Now, if we ignore this side of the question, and look at the material thus collected with the cold eye of the professional historian, what is it worth? We must recognise that it is 'drum and trumpet' history, a string of names adorned with picturesque incidents of migration and war. It is seldom that we can get much light on personalities, still more seldom that we can get any information on social and economic forces. We find, too, that chronology is weak. There are a few outstanding events (notably the battles of Akantamasu in 1826 and Jukwa in 1873) which are used as time-pegs; but when we are given a list of chiefs we cannot always be sure of the order in which they lived, and we can hardly ever be sure how long a chief reigned. We have to do much cross-checking between one tradition and another. These are limitations which we must accept.

On the other hand, although there is a natural tendency to glorify one's own side at the expense of the enemy, the traditions of different tribes corroborate each other to a remarkable extent. The elders of one town, for example, told me how the Ashanti once ordered them and another town to supply contingents to make up a military expedition. The expedition was a success, but their chief, named A, was killed in the moment of victory; and his successor, B, took over command on the battlefield, being formally enstooled on the army's return home. Subsequently I visited the other town, some fifty miles away, belonging to a different tribe, with no political connection with the first: it was apparently a pure accident that their troops on this one occasion had been brigaded together. The people of the second town gave me the same story, the details agreeing; and they mentioned that the chief of their colleagues was killed. I asked if they could tell me his name. They thought for a minute, and then said that his name was B, and his successor's name was A. In other words, they had got the two names reversed; and this very discrepancy seemed to me evidence that both narratives were entirely honest. Another instance is given by the story of Akwamu. I have told in this book how the Akwamu captured Christiansborg Castle from the Danes, an incident of which the Akwamu today are naturally very proud. They told me the story, their version being substantially the same as that given by Claridge from European accounts, but with one or two discrepancies in detail. At the end of the story they asked me triumphantly if I had ever heard that tale before? I replied that as a matter of fact I had, and asked them if they would like to hear the white men's version. Their faces fell somewhat, but they politely said they would; so I told them. When I stopped, they said, "Ah, yes; but of course you have one or two points wrong." Then an old man rose in his place and said simply, "I am a descendant of the chief who carried out that deed. I heard the story from my grandfather when I was a child. What the white man has just told you is exactly what my grandfather told me." And he sat down.

I am sure, therefore, that the traditional narratives I have collected are honestly related. I have always made a point of explaining before the narrative is begun, "I know there are some things you may not wish to tell a stranger. I may ask embarrassing questions in my ignorance. But if you say quite frankly that you do not want to tell me, I shall quite understand. Only please do not invent something merely to satisfy me." I believe that they have taken me at my word; I know that in many places they have done so. There are passages in tradition which are officially ignored: acts of cowardice or sacrilege, defeats which involved the loss of the Stool. These are never mentioned, and if necessary there may be a little judicious faking of a list of chiefs or a genealogical table to conceal the gap. Once or twice I have been given the official version of a tribe's history, and subsequently I have had the true version whispered into my ear behind locked doors, on condition that I promised not to reveal it to a soul or to make any use of it. In fulfilment of that promise I refrain from giving here any indication of what the information was, lest I should unwittingly give a clue to its source. I can say, however, that I have never had confidential information of this kind which would have affected general history; it has always had merely local importance.

Although this book thus incorporates more African material than Claridge, my judgments do not usually differ widely from his. I concur with him in many of his severe strictures on the mistakes of the British authorities on the Gold Coast. I think it only fair to point out here, however, that in past generations the British authorities on the coast were working under difficulties which we can hardly imagine. Tropical medicine was in its infancy. Cape Coast or Accra were as devoid of the comforts brought by modern science as the remotest bush village of today. Worst of all, the British officials were lonely with a loneliness surpassing anything to be found in the Gold Coast now. There are still plenty of lonely men in the bush. But even if in their ordinary routine they may not see another white face for weeks at a time, they know that not so very far away there is a district headquarters, where there will be a District Commissioner, and perhaps a doctor and a man from Cadbury's or the United Africa Company. If necessary they can go there and talk things over. But eighty years ago, British officials on the coast were few, and their service was often short. It was quite possible for a Governor to have no one at all to advise him who knew anything about the country, and no one whom he could spare to go into the bush for some weeks to find out what was happening inland. He had to make his decisions alone, on the basis of scanty and unreliable information. Even today it is not always easy for the Englishman in West Africa to be as calm and judicious as he would like to be. It is not surprising that Governors of a former generation sometimes made serious mistakes. This should in justice be borne in mind when we criticize the errors of Messrs. Pine or Simpson or Salmon or Pope Hennessy. More recent Governments can hardly claim indulgence on this ground.

I should like to express my thanks for the help I have received from paramount chiefs, chiefs and elders in many parts of the Akan country, who have given me information on their traditional histories, and in some cases have themselves collected for me the histories of their subordinate Stools. I have memories of so many such acts of kindness that it is better not to mention names.

I have other obligations. To my colleagues, Messrs. D. A. Chapman and V. Ayivor for help with Ewe history, and Mr. M. A. Ribeiro for help with Fante, and to the Rev. John Bardsley for introducing me to his engaging predecessor, the Rev. Thomas Thompson, A.M. To many friends who have contributed information on minor points, and to Messrs. K. Brakatu Ateko, J. Henley Coussey, J. C. de Graft Johnson, and R. Awoonor Williams for reading and criticizing the book in proof. To the late Captain Norman Young for allowing me to use the material he had collected in his researches among the Avatime people of Togoland. To Mr. G. B. Cartland, for guiding me in the history of the seven eventful years since I left the Gold Coast. Lastly, to the Gold Coast Government for opening to me its files and district record books, and to the Principal and Council of Achimota College for encouraging me to undertake the study and travel on which the book is based. I alone am responsible for the use I have made of my information, and nothing in the book is to be taken as representing the views either of the college, of the Gold Coast Government, or of the Colonial Office.

1948.

PREFACE TO THE SECOND EDITION

THOUGH the war delayed its publication until 1948, the typescript of this book was ready eight years earlier; I wrote most of it at desperate speed in the Gold Coast while awaiting a transfer to Mauritius. The concluding chapters had to be revised while the book was in the press to take account of the constitutional changes of 1946.

The British territory of the Gold Coast is now the independent State of Ghana, and the last three chapters of this edition, though they incorporate material from the last two chapters of the first edition, carry the story up to Independence Day. This edition is thus considerably longer than the first.

In those distant days of 1940, few of us expected that independence would come quite so soon. An attentive reader will see many signs that this book was written by an Englishman who assumed that British rule was likely to last for a long time. To go through the whole book altering such passages would mean an unconscionable amount of toil for author and printer, with very little gain for the reader. It seems better to leave the first thirteen chapters of the book much as they were, and leave the reader to make his own allowances. There may even be some interest in comparing the 1940 and the 1957 points of view. I have revised the reflections on education at the end of Chapter IX and on the Aggrey case in Chapter XI, and I have amended a few passages to take account of recent additions to our knowledge.

I have called the country sometimes the Gold Coast, sometimes Ghana, whichever the context makes appropriate. In the first thirteen chapters I have allowed the name Gold Coast to stand throughout.

I have to thank friends in the Ghana Office in London and in the Colonial Office for their help with sources of information, and the Comptroller of Her Majesty's Stationery Office for permission to reprint passages from the Coussey Report and other Stationery Office publications. Since the events recorded towards the end of the book have been matters of acute controversy, it is more than ever necessary for me to say that the account I have given is entirely my own, and is not to be taken as representing the views either of the Government of Ghana, or of the Government of the United Kingdom — nor have I any reason to suppose that it represents the views of Her Majesty's Opposition in either country.

1957   W. E. F. WARD

List of Authorities consulted

The more important authorities are asterisked

A.—WORKS CONTAINING FIRST-HAND HISTORICAL INFORMATION—

*R. S. Rattray: Tribes of the Ashanti Hinterland
*R. S. Rattray: Ashanti Law and Constitution
J. M. Sarbah: Fanti Customary Laws
*J. M. Sarbah: Fanti National Constitution
A. W. Cardinall: The Natives of the Northern Territories of the Gold Coast
*F. C. Fuller: A Vanished Dynasty—Ashanti
C. W. Welman: The Native States of the Gold Coast—Peki
*Carl Reindorf: History of the Gold Coast and Asante
M. J. Field: Social Organization of the Ga People
*E. F. Tamakloe: A Brief History of the Dagbamba People
St. J. Eyre-Smith: A Brief Review of the History and Social Organization of
    the Peoples of the Northern Territories of the Gold Coast
J. Withers Gill (translator): A Short History of the Dagomba Tribe
J. Withers Gill (translator): A Short History of Salaga
J. Withers Gill (translator): The Moshi Tribe—A Short History
Martin Wight: The Gold Coast Legislative Council
*J. J. Crooks: Records of the Gold Coast Settlements, 1750-1874
Louis Tauxier: Le Noir de Bondougou
G. D. Chamberlain: A Brief Account of the Brissa Language
*W. Bosman: A New and Accurate Description of the Coast of Guinea
B. Cruikshank: Eighteen years on the Gold Coast of Africa
*T. E. Bowdich: Mission from Cape Coast Castle to Ashantee
W. Meredith: Account of the Gold Coast of Africa
J. Dupuis: Journal of a Residence in Ashantee
Brackenbury and Huyshe: Fanti and Ashanti
J. B. Danquah: Cases in Akan Law
    (together with departmental reports, Blue Books and official files in the Gold
    Coast and in London, and * Parliamentary command papers on Gold Coast
    and Ashanti affairs from 1874 to 1901. The Gold Coast Government has
    also published an anonymous * Enquiry into the Constitution and Organiza-
    tion of the Dagbon Kingdom)

B.—OTHER WORKS—

A. W. Cardinall: The Gold Coast 1931
A. W. Cardinall: A Bibliography of the Gold Coast
Laws of the Gold Coast, 1920 and 1936 editions.
A. S. Southon: Gold Coast Methodism
F. D. Walker: Thomas Birch Freeman
R. S. Rattray: Ashanti
R. S. Rattray: Religion and Art in Ashanti
*W. W. Claridge: A History of the Gold Coast and Ashanti
Casely Hayford: Gold Coast Native Institutions
*A. B. Ellis: A History of the Gold Coast of West Africa
A. B. Ellis: The Tshi-speaking Peoples of the Gold Coast
A. B. Ellis: The Ewe-speaking Peoples of the Slave Coast
Lady Lugard: A Tropical Dependency
E. W. Bovill: Caravans of the old Sahara
Sir Alan Burns: A History of Nigeria
F. W. H. Migeod: The Languages of West Africa

13

S. Christaller: Dictionary of the Asante and Fante Language
M. Delafosse: Les Noirs d'Afrique
J. J. Williams: Hebrewisms of West Africa
*J. W. Blake: European Beginnings in West Africa
*R. H. Major: Prince Henry the Navigator
E. Prestage: The Portuguese Pioneers
D. Ogg: England in the Reign of Charles II
E. Lipson: Economic History of England
M. J. Field: Religion and Medicine of the Ga People
F. R. Irvine: Plants of the Gold Coast
*E. Martin: The British West African Settlements 1750-1821
Sir Hugh Clifford: The Gold Coast Regiment in the East African Campaign
*Lord Hailey: An African Survey
Martin Wight: The Development of the Legislative Council, 1606-1945
The Gold Coast Handbook, editions of 1924, 1927, 1937
Annual Report on the Gold Coast, 1946
Eva L. R. Meyerowitz: Akan Traditions of Origin
David E. Apter: The Gold Coast in Transition
P. T. Bauer: West African Trade
F. M. Bourret: The Gold Coast
Kwame Nkrumah: Ghana
Report of the Commission of Enquiry into Disturbances in the Gold Coast, 1948,
    Colonial No. 231
Statement by His Majesty's Government on the Report of the Commission of
    Enquiry into Disturbances in the Gold Coast, 1948, Colonial No. 232
Report of the Commission on the Marketing of West African Cocoa, Cmd. 5845
Report to His Excellency the Governor by the Committee on Constitutional
    Reform, Colonial No. 248
Statement by His Majesty's Government on the Report of the Committee on
    Constitutional Reform, Colonial No. 250
Report of the Commission of Enquiry into Wenchi Affairs (Accra 1952)
Report of the Constitutional Adviser (Accra 1955)
Report of the Achimota Conference (Accra 1956)
Constitutional Proposals for Gold Coast Independence and Statement on the
    Report of the Constitutional Adviser and the Report of the Achimota
    Conference (Accra 1956)
The Government's Revised Constitutional Proposals for Gold Coast Independence
    (Accra 1956)
The Proposed Constitution of Ghana, Cmd. 71
Government proposals in regard to the future Constitution and Control of
    Statutory Boards and Corporations in the Gold Coast, with the Report of the
    Commission of Enquiry into the Affairs of the Cocoa Purchasing Company
    Limited (Accra 1956)
Gold Coast Legislative Assembly Debates

A Note on Gold Coast Place Names

As a rough and ready guide to pronunciation it may be assumed
that vowels are pronounced as in Italian, and consonants as in
English. All vowels are tense, not slack as in Southern English.
There is a great difference between the African pronunciation of
the name *Aburi* and the English (not Scottish) drawl of 'Aboory'.
There is no accent in Gold Coast languages.

The vowel *a*, when preceding the vowels *i* or *u*, is pronounced like a French *é*, as in Aburi, Asiakwa. The combinations *gy* (in Akan) and *dz* (in Ga and Ewe) are pronounced like English *j* in *junk*; *ky* (in Akan) and *ts* (in Ga and Ewe) are pronounced like English *ch* in *church*. Final *n* is always nasal, more or less like English *ring*. *N* is also nasal when preceding *k*, as in the common name *Nkwanta*.

Accra (pronounced with the accent on the second syllable to rhyme with hurrah) is the Anglicized version of the Akan name *Nkran*. The people of Accra called themselves Ga. The *ga* are a kind of big black ant; not the aggressive and myriad driver ant, but a kind of ant three times as big, usually seen ambling peaceably along in parties of about a hundred. If they are interfered with they make a noise like a kettle boiling over, and immediately counter-attack; and their bite is very painful. The moral is plain; leave us alone and we will leave you alone; but touch us and look out for trouble. The Akan peoples call this ant *nkran*, and for some reason it is the Akan name, and not the native Ga name, that has become accepted in English usage.

The following are some common elements in place names:

-*su*, river (e.g. *Odasu*).

-*so*, upon (e.g. the common name *Beposo*, on the hill).

-*ase*, beneath (e.g. *Odumase*, under the *odum* tree).

Nkwanta, a fork in the road; *Nkwantanan*, cross-roads.

-*krom* (Akan), or -*man* (Ga), a town (e.g. *Amanokrom*, *Amasaman*).

Many names are really sentences, more or less abbreviated, referring sometimes to some circumstance connected with the town's beginnings. *Asiakwa* means 'we have stopped here in vain'. *Kukurantumi*, 'we have carried it (i.e. the stool) till we could carry it no farther'. *Kuntanase*, 'you have done your fighting; now sit down'. The common name *Brofo Yedru* means 'the white men are tough'; it usually marks the site of a British victory in some skirmish. Some names are less prosaic. *Chichiwere* means 'consolation'; *Nyamebekyere*, 'God will show'. There is a tiny village in Ashanti named *Mensofwefwenyame*, 'I too am seeking God'; and I once stayed in an Ivory Coast hamlet called *Kwasea-nni-adwene*, 'A fool has no sense'.

In this book I have kept to the well-known English forms of

familiar names such as Akim and Akwapim. I write the more accurate *Gyaman,* however, instead of the old-fashioned English form *Jaman*; and generally in less common names I use the more accurate form, e.g. *Kyikyiwere,* not *Chichiwere.*

CONTENTS

MAPS

ILLUSTRATIONS

CHAPTER I

THE FACE OF THE LAND

THE first European sea captains, coasting slowly and cautiously along the West African surf, named the different stretches of coast according to the principal cargoes they found there. Today, the very names of the Grain Coast and the Slave Coast are half forgotten; the French colony of the Ivory Coast exports only a negligible quantity of ivory; but the Gold Coast still contains some of the world's richest gold mines, and is an important source of supply. The Portuguese in the fifteenth century found gold within a few miles of the sea. Today nearly all the gold produced comes from inland. The great recent developments in the production have been made possible by the use of modern machinery for the extraction of gold from deep lodes; though river gravels still yield enough gold not merely to repay the small scale African prospector for his efforts, but to pay a dividend to London mining companies.

The modern British territory of the Gold Coast is composed of the two Colonies of the Gold Coast and Ashanti, and the Protectorate of the Northern Territories. After the war of 1914 a narrow strip of the adjoining small German colony of Togoland was attached to the Gold Coast under a mandate from the League of Nations, the greater part of the territory of Togoland, including its port of Lome, being assigned to the French. British mandated Togoland is administered as part of the Gold Coast. The British territory on the coast was gradually extended by a series of treaties with the African rulers during the first half of the nineteenth century, and the combined territory was proclaimed a Crown colony in 1874. Ashanti was annexed after a series of wars, and became a Crown colony in 1901, and the Protectorate of the Northern Territories was established in the same year.[1] The total area of the Gold Coast apart from Togoland is some 78,000 square miles; of this total the Colony and Ashanti are almost exactly equal in

[1] In this book I shall use the term 'Gold Coast' to mean the whole of the area under the one administration, including the two colonies, the protectorate, and unless otherwise stated the mandated area also; the four constituent parts shall be 'the Colony', Ashanti, the Northern Territories, and British Togoland.

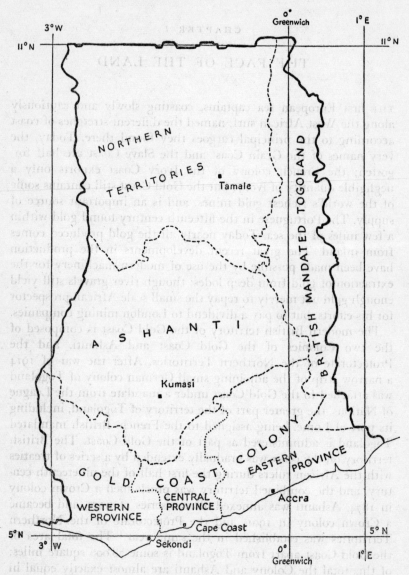

FIG. I. The Gold Coast—political divisions. The division of the Colony into three provinces has recently been changed: the Central Province has been abolished so that the Colony is now divided between the Eastern and Western Provinces only.

This map also shows the latitude and longitude.

containing 24,000 each, and the Northern Territories 30,000. British mandated Togoland contains 13,000 square miles.[2]

The frontiers of the Gold Coast were hastily drawn, in keen competition with France and Germany, during the scramble for Africa in the closing years of the nineteenth century. The result is that the Gold Coast has no natural unity, either from the point of view of physical geography or from that of population. Several of the important nations inhabiting the Gold Coast stretch into adjoining territories. The land of the Gyaman people stretches forty miles over the western border into the Ivory Coast; and in the Ivory Coast live the paramount chief and all but one of his immediate subordinates. The paramount chief of the Dagomba lives in Togoland, though as long as the British mandate lasts he is reunited to his people. The greater part of the ancient Moshi kingdom is outside the northern frontier. The south-east corner of the Colony and the southern section of British Togoland include a small outlying section of the Ewe people, most of whom dwell in French Togoland.

The surface of the land in this part of West Africa consists of an undulating plateau, falling in a series of steps to the coastal plain. The river Niger, rising in the mountains behind Sierra Leone, runs north-eastward, away from the sea, for 1,000 miles till it reaches the neighbourhood of Timbuktu; there it turns first south-eastward and then southward, and through its enormous delta falls into the Gulf of Guinea. The southern slope of the plateau in this great bend of the Niger is drained by several streams, the biggest of which is the river Volta. The Volta has a total length of some 900 miles. Its name was given it by the Portuguese, on account, it is said, of its meandering course. If so, the name is not very appropriate, for the lower course of the river runs in reaches of broad sweeping curves, rather unusually free from sudden loops and meanderings. The African nations of the low part of the basin know the river under the name of Firao. The Volta is formed by the junction of two main streams, the Black Volta and the White Volta, which rise about 200 miles south of Timbuktu and which flow south 200 miles apart, the Black Volta on the west and the White Volta on the east. As it approaches Ashanti, the Black

___

[2] That is to say, the Northern Territories are the size of Scotland, and Ashanti and the Colony together nearly the size of England.

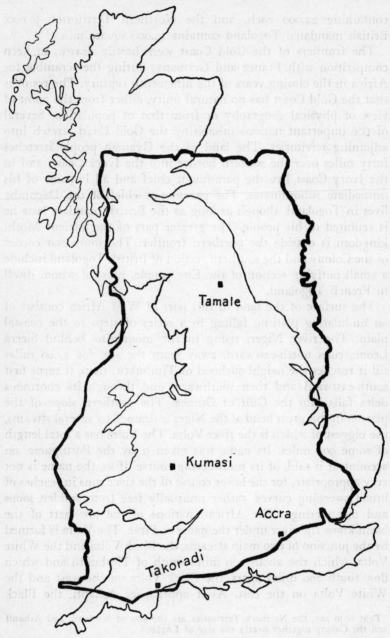

FIG. 2. The Gold Coast and Great Britain showing comparative sizes.

Volta is turned aside by a granite ridge, and in some confusion attempts to make its way eastward; eventually, after making an abrupt turn and retracing its journey first west and then thirty miles north, it succeeds in joining the White Volta at a point 250 miles from the sea, and the united river continues its southerly and south-easterly course to fall into the Gulf of Guinea not far from the eastern boundary of the Gold Coast. The river mouth is an estuary, with the inevitable bar. There is little in the way of a delta, though on the east there is a system of lagoons and wandering mangrove creeks, which may at one time have been connected with the river and have been silted up later. The Gold Coast bears exactly the same relation to the Volta that Nigeria bears to the Niger; it consists of the lower part of the Volta basin, together with the basins of a number of smaller rivers which take their rise south of the Black Volta bend.

There is no very high land in the Gold Coast. The sources of the Volta are only 1,200 feet above sea level, and the highest hills in the country are between 2,500 and 3,000 feet high. The most conspicuous feature on the physical map is the Kwahu plateau, which terminates in an abrupt scarp running for 180 miles from north-west to south-east, ending some forty miles from the sea due north of Accra. The Kwahu scarp shows in many places a sheer cliff face, rising several hundred feet above the forested plains at its foot. It throws out at right angles, to the south-west, a number of spurs; and the seaward end of the scarp is shod by the Akwapim ridge, which runs parallel to the spurs right away north-eastward into Togoland. The Volta cuts through the Akwapim ridge in a narrow and beautiful wooded gorge.

The Kwahu scarp is important for many reasons. It forms the south-west boundary of the Volta basin; its northern face is drained by the Afram, a tributary of the Volta, while the southern face gives rise to a whole row of smaller rivers flowing direct to the sea. On the geological map the Kwahu scarp is the edge of a large compact area of non-metalliferous 'Voltaian' rocks—clays, shales, sandstones, and the like—while its spurs and the valleys between them are composed of strips of various rocks, containing gold, manganese, aluminium and diamonds. The scarp is equally important in its influence on rainfall and vegetation. The prevailing wind for most of the year is from the south-west; it comes laden with

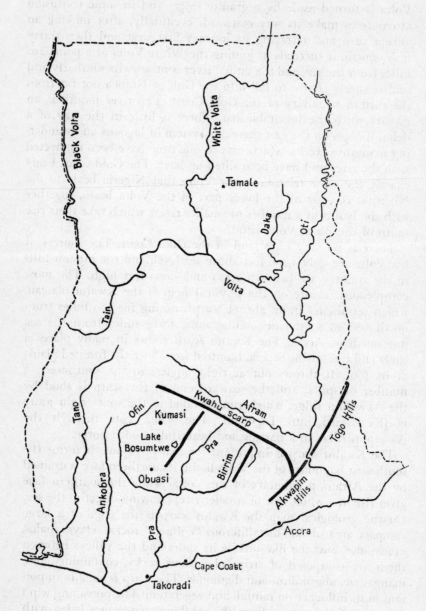

FIG. 3. The Gold Coast—Physical.

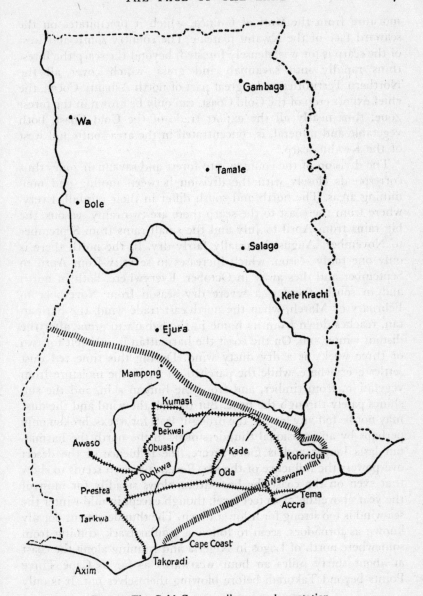

FIG. 4. The Gold Coast—railways and vegetation.
The hachured line marks the boundary of the closed forest zone, the cocoa-producing area. The importance of the Kwahu Scarp, marked in FIG. 3, is brought out in this map and in the linguistic map, FIG. 5.

moisture from the Gulf of Guinea, which it precipitates on the seaward face of the Kwahu plateau. The country south and west of the scarp is (or was) densely forested; beyond the scarp the forest thins rapidly into savannah and grass, which cover all the Northern Territories and a great part of north Ashanti. Cocoa, the chief export crop of the Gold Coast, can only be grown in the forest zone; thus nearly all the export trade of the Gold Coast, both vegetable and mineral, is concentrated in the area south and west of the Kwahu scarp.[3]

The division of the country into forest and savannah zones thus corresponds closely with the division between mining and non-mining areas. The north and south differ in their rainfall. Everywhere from the coast to the scarp there are two rainy seasons, the big rains from April to July and the small rains from September to November; August is usually fairly dry. In the north there is only one rainy season, which increases in severity from April to September and dies away in October. Everywhere, both in north and in south, there is a severe dry season from November to February or March, when the north-east trade wind, the harmattan, reaches down from its home in the Sahara to grope after the distant winter sun. On the coast the harmattan is only felt for two or three weeks as a dry dusty wind. During this time red dust settles everywhere, while the parched air sucks the moisture from vegetation, from timber, and from the human skin, and the sun shines palely through the haze. But though the wind and the dust may not be felt any longer, the drought lasts for weeks, broken only perhaps by an occasional thunderstorm. In the north the harmattan lasts longer and is more severe; the influence of the desert overpowers the influence of the sea. Recent research seems to show that even on the coast the harmattan blows steadily for most of the year above the 5,000 feet level, though except in mid-winter the sea-wind is too strong for it lower down. The thunderstorms, locally known as tornadoes, seem to follow a regular track, coming from somewhere north of Lagos in Nigeria and running along the coast at about thirty miles an hour westwards as far as Cape Three Points beyond Takoradi before blowing themselves out. It is only

[3] Not quite all. The Northern Territories have always had an export trade in cattle and shea butter, and since 1936 several mining companies have turned their attention to the newly-discovered gold-fields there.

the development of air transport that is causing the meteorology of the Gold Coast to be seriously studied, and there is yet a great deal to be learnt on the subject.

There is something of the same uncertainty over the question of zones of vegetation, a question so clearly bound up with that of climate, especially with rainfall. The Gold Coast is not primarily a forested land, though the economic importance of the forest zone (which happens also to be the mining zone) is so much greater than that of the rest of the country. The forest occupies a triangle, with its base on the western frontier and its apex touching the Volta about seventy miles from the sea. On the western frontier the forest stretches from the sea through three degrees of latitude; on the east, the Volta runs through less than twenty miles of forest country. Outside this triangular area there are isolated strips and patches of forest here and there on hill-sides and along river banks, but two-thirds of the country is savannah or grassland.[4] There is a grass strip along the coast, gradually widening from a few yards near Takoradi to fifty miles at the Volta. Nearly all Togoland, and the whole of the Volta basin, is grass or savannah.

The question is whether the forest area is naturally decreasing or not. There is no doubt that it is decreasing through artificial interference. A fifth of the forest has been cleared for cocoa farms, and the gold mines have cleared such large areas for firewood that they are beginning to feel considerably inconvenienced through the remoteness of fresh fuel supplies. But it is not certain, as has sometimes been stated, that in this part of West Africa there is a progressive desiccation taking place, so that the desert is advancing on the grass and the grass is advancing on the forest. The local encroachments on the forest that undoubtedly do occur are usually due to farming operations. Shifting cultivation is universal, and a farmer living just outside the forest is under a great temptation to cut into the forest when clearing a site for his new farm. The surface layer of forest soil is very rich in humus and has been protected by the canopy of trees against severe erosion. When first cleared it gives excellent crops. The trouble is that destroying the forest is easier than restoring it. In a clearing of this kind on the

[4] There are, of course, several subdivisions of this broad classification. Botanists speak of three types of Gold Coast forest—evergreen, deciduous and secondary; and of savannah forest, savannah, grass savannah and grassland.

edge of the grass, the forest cannot regenerate itself as it can in
an island clearing. The abandoned clearing is exposed to severe
erosion; it is invaded by grass, which begins to compete with the
forest saplings which are endeavouring to reassert possession. The
contest is unequal, for the annual grass fires sweep over it, killing
the young trees and shrubs but doing no permanent damage to the
grass population. These annual grass fires, which occur after the
harmattan has dried the vegetation, are the greatest obstacle to the
regeneration of the forest. Often they are lit by farmers to clear
the ground for the new season's crop, sometimes it may be that
they result from spontaneous combustion of the tinder-dry
herbage. They sweep over the country for miles, and only a few
species of savannah-dwelling trees with a specially thick bark can
stand against them. If only some means could be found of protecting land from fire it would be possible to maintain the forest
against this kind of destruction. In 1936 the rate of deforestation,
partly through encroachments at the edge and partly through
island clearings for cocoa, firewood, or food crops, was estimated
by the Government forestry department at 300 square miles a year
out of a total forest area of 18,000 square miles.

The climate, through its effects on human health and comfort,
is as important a factor in history as hills and vegetation. On the
coast itself the land and sea breezes mitigate the heat; but from
the sea to the northern edge of the forest a climate prevails in
which the range both of temperature and of humidity is very small.
It is exceptional for the thermometer to rise above 95° or to fall
below 65°; and for most of the year the daily range is from about
75° to 85°. The relative humidity is usually about 80°. Farther
north conditions are more extreme; the heat is hotter, the cool
weather is colder, and the relative humidity is much less. There
is no doubt that the equable damp heat of the forest and coastal
region is enervating, and the brisk dry heat and chilly nights which
the north enjoys for part of the year are healthier and more stimulating to Africans as well as to Europeans. The most trying time
of the year is the time just before the arrival of the rains, when the
clouds are banking heavier and heavier, there is a constant flicker
of lightning and rumble of thunder, and the air is heavy and life-
less. Much has been written about the unhealthiness of the climate.
The climate itself has been rather unfairly blamed. The constant

damp heat may weaken one's powers of resistance to disease, but the unhealthiness of West Africa is due mainly to the country's wealth of disease-bearing parasites. Malaria and yellow fever, both carried by mosquitoes, trypanosomiasis (sleeping sickness), carried by the tsetse-fly, and plague, carried by fleas, are all endemic in West Africa; and though in recent years much has been done by sanitation and preventive measures of various kinds to reduce the incidence of these diseases, we have not yet arrived at the day when by universal prophylactic injections or by the extermination of their insect hosts it will be possible to stamp them out altogether.

CHAPTER II

POPULATION AND PRE-HISTORY

VERY little is known about the pre-history of the Gold Coast. Pre-historic remains, though fairly numerous, are not such as to give us much knowledge of the prehistoric inhabitants.

The commonest relics are stone celts of neolithic type, which are found in many parts of the Colony and Ashanti. They are made of local stone, and are usually very short, only two to four centimetres long. Long celts of twenty centimetres or more in length are also found, though rarely. These celts are called in Ashanti *Nyame akuma* or God's axes; it is believed that they are thunderbolts, and are found where the lightning flash has struck the earth. They are believed to have magical powers. Here and there, however, a tradition is preserved that they are of human origin and were used as hoes. Rattray makes the very probable suggestion that the stone age in the Gold Coast overlapped the introduction of iron, and that the owner of a serviceable stone hoe would not be likely to throw it away to replace it by an expensive iron one until it was worn out; he thinks, therefore, that the short celts are the worn-down stubs of long ones, and that the long celts are so rare because they are the tools that were lost in forest or stream before being worn out.[1] The celts are of several types; Mr. C. T. Shaw[2] suggests a classification into eight types, based on the cross-section.

In addition to these celts, Gold Coast sites have yielded scrapers and hand-hammers, and large quantities of micro-lithic tools. There are also quantities of curious stone implements, rounded and flattish, usually about two inches in diameter and half an inch thick, with a bi-conically pierced hole. These stones are found sometimes singly, sometimes in hoards of as many as a thousand. Mr. Shaw remarks that "the purpose of these stones, together with the question of their age, is one of the most teasing problems of Gold Coast archæology. Possible uses include fire-making, personal

[1] Rattray's theory, however, will not easily account for all instances.
[2] Report on cave excavations; *Proceedings* of the Prehistoric Society for 1944 (New Series, Vol. X, pp. 1-67). I have made considerable use of Mr. Shaw's paper in these few paragraphs.

PLATE I   Forest country at the foot of the Kwahu scarp

(photo : C.O.I.)

PLATE II THE GOLDEN STOOL AND THE PRESENT ASANTEHENE, Sir Osei Agyeman Prempeh II. The Golden Stool, which takes precedence of the Asantehene, is lying on its side on its own chair of state, the upper surface facing the spectator.

(photo: C.O.I.)

adornment, net sinkers, digging-stick weights, currency, spindle-whorls, loom-weights, stone arrow-sharpeners, wire-drawing, in conjunction with bow-drill, bolas-stones, or cult objects." At several places in the Gold Coast there are outcrops of rock containing the long smooth grooves where countless implements have been ground and polished; and the earth round these sites is often full of debris.

Prehistoric pottery is found in several places. It resembles modern Gold Coast pottery in being made without a wheel and being fired in an open fire, not in a kiln. Several types have been described; the pottery is not found in well-stratified deposits, so that it is not yet possible to determine its date. Some types are definitely associated with stone axes and microliths, while others, more recent, are yet probably older than the present-day population.

There are also in many places remains of iron workings of uncertain antiquity. Iron is still smelted locally, but it is clear that the iron industry was formerly much more widespread. There seems no reason, however, to regard these remains as very ancient; they may indeed have been abandoned since the European traders brought European ironware into the country.

Very few prehistoric settlements have so far been discovered. In the forest in the eastern province of the Colony a few prehistoric earthworks have been found, usually consisting of a simple mound-and-ditch enceinte; excavation in the ditches has revealed little but pottery similar to that already known from Ashanti and elsewhere. The local people have no tradition of their origin, but they only settled in the district three hundred years or so ago.

West African archæology is still in its infancy. It seems clear that several different Neolithic cultures can be distinguished. One of these, characterized by wealth of microliths and stone axes, and absence of arrow-heads, occupied the Gold Coast and other coastal regions, while further inland there seems to have been more hunting and less digging. Presumably the different cultures imply different peoples; but we are not yet able to say when they lived or why they died.

We have no clue to the physical type of these earlier inhabitants. No very ancient prehistoric graves have been found.[3] It is possible

---

[3] One skull has been discovered in the Northern Territories whose measurements suggest ancient Egyptian affinities, but no clue exists as to its age.

B

that they were of a pigmy type; it may be that the universal belief in the *mmoatia* or little folk may arise from a folk-memory, as the belief in gnomes and ogres in Europe is said to arise from folk-memories of the pre-Aryan inhabitants and of subsequent Asiatic invaders.

We cannot speak with much more certainty when we come to the question of early contact between the Gold Coast and other parts of the world. The gold of West Africa was known to the ancient world from very early times, and no doubt some of the gold that went across the desert from the district vaguely known as Wangara came from Ashanti or other parts of the Gold Coast. Several attempts were made to circumnavigate Africa by Egyptians and Phœnicians, and it has been suggested that some of the expeditions may have visited the Gold Coast and even established trading settlements there. There is nothing improbable in the suggestion; but material evidence to support it is scanty. A few bronze wick lamps have been found in old gold-workings; the so-called Aggrey beads, so highly valued by the Gold Coast people, which have been found in the gold-bearing districts of the colony, may be of Carthaginian or Phœnician origin, though they are more likely to be medieval Venetian work; but so far no trace has been discovered of any ancient colony by the sea or near the mines. It seems then that there must have been some trade with Carthage or Phœnicia, and perhaps with Egypt; but we cannot yet say for certain that these nations established settlements on the Gold Coast.[4]

The most famous of early expeditions to West Africa is that made by Hanno the Carthaginian.[5] This man set sail from Carthage, probably about 500 B.C. or earlier, intending to found colonies along the West African coast and to circumnavigate the continent. An account of his expedition is preserved in Greek, probably somewhat abridged from the presumably Punic original. His course can be traced with fair certainty as far as the Senegal; from that point onwards it is difficult to make his description of the landmarks on the coast tally with the log of the number of days from point to point. For this reason it seems probable that his Greek translator has curtailed some of his tables of distances. Since

[4] Claridge, chapter II. Dr. Rendel Harris has some interesting arguments for Egyptian colonization founded on Gold Coast place-names; but without supporting evidence of other kinds, place-names are inconclusive.
[5] The question is discussed by Claridge in his chapter II.

it is impossible to make sense of the narrative of this later stage of
the voyage as it stands, accepting both the descriptions and also
the distances, there are two methods of interpreting the narrative,
according to which you prefer to accept. If you insist on his
information on distances you must conclude that he went little
past Sierra Leone; if you concentrate on identifying his landmarks,
and are content to assume that Hanno himself or his Greek
translator has abridged the table of sailing distances, it will seem
probable that he reached the Cameroons. In any case, there is no
reason to suppose that he landed on any part of the Gold Coast. If
we suppose that he passed it at all (assuming, that is, that he
reached the Cameroons), the Gold Coast must be part of the
unpromising shore which so terrified him because of the great
'burning' or surf.[6] If Hanno's voyage had any importance for the
Gold Coast at all, it can only have been as the beginning of a series
of voyages, some of which did visit the country.

In discussing the origins of the population of the Gold Coast
we are to an even greater extent in the realm of supposition. The
Gold Coast is part of the western Sudan, and over it for thousands
of years have flowed and ebbed the folk-wanderings of the African
races.

The origin of the Negro race is unknown. It may be that both
the African Negroes and the similar races of Melanesia spread outwards from a lost continent—Lemuria—sunk like Atlantis beneath
the ocean, and represented today only by Madagascar and some
groups of smaller isles. The original home of the race may have
been in Africa itself, somewhere near the great lakes. Negro traditions in West Africa agree in claiming that their nations arrived
at their present homes from somewhere in the east. It is impossible
to say how long ago the migration or series of migrations took
place. All we can say is that at the earliest moment when Egypt
and other nations of antiquity notice and describe to us Negro
peoples, these Negro peoples appear to be inhabiting much the
same lands that they or other Negro peoples are inhabiting today.

[6] Hanno speaks of a land so hot that no one could live there, and of rivers of
fire running into the sea. Early European voyagers had the same idea that the
land was too hot to inhabit. The incessant white surf was long believed to be
steam from the contact of the sea with the hot shore, and was called 'burning'
in English until the eighteenth century, as indeed it still is in German. Claridge
(p. 24) suggests another possible explanation, but this seems the likelier and
is simpler.

In other words, the settlement of the Negro race in Africa south of the Sahara had already taken place before the dawn of historical consciousness in Europe and the Near East.

It is probable, however, that West Africa was inhabited by an earlier race before the Negroes arrived. Apart from the existence of palæolithic implements and from the Gold Coast belief in the *mmoatia,* there is stronger evidence that the Negro settlers in West Africa found there in possession a different race. Several nations of the Sudan have a tradition that the original inhabitants were a race of short stature and reddish complexion.[7] Herodotus has a tale of certain young men from the Mediterranean coast who ventured southward across the desert; they came to a great river— doubtless the Niger—flowing from west to east, with crocodiles in it; the people who lived on its banks were below the normal height and were 'black'.[8] Delafosse and Lady Lugard regard this as evidence that at that time the southern edge of the Sahara was occupied by this earlier race, whom Delafosse calls Negrilloes. This conclusion seems rather strained: for not only do these people strike their discoverers as 'black', whereas according to Delafosse the Negrilloes were reddish, but a good deal depends on the meaning of the phrase used by Herodotus to describe their height.[9] Lady Lugard translates 'less than men of middle height', and goes so far as to identify the people with pigmies; but it seems unnecessary to read into the phrase more than that their height was below the average; and this average is presumably the average of Berber experience. It seems, in short, that the people in question are just as likely to have been Negroes, akin to the present inhabitants, as Negrilloes. There is, of course, just as much variation in height between different Negro nations as between different nations of Europe.[10]

[7] Delafosse, *Les Noirs d'Afrique,* pp. 11-13; Rattray, *Religion and Art in Ashanti,* pp. 26, 27, 35, 36; Dixon, *Racial History of Man* (quoted in Williams's *Hebrewisms of West Africa,* 28-30, with other authorities).
[8] Herodotus, II, 32. Delafosse (op. cit., 10, 11) mentions the possibility of identifying this river with Lake Chad, the Niger, or some western tributary of the Nile. But as the expedition started from Syrtis and kept bearing westward over the desert (πρὸς ζέφυρον ἄνεμον) it is hard to see how their description can mean anything but the Niger.
[9] ἄνδρας μικρούς, μετρίων ἐλάσσονας ἀνδρῶν.
[10] Hanno on his voyage met what he calls savage men, hairy. He tried to take some alive back to Carthage, but they were so wild that he had to be content with three skins. He mentions that his interpreters called them gorillas. It has been suggested that they were some species of ape, chimpanzee (or perhaps the

Whatever Negrillo element there may be in the present Gold Coast population has been completely submerged in the later waves of Negro settlers; so completely submerged that it is not even certain whether we can regard the short reddish-complexioned individuals who are sometimes seen as reversions to this presumed earlier type.

It seems fairly clear that the forest country of the Gold Coast was not settled by its present Negro inhabitants until recently—certainly within the last thousand years, and in some cases much more recently still. Most of the forest-dwelling tribes have traditions of a northern origin, though the places mentioned in their traditions are usually in the grass country north of the forest, either within the present Gold Coast or just outside it.

The principal people of the Colony and Ashanti is the Akan. The Akan occupy the whole of Ashanti, and the whole of the forest country west of the Volta in the Colony. They are divided into several nations, of which the Fante of the coast and the Ashanti are the two that have had most dealings with the Europeans. One Ashanti tribe stretches several miles into the Ivory Coast, and other nations of the Ivory Coast, notably the Baule in the north and the Agni in the south, speak languages which are clearly connected with the Akan languages of the Gold Coast.

From the linguistic point of view, the Akan of the Gold Coast fall into two main divisions, the Fante and the Twi. The two languages may be regarded as two forms of the same language, Fante being a softened form, with a tendency to modify the dental consonants of Twi into sibilants and to elide and assimilate its vowels. Both Fante and Twi, especially Twi, are divided into several dialects. Fante is spoken on the coast from near Sekondi to near Beraku, a distance of some eighty miles, and inland in a strip twenty to thirty miles wide. Farther inland it is replaced by the

gorilla, which was named by its discoverer in the belief that he had found Hanno's creatures) or baboon. Delafosse, however, makes the interesting suggestion that they were men. He points out (op. cit., 9) that the name given to these creatures by Hanno means "they are men" in the Wolof language of Senegal, which may have been the language spoken by the Lixitæ who supplied Hanno with his interpreters. It seems most unlikely that an experienced Cathaginian seaman should have been unfamiliar with baboons, which existed in Egypt. The chief interest of Delafosse's suggestion, however, is not in the identity of these mysterious creatures, but in the fact that if true it shows us the Wolof language being spoken 2,500 years ago in its present home. For another interesting conjecture see Bovill, *Caravans of the Old Sahara*, 16 n.

various dialects of Twi; and the Twi language in one form or another is spoken over the whole of Akim, Akwapim and Ashanti, as far north as the Black Volta. Twi is spreading as a *lingua franca* even east of the Volta, and one or two tribes who speak it as their mother tongue have established themselves on the left bank of the river. In the Ivory Coast Twi is replaced by Agni and other related languages, and the speech of some of the tribes in the west of the Colony may be regarded as a transitional form between Twi and Agni.

The grassy plains of Accra, stretching for sixty miles along the coast between the Akwapim hills and the sea, are the home of the Ga people. Their language has some affinities with the Akan tongues, especially in vocabulary; it has also considerable similarity to Ewe, which is spoken on the other side of the Volta. Ewe and Ga agree in using certain sounds, especially the consonant sounds *gb* and *kp,* which do not occur in the Akan languages. It has been suggested[11] that the Ga language has been formed by a mixture of Akan and Ewe. The language has two main dialects, the Accra and the Adangbe; one Adangbe-speaking tribe, the Krobo, has been pushing its way for many years north-westwards across the Akwapim hills into the forest country, buying land extensively from the Akan inhabitants.

East of the Volta lies the area occupied by Ewe-speaking peoples, which covers the south-east corner of the Colony, the southern section of British Togoland, and a very large area of the French colony of Dahomey. Ewe was the language of the ancient kingdom of that name before the French conquest.

The greater part of the Northern Territories is occupied by people speaking different forms of the Moshi-Dagomba language. The capital of the Dagomba kingdom is Yendi, just across the border in British Togoland; farther north are Mamprusi, Dagati and other tribes, all speaking languages related to Moshi and Dagomba. The centre of the old Moshi kingdom lies far to the north, outside British territory, but its language is spoken all over the basin of the White Volta.

Between the Moshi-Dagomba area and Ashanti is a strip along

[11] Migeod, *Languages of West Africa*, I, 40. Even if the language is a mixture of Twi and Ewe it need not follow, however, as Migeod suggests, that the people itself was formed by a similar mixture.

the left bank of the Black Volta where the language spoken is called Gonja or Gbanya. This language is one dialect "of a language which is spread over a considerable part of the Gold Coast and of Togoland, and is known by the name of Guang".[12] This Guang or Guan language is spoken in one form or another on the left bank of the Black Volta, on the Afram plains in the east of Ashanti, along the ridge of hills in Togoland, in Akwapim, and as far west as Winneba. Over the greater part of this large crescent-shaped area the Guan language appears to be tending to die out. The Guan-speaking people have for the most part been conquered by Twi-, Fante- or Ewe-speaking tribes, and use these languages for intercourse with the outside world, keeping their ancient mother-tongue for private use.

It is tempting to suppose that this widespread Guan language is evidence of the existence of a Guan nation or group of tribes which formerly inhabited all those territories where the Guan language is spoken today, and possibly others as well. Such a supposition would not be wholly untrue. Fante tradition records that the Asebu were in possession of the coast-lands when the Fante arrived, and were subjugated by the newcomers. The tradition of Agogo in Ashanti-Akim relates that when the first settlers established their home there they had to fight against a powerful ruler called Otara Fuom or Otara Finam, who ruled the whole of the land from the Volta to the neighbourhood of Kumasi. This man's name is Guan, and the Guan language is still spoken in the district. The Guan and Kyerepon people of Akwapim were only conquered by the Twi-speaking people of Akim in the first half of the eighteenth century. Further, the Guan language is certainly closely related to Akan[13] and related also to Ga and Ewe; and it seems that Guan uses word-forms which are older than the corresponding forms in Akan.[14]

But the question is complicated by the linguistic situation in the Gonja country. The Guan language in that region is not the language of the mass of the people, but of the ruling class. The mass of the people speak languages akin to Moshi.[15] The Gonja-speaking

[12] Professor Westermann's chapter IV in Rattray's *Tribes of the Ashanti Hinterland*, p. 126.
[13] Rattray, op. cit., preface, p. ix.; also Westermann, on p. 127 of Rattray's book.
[14] Op. cit., p. 127.
[15] Their languages, Vagale and its related tongues, form part of the Grusi sub-

class state that they found the Ashanti settled in the country when they arrived, and they married the Ashanti women. This they give as the explanation of the resemblance between their language and Ashanti. This would be understandable if the land were previously occupied by Guan-speaking people. But the mass of the people in the Gonja area today, speaking Vagale and other tongues not related to Guan, claim that they were the original inhabitants and were conquered by the Gonjas; so it would seem that Vagale, and not Guan, was the original language of this region. The leader of the conquest was a certain Jakpa, who is stated to have come with his men from Mande; which, if it does not mean that he was a Mandingo, at least means that he came from the west. Recent research has enabled us to date Jakpa's invasion fairly accurately at 1591 or very soon afterwards, and it seems probable that it was part of the convulsions which were caused by the Moorish conquest of the Songhai empire at that time.[16]

I shall discuss the complicated question of the history of this region later on[17]; for the present it is sufficient to note that the Gonja, and indeed all the other nations of the Northern Territories, are an exceedingly mixed race, and that their political organization has suffered frequently from invasion and conquest.

There are two areas in the Gold Coast where the linguistic situation is extremely complicated. One is the south-west corner of the Colony, the other is the district on the left bank of the Volta in that stretch of the river which forms the boundary between Ashanti and Togoland.

The coastal area west of the River Pra is occupied by a number of languages, more or less closely connected with Fante and Twi: Ahanta, Nzima, Evalue and Aowin; the thick forest and the lagoons on the lower reaches of the Tano have tended to restrict intercourse and so to multiply dialectical variations. The Gold Coast here touches the eastern fringe of an area in which different dialects and different languages are very numerous: Akan influence has been strong, and the Nzima language is tending to spread at

group of the Gur language-group; Moshi is one of the main languages of the Moshi-Dagomba sub-group: op. cit., 122,125.
[16] Rattray, *Tribes of the Ashanti Hinterland*, pp. 452, 516; Eyre-Smith, *Peoples of the Northern Territories*, pp. 11, 12; Meyerowitz, *Akan Traditions of Origin*, pp. 55-59.
[17] See pp. 129, 130.

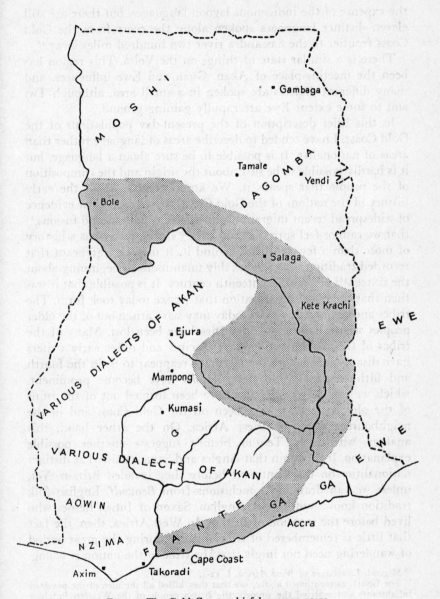

FIG. 5. The Gold Coast—chief language areas.

The shaded area is the region in which Guan languages are spoken or are known to have been spoken formerly.

the expense of the indigenous lagoon languages, but there are still eleven distinct languages spoken along the coast from the Gold Coast frontier to the Sassandra river two hundred miles away.[18]

There is a similar state of things on the Volta. This region has been the meeting-place of Akan, Guan and Ewe influences, and many different dialects are spoken in a small area, although Twi and to some extent Ewe are rapidly gaining ground.

In this brief description of the present-day populations of the Gold Coast, I have tended to describe areas of language rather than areas of nationality. It is possible to be sure about a language, but it is hardly possible to be sure about the origin and the composition of the people that speaks it. We know so little about the early history of the nations of the Gold Coast, we see such clear evidence of widespread recent migrations, invasions, conquests and fusions,[19] that we cannot feel sure that any tribe existing today has a history of more than a few centuries behind it. It may be significant that recorded tradition is so remarkably unanimous in beginning about the sixteenth or early seventeenth century. It is possible that it was then that the tribal organization that we see today took form. The tribes and nations that exist today may have arisen out of the older peoples whose names and identities have been lost. Many of the tribes of Germans mentioned by Tacitus and other early writers have disappeared before the Germans reappear to us in the fourth and fifth centuries; and new nations have become prominent, which we can only conjecture have been formed out of the ruins of the old. So it may have been on the Gold Coast and in the neighbouring lands of West Africa. On the other hand, this analogy with early Teuton history suggests another possible explanation. It is certain that Angles and Saxons existed as distinct nationalities on the Continent before they invaded Britain. Yet, unless we can draw any conclusions from *Beowulf*, English folk tradition knows nothing of Anglian, Saxon or Jutish heroes who lived before the invasion of Britain. In West Africa, then, the fact that little is remembered of tribal history during the great period of wandering need not imply that the tribe or the nation is young.

[18] Migeod, *Languages of West Africa*, I. 42-4.
[19] The Gonja, as mentioned above, say that they killed all the men of the previous inhabitants and married the women; the Brissa people of the Western Province of the Colony similarly claim descent from Ashanti men and the women of a previous race, the Eguanfo; see Chamberlain, *A Brief Account of the Brissa Language*, p. 5.

Rattray has shown[20] how most of the nations of the north originated, and has indicated the possibility that in Ashanti and the Colony the modern nations may have originated in much the same way. He has shown that among the Gonja, Moshi, Dagomba and other nations the national traditions are really the traditions only of a ruling minority; and that it is this small ruling class, and not the nation as a whole, that has carried out the migrations, invasions and conquests of which the whole nation nowadays regards itself as the successors. He has pointed out sufficient resemblance between the constitutions of these nations and those of the Akan and other peoples of the south to suggest that the invading strangers of the north were of the same stock as those who, "wandering on farther south, developed what are now the great Akan-speaking states". It may be, then, that in discussing the early history of the Ashanti, and others of the southern states, we are discussing states or nationalities which at that time did not exist. This is nothing more than a possibility; and the fact that many of the southern traditions explicitly state that the present occupiers found the land empty when they arrived[21] certainly tends to show that in these cases at any rate there must have been a more or less complete tribe with its tribal organization on the march.

Assuming for the present that the Gold Coast nations of today have existed in their present form for much longer than the three or four centuries of which their traditions are preserved, where do they come from?

Let us first consider the Akan. It is the all but universal tradition among the Akan that their ancestors came from the north. The Fante say that they came from Tekyiman; the Akim Bosome from Ejura; the Akwamu from Kong. There are two great centres of dispersion. One is the Adansi country, south-west of the lake. This is said to be the original home not only of the Adansi people of today, but of many of the Akim Abuakwa and of some of the people of southern Ashanti, including the important state of

[20] *Tribes of the Ashanti Hinterland*, preface, pp. xii.-xiv., xix.-xxi.; cf. *Ashanti Law and Constitution*, 64, 65.

[21] This is so, for example, at Apirede (Akwapim), Akyease (Achiasi, Western Akim), and Akim Soadru. The traditions of the Ashanti divisions "who came out of a hole in the ground" at Asantemanso clearly imply that the country was previously uninhabited; though there are difficulties in accepting this; see *infra.* p. 61. But on the whole it seems that the forest country was very thinly peopled, if peopled at all, before the arrival of the Akan and their kindred peoples. Asantemanso is close to Bekwai in Ashanti.

Mampon. The other centre is Asantemanso. This is today a tiny hamlet, of no importance save as a religious centre. Ashanti tradition relates that there was here a "hole in the ground", out of which emerged the ancestors of most of the peoples of southern Ashanti. They lived here in a great city for a time, and then as the pressure of the population increased, they dispersed to various places in Ashanti—Bekwai, Kokofu, Nsuta, Kumawu, Juaben, and others. Besides these Adansi and Asantemanso people, there are some other peoples today who claim to be autochthonous; they came down from the sky, or arose from the earth, or were created by God, in the very place where they are still living. But on the whole it is true to say that the general tradition among the Akan is that they came down from somewhere in the north.

It is tempting to make further conjectures. It seems to be accepted that the Akan left the grass country of the north under military pressure, but nobody knows who was the enemy. Claridge suggests the Fulani;[22] but the Fulani are not known to have become a military power until the eighteenth century, long after the peoples of the Gold Coast had reached more or less their present homes. It is possible that the invaders may have been Bantu. It seems that the Akan languages, like many other languages of West Africa, show traces of Bantu influence;[23] and from the distribution of these languages on the map it is possible to trace a course for the invading Bantu people.

A third suggestion has been made. It is that the Akan represent the section of the people of Ghana who refused to accept Islam in the latter part of the eleventh century, and who migrated south rather than accept a position of inferiority in the country which had been their own.

I think Claridge's suggestion of the Fulani unlikely, for a nation strong enough to drive into the forest the ancestors of the Akan would surely have left more traces of its presence than the Fulani have left in the Gold Coast of today. The other two suggestions, however, need consideration.

---

[22] *History of the Gold Coast and Ashanti*, 4-7. I think he goes too far in saying "it is commonly supposed" that the Fulani drove the Akan into the forest; and it is certainly not the case that the Fulani have been "migrating in a southerly direction for centuries". As far as this part of their migration is concerned, the direction is more easterly than southerly.

[23] Migeod, *Languages of West Africa*, II, 300-7.

Let us consider first the Bantu supposition. The Akan have a tradition that their ancestors were a race called the Nta or Ntafo,[24] who lived north of the forest in what is now the Gonja country. Since the features of the Akan languages which, according to Migeod, are signs of Bantu influence are common to all, it would seem that the Bantu influence must have been exerted at a time before the Ntafo had begun to disperse. This can hardly have been later than 1300, and may have been earlier by a century or more.[25] Similar Bantu influence is found in the various Mandingo languages; only the northernmost member of the Mandingo family, Soninke, being unaffected. This suggests that in the thirteenth century the Mandingo peoples were already occupying much the same situation that they occupy today; for they lie directly in the path of an invasion moving westwards from the Northern Territories of the Gold Coast.[26]

The alternative theory makes the Akan, or their immediate ancestors the Ntafo, one section of the people of Ghana, who migrated south rather than accept Islam. Ghana was a great empire of the western Sudan; it included both Negro and Berber nations, and reached a high degree of civilization. At its greatest extent the kingdom of Ghana held authority over the Berber state of Audoghast, which occupied the western trade-route through the desert and bordered the Mohammedan kingdom of the Two Shores. South of the Niger was a fringe of smaller Negro states, which inhabited the grasslands between the river and the forest; these also from time to time acknowledged the authority of Ghana, although it does not appear that any part of the present Gold Coast came under Ghana control. The capital city, after which the empire is named, was very ancient; it is said to have had twenty-two kings before the Hegira in A.D. 622. These kings are stated to have been 'white', which means Berber; and twenty-two more Berber kings ruled in Ghana after the Hegira. Then there was a revolution; the king was killed, and a Negro dynasty succeeded to power.[27] The

[24] Migeod, *Languages of West Africa*, I, 38, 41, 42.
[25] The most southerly branches of the Guan people had reached the sea before the Fante and the Accra peoples arrived in the fifteenth century or thereabouts. If we put their arrival at 1400 or 1450, we can hardly suppose them to have left the modern Gonja country later than 1300, especially if, as seems probable, they came down the Volta valley.
[26] Migeod, II, 299-306.
[27] Lady Lugard, *A Tropical Dependency*, 90-116; Bovill, *Caravans of the Old*

new kings were of the Soninke branch of the Mandingo race, and they ruled until 1076. In that year, the kingdom of Ghana was attacked by the Berbers who bordered it on the north-west, and suffered the fate which a wealthy pagan city must expect from Mohammedan conquerors who are fighting for their Faith and also

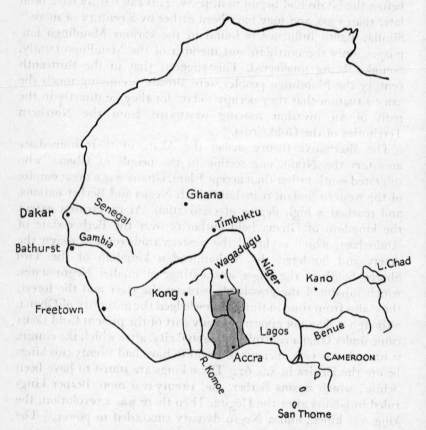

FIG. 6. The Gold Coast and West Africa.
The Gold Coast is shaded.

Sahara, 43-51, 57-66. There is a discrepancy about the date of the Soninke *coup d'état;* Bovill, 45, "in the eighth century", Lugard, 81, says before the Arabs visited it first in the eighth century. But Bovill, 33, 34, says that the first Arab visitor to Ghana came about 900. And twenty-two reigns after 622 would surely take us past the end of the eighth century.

for commercial supremacy. Ghana was destroyed, Islam was imposed on the survivors, and many of the people fled southward to escape it.[28]

These fugitives, it is said, were the ancestors of the Akan. But were they? It is true that there is a resemblance between the names Akan and Ghana, and that from the little we know of the customs of Ghana they seem to have been similar to those of the Akan. But we know very little. It seems that succession in the royal family went to the son of the king's sister. This matrilineal descent is the rule among the Akan of today; but it is also the rule in many other African nations; and indeed Akan tradition seems to regard it as a comparatively recent innovation as far as the Akan are concerned.[29] The few indications we have of their religion and of their burial and other customs also show some resemblance to Akan customs, but the resemblances are hardly specific enough, and the evidence is too scanty, to enable us to say decidedly that the Ghana people were allied to the Akan or Ntafo.[30]

On the other hand, there are reasons against connecting the Akan or the Ntafo with the people of Ghana. First, there is the silence of Akan tradition. It is hazardous to argue from silence, but the argument, when part of a series, may be worth considering. If the Ntafo really left Ghana about 1076 rather than accept Islam, they must have carried out a gallant march south-eastwards through some eight degrees of latitude, slipping between the Mandingo on their right and the Moshi on their left. Such an exodus would surely have left some trace in their tradition; but the traditions of Akan tribes invariably begin at a point close to the modern Gold Coast, and ascribe their movements to some local cause such as a local conflict or the pressure of growing population on food and water supplies. Mrs. Meyerowitz has collected some traditions which take us back to the region of Djenne and Timbuktu in the Niger bend, and she has fixed the foundation of the earliest Akan kingdom at 1295; but there is still a gap of two

[28] Bovill 64, 65; Lady Lugard, 110.
[29] Lady Lugard, 95-8; Bovill, 57-9; for matrilineal descent in Africa see Baumann, "Vaterrecht und Mutterrecht in Afrika", in the Zeitschrift für Ethnologie, 1926, 62-161. There is a well-known Akan story about a certain man called Abu, who began the custom of regarding his sister's children as his heirs because they were more dutiful than his own. The name is suspiciously like a piece of folk-etymology, but the story may show that the custom is not old among the Akan.
[30] Lady Lugard, 95-8; Bovill, 57-9.

hundred years and three or four hundred miles on which traditions
are silent.

Secondly, the resemblance of name seems only superficial. We
do not know what the people of Ghana called themselves; we do
not know what language they spoke. Until we know this, and until
the philologists have worked out the relationship between modern
Akan and the language of eleventh-century Ghana, arguments
based on the resemblance of name have no more weight than
Fluellen's comparison of Macedon and Monmouth. The name
Akan has a probable derivation from an Akan root *Kan*, meaning
first or leading; if so, the name of the people by which they call
themselves, as is so often the case all over the world, would be a
name meaning to express their superiority over other nations.[31]

Thirdly, the Negro part of the population of the Ghana empire
was more likely Mandingo than Akan. Its kings belonged to the
Soninke branch of the Mandingo race. The fugitives of 1076 took
refuge in the country between the Baule and the Niger, where they
built up another Soninke power which for a time expelled the
Berber conquerors from Ghana and reoccupied the city.[32] When
in 1240 the empire of Ghana and the capital city itself were conquered by the people of Melle, one branch of the Mandingo race,
the Malinke, was conquering the Soninke, another branch of the
same race.

Fourthly, if we assume that the Akan were part of the people
of Ghana, we are faced with two difficulties. One is, whereabouts
did they live, seeing that they were subjected, like their Mandingo
neighbours, to Bantu influence? According to Migeod,[33] among
the Mandingo tribes the Soninke alone, the most northerly, were
left more or less untouched by the Bantu invasion; from this it
would follow that the home of the Akan was somewhere well in
the southern part of the kingdom of Ghana, among the southern
sections of the Mandingo people. We have already seen that some
of the Soninke fled to the country between the Baule and the Niger;
a country which must therefore have been safe from the Moslem
invaders of Ghana. But the Akan, if they were part of the Ghana
kingdom and living well in the south of it, must have been there

[31] Christaller, *Dictionary of the Asante and Fante Language*, XIII; see also
143 s.v. *ga*.
[32] Bovill, 45, 58 n., 64, 65, 67, 68.
[33] II, 304.

already; so why should they move down to the Gold Coast to escape an invasion which never came near them? The other difficulty is that we have then another invasion to account for. The Ntafo lived in the modern Gonja country, and moved out of it because of the trouble they received from some invaders. Who were these invaders? Not the Fulani, I think, for the reasons I have already given. Not the Bantu, for their invasion had already passed, and had met the Akan or the Ntafo in their old home in Ghana. Not the various Moshi tribes, for they say that they found the Ntafo already settled when they arrived.[34] There is as far as I can see no answer to this question.

Since attaining independence, the Gold Coast has called itself Ghana, and official favour is shown to the theory that the Akan people of today are descended from the Ghana people of old. But the theory remains so far unproved, and I think the evidence is against it. In the strict sense, the true heirs of old Ghana are the Mandingo, not the Akan. Moreover, some of the Akan traditions collected by Mrs. Meyerowitz provide evidence for an alternative theory. They speak of a home in the Niger bend, between Djenne and Timbuktu, and Mrs. Meyerowitz suggests that the people were driven southward by a Muslim invasion of that district which is recorded by medieval Arabic writers as occurring in 1010. This theory seems to me quite acceptable. It is supported by direct evidence, which harmonizes with the other vague traditions on the subject which we already had. It avoids the main difficulties in the official theory, notably the long eastward march and the fact that the ruling people of Ghana was Mandingo, not Akan. And it provides an identification of the mysterious invader. The Djenne region may have been part of the Ghana empire; it was certainly part of the Melle and Songhai empires, which covered a wider area than that of Ghana—though those empires arose after the Ntafo had left the region. Whether the Djenne region was politically

[34] Rattray, *Tribes of the Ashanti Hinterland*. It is, of course, impossible to fix a date for the Bantu invasion. But as it did not affect the Soninke, it presumably happened before 1076, when the Soninke took refuge between the Baule and the Niger. The present state of our knowledge of old Ghana has been reviewed by M. Raymond Mauny in the *Bulletin de l'Institut Français d'Afrique Noire*, 1951, pp. 463-475. On pp. 438-462 of the same volume is an interesting account of the excavations at the deserted city of Koumbi Saleh, 330 km. north of Bamako, which may, or may not, have been the capital city. The still existing town of Walata, which is sometimes mentioned as Ghana's capital, cannot have been, for it was not founded till 1224.

subject to Ghana or not, it certainly shared in Ghana's culture. To this extent we can say that a direct link has been established between the old Ghana and the new, though there is so far no evidence of any connection between the Akan and the capital city of Ghana or the people of any region near it.

CHAPTER III

BEFORE THE COMING OF THE PORTUGUESE

ASSUMING that the Ntafo, the ancestors of the Akan, were settled somewhere in or near the modern Gonja country by about the year 1200, we must now discuss the movements of the Akan and other Gold Coast peoples from the thirteenth to the fifteenth centuries. We are still working largely by conjecture.

It must have been about 1200 that the Ntafo began to move southward. It was not a mass migration. The nation split into three main sections. The first to go were the ancestors of the Guan people of today. We can leave out of consideration for the moment the ancestors of the modern Gonja. If we may assume that the wide-spread Guan language indicates a widespread Guan nation, the course of its wanderings seems plain. The Guan-speaking area occupies the basin of the middle Volta and its tributary the Afram. It seems that the Guan came down the river, between the edge of the forest and the Togoland hills; when they came into the coastal plain through the Senchi gap, they turned westward and filled up the Akwapim hills, pushing on across the Densu until they reached the sea between Winneba and Cape coast. It is probable that they also occupied the Accra plains; for the Ga Mantse, the paramount chief of the Accra people, has a stool called the Guan stool, and though there is no record of how it received its name, it seems likely that it may have been taken in battle from the Guan. It is certain that the Guan were on the Akwapim hills, within sight of the sea, long before the Accra people arrived; and as far as we know the Accra plain was then uninhabited.[1]

---

[1] The Guan stool of Accra may, however, have been brought by a Guan princess who married into the Accra royal family about 1600. The Accra plain today is an area of grass savannah, very poorly watered, and apparently in process of becoming still more arid. But it is probable that 400 years ago it was well timbered, and therefore moister and altogether more habitable.

The traditions of the Fante and the small coastal states collected by Mrs. Meyerowitz have the effect of complicating the account I give of the three-fold migration, but as far as I can see my picture remains broadly true. Mrs. Meyerowitz has established the existence of a powerful state at Bono-Manso, about 100 miles north of Kumasi, as early as 1295; and she suggests that the destruction of this state by the Ashanti in 1742 sent crowds of refugees migrating

The next section of the Ntafo to leave were the ancestors of the modern Fante. They seem to have followed the line of the rivers Tano and Ofin. Fante tradition mentions Tekyiman, near the source of the Tano, as the home of the nation; so no doubt they made a long stay there. They appear to have reached the sea somewhere to the east of Cape Three Points, and to have worked eastward until they came in contact with the Asebu, one of the most westerly of the Guan tribes. The fighting that followed left the Fante in possession of the country round Cape Coast, in which the Asebu remained as a subject race.

The third and last section of the Ntafo to migrate were the Twi-speaking people. They came down towards the sea in between the Guan and the Fante. The Brong settled in the savannah country south of the Volta, between the river and the Mampon hills. The others went farther, crossed the Mampon hills and filled up the forest country of the Pra and Tano valleys, with the Kwahu scarp as their eastern border. The coast lands were occupied by Fante and Guan, but the Twi people came down to within twenty miles of the sea. The Akwamu, one of the most southerly of the Twi-speaking people, reached the neighbourhood of Nsawam, twenty-three miles from Accra, about 1600. By that time other Twi states were already being established by peoples farther inland.

The earliest Twi-speaking state to be established was apparently Adansi. The name of the state means 'housebuilding', and legend says that the Adansi were the first people in the Gold Coast to build mud or swish houses. If this implies that they were the first to settle down in permanent homes, it confirms other evidence that makes Adansi the senior Twi-speaking state. The founder of the Adansi state was Opon Enim; but it was the second chief, Ewurade Basa, that made it powerful. Ewurade Basa is related to have appointed one Kwae Mfrani as his *kyeame* or 'linguist'[2] instead of speaking to people direct; and other chiefs copied him

---

southward through the forest to establish new states on the coast. Mrs. Meyerowitz pictures the Etsi and others as peopling the coast from about 1300 onwards, and the first wave of the Fante arriving to struggle with them 300 years later.

[2] I use the customary term 'linguist', although the official so called has nothing to do with interpretation. He is a spokesman, whose business is to transmit speech between the chief and those with whom he is conversing, since no chief will speak direct on state occasions. The linguist is, of course, a very high official, and when delivering judgment in court, or when entrusted with diplomatic negotiations, has considerable discretion in conceiving the form of his message.

in this practice, which is universal among the Akan today. If this is based on a religious taboo, however, it seems unlikely that it should be so recent in origin. Perhaps the time of Ewurade Basa, the first great chief of the oldest nation, is used as a means of expressing immeasurable antiquity. The Adansi say that their ninth chief, Abu Bonsra, was contemporary with the Asantehene Osei Tutu, and reigned after Osei Tutu's death. His dates may be taken then as roughly 1700-35. Reckoning back from 1700 at an average of fifteen to twenty years for each chief, we get the very end of the sixteenth century or the beginning of the seventeenth as the date for the death of Ewurade Basa. We may roughly place the foundation of Adansi then at about the beginning of Queen Elizabeth's reign. This allows about three centuries for the migration from the original Ntafo country.

The first capital of Adansi was Adansimanso, which was close to the modern village of Mansia on the road from Fomena to Akrokyere. The Adansi people occupied the hill country of the Kwisa and Moinsi hills, which form a ridge running south-westward from the Kwahu scarp. In early times it seems that they tended to spread westward rather than eastward from their hill settlements, and they may have controlled the country as far west as the river Oda, fifteen miles from their capital at Adansimanso.

The valleys of the Oda and the Ofin, into which the Oda flows, were however the home of the Denkyera people. Their capital was at Banso or Bankasiesu, near the modern Obuasi. In Ewurade Basa's time the Denkyera were tributary to the Adansi; but they fought themselves free under the leadership of their chief Obuo-koropa. Ewurade Basa sent his son Apea Brenya to the Denkyera capital to collect the tribute. Apea Brenya got into trouble on the way through attempting to seduce a Denkyera woman; he was taken before the Denkyerahene, his beard was cut off, and he was bidden to take it home and show his father. The opinion of the Adansi council was that he had only himself to blame, and that the incident should be regarded as closed; but Ewurade Basa insisted on punishing the Denkyeras for their insolence. A punitive expedition was sent into Denkyera and a battle was fought near the confluence of the Oda and the Ofin, in which the Adansi were completely defeated. The Denkyerahene Obuokoropa and his successor Boa Amponsem carried the war into Adansi; Adansimanso was destroyed and the capital was moved to Dompoase, three miles nearer the hills. For a time the Adansi remained at Dompoase under Denkyera rule; but after a time the Adansihene Akora-folipan took his people across the hills into Akim. There they bought a block of land on the banks of the Pra, and settled for nearly a hundred years. In the time of the Asantehene Opoku Ware they took advantage of the destruction of the Denkyera power to return to their old home; and they fixed their capital at Fomena, where it still is.[3]

Meanwhile, having thrown off Adansi suzerainty, the Denkyera began to develop into a powerful kingdom. The Denkyerahene Owusu Bore was a great fighter, and conquered Sefwi, Wassaw and Twifu. This meant that he had pushed down the Ofin to its junction with the Pra, and even some distance down the Pra, no doubt until he came in contact with the Fante outposts; and he had crossed the watershed between the Ofin and the Tano and had conquered the middle course of the Tano itself. Instead of being a small state in the valleys of the Oda and the Ofin, Denkyera had expanded into a kingdom stretching from the Tano, or perhaps even the Bia, to the Anum, a distance of a hundred miles. The greatness of Denkyera lasted from the reign of Boa Amponsem till that of Ntim Gyakari; the first we may roughly date at 1660 and the fall of the second can be dated fairly closely at 1698. This century is the period of the gradual development of the Ashanti power to a point at which it stood out for the first time as the greatest of the Twi-speaking states.

Before dealing with Ashanti, however, we must glance at one other Twi-speaking state, Akwamu, and at Accra and other parts of the country.

Akwamu has one of the longest histories of any Akan state. The chronology of its traditions is a good example of the circuitous system of links that has to be used in Gold Coast unwritten traditional history. The only dates that can be fixed with certainty are those that are recorded in European accounts. One of these fixed points is the battle of Okai Koi hill in 1660, in which the Accra chief of that name was defeated by the Akwamu. Okai Koi came

---

[3] Adansi tradition. I use the term Denkyerahene, Adansihene, etc., to mean the chief or king of the Denkyera or Adansi people.

to the stool[4] very young, and was an old man at the time of his disaster. It was early in the reign of his father, Mankpon Okai, that the Akwamu first became a serious nuisance to the Accra. If we allow fifty years for the reign of Okai Koi, and ten for the short reign of his mother, Mankpon Okai's widow, we are left with 1600 as the date of Mankpon Okai's death. The Akwamu at this time were settled at Nyanawase, about twenty miles from Accra, on the slopes of the conspicuous Nyanao hill near the modern town of Nsawam. They had only recently settled there, under the leadership of their chief Ansa Sasraku I. There were six chiefs before him whose names are remembered, so that we may take 1500 as a rough date for the beginning of Akwamu chronology. In the time of the first chief they were living at Heman, not far from Cape Coast; but tradition claims that before his time they had lived at Kong (far away in what is now the Ivory Coast) and afterwards at Wam in Western Ashanti. They seem, then, to have come from the north-west; and had it not been that the Fante were already settled on the coast when they arrived, they would have reached the sea somewhere near Cape Coast or Sekondi. As it was, they were forced to turn eastward, and moved parallel with the coast until they settled at Nyanawase; Abakrampa and Asamankese are mentioned as stages on their journey from Heman to Nyanawase.

From their headquarters on the hill at Nyanawase, the Akwamu spread widely, and proceeded to build up a powerful kingdom. A section of the people had remained at Asamankese, twenty miles away to the north-west; and these two towns remained in close alliance. Nyanawase in particular was a very suitable site for the capital of a kingdom. It was on a steep hill, easily defended. It commanded the main trade route from Accra into the interior; it stood at the point where the little river Densu cuts a narrow gap into the hills and enters the coastal plain. Through this gap run

[4] The stool in the Gold Coast replaces the throne in Europe. But the stool is more than the throne. The stool on which a chief sat in his lifetime is consecrated after his death, and becomes the shrine for his spirit, which continues to guard his people. In some cases, such as the famous Golden Stool of Ashanti, a special stool is made and consecrated to be a collective shrine for the ancestral spirits of the whole nation. Such a stool, of course, is never to be sat on. As a rule, however, there is no one stool; there is a collection of carefully cherished ancestral stools, and the ordinary stool used by the present chief is destined in due course to be added to their number.

today the Accra-Kumasi railway and the trunk road from Accra to the north and west of the country. The Densu bridge at Nsawam is the point from which the modern roads radiate, as London Bridge was the focus of the roads in Roman Britain. The Akwamu, arriving from the west, and without Roman surveyors, may not have realized the full significance of the site they had chosen. To them, a more important fact may have been that the thick forest behind Nyanawase was almost uninhabited. They entered in and occupied the land; and the whole of the country from the Kwahu scarp to the Pra river became Akwamu.

It was under the stimulus of European trade that the situation of Nyanawase began to produce its full benefits. From their hill-top the Akwamu looked eastward over the forested ridges of Akwapim, the centre of the southern Guan states, and southward over the pale grassy plains to the sea. The plains also were thickly peopled. They were dotted with Guan villages, and here and there rose isolated dark hills, on which the Ga people, newcomers like the Akwamu themselves, had built their towns, from which they were beginning to rule the Guan inhabitants of the plain. On the seashore far away there was a string of tiny fishing villages;[5] and among them stood already a small Portuguese fort. Already this little trading station was making its influence felt. The paramount chief of the Accra people had actually moved his headquarters away from the hills down to the seashore in order to be on the spot for dealing with the white men, who seemed to have no taste for leaving the shelter of their stone walls. His bold move seemed to be succeeding; as the sole agents for the white men in that part of the country, he and his people were becoming rich and powerful. All the people of the plains were beginning to regard him as their suzerain. The Akwamu in their turn began to acquire wealth, some in peaceful trading with the Accra folk, some by less peaceful means, waylaying and robbing Accra traders who ventured inland. As time went on, they extended their raids into the grass country, which was the home of the Accra traders; and they became bolder and bolder, and more and more of a nuisance, until matters came to open war between Accra and Akwamu.

[5] Mr. A. P. Brown's researches have shown that the fishing industry along the Ga coast is of recent growth. Seafishing only seems to have begun in the latter half of the eighteenth century, though no doubt the easier lagoon-fishing is far more ancient.

The Ga people, of whom the Accra were one branch, were new-comers from Nigeria. They are divided into many small tribes, and into two main groups or branches, the Accra and the Adangbe. It seems probable that the Accra group came by canoe[6] along the coast, while the Adangbe group migrated by land. Their earlier home in Nigeria is uncertain; Benin, Bonny and Ile Ife have been suggested, but the only point on which Ga tradition is strong is that their home lay to the east, between two large rivers.[7]

The Adangbe settled on the west bank of the Volta, where a number of isolated kopjes stand out from the plain a few miles in advance of the Akwapim ridge. On these rocky outposts, the Krobo and Shai hills, and others, they established their religious and political centres and proceeded to dominate the agricultural land beneath. The Accra, whether they came by canoe or overland, settled farther west, where the Akwapim ridge approaches the sea. I have shown reason for thinking that the plain was already occupied by Guan settlers; but the Accra established themselves on the foothills of the ridge, which near its western end is lower and less steep.

The date of the Ga invasion can hardly be much earlier than the beginning of the sixteenth century. The Adangbe may have been fixed on the Krobo rock some time before the Accra settle-ment. The first Accra chief was one Ayi Kushi, and Mankpon Okai, who must have died about 1600, was the fourth; so Ayi Kushi's date can hardly have been earlier than 1500. It may be that some other sections of the Ga people had preceded the Accra by a few years; but not by long. The Accra capital was fixed first at Ayawaso, on a long saddle of hill eight miles or so from the sea; but before long it was moved to the site of the present town so as to be handy for trading with the Portuguese. From that time onward the power and wealth of Accra began to grow. Other Ga tribes, who claimed to be senior to the Accra, were forced to accept Accra leadership; and one after another they followed the Accra example and moved their towns from the hills down to the sea-shore. By 1600 Accra was well on the way towards becoming the capital of a Ga federation which covered nearly the whole of the

[6] Or, as Dr. Field suggests, along the beach.
[7] Ga tradition is contained in Reindorf's *History of the Gold Coast and Asante*, though often his is only one of rival versions. Other Ga traditions have been printed by Dr. Field in her *Social Organization of the Ga People*.

plains as far east as the Volta, and which threatened to dominate the Adangbe and the Guan on their hills.

Adansi 1550, Denkyera 1600, Akwamu 1500, Accra 1500—how recent it all is! The Ewe people and the ruling class among the Gonja did not arrive until the seventeenth century. There is no nation now dwelling in the Gold Coast which has been in the country much longer than the European. It may have been merely a coincidence that so many tribes were set wandering southward into the forest just at the time when the first Portuguese seamen were clawing their laborious way from cape to cape round the West African shore. It hardly seems possible that the news of the Portuguese arrival can have helped to attract them into a land which had hitherto been almost, if not quite, uninhabited. And yet, recent though these African states are, their traditions go back to a time before the Songhai had conquered the empire of Melle.

Whatever the cause may have been which set them adrift from their earlier homes, it cannot have been this conquest, much less the subsequent conquest of Songhai by the Moors. Similar migrations were taking place farther east. The Yoruba may have arrived at their religious centre Ile Ife in Nigeria some time after A.D. 1000 as part of a great movement of peoples which affected the Hausa, Nupe and others, as well as the Yoruba themselves. It is possible that the Ga people of the Gold Coast were themselves displaced by the Yoruba, and moved first farther south to Benin or Bonny and then westwards to their present home. The general result of it all was that the forest lands became fairly thickly peopled by nations arriving from the grass lands to the north.[8]

The homeland of the Ashanti is the district around Lake Bosomtwi, the only true lake in the Gold Coast. The lake is roughly circular, five miles in diameter; it lies in a deep cup in the Kwisa hills, about eighteen miles south-east of Kumasi, the modern capital of Ashanti. The steep wooded sides of the lake, rising 500 feet from the water, are seamed with stony torrent beds, but very few permanent streams enter the lake, and none leave it. The lake itself seems to have been discovered by the Ashanti only recently; in the reign of the Asantehene Oti Akenten, about the middle of

[8] Niven, *Short History of Nigeria*, 39-41, 64-8.

the seventeenth century, showing that not only the Ashanti themselves, but also the Adansi and other peoples were living within a
few miles of the site of their present habitat. This being so, it
seems strange that the date was not known earlier. But it is
surrounded by very thick forest and lies in a very sudden
depression of the ... the hills, and moreover it seems certain
that at that time the lake must have been much smaller than it is
now.

The Ashanti route for the country round the lake, is ...
the beginning of customs, and according to Ashanti tradition
their most important settlement in this region was Asantemanso,
between Bekwai and Asumenya. Most of the important divisions
of Ashanti, according to them, are that they came out of holes in
the ground at Asantemanso. At first this would mean, so that
Asantemanso, the name given to the town, is an expression in a ...
told from ... which is found elsewhere in Ashanti tradition, the
town of ... emerged ... but severely even the words and its appear
... ird could and ... without attempt to represent. ... but one
is the ... not be ... ind of the forest. It is not very strong on
the ... under usually seen ... to ... ... top ... ...
to this part of the country is not a ... ... and in time
went on and the populating increase, before ... ... a second town arose
at ... ... Asantemanso and eventually other was a more ambitious
migration and then ... ... Bekwai, Juaben, Kumawu and
other towns of course, say the Asantehene ...

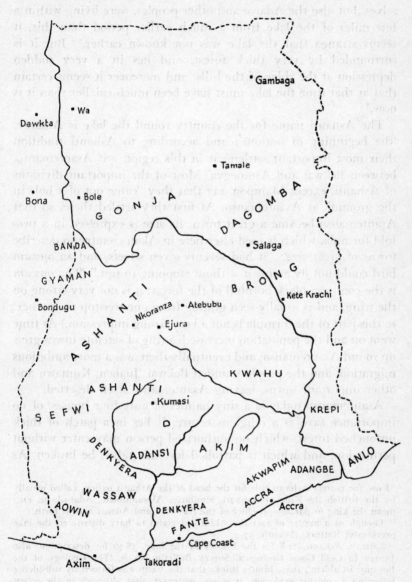

FIG. 7. The Gold Coast—chief tribal divisions.

the seventeenth century.[9] Seeing that not only the Ashanti themselves, but also the Adansi and other peoples, were living within a
few miles of the lake from a much earlier period than this, it
seems strange that the lake was not known earlier.[10] But it is
surrounded by very thick forest, and lies in a very sudden
depression at the ridge of the hills; and moreover it seems certain
that at that time the lake must have been much smaller than it is
now.[11]

The Ashanti name for the country round the lake is Amanse,
'the beginning of nations'; and according to Ashanti tradition
their most important settlement in this region was Asantemanso,
between Bekwai and Asumegya. Most of the important divisions
of Ashanti, except Mampon, say that they "came out of a hole in
the ground" at Asantemanso. At first they settled there, so that
Asantemanso became a great town; its size is expressed in a twofold formula, which is used elsewhere in Akan country to describe
towns of great size: "it had seventy-seven streets, and an *onwam*
bird could not fly across it without stopping to rest." (The *onwam*
is the common black hornbill of the forest; it is not very strong on
the wing, and is usually seen gliding from one tree-top to another;
so this part of the formula is not a very strong impression.) As time
went on and the population increased, a ring of satellite towns grew
up round Asantemanso; and eventually there was a more ambitious
migration, and the people founded Bekwai, Juaben, Kumawu and
other important towns, leaving Asantemanso itself deserted.

Asantemanso today is a tiny hamlet of only four houses, of no
importance save as a religious centre. It lies in a patch of thick
untouched forest, which no authorized person may enter without
permission, and which is patrolled lest this taboo be broken. As

[9] I use the correct Ashanti title for the head of the Ashanti nation, called usually
by the British the King of Ashanti. Similarly, Akwamuhene, Adansihene, etc.,
mean the king or paramount chief of the Akwamu and Adansi and so forth.
[10] Though as a matter of fact the Akim did claim to have discovered the lake
previously; Rattray, *Ashanti*, 57.
[11] Rattray, *Ashanti*, 54-8 for the history of the lake, 58-76 for description; also
Junner in Gold Coast Geological Survey Bulletin No. 8, 'The Geology of the
Bosumtwi Caldera', 1937. Junner thinks that the basin was formed by subsidence
following a volcanic explosion. It seems, moreover, that although in the recent
past the lake was much smaller than it is now, at a more remote period its water
level was more than 100 feet above the level today (Junner, pp. 14, 15, 44).

the traditional place of origin of the Ashanti, it is the most sacred place in the country.[12]

It is difficult to know what meaning to give to this legend of the hole in the ground at Asantemanso. No doubt this place was the most important of the early settlements of the Ashanti, and it may have been a place of refuge when the Ashanti were being attacked by Denkyera or others. But of the seven matrilineal clans[13] into which the Ashanti, like other Akan nations, are divided, only two, the Aduana and Oyoko clans, come from Asantemanso, and it is related by the tradition of Asumegya[14] that when these two clans emerged from the earth there was already an Asantehene. Moreover, the tradition of the Gyaman people[15] tells that they were driven from this region to their present home in the Ivory Coast long before the period of the exodus from Asantemanso. Perhaps we may regard the Asantemanso settlement as the earliest *synoecism* of the peaceful Ashanti farmers, but it is unsafe to place more weight than that on the legend.

The Ashanti were certainly subject to the Denkyera state after Denkyera itself had thrown off the power of Adansi. There were four reigns of Ashanti chiefs during this period of vassalage, which was ended by the great Asantehene Osei Tutu, who began his reign about the year 1695. The first reign was that of the two joint rulers Twum and Antwi; then came Kobia Amamfi, in whose time the settlement at Asantemanso is placed by Asumegya tradition. It is with the third chief, Oti Akenten, that Ashanti began to develop into something more than a nation of peaceful farmers and hunters in the lake region. He fixed his capital at Kwaman, and began to make war on the Doma people to the north. The Doma were an Akan people; a century before Oti Akenten's time, their chief Adu Bini had abandoned his home and had retired westward, to what is now the Ivory Coast, before the attacks of

[12] For a description of the sacred grove at Asantemanso (which he calls Santemanso) see Rattray, *Ashanti*, chap. X, and *Ashanti Law and Constitution*, chap. XVII.
[13] Rattray, *Ashanti Law and Constitution*, chap. VIII.
[14] Ibid, 131ff.
[15] The Gyaman tradition is related in Tauxier, *Le Noir de Bondougou*. There were eight chiefs of Gyaman between Adu Bini, who moved to the Ivory Coast, and Abo Kofi, who was defeated by Ashanti about 1735. We cannot place Adu Bini later than the middle of the sixteenth century, whereas the Asantemanso settlement must have been made about 1620. It is clear that the Ashanti were a fighting power before Asantemanso rose to prominence.

some earlier Ashanti warrior chieftain whose name is now lost. Although Oti Akenten failed to dislodge the remainder of the Doma and to force them to follow their kindred westward, he made sufficient of a reputation for himself and his people to attract the main body of the Asantemanso settlers northward to serve under him, and he and his people became the nucleus of the Ashanti confederation.

It is clear that this account is very imperfect. The Gyaman tradition[16] shows that there was a previous war between the Doma and the Ashanti. Perhaps the Doma, like the Ashanti themselves, served Denkyera; but it seems more likely that the Ashanti had been a military power a century before, and that they had been subdued by the Denkyera through a series of events which are forgotten. Our knowledge of the Ashanti beginnings is very limited; it happens that research into Ashanti history has so far been carried out in the southern area, which was peopled from Asantemanso. Research is needed among the peoples of northern Ashanti before we can begin to form a clear idea of the rise of the Ashanti people. It is, however, unlikely that this research will reveal much; for Osei Tutu made a law that for any member of a tribe which had become part of the Ashanti confederation, it was a punishable offence to relate the earlier, pre-confederation period, history of his own tribe. This law seems to have been effective in south Ashanti, and there is little reason to hope that it may have been less effective in the north.

We have been led forward to a period beyond the arrival of the Portuguese. We have seen that the Portuguese landed on the Gold Coast at a time when the nations who people it to-day were themselves just arrived or still arriving. The Guan may have been settled by 1350. The Fante were probably not far behind them, and we may suggest 1400 as the date for the Fante occupation of the coast. The end of the fifteenth century seems to have been the

[16] Mentioned above. The Doma are also known as Domina. The name Gyaman is formed from two Akan words, *gya* to leave, and *oman*, a nation or people. It is the name given by the Ashanti to the Doma who retired to the Ivory Coast leaving the rest of their people behind. It suggests indeed that it may have been originally a nick-name applied to the Gyaman chief Adu Bini, who left the bulk of his people behind him; the name seems more appropriate when applied to a chief, who leaves behind him the people he is responsible for, than to a people, who leave only their country. The word *oman* can only mean a nation, not the land in which the nation dwells.

time of the great migrations within the Gold Coast itself. At that time the Ga were arriving from the east, the Akwamu from the north-west; the Adansi were beginning to 'build houses'; and the Ashanti, not yet under foreign rule, were engaged in their first struggles to clear for themselves an area in which to settle. Farther north still, the Moshi and Dagomba warrior bands were establishing their rule over the earlier peoples, the Isala and others; and it may have been as a result of this invasion that the Gonja were being forced to admit Isala and Vagale settlers in such large numbers. In a very real sense, we may take the end of the fifteenth and the beginning of the sixteenth centuries as the beginning of Gold Coast history.

CHAPTER IV

EARLY EUROPEAN VOYAGES TO THE
GOLD COAST

THE first European seamen to visit the Gold Coast were the Portuguese.[1] At the beginning of the fifteenth century Prince Henry of Portugal, who won for himself the honourable nickname of 'the Navigator' for his interest in exploration, had conceived his plan of exploring the West African shore. The Western Sudan was known as the home of a civilized Mohammedan empire, and was rich in gold, ivory and pepper.[2] There was no possibility of penetrating to the land of gold by the trade routes across the Sahara, and it may be that Prince Henry had hopes of tapping the gold supply near its source by finding a sea route. It seems certain, however, that love of exploring for its own sake and the desire to preach Christianity in pagan Africa were two strong motives in his life work.

It was in 1419 that Prince Henry established himself in his headquarters at Sagres and began his life work of organizing exploring expeditions along the West African coast. In 1418-20 Madeira was discovered, or rather rediscovered,[3] and then Prince Henry set himself to explore the coast of the mainland. For a long time Cape Non had been regarded as the southerly limit of European and Arab knowledge, but a generation before Prince Henry's time Cape Bojador had become known to European geographers, though it was rarely visited. Cape Bojador was a formidable obstacle. It was protected by a dangerous reef and by heavy surf; it could only be passed by standing well out to sea. Land and sea alike beyond Cape Bojador, moreover, were well known to be inhabited by devils and utterly uninhabitable by men; and anyone who escaped the

---

[1] The story of the exploring and trading ventures by French seamen in the fourteenth century (Claridge, I, 48-53) may now be considered as disproved: J. W. Blake, *European Beginnings in West Africa*, 2-3; R. H. Major, *Prince Henry the Navigator*, xxiv.-li., 117-33.

[2] Not the pepper of the East Indies, but an indigenous species, called by early European traders Malaguetta pepper or grain of paradise. It is this crop that gave its name to the Grain Coast, now called Liberia.

[3] It had been accidentally discovered by an Englishman some 75 years before and had not been altogether forgotten.

THE FORT AT ANOMABU
(photo : P. Redmayne)

PLATE III

PLATE IV   DUPUIS AND THE ASANTEHENE MAKING THE TREATY.   From a drawing by Dupuis himself. The Asantehene has left his chair of state, which may be seen on the dais in the centre of the picture; amid general acclamation he is brandishing his sword before Dupuis in token of military alliance. The Asantehene's state umbrella is being brought forward, so that he may retire under it and return to his seat.

devils would be scorched black by the increasing desert sun. In 1433 the Portuguese captain Gil Eannes set out to try to pass the cape; but he turned back unsuccessful, and put in to the Canaries and returned to Portugal with a cargo of slaves. Prince Henry immediately sent him back with orders to pass Cape Bojador at all costs, even if he went no farther. This time Gil Eannes stood boldly out to sea when he sighted the cape, and made his landfall again on the coast beyond. This feat was the decisive event in the Portuguese exploration; it finally broke the fear of the unknown which had held their seamen back so long.

From this time onwards progress was steady. In 1442 the first gold and slaves were brought to Portugal from Rio d'Ouro; next year the Portuguese reached the old Carthaginian station of Arguin, where they built their first fort. In 1445 the voyages received a fresh impetus; Nuno Tristram passed beyond Cape Mirik and reached beyond the desert to a land of green trees. So the desert did not go on for ever. Now, every year brought fresh discoveries: the Senegal in 1446, the Gambia two years later, and Sierra Leone in 1460, a few weeks after Prince Henry's death.[4]

A voyage undertaken in 1461 or 1462 reached a point a few miles beyond the site of the modern town of Monrovia, the capital of Liberia. In 1469 the king of Portugal made a contract with a certain Fernão Gomez,[5] by which Gomez was to monopolize the Guinea trade for five years in return for an annual rent of 500 ducats and an undertaking to explore a hundred leagues of new coastline every year.[6] It was under the terms of this contract that the Gold Coast became known to Portuguese seamen. Soeiro da Costa discovered the river which was named after him; it is the Comoe river, which flows into the sea at Grand Bassam on the Ivory Coast, and which may in one sense be regarded as a Gold Coast river, since its upper course forms the western frontier of the Twi-speaking people of Ashanti and Gyaman.

[4] Sierra Leone, the Lion Mountain, is usually stated to have been named from the roaring of thunder among its wooded ravines. This may be so; but it is worth pointing out that from one point in the river as you come upstream to the anchorage, the mountain does look exactly like a lion lying down, his head and mane to the right, haunches immediately behind the town, and tail stretched straight out to the left. The resemblance vanishes in a few moments as the mountain becomes foreshortened.
[5] I give this and other names in the Portuguese form: Fernão, Diogo, João instead of Fernando, Diego, Juan and so forth, in which they are usually seen.
[6] The Portuguese league is about four miles.

In January 1471 two of the captains employed by Fernão Gomez, named João de Santarem and Pedro de Escobar, reached the Gold Coast itself. They rounded Cape Three Points[7] and came to land somewhere between the cape and the next landmark, the much smaller Cabo Corso, now Anglicized into Cape Coast. The exact place of their landfall is unknown; but the village of Shama, at the mouth of the river Pra (called by the Portuguese the Rio São João) became the base of Fernão Gomez' trade in this district. The whole region between Cape Three Points and Cape Coast was so rich in gold that the coast received the name of the Gold Coast, and such a busy trade in gold dust sprang up that Gomez soon made his fortune.

The contract with Fernão Gomez expired in 1474, and the monopoly of the Guinea trade was taken over by the government. Gomez was granted a coat of arms and the surname of Mina in commemoration of the gold mine he had discovered; and the Portuguese government decided to establish a fortress on the Gold Coast to secure the trade against foreign competition or against interruption by hostile tribes. For this purpose the site at Shama was rejected in favour of a site twenty miles farther east, and there the Portuguese built their great fortress of São Jorge da Mina.[8]

The expedition for the purpose of building the fort was dispatched on 11th December, 1481, under the command of Don Diogo de Azambuja. It consisted of ten caravels and two transports, with a small pinnace; it was manned by 500 soldiers and seamen, with 100 engineers and workmen for the building operations. The site was already chosen, the plans made, and all the stone and timber and material of other kinds was ready cut and dressed; all that remained was to assemble the pieces on the spot. Speed in

[7] So called because from the sea it consists of a broad low base with three sharp-pointed knolls in a row.
[8] The origin of the modern English name Elmina is uncertain. The native name is Ednaa or Edinaa; but it would have been quite exceptional for the Portuguese to use a native name, and it seems more likely that Edinaa is a corruption of Elmina than vice versa. As Bosman (41, 42) points out, there are no mines very near the town. He is probably right in suggesting that the Portuguese called the whole region Mina because of the abundance of gold in use. This is supported by the grant of the name Mina as a personal name to Gomez. It is not unlikely that the name of the region should come to be applied particularly to the headquarters of the region. The name São Jorge da Mina had already become St. George d'Elmina in Bosman's time 200 years later.

erection was naturally regarded as most important, since no one knew what opposition might be raised by the inhabitants.

The caravels sailed from Lisbon, with instructions to pick up the two transports, with their cargo of building materials and artillery, in the bay of Bezeguiche, the modern Dakar. The transports, being presumably much slower vessels, had already sailed. They were old ships,[9] and Azambuja had orders to break them up after they were unloaded, in order to give support to the rumour, which was being industriously spread by the Portuguese government, that the current along the Guinea coast made it impossible for ordinary tubby cargo ships to return thence to Europe. The caravel, a long and narrow ship with three lateen-rigged masts, and a stern-castle, was a Portuguese invention and hitherto a Portuguese monopoly; and the government hoped thus to discourage foreign competition in the Guinea trade.

There was a foundation of truth in this story. It was much easier to sail from Portugal to Guinea than to return. The northern equatorial current on its return journey to the equator sets gently southward from Gibraltar to the Canaries. From near the Canaries to Sierra Leone there are always "the orderly clouds of the Trade and the ridged roaring sapphire thereunder". Beyond Sierra Leone there are the equatorial calms, but the Guinea current, a sort of back eddy of the cold Benguela current, flows slowly eastward into the great gulf. The prevailing wind throughout the year, except for the few weeks of harmattan, is south-westerly; the south-east trade winds being apparently deflected by the attraction of the great heated land mass of the western Sudan. As the general trend of the coast, east of Cape Three Points, is east-north-east, the prevailing wind, like the current, is foul for ships returning to Europe.[10] No doubt the caravel was a handier vessel for the Guinea trade than the ordinary cargo ship used in European waters; but expert seamen knew that to say that none but a caravel could hope to return safely was to exaggerate grossly.[11]

Azambuja, sailing from the Tagus on 11th December, made his

[9] Prestage, 201.
[10] Blake, 13, 14.
[11] Prestage, 200, 201. After the discovery of America it became customary to avoid these difficulties of winds and currents by visiting the West Indies before returning to Europe—a practice which was greatly encouraged by the slave trade, though it began merely as an expedient in navigation.

rendezvous at Cape Verde twelve days later, and having picked up his transports, which must have slowed the pace of his fleet, reached Cape Three Points on 19th January. The captains in his fleet included several of the best Portuguese seamen of the day, among them Bartholomew Diaz, the future discoverer of the Cape of Good Hope; and it is probable that one of his ships had on board as an officer a still more famous seaman, Christopher Columbus.[12] On arriving at Mina, Azambuja found that the people were already busily trading with a Portuguese ship in the roads. No time need be spent in laboriously persuading the people that the Portuguese were come on a friendly errand. Friendly relations already existed.

The next day Azambuja and his officers went ashore in full dress to meet the chief of the place, whose name is given as Caramansa. (Claridge suggests that this is a version of the Fante name Kwamin Ansa; but it may be that the Portuguese were accustomed to add 'mansa', the Mandingo word for 'chief', to chiefs' personal names: we find Gumimansa, Nomimansa, Battimansa and Casamansa, as well as this Caramansa, mentioned in their accounts.) Mass was said under a great tree, and afterwards Azambuja held a state interview with Caramansa and his elders. The chief was unwilling to have a permanent Portuguese post established, and showed skill in countering Azambuja's arguments in favour of the plan. The Portuguese, of course, had slurred as lightly as possible over the benefit that a fortress would be to their own commerce, and had dwelt on the benefits that the Elmina people would receive. Caramansa, while willing to listen to the preaching of Christianity, and still more willing to continue friendly business relations with the Portuguese, told Azambuja that his men would never endure the climate, and that a permanent Portuguese garrison would be less likely than visiting Portuguese merchants to remain on friendly terms. Azambuja was forced to show more of his hand; and with a judicious mixture of threats and promises he succeeded in getting Caramansa to give a reluctant consent.[13]

Next morning the work of building began; but it was soon

---

[12] Claridge, 43, 44.
[13] Azambuja seems to have made the common European mistake of expecting Caramansa to give an answer on the spot. No Akan chief (presumably Caramansa was a Fante, or else an Efutu) can possibly answer without consulting his council; but Azambuja was strong enough to override constitutional etiquette.

interrupted by an incident which seemed to illustrate the truth of Caramansa's forebodings. The Portuguese workmen began to quarry the rock for the foundations of their fortress. They began working in a rock which was sacred to the Elmina people as the home of the god of the little river Benya. The people attacked them, and several men were wounded before Azambuja succeeded by gifts and apologies in pacifying the crowd. It was clear to all the Portuguese that the sooner the fort was in a state of defence the better. The work was pushed on as fast as possible, and in three weeks' time the main tower was one storey high and the curtain walls were high enough to shelter the workmen and the garrison. When the fort was finished, Azambuja himself stayed behind with a garrison of sixty men, and sent the fleet with the rest of the men back to Portugal, well laden with gold and slaves. The fort was named São Jorge da Mina; four years later, in 1486, it received from the king the privileges of a municipality. A daily mass was said in its chapel for the soul of Prince Henry. At his retirement, Azambuja was granted the augmentation of a castle to his coat of arms; while the king added to his royal titles that of Lord of Guinea.[14]

Elmina Castle, as it is usually called today, lies at the mouth of the little river Benya. The Benya drains a mangrove lagoon, and is prevented from flowing south directly into the sea by a low ridge of rock which projects from the sandy shore. It therefore turns east, and flows parallel with the coast, only a few yards away, finally falling into a small bay which is formed by the erosion of the sandy foreshore beyond the rocky spit. The castle stands on the point of the rock, between the river and the sea, and occupies the whole of the point, so that it is protected on three sides by water. West of the castle lay the town, and it was on this west face, the only land face of the building, that the most elaborate defences were constructed. The ditch, which was dry except close to the sea, was

[14] Major, 324; Prestage, 203-4; Claridge, I, 47. In the animistic religion of the Gold Coast almost every river, rock, hill, or other natural feature has its indwelling tutelary spirit to whom prayers and sacrifices are made. Unconscious tampering with such sacred sites by Europeans has often caused trouble. The Benya rock was a small one and was to be almost entirely occupied by the European's erection; no wonder the people objected. I cannot accept Major's statement that the riot came about because Azambuja had not given sufficient gifts to the chief. Only an insult to their religious feelings would, I think, have roused the people so very soon. Claridge sees this.

crossed by a drawbridge to the main west gate. By the drawbridge
stood a tall octagonal tower, in which were the governor's quarters.
The ditch was deep and wide, cut in the living rock, and heavy
batteries were constructed to command the approach from the
town and to defend the seaward face of the castle. The river mouth
was turned into a harbour for caravels and galleys, and a small
fleet of galleys was permanently based at Elmina, the calm tropical
water being suitable for these fair-weather vessels.[15]

Besides building their headquarters at Elmina, the Portuguese
built several smaller forts, at Axim, Shama and Accra, and hoped
to monopolize the Guinea trade. But from the very first, their
monopoly was challenged. Spain claimed a share in the Guinea
trade, and not only Spanish interlopers, but also official Spanish
expeditions, engaged in the trade with Mina before the end of
the fifteenth century. Portuguese and Spanish pilots, in spite of the
Portuguese government's attempts to keep all information on
West African affairs secret, revealed their technical information to
Genoese, Flemish and even English seamen.[16] The Spanish rivalry
was soon settled. By a treaty in 1480, Portugal surrendered the
Canary Islands to Spain, and the Spanish government in return
undertook to forbid its seamen to interfere in the Guinea trade.[17]
It seems that this prohibition was for some time not completely
effective; but before long the superior attractions of the New
World drew off the attention of the Spaniards from Guinea.

The danger from other rivals was not so easily disposed of. As
early as 1480 the Portuguese government protested to Edward IV
of England against a forthcoming English expedition; the protest
was made just in time, for the ships lay ready to sail in the Thames.
Flemish merchants had already obtained a fairly detailed knowledge of the coast and of the trading prospects; and it is possible

[15] Elmina castle as it stands today is greatly altered from its original appearance
owing to the improvements and extensions carried out by the Dutch. The long
gallery which bisects the ditch, the handsome arcade on the north side of the
great tower, the strong battery of guns overlooking the river and most of the living
quarters, are Dutch work. Blake has shown (following Santarem) the improbability
that the so-called Bastion de France at Elmina is really of French origin. In
Portuguese times the land between the lagoon and the sea, right opposite the
main gate of the castle, was occupied by part of the town, and remained so until
1873. The town, being divided by the river Benya into two parts, which formed
parts of two different states, was called by the Portuguese the village of Two Parts.
[16] Blake, chaps. II and III.
[17] Blake, 52, 53.

that before the Portuguese protest was received in London there had already taken place one successful English expedition. Only ten years after the building of the fortress at Elmina, French raiders captured a caravel returning thence to Portugal with a cargo of gold. Soon after the beginning of the sixteenth century, French activity on the coast increased greatly, and until the middle of the century the French were the greatest threat to the Portuguese trade. The Portuguese did all they could to maintain their monopoly. They organized a convoy system for the gold fleets which sailed twice a year from Elmina to Lisbon; they kept local fleets of caravels and galleys to patrol the Guinea coasts; and any foreign seamen who were caught by the Portuguese trading on the coast were executed as pirates. But the task of maintaining a monopoly of the trade over such a long coastline was an impossible one. Their fortified posts were too few, and their naval patrols could not be adequate. Though there are few good harbours on the West African coast, there are plenty of creeks and small coves in which illicit trade can be carried on by ships' boats, as the British found in the nineteenth century when they undertook the task of stopping the slave trade. The Portuguese forts were mainly dependent for their provisions on supply fleets from home; and the cost of the organization for maintaining the forts and the local fleets was a heavy burden on the revenue of the trade. The Portuguese had no control whatever over the African inhabitants beyond the range of their guns; and they depended on African goodwill not only for their own trade, but largely also for information about foreign interlopers.

Moreover, although the trade in gold, slaves, ivory and pepper of West Africa was very valuable, the Portuguese merchants were expanding their interests so rapidly that Guinea was no longer their main field. The discovery of Guinea had from the first been only a by-product of the search for the sea route to India; and after Vasco da Gama's successful Indian voyage and the Treaty of Tordesillas of 1494, Portugal had open to it the trade not only of East Africa, but of India, the East Indies and Brazil. It was natural that the government's interest in Guinea should fall off when there were such rich alternative markets; and in fact it seems that during the sixteenth century the Guinea trade was a good deal neglected by the Portuguese government. Their officials and garrisons were relieved every three years; but they were far from home, and many of them needed much more supervision than they could possibly receive. From time to time the home government was stirred by unsatisfactory reports from the Coast to attempt reforms; but the reforms did not last long.[18] After about 1530, the value of the Portuguese trade on the Guinea coast gradually declined.

The first serious attack on the Portuguese monopoly was made by the French. French privateers raided the Guinea fleets, and traded along the coast for gold, ivory and pepper. Between 1500 and 1531, 300 Portuguese caravels were captured on the Guinea trade route by French raiders,[19] and from 1530 onwards French trade steadily increased on the Guinea coast in spite of the efforts of the Portuguese.

The first English voyage may have taken place as early as 1479, and as we have seen, it was only an official Portuguese protest to Edward IV that prevented a strong English expedition from sailing to Guinea the following year. But after this there is no record of English voyages to the Gold Coast[20] until 1553. In that year a fleet of three ships sailed from Portsmouth under captain Thomas Windham, piloted to the Coast by Antonio Pinteado, who had been a Portuguese naval officer, and had until a short time previously been in command of a Portuguese squadron on the Guinea coast. They came to the Gold Coast, and traded both east and west of Elmina, buying 150 pounds weight of gold. Then Windham insisted, against Pinteado's advice, on going to Benin for pepper; and in the Niger creeks they lost so many men from fever that the survivors thought no more of trade, but only of escaping while they could. Both Windham and Pinteado died, and only forty men reached England out of the 140 who sailed; but the gold they brought was enough to induce others to follow them.[21]

Next year John Lok visited Guinea with a small fleet. He took three months to reach Cape Three Points, and arrived at Shama on

[18] Blake, 99-105, 177-81.
[19] Blake, 107.
[20] Though William Hawkins sent more than one expedition to Sierra Leone and the Grain and Ivory Coasts about 1530. He was mainly interested in the Brazil trade, and the Gold Coast was out of his way, whereas the regular route to Brazil lay past Cape Verde, and the seas between Cape Verde and Sierra Leone were the junction of the routes to Brazil and the East Indies.
[21] Blake, 143; Claridge, I, 60-2.

12th January, 1555. Here the squadron was fired on by the small Portuguese fort, and after returning the fire Lok passed farther east to Cabo Corso or Cape Coast. Cape Coast at this time was a village of about twenty houses, probably a newly-established fishing settlement.

They traded here and at Kormantine and Beraku, which was the most easterly point they reached. After a month on the coast they turned homewards, calling at Shama for gold, from which it would seem that the Portuguese garrison had left the fort unoccupied, if indeed it had not been silenced by Lok's fire a few weeks earlier. They reached England five months later with a rich cargo of gold and ivory and pepper. They had lost twenty-four men, but the voyage had been a great success from the financial point of view.[22]

From this time onwards English voyages became frequent, and in spite of vigorous Portuguese protests, both French and English interlopers traded busily on the Gold Coast. William Towerson made three voyages in 1555, 1556 and 1558, and on his first voyage he joined with a French squadron not only in trading but in fighting a combined action against a Portuguese patrolling fleet. In 1561 a combined Anglo-French fleet sailed as a joint enterprise from the beginning. These Anglo-French alliances did not last long; they were only assumed for fear of the local Portuguese fleets, and they always tended to dissolve through commercial jealousy.

But no amount of Anglo-French co-operation could outweigh the advantages which the Portuguese possessed in having two fortified bases on the Gold Coast itself. In Lok's first voyage there had been talk of establishing an English fort at Kormantine[23] and in 1556 Towerson had considered the possibility of building at or near Kommenda. In 1561 a number of English merchants formed themselves into a syndicate called the Company of Merchant Adventurers for Guinea; they included Sir Thomas Lodge, Lord Mayor of London, Benjamin Gonson, treasurer of the navy, and William Winter, one of Elizabeth's most trusted officers; and they

[22] Blake, 147; Claridge, I, 62-4. Shama was hardly to be reckoned as a fort; it was a trading post and provisioning station for Elmina and Axim; there were only two or three Portuguese there, and one or two small guns. For English and French voyages after 1555 see Blake 150-75.
[23] Blake, 155; Claridge, I, 62.

had the secret support of Cecil and the queen herself.[24] The syndicate proposed to send out John Lok to survey a site for a fort, but he refused to sail in the ship they offered him, on the ground that she was unseaworthy; and the expedition which went without him was so harried by the Portuguese that it could do nothing. In 1566 and again in 1570 plans were suggested for building an English rival to São Jorge da Mina, but they came to nothing.[25]

Without a base on the Gold Coast, the English had little hope of running a regular trade at a profit. Individual ships or expeditions might be lucky, but taking the trade as a whole the risks were too great. The gold area of the coast was only 150 miles long, from Axim to Winneba.[26] It was difficult to cruise on such a short stretch of coast for a month or so without coming into conflict with the Portuguese patrols. They were not always to be feared by a strong squadron, but their swift oared galleys armed with bow guns could be very deadly in a tropical calm against sailing ships which had much ado to keep steerage way. Apart from the Portuguese, there were other risks. There was fever and dysentery, not to mention scurvy, as captain Windham found. The supply of gold was not unlimited, and the out-going ships often had to race each other like the nineteenth century tea clippers as soon as they reached Cape Three Points. The first ship to arrive on the coast skimmed the cream of the market, the others often had to go short. Above all, the foreign interlopers, like the Portuguese themselves, were entirely dependent for their trade on the goodwill of the coast tribes. Here again they were at a crushing disadvantage through having no base of their own. The Portuguese were often unpopular, and many a chief would gladly have sold to the French or the English, if only to spite the Portuguese. But the Portuguese were always there, and it was unwise to spite them; so that often it happened that people who would have been willing to trade with the interlopers were afraid to. Moreover, the interlopers were not always welcome, even when compared with the Portuguese. The

[24] Blake, 163-4; Elizabeth hired four royal ships to the syndicate, though it was given out that they had been sold outright. The royal navy was to have one-third of the profits of the syndicate's trade. Elizabeth, of course, could not afford yet to defy Portugal or Spain.
[25] Blake, 173-5.
[26] Blake, 80; the Cabo das Redes seems to have been near Winneba; it is rather less than half-way from Elmina to the Volta, and has a hill immediately to the west of it, both of which details suit Winneba.

misdeeds of one English or French captain were revenged on his countrymen who came after him, as was found by Towerson on his first voyage and by George Fenner in 1567. Both these captains found their trade spoilt because previous English visitors had raided the coast for slaves.[27]

Partly for these reasons, and partly no doubt because of the greater attractions of the Spanish Main, the English interest in the Gold Coast waned after 1571.[28] For some little time before that, the English had been thinking more of slaves than of gold. John Hawkins's first slaving voyage was in 1562, and for a few years afterwards the slave trade was very popular among the English merchants. But the Senegal coast, and not the Gold Coast, was the chief area of this early English slave trade.[29] In 1576 the Elizabethan government signed a treaty with Portugal whereby English trade was admitted to Madeira and the Azores, and although Barbary and Guinea were not mentioned in the treaty there seems to have been an understanding that English merchants would be permitted on the Barbary coast as long as they kept away from Guinea.[30] At the close of the century, when Ancient Pistol declaimed for the first time on a London stage:

"I speak of Africa and golden joys",

as far as English seamen were concerned the golden joys he spoke of were already over. The phrase with its brave memories fits well with the tags and shreds of old stage plays that make up so much of Pistol's vocabulary.

The Portuguese did not long enjoy uninterrupted their freedom from English interlopers. The French still came to the Gold Coast, though not in such numbers as formerly. In 1580 Portugal was conquered by Philip II of Spain, and the Portuguese possessions in Brazil and on the African coast were thus thrown open to attack from Philip's revolted subjects of Holland. The first Dutch voyage to the Gold Coast was made in 1595, and was speedily followed by others, in spite of stout Portuguese opposition. The people welcomed the Dutch, as they had welcomed the English; and the

[27] Blake, 169; Claridge, I, 65-8.
[28] Blake, 169-72.
[29] After Hawkins's disaster at San Juan d'Ulloa in 1568 the slave trade as far as the English were concerned dwindled, not to revive until 1630. There was no market for English-supplied slaves in the New World as yet.
[30] Blake, 189.

Dutch determined to establish their own bases in the country. In 1598 they settled at Mori, Butri, Kormantine and Kommenda, so that the great Portuguese fortress at Elmina was now contained with a pair of Dutch settlements on each side; the Dutch settlements, however, were merely small affairs of earthworks and a fortified house, mounting one or two small guns each.

The new masters of the Portuguese settlements on the Gold Coast were much more interested in the East Indies and in America than in the dwindling supply of gold and slaves that came from West Africa. In the last years of the sixteenth century Loanda began to outdo the Guinea coast as the chief source of slaves, and in 1645 slaves began to go to America from the Portuguese settlements on the Mozambique coast. Near Elmina, the tunnels of one of the few mines in which gold quartz was being worked collapsed and buried the miners,[31] and naturally the African workers attributed the disaster to an angry god, and refused to reopen the mine. Next year, in 1623, the Portuguese sent an expedition up the river Ankobra to build a fort and work a gold mine in the Aowin country. For a time it looked as though this enterprising expedition, the first European attempt to establish bases inland, was going to meet with the success it deserved. A small fort was built fifteen miles up the river, and was defended against the attacks of the Aowin with their poisoned arrows. After peace had been made, a promising mine was opened, and for some years gave a rich yield of gold. But in 1636 there was an earthquake; the mine tunnels fell in, and several Aowin villages suffered. The people turned against the Portuguese[32] and killed those around the head of the mine; the fort itself was destroyed by the earthquake, and the survivors of the garrison abandoned the ruins and retired to Axim.

Meanwhile the Dutch increased their attacks, and formed the plan of capturing Elmina itself and expelling the Portuguese from the coast altogether. In December 1625 they made their first

[31] Claridge, I, 86, 87. Most of the gold was alluvial, obtained by washing river sand. This hill was the residence of a local god.
[32] Claridge, 90, 91. The Ankobra mine also was sunk in a sacred hill, and the Aowin had been at first most unwilling to give the Portuguese permission to dig there. In the end, however (Claridge, 88), they had consented; and it was no doubt to this consent that they attributed the damage done by the earthquake to their own villages. They took the natural course of burying alive in the mouth of the adit all the Portuguese survivors they could catch as a sacrifice to the god.

attempt on Elmina. A force of 1,200 Dutch troops and 150 Africans landed at Ampeni, six miles west of Elmina; but before they had time to form up they were attacked and completely defeated by the Elmina townsfolk, and the survivors escaped to their ships.

Events on the other side of the Atlantic were meanwhile bringing the English to think of resuming their trade on the Gold Coast. English settlers were establishing themselves in the West Indies; they settled in Bermuda in 1609, Barbados in 1627, and soon afterwards in Antigua and other islands. The English now had sugar plantations of their own, and slaves were needed to work them. The result was a revival of the English slave trade. In 1618 an English company was formed under royal charter, called the Company of Adventurers of London Trading into Africa; but the company was not successful and the charter lapsed. In 1631 another royal charter was granted, giving the company the monopoly of English trade over the West African coast from Cape Blanco to the Cape of Good Hope; thus setting up a direct challenge to the new Dutch West India Company, which had been established by the Dutch government only two years before with exactly the same field of operations.[33]

The slave trade now began in full swing, and Dutch and English strained every nerve to establish their position on the Gold Coast so as to control the source of supply. The Dutch enlarged their trading post at Mori and converted it into a strong stone fort, and they built a small outwork at Queen Anne's point between Mori and Cape Coast. The English company built a fort at Kormantine, thus belatedly carrying out the suggestion made to John Lok eighty years before. Dutch and English rivalry on the Gold Coast was becoming as keen as their rivalry in the East Indies. In both areas there was a rich trade to fight for.

The Dutch were determined to capture Elmina. Their defeat at Ampeni had shown them that they had to contend not only with the guns of the fortress but also with the supporting warriors of the Portuguese sphere of influence. The Dutch governor at Mori began a careful campaign of propaganda to deprive the Portuguese of this support. By 1637 he had succeeded in getting nearly all the coast tribes to promise help against the Portuguese and the Elmina

[33] Claridge, 89, 90.

people: a work which was probably not very difficult, for there was a long-standing enmity between the Elmina people and most of the surrounding Fante tribes, especially the people of Kommenda.[34] Having obtained these promises of help, the governor wrote to the West India Company urging them to make a fresh attempt on Elmina. The Company forwarded his letter to Count Maurice of Nassau, who was in Brazil with a strong fleet and an army for harassing the Spanish and Portuguese possessions there. He decided to come himself to the Gold Coast, and arrived off the coast on 25th June, 1957, with nine ships and 800 troops. He met Nicholas Van Ypren, the governor of Mori, at Kommenda, and on 24th August the joint forces left Kommenda with a fleet of 200 war canoes in support. On the morning of the 26th they disembarked at the mouth of a small lagoon at Cape Coast[35] and began the march towards Elmina.

The distance from the landing-place to Elmina is eight miles. About midday the troops reached the Sweet River, two miles from Elmina, and there they halted while scouts went forward to reconnoitre. Colonel Coine, the commander of the troops, saw that the only way of taking the fortress was by gaining possession of St. Jago hill on the north side of the Benya, which commanded the fortress, and from which heavy guns could bombard the weakest side of the defences. This hill had formerly been crowned by a chapel dedicated to St. James; but the chapel had recently been re-erected within the walls of the castle. The hill was defended by a thousand of the Elmina men, and Coine sent a detachment to attack it. The first attack failed; but the Elmina men, thinking that the battle was over, left their position, and a second party of Dutch carried the hill without much loss, and held it against counter-attacks. Coine at once brought some heavy guns to the hill-top and opened fire on the castle, while his allies from Kommenda crossed the river and attacked the town. The Portuguese were in great difficulty; they had only thirty European troops to garrison the castle, and many of them were ill; while the

---

[34] Claridge, 91; in describing the Dutch capture of Elmina, Claridge follows the account of Barbot and Dapper, the Portuguese version being much less plausible. The enmity between the Elmina people and their neighbours may have begun in Portuguese times through commercial jealousy; but it has been often reinforced since by other events.

[35] The lagoon was then open to the sea; the entrance is now closed by a sand bar.

attacking force, even after its losses at St. Jago hill, must have been nearly a thousand strong without counting the African troops. The Dutch gunfire from the opposite hill was doing little damage, the range being too great; but the Portuguese could make no reply, for on that side of the castle they had only two small guns to command the river crossing. If the Dutch chose, they could bring their battery to the foot of the hill and settle down at leisure to make a breach, quite safe from any Portuguese fire. The Dutch, on the other hand, were short of food, for they had brought only three days' rations with them from Cape Coast.[36] Accordingly, at daybreak on the 27th Colonel Coine summoned the fortress to surrender, and allowed the governor only one day to consider his position, instead of the three days which he requested. Next day the answer was delayed; whereupon Coine brought his guns to the foot of the hill and opened fire once more. Then the Portuguese governor surrendered; and next morning he and his garrison marched out, leaving the castle and all its stores to the Dutch. The Portuguese troops were put on board the Dutch ships and landed on the Portuguese island of San Thome.[37] A white stone let into the pathway outside the main gate of the castle marks the spot at which the Portuguese governor handed over the keys of the castle to Colonel Coine.

The Dutch now made Elmina their headquarters. Fort San Antonio at Axim refused the summons to surrender, and the Dutch left it alone for the time being; but in 1640 Portugal revolted against Spain and regained its independence, and immediately got into a war with Holland over Brazilian affairs. The Dutch took their opportunity, and in 1642 they captured Axim and expelled the Portuguese from the Gold Coast altogether. By the treaty of peace the Portuguese gave up their claims on the Gold Coast and in return the Dutch gave up theirs in Brazil.

Thus the Portuguese rule on the Gold Coast was ended, after their flag had flown 160 years.[38] They had left their mark on the country. Both in the Gold Coast languages and also in 'pidgin'

[36] This shortage of food can surely have been only a temporary inconvenience; for the Dutch fleet was lying off the shore, and its communications with the land forces were not interrupted.
[37] Claridge, I, 91-100. The Portuguese account as quoted by him certainly seems improbable enough.
[38] The Portuguese retained their interest farther east on the Slave Coast; and from 1679 to 1682 they even hoisted their flag again at Christiansborg near Accra.

English as spoken on the coast there are many Portuguese words;[39] but their best memorial is the long list of useful plants they introduced to the country from their other tropical possessions. They brought oranges, lemons, limes, rice and the sugar-cane from the Far East, and maize, tobacco, pineapple, cassava and guava and other fruits from America. It was the Portuguese also who introduced cattle to the coastal areas, which were inaccessible to cattle from the northern Sudan because of the tsetse belt.

In mission work, which was so important in the mind of Henry the Navigator, the Portuguese were not as successful as they were in some other parts of Africa, notably the Congo. The priests who came with them did not succeed in establishing an African Church, though it is said that some of the pagan ritual in the Elmina district shows, or formerly showed, traces of being influenced by Catholic ceremonial. When the Portuguese lost control of the Gold Coast the Catholic missionaries likewise departed; it was impossible for Catholic priests to work in an area controlled by seventeenth century Dutch Calvinists. The Dutch on the whole made no attempt to evangelize the African population, but contented themselves with supplying chaplains for the needs of their own staff. From the point of view of Christian influence in the country as a whole, the replacement of the Catholic priest by the Dutch predikant was a great loss.

[39] E.g. in Twi, *asepatere* (shoe), *krata* (paper), *osekan* (knife), *prako* (pig); in 'pidgin', *palaver*, *piccin*, *fetish*, and the ubiquitous *dash*.

CHAPTER V

THE EUROPEANS ON THE GOLD COAST DURING THE SEVENTEENTH AND EIGHTEENTH CENTURIES

AFTER expelling the Portuguese in 1642, the Dutch took steps to establish a monopoly of their own. They greatly enlarged and strengthened Elmina castle, in particular building a strong sub- sidiary fort on St. Jago hill and taking extraordinary precautions to keep its garrison secure. Bosman, writing in 1701, says, "Before any Fort was built upon St. Jago, that Hill was of great Service; 'twas from thence we chiefly obliged the Castle of St. George to Surrender, for our Cannon Planted there perfectly Commanded the Castle; wherefore we ought to be nearly concern'd for the Defence and Preservation of this Fort and Hill, for these once lost, the Castle of St. George could not hold out long; and accordingly therefore as much Care is always taken of this as of the Castle itself, there being always an Ensign left there with a good Garrison under his Command." They built forts at Shama and Butri to replace the small trading posts that already existed, and they built 'lodges' or trading posts at Accra, Anomabu, Kormantine and perhaps Cape Coast.

But the profit to be gained from the slave trade was too great for other nations to allow a Dutch monopoly. The English company already had a footing on the coast, and Swedes, Danes, French and Germans soon came to share in the scramble for wealth. The English company already held its fort at Kormantine, built in 1631; but the English were so occupied by their political troubles at home that for a good many years they were not able to extend their footing, and other nations got ahead of them on the Gold Coast.

The Swedes, having emerged from their Thirty Years' War while the English Parliament was still negotiating with its captive King, were first in the field. They sent an expedition to the Gold Coast in or about 1652, and built lodges at Takoradi, Cape Coast and Osu near Accra.[1] In 1657, however, they were driven out of all their positions by an expedition sent by King Frederic III of Denmark, and never again held any settlement on the Gold Coast. The Danish expedition also built a small new fort only three-quarters of a mile east of Cape Coast at the village of Amanfro, either to protect Cape Coast itself from the Dutch of Mori, or to command the eastern end of the Cape Coast roads. Takoradi was soon abandoned, the fort at Amanfro was sold to the English twenty years later; but the fort at Osu was enlarged and strengthened by the Danes, and under the name Christiansborg became their chief post on the Gold Coast.

By this time the Commonwealth was firmly established in England; and in 1651, the year of Cromwell's 'crowning mercy' at Worcester, the English company's charter of 1631 was confirmed. Next year the Commonwealth government sent out a frigate to protect English trade on the Guinea coast against Dutch attacks, and diplomatic protest was made to Sweden against Swedish inter-ference with English trade. The first Anglo-Dutch war of 1651-4 caused on the whole much more loss to Holland than to England; but as far as the Guinea trade was concerned the English losses were heavy enough. The English were finding that the possession of one fort at Kormantine was of little help against the Dutch with their magnificent castle at Elmina and strong forts also at Axim, Butri, Sekondi, Shama and Mori, not to mention lodges elsewhere. In 1650 the Dutch took another step by replacing their lodge at Accra by a strong fort. It seemed that unless the English made a mighty effort they would be squeezed out of the Guinea trade altogether by the Dutch, as they had already been squeezed out of the East Indies spice trade.

Peace was made with the Dutch in 1654; but there was no peace on the Guinea coast; then, as in Portuguese days, peace treaties lost their force south of the Tropic of Cancer.[2] The Dutch were aiming

[1] It may be that this energetic party also took the Dutch lodge at Anomabu, only to lose this with the rest to the Danes five years later. The eary history of Cape Coast is very obscure. There may have been a lodge there in Portuguese times, which the Dutch abandoned soon after their capture of Elmina. This lodge was reoccupied by the Swedes, and certainly taken from them by the Danes in 1657 or 1658. It is uncertain what happened to it in the next few years; it may have been abandoned by the Danes because they preferred Amanfro, or it may have been taken from them by the Dutch or by the Efutu people in whose land it stood. In any case, it was replaced by a castle, built by the English, in 1662.
[2] Blake, 160, 162.

at monopoly. They regarded themselves as entitled by right of conquest to the same monopoly which the Portuguese had claimed. They were unable to drive the English off the coast altogether, but they steadily attacked every English ship they could, and imprisoned the crews at Elmina just as the Portuguese had done. The English, being the weaker party, seem to have had a theory that the Dutch were entitled to a monopoly of the trade at their own stations, but not at other places; thus in 1662 they protested against Dutch attacks made on English ships at Kommenda and Cape Coast, on the ground that the Dutch had no trading station at those places and thus could not be injured by others coming to trade.[3] To this it might be replied that Kommenda is only ten miles, and Cape Coast eight miles, from Elmina, and trade carried on there must tap the sources of the Elmina prosperity; and it is very doubtful if the English would have maintained their theory if they had had any prospect of being able to exclude the Dutch from the Gold Coast.

In 1662 the English trade with the Gold Coast was placed on a new footing by the formation of a new company called the Company of Royal Adventurers of England Trading to Africa, which included James, Duke of York, brother of Charles II and afterwards himself king. The importance of this step is that the Duke of York and many other important people were interested, and the Company was sure to have the ear of the government. Its charter gave it the monopoly of trade, not merely from Cape Blanco, but from the Straits of Gibraltar to the Cape of Good Hope. It was to supply 3,000 slaves a year to the West Indies, and was to take over the fort at Kormantine and build new forts or lodges at Cape Coast, Anashan, Egya, Kommenda, Winneba and Accra. Cape Coast was to be its headquarters.

The new company lost no time in beginning its work. In 1662 or 1663 it built Cape Coast castle, and in 1663 built lodges at Anashan, Egya, Kommenda and Winneba. The fort or lodge which the company's charter obliged it to build at Accra was not built till ten years later, by which time the company which had been started with such pomp was defunct and was replaced by its

---

[3] Claridge, I, 107-8. Monopoly was, of course, the aim of every trading nation at that time; the English would have monopolized the Guinea trade if they had been able.

successor. The more energetic its measures, the more stubborn was the resistance of the Dutch. They incited the African inhabitants to attack the new English lodge at Winneba and the English fort at Kormantine; they formally protested against the English violation of their monopoly, claiming that they had won from the Portuguese the right to exclude every other nation from the Gold Coast. This formal protest was followed by a surprise attack on the English fort at Cape Coast, and both this fort and the lodge at Egya were taken. The attack on Kormantine failed, as an English ship arrived in time to relieve the garrison. While the Dutch were thus irritating the English commercial interests in Guinea, the English were consoling themselves by landing troops to conquer the Dutch colonies in North America; and the merchants in both countries grew tired of such a peace. In 1665 open war broke out; but already the English government had secretly dispatched captain Robert Holmes with a fleet to cruise all down the West African coast and take reprisals against the Dutch for these attacks on English shipping.[4] Holmes began by taking the Dutch fort at Goree, and on 9th April he arrived at Takoradi. Here the Swedes, and later the Danes, had held a small post; but it had been abandoned about 1660, and the Dutch had thereupon occupied the site and built a small fort called Fort Witsen.

Holmes now began a rapid triumphal progress. He took Fort Witsen without any trouble, and in the next few weeks took the forts at Shama, Cape Coast, Mori, Anomabu, Egya and perhaps Axim also; and arrived back in England, having done what he was sent to do. It may, however, be typical of the government of Charles II that Holmes's fleet did not include transports to provide the restored English forts and the newly-taken Dutch ones with an adequate garrison. His expedition was in fact nothing but a raid in the old Elizabethan tradition.

The States of Holland were not likely to submit to this treatment. Admiral de Ruyter was at Gibraltar with thirteen ships, and

---

[4] For these operations see Claridge, 108-15. This was not Holmes's first visit to West Africa; Dryden, in *Annus Mirabilis*, written in 1666, speaks of Holmes, "who first bewitch'd our eyes with Guinny gold", and on 24th August, 1661 Pepys "called to Sir W. Batten's to see the strange creature that Captain Holmes hath brought with him from Guinny". It was a "baboon", so intelligent and "so much like a man in most things" that Pepys had much ado to accept it as a beast at all. It sounds like a chimpanzee, a species which is still found on the Gold Coast.

as soon as the news of Holmes's exploit reached Holland, orders
were sent to him to abandon the Mediterranean[5] and restore the
Dutch to their old position on the West Coast. He retook Goree in
October, Takoradi in January, and Anashan, Kormantine, Kommenda, Winneba, Shama, Mori and Anomabu in the next few
weeks. Egya was blown up by the English garrison.[6] The Dutch
authorities begged him to retake Cape Coast, saying that the loss of
Cape Coast might so discourage the English that they would retire
from the Coast altogether and leave the Dutch in possession. But
de Ruyter, after reconnoitring the castle and discovering that the
place would have to be stormed not merely in face of its military
strength but also in face of a hostile people, declined to make the
attempt, and in February departed. He had done enough, in spite
of his failure at Cape Coast; he had taken every other post that the
English had, and had garrisoned them so strongly that nothing
but an expedition in force could hope to recapture them. And war
was not declared until March 1665, by which time de Ruyter was
in mid-Atlantic on his way from the African coast to the West
Indies.[7] Pepys recorded bitterly in his diary "the news of our being
beaten to dirt at Guinny by de Ruyter with his fleete".[8] As he said,
it was "most wholly to the utter ruine of our Royall Company",
which after petitioning for compensation from the Government
for its losses from de Ruyter, gave up the business and surrendered
its charter in 1672.[9]

The treaty of Breda, which ended the war, left only Cape Coast

[5] He received his orders early in September and sailed a few weeks later; Corbett,
England in the Mediterranean, II, 337.
[6] They were sure that the Dutch would occupy the place, and hoped that their
mine would blow up the Dutch troops that entered. But the Dutch ignored the
small building and went straight on to Kormantine.
[7] The news of Holmes's raid did not reach England until September; Pepys
records it on 29th September, 1664. Holmes did not return direct to England,
but went from the African coast to the other side of the Atlantic, where he
was in time to assist in Captain Nichols's conquest of the Dutch colony of New
Amsterdam in August. De Ruyter likewise went from Africa to America; he
attacked Barbados in April 1665 and was repulsed; from there he went on
to Newfoundland and returned home by the northern route, picking up the
Dutch Levant and Indies fleets and escorting them home via Norway. He did
not reach Holland, anxiously awaited, till August (Ogg, *England in the reign of
Charles II*, I, 290).
[8] 22nd and 24th December, 1664.
[9] The Company had other difficulties; it could not induce its shareholders to pay
up the whole of their investment and so was constantly short of capital; the
expenses of the slave trade were heavy, and its customers wanted long credit,
and it was always harassed by the Dutch (Ogg, I, 230; Lipson, II, 355).

in English hands. But the English had no intention of sacrificing the capital that had been invested in the Guinea trade; and in 1672 a new company was formed, called the Royal African Company, with a still more imposing list of shareholders than its predecessor's. Like the earlier company, it received a monopoly charter, and it determined to enforce its monopoly more strictly than the earlier companies had done. The Royal Adventurers had granted licences so freely to non-members that the trade had been virtually open to any Englishman on payment of a fee. The Royal African Company raised the licence fee to 40 per cent of the value of the freight carried in the interloper's ship, a prohibitive tariff. This raised a storm of protest; the West Indian planters complained that the price of slaves had doubled, and similar complaints came from consumers of other African produce—ivory and dyewood—and from the manufacturers of trade goods for the African market. After years of wrangling in parliamentary committees and elsewhere, the matter was decided by a statute, which laid down in 1698 that the licence fee was to be reduced to 10 per cent, which was to be paid to the Company for the upkeep of the forts on the coast.[10]

The Royal African Company, like its predecessor, began its operations with too little capital; but it began energetically enough. It bought Cape Coast castle and two other forts at Sierra Leone and the Gambia for £34,000; it built a new fort at Accra, which it named James Fort in honour of the Duke of York, and forts also at Kommenda and Anomabu. In its first season it brought home a great quantity of gold, from which the first guineas were struck by the Mint.

It is evident from these constant struggles that the Guinea trade was booming. This was because there was a new and expanding market for slaves in the West Indies and North America. In Portuguese days there had been a regular slave trade with the Spanish and Portuguese possessions in the New World; but the trade was a Portuguese monopoly, protected not merely by Portuguese regulations and prohibitions in Guinea itself, but by the strict refusal of the Spanish and Portuguese governors and planters in tropical America to buy slaves from any foreign dealer. In the reign of Charles II the English ambassadors at Madrid were

[10] Lipson, II, 355-60.

making constant efforts to induce the Spanish government to throw open the slave market to English shipping;[11] but the Spanish market was no longer the only market for slaves. The English had occupied Barbados, St. Kitts, Antigua, Tobago and others of the Caribbean islands, before the Commonwealth; the Commonwealth forces captured Jamaica in 1655; the Bahamas were occupied in 1670. The staple crop for export was sugar, which needed a large supply of slave labour; and the demand for slaves was so great that every commercial nation in Europe began competing for a share in the trade. Not only West Indian sugar but also Virginian tobacco depended on a constant line of slave ships speeding westwards on the wings of the trade wind; most of them flying the flag of England or of Holland, the leaders of European freedom.

The Gold Coast received its name from the Portuguese, at a time when gold was by far the chief item in its trade. In the eighteenth century it would have been even more appropriately named the Slave Coast, had not that name already been bestowed on the coastline between the Volta and the Niger. The trade increased greatly when the Treaty of Utrecht in 1713 gave the British the right to supply 4,800 slaves a year to Spanish America, over and above the large numbers which they were already exporting to the British West Indies and North America.[12] The size to which the trade developed can best be seen by figures. It was estimated that between 1680 and 1700 the Royal African Company exported 140,000 slaves, and interlopers exported 160,000 more. Between 1700 and 1786, the island of Jamaica alone received 610,000 slaves from all sources. At the end of that period, the annual slave trade was estimated at 38,000 British, 20,000 French, 10,000 Portuguese, 4,000 Dutch and 2,000 Danish, 74,000 in all. There were 192 British ships employed in the slave trade in the year 1770. One slave in every eight died at sea, and two more died within a few months of their arrival in the plantations, so that sometimes not more than half the slaves exported from Africa survived to live laborious days in the New World.

[11] Ogg, II, 667.
[12] This Asiento concession had formerly been held by the Dutch, and subsequently by the French, from whom it was transferred to Britain in 1713. The concession was granted to the South Sea Company, but the company suffered greatly from the 'Bubble' slump, the concession was not profitable, and it was surrendered in 1750; Lipson, II, 367-70.

Not all of these vast numbers came, of course, from the Gold Coast. The French obtained most of their slaves in Senegambia and on the Slave Coast; the Portuguese drew theirs from Angola and Mozambique as well as from the Gold and Slave Coasts; and the British did not by any means confine their attention to the land west of the Volta. Most of the Dutch, and almost all the Danish slaves, probably came from the Gold Coast. But even if we assume that only half these slaves were from Gold Coast ports, an annual export of 35,000 is a heavy drain on the population of a country the size of Britain.

The supply of slaves to the ships was entirely in African hands. Both here and on the Slave Coast the Africans jealously guarded their monopoly of the trade. On the Slave Coast the king of Dahomey was paramount, and refused to allow any European coastal forts. He collected slaves in inland depots, and the European dealers had to buy them there. On the Gold Coast the shore was controlled by a number of comparatively small states, who encouraged forts on the coast for two reasons; first, to prevent the Europeans from penetrating through their territory and coming into direct trading relations with the more powerful inland nations such as Ashanti or Akwamu, and second, to have the aid of the European garrisons in case of attacks from these powerful inland rivals. In both countries the motive was the same, though the difference in political conditions led to entirely opposite policies.

The supply of slaves was controlled by Accra or Fante middlemen, who sent their agents inland to buy slaves from the wholesale dealers. The Ashanti sent most of their slaves down to the great depot at Manso, some thirty miles from Cape Coast on the Kumasi road. At Manso and similar staple towns the slaves were bought by the middlemen from the coast, and drafted down to smaller depots in the coast towns themselves. Every castle had its storehouses for slaves, where they were kept by the European agents who bought them in the local slave market, until the ships came to take them across the sea.

The Europeans themselves lived a sufficiently miserable life. The chief British officials were reasonably well paid, and though they were forbidden to engage in private trading, it seems that the prohibition was often ignored. But they had little other comfort.

There was little love lost between the European officials and the African townsfolk, and the officials often had to live pent up inside the forts and could never go far afield. They were supplied with some provisions from Europe,[13] and supplemented these with what they could buy in the local market. Bosman thinks little of the local markets' resources:

"For Food, what is here to be gotten for the common people besides Fish and a dry lean Hen? And, indeed, were he able to pay for better, here is nothing proper for a weak Stomach; for all the Oxen and Cows, Sheep and Hens, are dry lean and tough: so that a sound Man, not to mention an infirm one, hath enough to do to eat them. So that the best . . . that the poor Sick can get here, are Culinary Vegetables and Spoon-Meats; the Director and the Chief-Factor are abundantly furnished with the former, but they are not in every Bodies reach."

But perhaps in this passage Bosman is speaking too strongly; elsewhere he speaks of the kingdom of Saboe, which "produceth in great abundance, Corn, Jammes, Potatoes and other Fruits of the Earth; with which and Palm-Oil about an hundred Canoas are daily laden at Mouree, bound for Axim and Accra". If badly off for food, the Europeans seem to have been well provided with drink; Bosman and other contemporary writers describe the heavy drinking as characteristic of European life on the Coast, "by which excessive tipling and sorry feeding," says Bosman, "most of the Garrison look as if they were Hag-ridden". Tropical medicine was in its infancy; the dangers of malaria and yellow-fever mosquitoes, and of unboiled water, were unknown. The evening mist, and what Bosman calls the "odious Mixture of noisome Stenches" coming from congested seaside villages whose chief industry was fish-curing, were regarded as the source of malarial fever, and these naturally could not be avoided. The danger of chill from sudden drops in the temperature was known, but not always sufficiently guarded against. It is not surprising that the mortality from malaria, yellow-fever and other tropical diseases was appalling. In 1821 thirteen Europeans out of fifty-two living in Cape Coast died; three years later 295 died out of the garrison of 600 in the course of a few months; in 1826 the House of Commons was informed

[13] "Beef, Pork, Bread, Flour, etc.", says a document of 1781; Crooks, 48.

that during a period of nine quarters 1,567 troops had been sent to
the Gold Coast, of whom 905 had died of disease. Bosman estimates
that during his service on the coast at least one English agent, and
factors innumerable, died every year. The Danes had twenty-four
governors in fifty years, from 1700 to 1750; and all but four died
in harness.[14] The Coast acquired an evil reputation, and it became
hard to engage good men to serve there. Many of the troops were
convicts, many of the officers were far from being the best type of
European soldier or statesman. They failed to win the confidence
of the Africans with whom they had to deal, and a general
atmosphere of suspicion and sharp practice made life on the Coast
still more miserable.[15]

The forty years which followed the duel of Holmes and
de Ruyter were the period when the scramble for trade and territory was keenest. The English company had forts at Cape Coast,
Kommenda, Anomabu and Accra, and soon afterwards built small
forts at Winneba and Sekondi. The Dutch held Elmina, Accra,
Axim, Butri, Mori, Sekondi, Shama, Kormantine and Takoradi;
and were still expanding their possessions. In 1667 they built a fort
at Beraku, in 1688 at Kommenda to compete with the English
there; earlier in their career they had built three forts, Duma,
Elise Carthago, and Ruyghaver, on the river Ankobra, with
the idea of controlling the Aowin mines which had attracted the
Portuguese several years before. But they had no better luck than
the Portuguese, and they soon abandoned the attempt. In 1697
they began building a fort at Apam near the English fort at
Winneba. The work went on so slowly under continual opposition
from the people that the fort was named Leydsamheid or Patience.
The English about the same time built a fort at Dixcove near Cape
Three Points.

In 1679 the Portuguese tried to re-establish themselves. The
Danish governor of Christiansborg was murdered by one of his
officers, and the murderer sold the castle to the Portuguese, who

[14] Claridge, II, 586-7.
[15] Bosman says that the English agents cheated their men by selling liquor at
double its value. Salaries were paid in a depreciated local currency, and men
were constantly in debt to the company they served. Cruikshank (I, 28-9) gives
several instances of incompetence and brutality among the European officials,
which may or may not have been typical, though he himself seems to have
thought them so. But see also note 23 on p. 201, which shows that things were
not always as bad as this.

garrisoned it from their troops at San Thome.[16] But the Portuguese investment was unprofitable, and the Danes bought the castle back a few years later. When the Danish fort Frederiksborg at Cape Coast was sold to the English in 1685 Christiansborg was the only Danish possession left on the coast.

Apart from a short-lived venture by the French[17] the only other European nation that settled on the Gold Coast was Brandenburg. In 1682 the Elector of Brandenburg[18] sent an expedition to the district round Cape Three Points, where they built an imposing fortress, named Gross Friedrichsburg,[19] and two smaller posts, fort Dorothea at the village of Akwida and a redoubt at the village of Takrama. The last was intended to guard an important watering-place and to make an income by charging fees to ships watering there.

The Brandenburgers laid claim also to the site of the English fort at Dixcove. The Brandenburg settlements had a troubled career. Not only did they carry on skirmishes with the English interlopers at Dixcove, but they were in continual difficulties with the villagers and with the Dutch. Two of their governors were killed; and the Dutch author Bosman, writing of conditions in 1698, says, "I very much doubt whether ever they will regain the Mastery, for the Negroes having once got the upper-hand will sufficiently Lord it over them." In 1708 the Brandenburgers abandoned their forts; Gross Friedrichsburg, after being intermittently occupied by the local chieftain for some time, was taken by the Dutch in 1725.[20]

The kaleidoscopic changes in the occupation and ownership of the forts on the coast during the seventeenth and eighteenth cen-

[16] An island in the east end of the Gulf of Guinea, on the Equator; still a Portuguese possession.
[17] In 1688; they established a factory at Kommenda which was destroyed by the Kommenda people a few months later; Claridge, I, 125-6. It is interesting that exactly a hundred years later the French made a second attempt which lasted six years. They were, of course, well established farther north on the Senegal.
[18] The Electorate of Brandenburg became the kingdom of Prussia in 1701.
[19] Sometimes known by its Dutch name of Groot Fredericksburg. The imposing ruins of this fortress are a favourite place of pilgrimage for passengers on German liners putting in at Takoradi. Some years ago the German government sent a cruiser to remove some of the guns and take them to Germany. The people of the village below the castle still talk of the strength and determination of the German sailors, who manhandled the guns, refusing all assistance from the people, and took them off from the cove in their boats.
[20] Bosman, 7-11; Claridge, I, 203-6.

FIG. 8.
The European Forts on
the Gold Coast.

turies are wearisome and confusing to follow in detail. Forts were built, abandoned, sold, attacked, captured, exchanged; thirty-five villages on the present Gold Coast were at one time or another chosen as sites for some sort of fortified posts. In dignity and strength they ranged from imposing places like Elmina, with six satellite redoubts linked in one system of defence, to places like the English fort at Anashan, "where the intire Garrison consists of one whole English-man, who lies there; is it possible for him to preserve the Honour of the Flag?"[21] Portuguese, Dutch, English, French, Swedes, Danes and Brandenburgers, and once or twice the African chieftains, reigned proudly over bastions and batteries, and reproduced on African soil the engineering of Vauban and the militarism of Corporal Trim. The story of the sieges, blockades, surprises and changes of ownership is best summarized in a table.[22] One incident, the capture of Christiansborg by the Akwamu from the Danes in 1693, though not typical of the fortunes of the European forts,[23] is worth relating.

Christiansborg, like all the European posts, was a trading station, and in time of peace was open to the African public for buying and selling: buying of guns, cloth, spirits and miscellaneous fancy goods, selling of gold, ivory, pepper, and above all, slaves. In 1693 the Danish garrison was reduced by death and disease to twenty-five men fit for service; and an Akwamu named Asameni conceived the idea of capturing the fort by stratagem. Asameni was well known to the Danish garrison; he had at one time been in the English service,[24] but had set up as a trader on his own account. He specialized in the business of an agent for parties of traders from the interior who wanted introductions and an interpreter in their business with the white men.

[21] Bosman, 56.
[22] The table forms Appendix I at the end of this book, p. 414.
[23] Though no fewer than ten forts were at one time or another taken by Africans, either by the local people or by invaders (Ashanti and Akim). The list is as follows: Winneba, 1663 and 1679; the French lodge at Kommenda, 1688; Christiansborg, 1693; Ruyghaver, c. 1680; Dorothea, c. 1690; Orange (Sekondi), 1694; the English fort at Sekondi, 1698; Amsterdam (Kormantine), 1807; Leydsamheid (Apam), 1811; and the small Portuguese fort at Accra, 1578. Forts Amsterdam and Leydsamheid were taken by the Ashanti and the Akim respectively, the others by the local people. These two and Christiansborg were considerable places, the others were small forts. In addition to these, Dixcove, though not actually stormed, was forced in 1695 to come to terms with the local people.
[24] Claridge says he had been a cook in English service.

In this capacity Asameni came to the Danish governor and told him that he was going to bring a large party of Akwamu traders to buy firearms; the weapons were urgently needed, he said, and the men would pay a good price if necessary. A few days later he arrived with a party of eighty men. They entered the shop on the ground floor of the courtyard and began examining the guns for sale; and presently they asked to be obliged with a charge of powder apiece, so that they might test the guns with a blank charge before buying. This was customary, and the clerk provided the powder; but every man had brought a bullet tied up in the corner of his cloth, and all the guns were rapidly loaded. The garrison was overpowered; the governor, who was in his room above the shop, heard the noise and ran down with drawn sword to investigate, but was attacked and wounded. He defended himself with his sword as well as he could, but seeing the position was hopeless he jumped from a window and ran, with a broken arm and several wounds, along the beach to the Dutch Fort Crèvecœur, two miles away.[25]

Asameni now took over the governorship of the fort, nominally at least in the name of the Akwamuhene; and held the place for several months. He wore the governor's uniform, traded freely with English and Dutch, entertained visiting sea-captains and his European fellow-governors, and was prodigal in his expenditure of powder in salutes with his big guns. Eventually, the Danes sent out an expedition to retake the castle, and through the mediation of the Dutch of Fort Crèvecœur, Asameni agreed to haul down his flag and cede the castle to the Danes for the sum of £1,600. He had taken £7,000 worth of trade goods when he captured the place; and he refused to consider the suggestion that he should restore this or pay any compensation; so his enterprise was a lucrative one.

The unfortunate Danish governor, whose stay in Fort Crèvecœur had been embittered by the daily view of the castle of which he had been in charge, embarked with a heavy heart on the Danish

[25] This account is taken from Bosman, 67-8, and Claridge, I, 127-30, but Akwamu tradition of today confirms it in all essentials. The Akwamu believe that the governor was killed by Asameni's men. The keys of the castle, an enormous heavy bunch, are still preserved in the Akwamu treasure. Asameni's flag was white, with a device of an African warrior, proper; this, alas, is not preserved with the keys.

ships to stand his trial in Denmark. But he never came to trial; for the ships' companies were so depleted by the garrison they left in Christiansborg that the ships were soon captured by the English pirate 'Long Ben' Avery, who took them to the pirate lair at the island of Principe[26] and made the whole company walk the plank. Asameni had a better fortune; he became a chief in his native country of Akwamu, and his descendants are alive at this day to testify.[27]

Of the many local wars between the different European nations, and between the Europeans and the local tribes, few are of any real importance. In 1694 a war broke out between the Dutch and the Kommenda people, which led to a long-standing feud. The Kommenda people had never agreed to the establishment in their town of the Dutch Fort Vredenburg; and when the Dutch began mining for gold in a sacred hill, they took up arms and stopped the Dutch operations. The Dutch commander collected a force from Elmina and began making reprisals; and the Kommenda people countered this by inviting the English to return and occupy a fort that they had abandoned some years before. The English came, to the great embarrassment of the Dutch; for the English fort when restored was stronger than Fort Vredenburg.

The Dutch now saw that the situation was serious; and they spent £5,000 in hiring a large force from Elmina and Cape Coast to supplement the party of Elmina men that they already had. So large was the contingent that the Dutch commander conceived the plan of settling first with the people of Kommenda and then passing on to deal with the people of Asebu and Fante; and he was imprudent enough to say so. The result was that the Asebu and Fante at once anticipated him by mobilizing their troops, and the Dutch with their Elmina allies were utterly defeated. They made great efforts to recover their position; they secured allies from one section of the Kommenda people themselves, and also from other neighbouring tribes; but in one case through treachery, in another through dissensions, in a third through the sudden outbreak of another and much more serious war in the interior, their allies were useless to them. The Dutch and their auxiliaries were defeated a second time; Fort Vredenburg itself was strongly

[26] Principe, near San Thome, was a favourite pirate haunt.
[27] The Akwamu, like all Akan nations, reckon descent through the female line.

attacked, and in the end the Dutch considered themselves lucky in being able to secure peace on reasonable terms.[28]

The importance of this war lies in the permanent antagonism which it brought about between the Elmina people and their neighbours. The remote origin of this feud is lost. Ever since the Ashanti came to power the Elmina people have claimed to have some connection with Ashanti; but it is impossible to say what the connection may be. There are many grievances which embittered the feeling between Elmina and the towns in the surrounding country; but a sufficient origin for the feud is probably to be found in the fact that the Elmina people were for 150 years almost the sole agents for the white men, and roused commercial jealousy among their neighbours. However this may be, at the close of the seventeenth century we see Elmina isolated from the surrounding country, and completely identified with the Dutch interest against Kommenda, Cape Coast, Anomabu and a large part of the coast lands. The English, whose own relations with the local tribes were far from happy, on this occasion intrigued successfully against the Dutch, and for a time managed to pose as the leaders of a con-siderable African confederation against the Dutch and their Elmina auxiliaries.

During the seventeenth and eighteenth centuries the coastline from the mouth of the Tano to the mouth of the Volta was divided into a large number of petty states. From the Tano to the Ankobra were the two states of Adouir and Ankober. Between the Ankobra and the Pra were Axim, Ante or Ahanta, Adom and Jabi. Between the Pra and the river Benya at Elmina was the more powerful state of Kommani or Kommenda, and the twenty-mile stretch of coast from the Benya to the so-called Iron Hills a little east of Mori was divided about equally between Fetu and Asebu. The Fante coast reached from the Iron Hills to a point a little east of Tantumkweri, coinciding roughly with the present administrative boundary between the Saltpond and Winneba districts; the length of the Fante coast was about twenty-five miles. The Devil's Mount at Winneba was the approximate boundary between the small kingdom of Akron and the much larger one of Agona. The state

---

[28] The complicated story of this war and the intrigues which accompanied it is in Bosman, 26-41 (Bosman was himself in command of the successful defence of Vredenburg), and Claridge, I, 146-54; on 144 Claridge hints at the nature of some of the old scores that the Dutch had against Asebu and Fante.

PLATE V "The white man brings his cannon to the bush": Hausa artillerymen bringing the guns across the Pra in the 1874 campaign

(Illustrated London News)

PLATE VI

THE BATTLEFIELD AT ABAKRAMPA

(*Illustrated London News*)

of Agona ended near the Sekumu lagoon; thence to the Sango lagoon was Accra, and east of that was Ningo. In Bosman's time Accra and Ningo were counted as part of Akwamu.

These states were all small, and although the capitals in most cases were a little inland from the sea, their territory was only a few miles broad. It is interesting to compare this list of fourteen sea-board states with the list of states which occupy the same stretch of shore today. Passing, as in the first case, from west to east, they are: Western Nzima, Eastern Nzima, Upper and Lower Axim, Upper and Lower Dixcove, Ahanta, Dutch and English Sekondi, Shama, Kommenda, Edinaa, Oguaa, Nkusukum, Anomabu, Ebiram, Winneba, Gomoa Asen, Ga, Prampram and Ada: twenty-one in all, which may be perhaps reduced to nineteen by omitting Prampram and Ada, which lie east of the village of Ponni (Kpone or Kpong), the easternmost village mentioned by Bosman. Of these nineteen states four bear the same names as those in the earlier list: Axim (now divided into two), Ahanta, Kommenda and Ga or Accra. Three states in the earlier list, Gwira, Agona and Asebu, still exist today under those names as inland states, having lost their outlet to the sea. Oguaa, Anomabu, Nkusukum and Ebiram are Fante states, occupying the same region as Bosman's 'Fantynean land', where even in his day "every part of Fantyn hath also its particular Chief, who will sometimes scarce own himself subject to the Braffo, who hath the ineffectual name only of Supreme Power". No fewer than eight of the modern states take their names from European settlements: two at Dixcove, two at Sekondi, Shama, Edinaa (Elmina), Oguaa (Cape Coast) and Winneba—striking evidence of the disintegrating effect of the centuries of European conflict.

The inland states known to Bosman were Aowin, Wassaw, Denkyera, Adansi, Ashanti, Akim, Akwamu, all of which exist under the same names today; Encasse and Juffer, which he describes as subject to Denkyera and bordering upon Kommenda; and Akane. Encasse and Juffer have presumably been absorbed by Wassaw, and it is doubtful whether the Akane which he mentions existed as a separate state at all; its name is still in use as a general term for the Twi- and Fante-speaking nations.

The European forts along this coast all stood on land which was rented by the Europeans from the local tribes. A written agree-

D

ment was made with the chief and his elders; in local parlance this document was called a Note. The rent for Elmina castle was two ounces of gold a month, increased to four ounces at the end of the seventeenth century; James fort, Accra, paid two ounces, and Cape Coast and Anomabu paid four ounces each. An ounce of gold was valued at £4. Beside the rent which was paid to the ground landlord, stipends were paid to other influential men in the towns; thus, in a return of 1820 we find such payments as these: "Quamina Amoa, River Cabboceer[29]—Company's Pay £18, Equal to Sterling £12. Useful in facilitating the communication over the river.[30] . . . Coffee Sam, Captain of the Town—Company's Pay £24, Equal to Sterling £16. The next man of the most influence, of great use in case of disturbance between the natives and the garrison, or with the shipping. . . . Braffoes and Curranteers of Fantee, for water custom. Company's pay £36, Equal to Sterling £24. These people are the supreme chiefs of the Fantee country. By assembling the chiefs of Abrah and Murram, they can at any time shut all communication between inland Fantee and the waterside . . . " In this year, 1820, the total amount paid in rents and stipends by the British forts alone was over three thousand pounds sterling, nearly five thousand in local currency.[31]

At this point it is as well to discuss the nature of these chiefs, 'Braffoes, Caboceers, Curranteers', as they were called formerly, and of the constitution which regulated their position. The constitution of the Akan and other Gold Coast nations is a subject of great political importance still. The Government is constantly under suspicion of ignoring it or of deliberately violating it; and it is this suspicion which renders Indirect Rule, Native Administra-

[29] 'Cabboceer' is the Portuguese *caboceiro* or captain. 'Braffo' and 'Curranteer' are corruptions of Fante terms. *Obrafo* is a general term for a distinguished man: it also means a Lord High Executioner, and this may have been its original sense. In the eighteenth century a certain Eno Baisie Kurentsi was the founder of a dynasty of powerful chiefs in Anomabu; 'Curranteer' is a corruption of his family name, which the Europeans supposed to be a title. I am indebted to Mr. M. A. Ribeiro for this information.
[30] The Ankobra.
[31] Crooks, *Records of the Gold Coast Settlements*, 126-34. Sums of money were usually reckoned in gold dust. The commonest weights used in reckoning were the ackie, 5s., the ounce, £4, the benda, £7, and the pereguan, £8. The Akan had, of course, a much bigger list of gradations: Rattray (*Ashanti*, 320-1) gives fifty-nine weights ranging from a third of a penny up to £80; Christaller gives thirty-nine, ranging from ¼d. to £24. The benda and the pereguan are two of these Akan weights. Many of the weights, represented by their equivalents in modern sterling, are still used for purposes of reckoning.

tion, Stool Treasuries and Direct Taxation such thorny subjects of discussion. Unjustified though this suspicion is today, it is a natural result of long years of negotiations in which the Government of the day did frequently show itself ignorant or careless of the constitutional principles on which the Gold Coast tribal life is regulated; and only time can dispel it. The chief misconception which has been made is that the chief of a Gold Coast tribe is a despot, or at least that he has a large prerogative. All writers, from Bosman's time onwards, who have come into close contact with Gold Coast rulers have pointed out the contrary; but in negotiations with these rulers, European commanders have constantly made Azambuja's mistake of expecting them to decide and to act without an opportunity of consulting their constitutional advisers.

The native constitutions of the Northern Territories differ greatly from those of Ashanti and the Colony. The Northern system will be discussed later when dealing with recent developments in that part of the country. The description in this chapter applies only to Ashanti and the Colony. There are, of course, variations from one nation to another, but the general principles are the same.

The unit of society is the family, whether this is matrilineal as among the Akan or patrilineal as among the Ga. Family ties are very strong, and are strengthened by the system of ancestor-worship. The ancient division of the Akan into seven 'families' with a number of sub-divisions is becoming ignored in modern times, and the family of today is more narrowly defined. Even so, it is much wider for everyday reckoning than the English family; and in spite of the impact of European commercialism it is so far holding together with admirable tenacity. In commercial life, for example, brothers, sisters, uncles and other relatives claim and receive constant payments from the salary of a clerk or other wage-earner; and conversely, any member of the family who is out of work is supported by his relatives. In country districts, the family is the holder of land. The village land is divided among the families living in the village; and each family sub-divides its land among its members.

The village is governed by a council of elders, composed of the heads of households or families in the village. The council elects a headman, who has over the village the same sort of power that each head of a household has over his own people. It is important to observe that this is a limited power; limited by the fact that it must be used reasonably and in accordance with the general sense of the group. Rattray,[32] describing the Ashanti system, says:

"The authority vested in the uncle is in virtue of his position as chosen representative of a group, bound together by the common tie of blood. The power which he possesses is very great, but its force and ultimate sanctions lie in the fact that it is a kind of corporate authority in which all the blood relations have a voice. He administers an estate in which every member of his kinsmen has a stake, but in which his position really does not confer on him any special monopoly. His status is in these respects, as I have already suggested, exactly similar to that of the Chief."

The village headman is chosen to be *primus inter pares*; he stands to the members of his village in much the same relation as he stands to his own household or family. He cannot, of course, interfere with private family affairs; but in his dealings with the heads of households he stands in the position of a head of a household who has under him a number of grown-up kinsmen whom he is bound to consult. The village headman presides over the council of elders, and naturally, by reason of his personal reputation, makes weighty contributions to the council's discussions. But he cannot overbear the council's opinion, nor can he take an arbitrary decision without the council's support. In a contested question, there is no 'division' of the British type, with its mechanical counting of heads. The head of the council allows the discussion to continue until all opinions are sufficiently expressed and the general sense of the meeting has emerged; and then he expresses this general sense as he conceives it, and the matter is closed. I find this African way of handling a meeting extremely impressive. A tactful chief sits patiently and attentively listening while the elders round him are excitedly debating. Occasionally he interjects a few quiet words, but for the most part his impassive demeanour contrasts strongly with the eager oratory and the passionate gestures all around. To an outsider it seems that the conflict of views is

---

[32] *Ashanti Law and Constitution*, 18. In Ashanti, a man is the head of a family consisting of his own younger brothers and sisters, and of his sisters' (not his brothers') children. Hence the mention of the 'uncle' in the passage quoted.

irreconcilable; but the chief has gauged the sense of the meeting. When he begins to speak there is a hush. His speech closes the discussion; it is received with quiet approval, all excitement and opposition vanishes, and the meeting passes to the next business.

Clearly, however, a chief or headman can only possess this control over a meeting if he is a man of tact and discernment. If he tries to obtrude his own opinion, or if he errs in interpreting and expressing the general opinion, there will be trouble. His power lies precisely in this fact, that when he speaks in his official capacity it is not himself, but the general voice speaking. A chief has no opinion of his own; he can only express the opinion of his people, and from this it follows that he can express no view until he has a chance of finding out through formal discussion what his people's view is.

This characteristic of chieftainship is found in chiefs of all grades. The village headman is a member of the council of a higher division; the chief of the division is a member of the council of still higher rank; and ultimately the highest sub-chiefs are members of the national council, presided over by the paramount chief. From the paramount chief downwards all must consult their people and express their people's opinion, not their own. Their position as representatives of their people is more like that of a member of a Russian Soviet, or of a British trade union delegate, than that of a British member of parliament. The Gold Coast representative system would be too slow for working in modern Europe, but it suited well enough the leisurely tribal life, in which sudden emergencies were almost unknown, and wars were threatened and declared with an amount of formal punctilio reminiscent of the days of Froissart. It may be necessary to modify it to suit modern conditions,[33] but we cannot afford to destroy it; and the principle of the chief's direct responsibility to his advisers and people is vital to the system.

We have no space to discuss the religious basis of African society on the Gold Coast.[34] The whole political organization is inextricably interlocked with religion. Every family is united in its worship of the common ancestors. Every tribe is united by a similar

[33] See below, chap. XIV.
[34] See e.g. Rattray, *Ashanti*, chaps. IV.-X.; Field, *Religion and Medicine of the Ga People*, chaps. I. and IX.

common worship, either of some eponymous ancestors or of some tribal gods or other spiritual influences.[35] The chief has priestly functions, centring especially in the ancestral stools. The blackened stools of the dead chiefs are kept in a special house, to which only the chief and a few distinguished elders have access. At frequent and regular festivals, the stools are visited, and sacrifices and prayers are made to the ancestral spirits inhabiting them. Once a year there is a greater festival, called the Odwira by the Akan, and variously named by other nations, at which the new season's harvest is thankfully received and the spirits of the nation's dead are honoured. In this festival also the chief has a leading part to perform.[36]

The chief is chosen from one special family; in some nations there may be two or more families from whom the choice may be made, and as far as possible the choice falls upon each in rotation. Where there is only one royal family, the hereditary principle is followed as long as the next heir is not clearly unsuitable; if he is, the elders who are the constitutional electors have power to pass him over and choose another from the same family. A chief may be constitutionally deposed, and depositions are frequent.

It was to people living under this well-developed constitution that the Europeans came, with their individualism, their emphasis on money, and their preconceived idea that a barbarian chieftain must be a despot. As the Europeans, whose military power and restless energy were on the West Coast so much more conspicuous than their culture, came competing for trade and for sites for their trading-posts, it is not surprising that they were a powerful force in disintegrating the tribal structure among the coast peoples. We have seen how the political units on the Gold Coast split into smaller divisions, as factions developed and energetic traders like Asameni raised themselves into political authority. The Europeans came in time to place more and more weight on the slave trade, and their keen demand for slaves naturally stimulated the supply. Domestic slavery existed among the Gold Coast nations; but such

---

[35] I avoid the word 'fetish'. I use the unsatisfactory phrase 'spiritual influence' to cover such cases as that of the famous Golden Stool of Ashanti, which contains "the *sunsum* (soul or spirit) of the Ashanti nation".
[36] For the chief's priestly functions see Rattray, *Ashanti*, chaps. V.-X., *Religion and Art in Ashanti*, chap. XII.; Field, *Religion and Medicine of the Ga People*, p. 3; according to Dr. Field, all Ga chiefs were originally priests.

domestic slaves were regarded to a very considerable extent as members of their master's family,[37] and there would be very strong opposition to the idea of selling them into plantation slavery beyond the seas, even if the numbers available had been sufficient. In any case, the numbers were far from sufficient; and to supply slaves in sufficient numbers for the white man's demands, a whole crop of wars broke out among the nations of the interior, the chief object of which was the capture of hordes of prisoners. The slave trade was one of the principal stimuli leading to the growth of the Ashanti military power; though Ashanti never reached such a pitch of cold-blooded efficiency as a slaving state as did the neighbouring kingdom of Dahomey.

[37] Rattray, *Ashanti Law and Constitution*, chap. V.

CHAPTER VI

THE NATIVE STATES 1600 TO 1733

THE seventeenth and early eighteenth centuries are the period of
the great *Völkerwanderung* of the Gold Coast peoples, of migrations within the Gold Coast itself, of wars and the consolidation of
states. In describing the history of the Gold Coast during this
period it is hopeless to try to concentrate on one main topic. The
nations were in the melting-pot, and it was impossible at that time
to foretell which, if any, would rise to a leading position in the
country. In this chapter, therefore, we must be prepared to cover
a wide area of ground and describe the early years and the
establishment of the states which were destined to play a great
part in later history. We shall deal with Ga, Akwamu, Akim,
Ashanti, Ewe and Dagomba.

Ga

The Ga state of today is a modern growth. The Ga people, as
we have seen, came from the east in small parties, probably about
the beginning of the sixteenth century. They seem to have settled
originally on some of the low hills rising out of the plain, but either
for trade or for defence they left the hills and settled on the sea-
shore. In the case of Accra itself, this move probably took place in
the reign of Okai Koi (1610-60); earlier chiefs lived on the hill
Ayawaso, eight miles from Accra, and his mother, who reigned as
queen, was killed by a rebellion while engaged in sinking a well on
the hill Akai Kai, which suggests that the capital at that time was
still inland. It is evident, however, that the Accra people were in
the habit of visiting the coast long before that; for there was a
Portuguese fort at Accra from about 1500 to 1578, when the Accra
destroyed it. There are today seven main Ga towns, each on the
coast, but having migrated from a hill-station a few miles inland.
Each town has a long narrow strip of country dependent on it,
running back into the Akwapim hills; and the *contadini* invariably
flock into the *citta* for their religious festivals.

The religion of the Ga shows that the present population of the
Accra plain is a mixed one. In every town there is a twofold

hierarchy of gods; the gods which the Ga invaders brought with
them from the east have settled down among the aboriginal gods
of lagoon and rock. Many of the religious songs of the lagoon-gods
are in the Obutu language, which is a dialect of Guan,[1] quite
distinct from Ga; a fact which almost certainly shows that the
songs, and the gods whom they honour, are older than the Ga
invasion.[2]

It seems then that, although Ga tradition records little or nothing
of any conquest, the Ga of today represent a military aristocracy
which has assumed overlordship over an older Guan or Obutu
population. Dr. Field points out that chiefs in the Ga country owe
their secular power to the fact that they originally were, and still
are, priests; and she considers that the Ga people were originally
governed solely by priests, without any secular political
machinery.[3] If so, it is likely that it was the process of conquest
which led to the development of the chieftainship; especially as no
sooner had the Ga conquered their new home than they themselves
had to stand on the defensive.

Their new enemies were the Akwamu. We have seen that the
Akwamu were settled within sight of Accra on the Nyanao hill.
Under the rule of Okai Koi the Ga rapidly consolidated their
power under the suzerainty of Accra; and it was not long before
they came in serious conflict with Akwamu. The Akwamu were
pressing southward, the Ga were extending their power northward
on to the fringes of the Akwapim hills, whose Guan inhabitants
were so akin to the Obutu of the Accra plains. In the last years of
the sixteenth century friction began between the two peoples, and
it became more and more serious as time went on.

Had the Ga remained united, it is possible that they might
have kept the Akwamu at arm's length. The unification of the Ga
nation, however, was too recent and artificial; and Okai Koi himself seems to have been a headstrong and violent man, too violent
for statesmanship. Apart altogether from the aboriginal Obutu
population, the Ga themselves were deeply divided. Accra, like the

[1] It is dying out, and at the date of Migeod's *Languages of West Africa* (1911)
was already much overlaid with Fante and Twi.
[2] Field, 1-3, 10-11, 77 and elsewhere; also *Social Organization of the Ga People*,
82-4.
[3] Field, 3. The point is further developed in *Social Organization*, 71-84 and
elsewhere.

other towns, consisted of several separate quarters,[4] each perhaps representing a separate settlement; and there was little national feeling to unite different towns together. Okai Koi had obtained his headship largely by force and the threat of force. He had fought against Labadi, which claimed to be senior to Accra,[5] and he had deeply offended the people of Asere in Accra itself, which claimed to be the senior quarter of Accra. Farther afield, too, he had made himself and his new Accra state feared rather than respected. The consequence was that when the continual border fighting with the Akwamu blazed up into a full-sized war, Okai Koi found that he could not depend on having a united people behind him.

The decisive battle took place in 1660 at Nyantrabi, some twelve miles north of Accra, near the site of the old Accra capital of Ayawaso. The disaffected sections of the Ga army went into battle with a private understanding with the enemy, to the effect that they would take no part in the fighting. The whole strength of the Akwamu army therefore was concentrated against the personal following of Okai Koi, and he saw that all was lost. The story goes that he called his chiefs round him, and in their presence he painted one side of his body with white clay and the other with charcoal; then he laid his curse on them for their treachery. If his body fell with the white side up, Accra would have victory and prosperity; if with the black side up, Accra would for ever be disunited before its enemies, as it had been that day. Then he sat on his throne and shot himself before them all; his body fell with the black side up; and they saw that the curse was come upon them, and fled.

Okai Koi was dead, and his body was buried near the place of his death; but his curse lived on. His son and successor, Ashangmo, carried on the war and for several years put up a gallant defence against the Akwamu; but eventually he found that the nation was so riddled with dissension and despair that further fighting was useless. In 1680 he rallied round him the strongest elements in the people, and abandoned the Accra plain to the enemy; he and his men marched eastward, retracing the course of their immigration

---

[4] Field, 2, 3, 39, 40, 64, 65, 77, 84-7. In Accra itself there are seven quarters.
[5] Field, 39. The original settlers in Labadi claim to be the first of the Ga people to arrive in this part of the country.

150 years earlier, and conquered for themselves a new home at Little Popo[6] on the coast of Dahomey. Here the Ga settlers had at first a difficult time. They had forced their way past the Ewe settlers of the Keta district, and they were naturally at once involved in continuous frontier disputes. The situation became easier when they came to terms with the powerful kingdom of Dahomey; in return for accepting a position of vassalage, they obtained a safe northern boundary, and had thenceforth merely to maintain themselves against the Anlos on the west and the Whydah people on the east, which they did with fair success.

Meanwhile the Accra plain fell under the overlordship of the Akwamu, whose desire for European trade was supplied by the building of three forts, the Dutch and English forts at Accra and the Danish fort at Osu. The remnant of the Ga people flourished through the great increase of the slave trade. In Bosman's day the Akwamu were constantly engaged in war with the surrounding peoples, and great flocks of prisoners were brought down to the forts to be sold as slaves.[7] From about 1680 to about 1730 the Akwamu authority was unchallenged, and the European commanders competed against one another for the favour of the Akwamuhene.[8]

Akwamu

Akwamu tradition is strangely silent on this great period in Akwamu history, and it is difficult even to reconcile the names of the chiefs of Akwamu as recorded in Akwamu tradition with those recorded by Bosman and other outside observers. This may be partly because the Akwamu had a custom of appointing not only an Akwamuhene but also a deputy; it was usual, but not invariable, for the deputy to succeed to the stool.[9] Bosman noticed that "the Aquamboean Government was administered by two, viz. the Old and Young King"; and it is clear that the young king or deputy was commonly in command of the army.

After conquering Accra the Akwamu ruled from their capital at Nyanawase a great and increasing part of the Accra plain, and

[6] Also called Aneho or Aharamata; Bosman, 69.
[7] Bosman, 70.
[8] Early in the eighteenth century the Ga revolted against the Akwamu with the help of the Dutch; but the Danes supported the Akwamu.
[9] Akwamu tradition.

also the Akwapim ridge and the greater part of the plain between
the Kwahu scarp and the left bank of the Birrim.[10] Commercially
they were in an exceedingly strong position. The European forts
at Accra and Osu were the easternmost of all the forts on the
Gold Coast at that time, and the Akwamu had a monopoly
of the trade with them and of the trade routes leading into the
interior.

The Birrim valley is rich in gold, and Bosman records that at
Accra alone "sometimes more gold is received than on the whole
Coast besides". He goes on, however, to mention a hindrance to the
development of the Akwamu power, which was later on to destroy
it. The trade of Accra "would be yet enlarged if the Negroes
of Aquamboe and Akim could agree, as they generally are at
difference; the latter pretending a Feudal Right over the former,
and subsequent thereto demanding an Annual Tribute of them;
which the Aquamboeans will by no means submit to, as knowing
very well that a Concession of that Nature may in time cost them
their whole Country".[11] The Akim were pressing down from the
north-west behind the Akwamu, and beginning to compete with
them for ownership of the Pra and Birrim valleys. The claim to
tribute means that the Akim must at some time or another have
inflicted a serious defeat on the Akwamu. Akwamu tradition is
silent on the subject of this defeat. According to the Akwamu, the
founder of the Akim state or of one of its main sections[12] came
into Akwamu territory as a fugitive, and was given land by the
Akwamuhene. After he had settled, other Akim settlers came from
Adansi to join him, until there was a strong Akim colony in the
inland districts of the Akwamu land. It is certain that the Akim
immigration was a gradual piecemeal one; and no doubt, as in
the case of the early friction between the Akwamu and the Ga,
there was a good deal of desultory fighting with varying result
before the Akim were strong enough to expel the Akwamu
altogether.[13]

[10] Akwamu tradition; the Akwamu give the names of a long list of villages in
the district which were then Akwamu villages, and the present inhabitants of
many (though not all) of those villages admit their Akwamu origin.
[11] Bosman, 69.
[12] The Akim Abuakwa; Akwamu tradition.
[13] There is no great discrepancy between the Akim and the Akwamu accounts.
Begoro tradition has preserved the memory of 'many battles' between the invading
Akim and the nearer Akwamu villages.

Akim

The Akim nation is divided into three sections, the Akim Abuakwa, the Akim Kotoku and the Akim Bosome. The early history of the three sections and of their relationship is obscure; and old European records commonly ignore the distinction between the three sections and talk vaguely of 'chiefs of Akim', as if the Akim were a confederacy like the Fante.

All three sections of the Akim agree in tracing their origin to Adansi, though the Kotoku and the Bosome remember an earlier time when they were living farther to the north.[14] The Abuakwa lived near Kokobiante,[15] the Kotoku and the Bosome near Ahuren.[16] They appear to have been subordinate divisions of the Adansi, and migrated to Akim either in the time of the Denkyera war of independence, when the Adansi stool itself moved to Akim, or else fifty years or so later, in the troubles that arose between Denkyera and the rising power of Ashanti.[17] Akim tradition is clear in describing their migration as a series of wanderings, carried out by small parties at different times, all moving generally east and south into country which was thinly peopled. These parties were small splinters of the great Adansi state, and it was only after their settlement in Akim, in some cases long after, that they organized themselves into new states.[18]

The Akim Abuakwa count four predecessors of their chief Ofori Panin, who first migrated from Adansi; but it is with Ofori Panin that the modern state of Akim Abuakwa really begins. There was apparently a nucleus of Akim settlers, under a certain Kuntunkrunku, even before Ofori Panin's time; but Ofori Panin came into favour through his wisdom as a judge and was chosen to

[14] The Kotoku in Denkyera country, the Bosome at Ejura.

[15] This was the home of what is now the paramount stool.

[16] Ahuren is a few miles south-west of the lake. The Akim themselves claim to have lived at Ahuren; but the comment of the Ahuren elders on this claim was: "No, they never did. But they lived at Omanso, only five minutes' walk away, and naturally they remember the name of the bigger town Ahuren rather than that of a small suburb like Omanso."

[17] Out of eleven of the principal divisions of Akim three came before Ntim Gyakari's time, four at that time, and four later. Ntim Gyakari of Denkyera ruled till about 1695; traditions of Kibi, Oda, Akim Soadru, Begoro, Kukurantumi, Otwereso, Asiakwa, Wankyi, Abenase, Anamase and Manso.

[18] For examples we may take three of the principal divisions of the Abuakwa and two of the Kotoku: Asiakwa and Kukurantumi swore allegiance to Abuakwa about 1720, Begoro about 1750, Anamase swore allegiance to Kotoku about 1780, and Abenase as late as 1860. These dates in the traditions can be approximately fixed by allusions to reigning chiefs and contemporary events.

succeed Kuntunkrunku as head of the growing Akim contingent. It seems to have been during the wars between Denkyera and Adansi that Ofori Panin migrated to Akim. He came as a young man and seems to have been still ruling about 1730, so that he must have lived to a great age.[19]

The Akim Kotoku at that time lived a more varied existence. Whereas the Abuakwa moved straight from Adansi into the Akim country, the Kotoku did their best to maintain themselves farther north. Here they felt the force of the growing Ashanti power, and they moved from place to place on the hills, sometimes to escape the Ashanti menace, sometimes being moved by the Ashanti to suit Ashanti convenience. Eventually, having travelled from Ahuren to Ejisu, Kotoku in Ashanti-Akim, and then to Akim Kotoku, they built themselves a new capital at Oda between the Pra and the Birrim.[20] Both these sections of the Akim, in fact, were in a dilemma. Before them lay the Akwamu, behind them lay the growing power of Ashanti; their problem was to find a home in between. The Abuakwa chose to settle in the more thinly-settled parts of the Akwamu country, and for the time being at least to keep on friendly terms with Akwamu; the Kotoku preferred to cling to the hills and risk hostilities with the young state of Ashanti.

The Akim Bosome section is the smallest of the three. It lived in close connection with the Kotoku near Ahuren, but did not share in the Kotoku wanderings. The Bosome seem to have stayed in the Ahuren district and served Ashanti until the end of the eighteenth century, and then to have come straight south to their present home. By their own account they were settled near Ahuren before ever the Abuakwa left Adansi.[21]

About 1700, then, the valleys of the Pra and its tributary the Birrim were fast being filled up by a wave of migration from Ashanti and Adansi; the Akim newcomers were beginning to organize themselves into states; and it was only a matter of time before they were certain to find themselves driven into hostilities with the Akwamu.

The decisive clash came in 1733. Apart from the desire of the

[19] Akwamu tradition.
[20] Kotoku tradition. This Oda is not the present town of the same name, which is a much more recent foundation, named after the old one. Old Oda is deserted.
[21] Bosome tradition.

invading Akim for land, and possibly for the European trade which the Akwamu were monopolizing, there is general agreement on the incidents that provided the occasion of the outbreak of war.

The war was remarkable for the wideness of the coalition which fought against the Akwamu. It included Akim Abuakwa and Akim Kotoku,[22] Agona, Obutu, Gomoa, Accra, Fante and the Dutch of Fort Crèvecœur at Accra.[23] The truth is that, as the Akwamu themselves relate with a sort of gloomy pride, they had been thoroughly bad neighbours to all around them, and every neighbouring state jumped at the chance of expelling them, since every one had its own grievances. The fullest account is preserved in the Akwamu tradition, though Kotoku tradition confirms it in all essentials.

According to the Akwamu there were four main causes of the war. In the first place, Akwamu parties had made a practice of waylaying and robbing Akim and Fante traders and selling them as slaves to the Dutch. This practice was locally known as panyarring, a word taken from the Portuguese, and was commonly detested because of the general insecurity it caused to trade; the slave trade acquired a small temporary fillip at the cost of a long-enduring setback to every other kind of trade.

The second cause was that the Akwamuhene insulted Firempon Manso, the Kotokuhene. Firempon Manso's sister had married the Akwamuhene,[24] and her husband made it unnecessarily plain that he wished to have nothing to do with his wife's relatives. Firempon Manso, swearing an oath that he would follow the Akwamuhene "even if he flew to the sky", prepared for war, and had recourse to the time-honoured parable of the bundle of sticks, only to be broken when the bundle was untied. The Fante and Ga chiefs to whom the bundle was sent agreed to ally themselves with the Kotoku in a joint attack on the Akwamu.

The third and fourth causes were connected with two headstrong young men of the royal family of Akwamu. All accounts agree in

[22] But not Akim Bosome, who according to their tradition were still in Ashanti at this time. Bosome tradition, which is a very full one, is silent about this war.
[23] This list is the one given by the Akwamu traditions of Asamankese; other lists omit one or other of the names.
[24] So the Akwamu say; the Kotoku say that she had married the heir, not the Akwamuhene himself. It is perhaps worth mentioning that this is the only discrepancy between these two enemy accounts of these events, though the Akwamu account is the fuller.

describing their evil-doing; they terrorized the whole countryside, and were particularly fond of practising their marksmanship on harmless passers-by. The Akwamu chief of Asamankese complained to the Akwamuhene about their behaviour, but in vain; and then they killed the niece of another distinguished Akwamu war-captain, and he swore to be revenged. This raised up a section of the Akwamu people themselves against the paramount stool.

The Dutch of Accra now heard rumours of the approaching war, and offered their mediation; and at last the Akwamuhene began to realize the danger of his position. He arrested his two nephews and handed them over to the Dutch for safety. When in Fort Crèvecœur the two young men asked permission to have razors to shave themselves; and the Dutch, suspecting nothing, gave permission. They promptly cut their throats, and the unfortunate Dutch commander sent to tell the Akwamuhene the news. The Akwamuhene refused to believe it until the news was confirmed by a second messenger; and then he swore that the whole wealth of Europe would be insufficient compensation, and declared war. The Dutch acted promptly. They supplied not only powder, ammunition and muskets, but also some small cannon, to the allies,[25] and did their best to bring into the alliance the Accra people who were still under Akwamu overlordship.[26]

Little is remembered of the details of the war. It lasted a year and three months, and the Akwamu remember Firempon Manso of Kotoku as the mainstay of the enemy coalition. According to them, the Kotoku and some of the allies formed two armies, which were defeated one after the other near Jukwa.[27] Then there was a year's pause, busily occupied by the Dutch and the Accra people in forming a stronger alliance, which advanced into the heart of the Akwamu country and attacked their capital of Nyanawase. Then ensued the decisive three months' campaign. The Asamankese people and some other divisions of Akwamu refused to fight,[28] and actually supplied the enemy with munitions. The allies defeated the Akwamu once, and then the allied army dispersed; so the Akwamu rallied, and turned against the nearest enemy con-

[25] Three of these are still preserved at Asamankese.
[26] Akwamu tradition.
[27] Akwamu tradition; Jukwa is near Cape Coast, so it would appear that the Akwamu had taken the offensive into Agona country.
[28] Asamankese tradition, confirmed by Akwamu.

tingent, that of Accra. The news of the Accra defeat brought about a hasty reconcentration of the allies, spurred on by the indefatigable Firempon Manso. The decisive battle took place on the banks of the tiny river Nsaki, twelve miles north of Accra, where a tall tree is still pointed out as marking the place where the Akwamuhene stood to watch the battle. The Akwamu were fatally short of men; and after three fruitless appeals for reinforcements, their general advised the Akwamuhene to retreat while he could. They marched fifty miles north-eastward to the Volta, on the advice of their general, who was familiar with the river country; it must have been an unpleasant march, with enemy country on their left flank all the way and the country they were marching through inhabited by Ga tribes in revolt against them. They reached the river somewhere near the modern Senchi ferry, the enemy hard on their heels; there were no boats, and their general's familiarity with the district did not extend to a knowledge of the fords. It seemed as if all were lost; but in the nick of time their god Ayesu took on him the form of a wild pig and trotted ahead of them to reveal a ford; the whole army splashed across behind him, and by the time the enemy scouts appeared on the river bank they were safe on the other side.[29]

The stool and the army were safe; but the war was lost. Accra recovered its independence. The whole of the forest country of the Pra and the Birrim fell to the Akim. The Guan and Kyerepon of the Akwapim ridges commended themselves to the victorious Akim; and a long list of Akwamu villages, headed by Asamankese, accepted Akim protection and overlordship.[30] Nothing shows more clearly the extent of the disaffection among the Akwamu themselves than a comparison of the present Akwamu country on the other side of the Volta with the size of the country they formerly ruled, in what is now Akim. The Akwamu villages that became part of Axim lie in a great semicircle some thirty miles in diameter

[29] This picturesque story is the Akwamu version; other versions say that a daring Akwamu hunter ventured across at the risk of his life; the people stood on the bank expecting to see him swept off his feet, and as he seemed to be getting out of his depth, they called anxiously, *"San akyi!"* ("Come back!"). This is the origin of the name Senchi.

[30] Akwamu tradition gives a list of nineteen, many of which have several other villages dependent on them. Most of these nineteen villages, though not all, still remember their Akwamu origin. This list is greatly extended by various Akim traditions.

in the modern district of eastern Akim Abuakwa; the area now subject to the Akwamuhene is not more than a quarter of this. The Notes for the three forts at Accra and Osu fell into the hands of the Akim, though as events turned out they did not hold them for long.[31]

The Guan and Kyerepon of Akwapim came under the overlordship of the Akim, who lent them a general, Kwao Safori, to command their contingent against the Akwamu. After the war they were organized into an Akan state, with a royal family of Akim descent; since that time the state of Akwapim, though independent, has been on terms of close friendship with the Akim.[32]

Ashanti

Oti Akenten had laid down the lines for the future development of Ashanti. It was under him that the Ashanti became a military people, spreading far and wide from Asantemanso and similar centres, and conquering neighbouring tribes to provide themselves with land.

Oti Akenten died about 1660, about the time of the Akwamu conquest of Accra. He was succeeded by Obiri Yeboa, his nephew, who carried on his uncle's policy of military advance. In his time the Ashanti tribes formed themselves into a regular confederation, with Obiri Yeboa as their head and his capital town of Kwaman as the capital of the confederation. Little is known of Obiri Yeboa's reign apart from the circumstances in which his successor was chosen.

The succession should pass to a younger brother, or failing a brother to the son of a sister.[33] Obiri Yeboa had no brothers, and only one sister, Manu Kotosii, who was childless. She went to Tutu in Akwapim, then under Akwamu rule, hoping to obtain from the famous god of that place a charm to give her a child. She did; and a son was born, whom in gratitude she named after the god

[31] Though in general this episode is so well documented by supporting tradition there is one strange gap: the name of the Akwamuhene at the time. The Akwamu themselves say it was Obuaman Darko; everybody else says it was Ansa Sasraku. There have been four chiefs of that name in Akwamu, and it may be that Obuaman Darko may also have been called Ansa Sasraku; or it may be that another Ansa Sasraku has been omitted from the Akwamu list.
[32] Akwapim tradition; the tradition, that is, of the royal family of Akropong, descended from the Akim.
[33] Under the Akan matrilineal system.

who had given him to her. This son was the famous Osei Kofi Tutu, usually known as Osei Tutu, the real founder of the Ashanti power.[34] When Osei Tutu was a boy, his uncle Obiri Yeboa sent him to be educated at the court of Boa Amponsem the Denkyera-hene; for the Ashanti were still subject to Denkyera, and paid an annual tribute.

While at the Denkyera court, young Osei Tutu got into trouble. He had an intrigue with a woman called Ako Abena Bensua, the sister of the Denkyerahene, and when she was discovered to be pregnant, Osei Tutu had to flee for his life. He took refuge in the Akwamu country, the country which his mother had visited before he was born; and he became on good terms with the Akwamuhene.

While in Akwamu, Osei Tutu formed a friendship which was to be the deciding factor in his career. This was with a priest called Kwame Frimpon Anokye. This man is stated by most tradition, including some at least of the Ashanti traditions, to have been a native of Awukugua in Akwapim, the chief town of the old Kyerepon state. His descendants today, however,[35] claim him as an Ashanti, and say that, like Osei Tutu himself, he was the son of an Ashanti mother and an Adansi father; his father, like Osei Tutu's father, came from Akrokyere. They explain his connection with Awukugua by saying that he went there to study magic and medicine. The two men became close friends; and when the news came to Osei Tutu that his uncle Obiri Yeboa had been killed in battle against the Doma, and that he had been chosen to succeed him, Okomfo Anokye determined to go with him back to Ashanti. The Akwamuhene gave them an escort of thirty[36] men from Anum, who settled in Ashanti and whose descendants still live there.

This alliance between Osei Tutu and Okomfo Anokye had far-reaching consequences for Ashanti. Both of them were very great men, though it is impossible now to distinguish between them.

[34] This story, with slight variation, is well known all over the country. The Akwamu say that it was not Tutu in Akwapim that she visited, but their priest Tutu Aban in Nyanawase. Osei Tutu's father was an Adansi man called Owusu Panin from Akrokyere.
[35] He was the founder of the stool family of Agona in Ashanti; Rattray, *Ashanti Law and Constitution*, chap. XXIV. He has also left descendants in the Awukugua district. I have been given his name also as Kwame Agyei Frimpon; he is always called, however, simply Okomfo Anokye, *Okomfo* meaning 'priest'.
[36] So the Agona (Ashanti) tradition given by Rattray (p. 272); the Akwamu say they gave him 300 men.

Their name is so great in Ashanti today that all laws and customs are ascribed to Okomfo Anokye, and the foundation of the Ashanti kingdom or confederacy is attributed to Osei Tutu, although even from the little information we have about earlier rulers it is plain that the general lines of his policy had been laid down by Obiri Yeboa. It was Obiri Yeboa, for example, who began the organization of the Ashanti confederacy. But Osei Tutu carried out that policy so much more thoroughly and successfully that the Ashanti today ascribe its success to Okomfo Anokye's magic.[37] The magical element is very strong in the Osei Tutu and Okomfo Anokye legend. It is easy to say that the magic has obscured the truth and made it impossible to believe the legend as it stands. But miracle-stories do not grow up round nonentities; and the very predominance of the magic in the legend shows that the contemporaries of these two men felt that their deed were more than human. For this reason, apart from the picturesqueness of the story, I shall not attempt to suppress all the mythical elements, though I hope that something of the greatness of these two men will appear in the bare narrative of their deeds.

The position in Ashanti when Osei Tutu and Okomfo Anokye arrived was as follows. The settlement at Asantemanso had been broken up, and Juaben, Kumawu, Nsuta, Kuntanase, Bekwai and others had been founded. These small states, with Mampon, which came from farther south (from Ahinsan in Adansi) were united in a loose alliance, but they were all still subject to Denkyera and paid tribute: Mampon and others sent red clay, Juaben sent plantain fibre and Osei Tutu's own people sent firewood.[38] Oti Akenten's town of Kwaman was the northern outpost of the Ashanti,[39] and the Doma, against whom Oti Akenten and Obiri Yeboa had fought so much, still held villages within four miles of it. Some other Ashanti chiefs, notably Nsuta, Juaben and Mampon, were pushing northward into the hills away on the right wing of the Ashanti advance; but the stubborn resistance of the Doma was holding up the centre. Fifteen miles to the south were Bekwai and Asumegya,

[37] For example, Anokye's success in bringing about the confederation of the independent Ashanti chiefs was regarded as magical; Rattray, p. 273.
[38] Ahuren tradition.
[39] Mampon and Juaben were established in the hills slightly to the north and several miles to the east, though neither had reached its present situation. Kwaman, on the other hand, lay in the plain on the direct northward line from Adansi along which any considerable advance must be made.

keeping watch on the Denkyera; no help could be looked for from them in the northward advance. Adansi, formerly a powerful state, had been greatly weakened by its wars with Denkyera, and by the loss of so many of its people who migrated to form the new states of Akim and Ashanti; and the Adansi, like the Ashanti themselves, were subject to Denkyera.

Clearly the first task was to break the resistance of the Doma, against whom Oti Akenten and Obiri Yeboa had both fought, and by whom the latter had been killed in battle. But the experience of the previous Doma wars had shown that this could only be done by using the full strength of the Ashanti people. No ephemeral alliance would suffice; a permanent military league must be established. The nucleus of such a league already existed in the fact that five of the most powerful chiefs of Ashanti were of the same family as Osei Tutu.[40] The problem was to bring into the league the other powerful chiefs who were of different families. As the cohesive force of the family is a spiritual one, the belief in the descent from a common ancestress, and the community of existence between the living members of the family and the countless spirits of its dead members, the cohesive force of any artificial league must be likewise a spiritual one. If Ashanti was to hold together as a permanent unity, it must be unified by means of a common worship. This task Okomfo Anokye accomplished; and no one but a priest, and a priest of extraordinary genius, could have accomplished it.

To say this is not to deny the force of economic motives. Strategically and economically it was intolerable that the Ashanti should be squeezed in between the Denkyera and the Doma, as it

[40] The Ashanti, like other Akan peoples, are divided into a number of families or clans, matrilineal or exogamous. In Ashanti there are eight of these clans, in Fante there are seven; and many of the names are identical. For a description see Rattray, *Ashanti Law and Constitution*, chap. VIII. The point that is important for our purpose is that this clan organization runs right through the Akan people, and an Ashanti, an Akim, an Akwamu, or a Fante who happened to be of the same family or clan would recognize the tie of blood even if they were complete strangers to one another and lived a hundred miles apart. The Akan word *abusua*, which is the word for such a matrilineal family or clan, has a secondary meaning of 'blood', as used in the term 'blood-relationship'. The *abusua* is regarded as being descended from a common ancestress, perhaps ultimately from some totem. It has a spiritual unity and is one of the fundamental elements in Akan society. Thus, chiefs belonging to the same *abusua* would feel that "blood is thicker than water", and though not legally bound to aid one another in war, would readily do so.

was intolerable for the Akim to allow themselves to be squeezed
in between the Ashanti and the Akwamu. No doubt the ties of
common language and customs, and the pressure of a common
enemy, would have been sufficient to unite all Ashanti in a temporary alliance, as they were sufficient to unite the Hellenes. But
if Ashanti were to succeed, where Hellas failed, in permanently
uniting into a nation, only spiritual means would suffice.

The magical or religious ceremonies which Okomfo Anokye
employed, and which are remembered today in such detail, no
doubt followed on long weeks or months of patient diplomatic
negotiations, by which the desire for unity was aroused.[41] Anokye
made some 'medicine' and mixed it with palm wine, and all the
Ashanti chiefs drank it; under his instructions, Osei Tutu made
new swords for his army officers, and each swore an oath to fight
to the end. Still some of them were not satisfied, for their last war
against the Doma had ended in disaster; and this in spite of the
fact that Anokye's own elder brother, who was also a priest, had
promised them victory. Anokye succeeded in overcoming their
fears, and under the leadership of Osei Tutu the Ashanti forces
were victorious over the Doma, and then over the people of Tafo;
the Doma chief was spared and appointed to a position in Osei
Tutu's household, and the Tafo chief was killed.

The campaign was over, and Osei Tutu's leadership in war had
justified itself; but now came the critical moment. Was the alliance,
its immediate objects being attained, to break up again? Okomfo
Anokye determined that it must not. He set to work to unite the
Ashanti people by providing a common stool, in order that the
whole nation might be united in the same way as each section was
united through its common stool. He began by taking three
cuttings of the *kumnini* tree[42] and planting one each at Kwaman,
Juaben and Kumawu. Those at Juaben and Kumawu died, the one
at Kwaman lived; and this was taken as a sign that Osei Tutu was
the leader chosen by the gods to be the permanent head of the
nation. Henceforth Kwaman was known as Kumasi, 'under the
kumnini tree'.

Having settled this point Anokye set to work in earnest, and the

[41] These negotiations unfortunately are forgotten. For Anokye's magic and the
Doma campaign, see Rattray, *Ashanti Law and Constitution*, 273-5.
[42] 'Kill-the-python' tree; *Lannea acidissima*, Irvine, 258. It is a smallish or
medium-sized tree with compound leaves.

culmination of his efforts was the institution of the Golden Stool.[43]
One Friday a great gathering was held at Kumasi; and there
Anokye brought down from the sky, with darkness and thunder,
and in a thick cloud of white dust, a wooden stool adorned with
gold, which floated to earth and alighted gently on Osei Tutu's
knees. This stool, Anokye announced, contained the spirit[44] of the
whole Ashanti nation, and all its strength and bravery depended
on the safety of the stool. To emphasize this he caused Osei Tutu
and every distinguished chief and queen-mother present to give
him a clipping from their nails and from their hair; all these were
mixed into a paste with 'medicine' and smeared on the stool, and
the remainder was drunk by the contributors as a sacramental
drink.[45] Whatever we may think of the heavenly origin of the stool,
the fact remains that somehow or other Okomfo Anokye succeeded
in impressing on the national consciousness that henceforth
Ashanti was a nation, linked by a common mystical or religious
bond, of which the Golden Stool was the visible symbol. This was
the origin of the famous *Sika Agua Kofi*, 'Friday's Golden Stool'
of Ashanti, which in spite of many vicissitudes still survives today
with its unifying power unimpaired.

The newly-united nation was soon called on to face a crisis
severer than that of the Doma war. The Denkyera, who were still
the overlords of Ashanti, were beginning to think that this new
national feeling that was growing up among their subjects was
dangerous and should be broken before it went too far.

The Denkyera, like the Akwamu, had a bad reputation as rulers;
they were hated as well as feared, and their subjects lived always
on the edge of revolt. (Perhaps the main reason why the Ashanti
state has lasted so well is that it has been an exception to the
general rule that a conquering state bleeds its conquered provinces
and drives them to despair. We have already seen this happen in
the case of the Ga and of the Akwamu; now we see it also in the
case of the Denkyera. Ashanti, on the other hand, probably
through Okomfo Anokye's statesmanship, always tried to incor-

[43] Rattray, *Ashanti*, 288-90.
[44] The Akan distinguish between the *sunsum*, that is, the personality, character,
energy, and the *kra*, which is the individual soul which enters the body at
conception and leaves it at death. It was the *sunsum* of the Ashanti people that
was contained in the Golden Stool; not the aggregate of their *akra*.
[45] By this means the *sunsum* of each contributor was provided with a resting-place
or anchorage on the Golden Stool.

porate conquered provinces into the Ashanti confederacy, giving
their chiefs seats on the great council of state, and leaving them
as free as possible in their internal affairs.) After the wars under
Obuokoropa, in which they had freed themselves from the Adansi,
the Denkyera had grown into a powerful military state under their
warlike chief Owusu Bore, and had brought under their rule Sefwi,
Twifu and Wassaw, as well as Adansi and the Ashanti.

The old Denkyerahene Boa Amponsem, whom Osei Tutu had
served as a young man, was dead. Under him Denkyera had been
the principal state for the Dutch traders; its gold was abundant,
and remarkably pure,[46] and its wars with surrounding kingdoms
had made it as important a source of slaves for Elmina as Akwuma
was for Accra. It seems certain that Ashanti was determined to
assert its independence in any case, and there were also immediate
occasions of the war. The Ashanti wanted access to the sea and to
the coast trade in salt and European goods, especially guns and
powder, which were rare among them at that time.[47] Their most
convenient ports were Cape Coast and Elmina, but the road to these
places lay through Adansi and Denkyera territory. There was a personal quarrel between Osei Tutu and the Denkyerahene Bosianti.
And the Adansi had rebelled in vain against the Denkyera and had
fled to Ashanti for protection, which had been given them.

The Ashanti prepared for war, and began buying firearms from
the Dutch, which the Denkyera actually allowed to pass freely
through their country, knowing that they were going to arm their
enemies. Bosianti offered money compensation for the injury he
had done Osei Tutu, but Osei Tutu declined it, and continued his
preparations. In the middle of this period of tension Bosianti died,
and was succeeded by a young man called Ntim Gyakari, who is
sometimes said to have been the son of Osei Tutu and Ako Abena
Bensua the Denkyera princess.[48] Ntim Gyakari chose this most
unpropitious time to demand a greatly increased tribute from
Ashanti. He sent a great brass pan and demanded that it be
returned to him full of gold dust, and accompanied by the favourite

[46] Bosman, 73, 74.
[47] Adansi tradition; this may also perhaps be inferred from the story that
Okomfo Anokye had new swords and a shield made for the Doma war (Rattray,
Ashanti Law and Constitution, 273-4). The Ashanti had hitherto used swords
and bows and arrows, with shields.
[48] Rattray, 275, and Adansi tradition.

wife of each of the Ashanti chiefs.[49] Such an apparently insane demand may have been intended to provoke the Ashanti into instant war before they had completed their preparations. If this was its purpose it succeeded. The Ashanti refused the demand, declared war, and set Okomfo Anokye to open the campaign with his magic.

The Denkyera war lasted between one and two years[50] and resulted in the complete overthrow of Denkyera and the establishment of Ashanti as a first-rate power. War broke out about the beginning of the year 1699,[51] but it is clear from the course of the campaign that the Ashanti were far from ready.

Okomfo Anokye began the war by a spirited duel in magic with the chief Denkyera magician, and announced at the close of it that with proper precautions victory was sure.[52] Three brave men volunteered either to be sacrificed or to sacrifice themselves in the battle in order to ensure victory[53] and Boahinantuo, chief of Mampon, was chosen as commander of the Ashanti forces.

Nevertheless, the Denkyera army was over the frontier before the Ashanti were mobilized, and the decisive battle of the first campaign was fought on Ashanti soil and only ten miles from Kumasi. The Ashanti victory was due mainly to the splendid resistance of the forlorn hope, which sacrificed itself almost to the last man to gain time for the main army to gather. The invaders advanced to the little village of Adunku, where they halted for the night, and captured a prisoner who was found inspecting his hunting traps. The prisoner turned out to be the chief of Adunku, and his capture gave the alarm. The Adunku men at once turned out to recapture him, and for seven days maintained such a resistance that the main Denkyera army was only able to advance eight miles to the village of Feyiase.[54] Feyiase was the scene of the

[49] Rattray, 170; this story is the one commonly given in Ashanti. Sometimes the demand is said to have included also one finger from every Ashanti chief.
[50] Adansi tradition.
[51] Claridge, I, 194-5.
[52] Rattray, 276-7.
[53] Tweneboa Kodia of Kumawu, Duku Pim of Ejisu, and Bobie of Bonwere; Rattray, 277. Rattray says that Duku Pim was sacrificed before the battle and the other two killed in the fighting. This is the Agona tradition, and Kumawu tradition (ibid., 219-20) supports it, but it is sometimes said that all three were killed in battle.
[54] Adansi tradition. The Adansi took no part in this war but watched it from their refuge in Akim.

decisive battle of the campaign; it was long and dubious until one of the most important Denkyera commanders abandoned his place in the line and the Ashanti broke through.[55] The Denkyerahene himself, Ntim Gyakari, was seated playing wari[56] in his tent, shackled with golden fetters round his ankles to one of his wives. The Juaben men broke in, the first blow aimed at the Denkyerahene was intercepted by a heavy gold bangle he was wearing on his arm, and then he was made prisoner.

The battle of Feyiase was a decisive victory for the Ashanti, especially as it had been crowned with the capture of the enemy general who was, of course, executed. But Feyiase was after all merely a successful repulse of an invasion, and must be followed up before the war could be regarded as ended; more especially as the Ashanti commander also had died of his wounds received in the battle.[57] Ntim Gyakari was succeeded by Boadu Akefun who, according to the Ashanti tradition, swore to serve Ashanti. Whether this oath was sworn and then repudiated, or whether (as seems more likely) it was not sworn at all, Osei Tutu determined to take the offensive against Denkyera, and he did this in the following year. The Ashanti advanced into Denkyera and utterly defeated the Denkyera in a battle fought on the banks of the Ofin river. All Denkyera territory on the left bank of the Ofin was annexed by Ashanti; Wassaw and Sefwi profited by the Denkyera defeat to throw off their allegiance, and the ruin of Denkyera was complete.

Before considering the work of Osei Tutu and Okomfo Anokye in organizing the Ashanti kingdom, it is convenient to push ahead with the remaining political events of the reign. Among the great booty which was brought from Denkyera to Kumasi one capture was particularly important. This was the Note by which the Dutch agreed to pay rent for Elmina castle. It had passed from the Elmina people to the Kommenda, and from them to the Denkyera; and now it was taken by the Ashanti. The capture of this Note brought Ashanti directly into coast politics; it is even possible that it may be the origin of the belief that Elmina is an ancient Ashanti

[55] Adansi tradition, which says that there was treachery afoot.
[56] This story is universally known all over the country. Wari is a game of skill very popular in the Gold Coast; see Rattray, Religion and Art in Ashanti, 382-90.
[57] Rattray, Ashanti Law and Constitution, 236, 237.

settlement. The payment of rent for Elmina automatically passed henceforth to Ashanti.[58]

The Denkyera war involved Ashanti in further fighting. The Akim had taken part in the war as allies of the Denkyera, and Bosman records[59] that they lost 30,000 men, "besides that a great Caboceer of Akim, with all his Men, were cut off". Early European allusions to Akim draw no distinction between Abuakwa and Kotoku, and we have to decide in each case which of the two is meant. In this case it is the Kotoku. The Abuakwa were settling farther south, well away from the Pra, and in contact with the Akwamu rather than with the Ashanti. The Kotoku, on the other hand, were settled near the Pra, which was the war area. The Akim were defeated, and became tributary to Ashanti, paying an indemnity and handing over hostages.[60] But the Akim Kotoku were not crushed. There was difficulty over the payment of the money, and Osei Tutu determined to send another expedition against the Akim to reduce them to complete subjection. This expedition took place either in 1720 or in 1731; there seems no means of deciding between these dates, the first of which is given by Bowdich[61] and the second by Claridge and Fuller. It was a disaster for the Ashanti. The Akim allowed the main Ashanti army to cross the Pra unopposed, but somehow learned that Osei Tutu himself was to cross the river in the rear of his army, and prepared an ambush. The Akim opened fire just as Osei Tutu's hammock was entering the river; the king himself was shot, and a second bullet killed him; his dead body fell into the river and was never recovered. The escort, which was two or three hundred strong and included all the general staff of the army, was killed to a man, and the Ashanti army returned hastily to Kumasi.[62]

[58] Claridge, I. 197-8.
[59] 76.
[60] Claridge, I, 198-200. This war is recorded in Kotoku tradition; the Kotokuhene at the time was Afosu Apenten.
[61] Bowdich was calculating from information given him at the time of his visit to Kumasi in 1817. I do not know why Ellis (History of the Gold Coast, 89) and, following him, Claridge, say so definitely that it was in 1731. But since Opoku Ware's punitive expedition took place about 1734, 1731 seems far the more probable date.
[62] On their return home, the triumphant Akim commanders were first fêted as heroes and then severely punished for what was regarded as a dirty piece of work.

The chronology of the various early Akim wars is obscure. Piecing Ashanti, Adansi, Kotoku and Abuakwa tradition together, I suggest the following list; dates, of course, are only approximate: I: 1700, Kotoku (Kotoku tradition).

Nothing is more significant of the solid nature of Osei Tutu's and Okomfo Anokye's work than that the Ashanti state survived this disaster, and that there was no talk of its dissolving into its component members. Had Ashanti remained merely a military league, the crushing blow which deprived it not only of its head but of almost all its nobility would probably have been fatal. But Ashanti was not merely a military league; thanks to Anokye's work it was an organized state. Sir Francis Fuller has spoken of Anokye as the Ashanti Cardinal Wolsey. I think it would be better to compare him with the great American statesmen who determined that the united colonies which had successfully asserted their independence of Britain should remain united. Anokye was a statesman of genius. He succeeded where the Hellenes of old had failed: he brought his people triumphantly through their war of liberation and he held them together afterwards.

It is important to notice that Ashanti was an organized state. It is sometimes spoken of in English as the Ashanti confederacy, but the term confederacy is apt to be misleading. It may have been the case that before the institution of the Golden Stool it was merely a confederacy, the members of which had joined for a specific purpose, while retaining their full sovereign rights. But

II: 1720 or 1731, Kotoku (since the enemy was presumably the same as in the first war; submission then promised had not been fulfilled. Moreover, Asumegya tradition records that Ofosu Apenten was the enemy chief, and he was Kotoku-hene). But according to Abuakwa tradition, the Abuakwa were also involved in this war. III: 1734, Abuakwa and Kotoku. This was Opoku Ware's first war. The Notes for the Accra forts were captured; therefore the war must be later than 1733, when the Akim Abuakwa captured them from the Akwamu. Akwamu tradition says that their arch-enemy Firempon Manso of Kotoku was reported by them to Opoku Ware, who executed him. Is it possible that this is Frimpon Ampim, who was one of the enemy generals whose heads were preserved in Kumasi? (Rattray, *Religion and Art in Ashanti*, 132). IV: Abuakwa and Kotoku. This was Opoku Ware's second war, about 1740 (Adansi tradition; Fuller, 26). The Adansi call this the *Ahantan* war, that is, the swaggering war, because the Akim, to show their scorn for the enemy, went into battle wearing sandals instead of barefoot. Three consecutive chiefs of Akim Abuakwa—Bra Nkante, Pobi Asumanin and Owusu Akim Tenten—were killed by the Ashanti (Rattray, 132 and Adansi tradition); the last two in this war, and the first presumably in the previous war. The chief battle in this war, according to the Adansi, was fought at Peminase (east of the lake). V: 1745. Bowdich (187) says that "the king of Akim" went to war with his neighbours, having received permission from the Asantehene to do so, and having promised half the spoil to the Asantehene. He did not keep his promise, was attacked by the Asantehene Kwasi Obodum, and blew himself up in despair, together with several of his officers. Neither Abuakwa nor Kotoku tradition, nor (more strangely) Ashanti tradition, records the name of this chief, and it is impossible to say whether the Abuakwa or the Kotoku, or both, were involved in the war.

after the institution of the Golden Stool[63] the members of the Ashanti confederacy had parted with some of their sovereignty. "The family had expanded into the clan, both had merged into the tribe, now the tribes were to merge into the nation under a King; but the king stood in the same relation to the great *Amanhene* as they had previously stood to their sub-chiefs, as sub-chiefs to village headmen, as village headmen to the family heads, and as the family heads to their respective households."[64] The chiefs of the separate divisions henceforth sought, and were required to seek, recognition by the Asantehene. They swore allegiance to him and accepted a position with remarkable similarities to that of a feudal tenant in medieval Europe to his lord. It is true that they were jealous of their rights, and always ready to cast off their allegiance to the Asantehene if he infringed the customary limits of his prerogative. But however limited the prerogative of the Asantehene might be, it existed: and its existence was safeguarded by the same forces that safeguarded its limitations—custom and religion.[65]

Osei Tutu was dead, and was succeeded by his grand-nephew Opoku Ware; the Akim campaign came to a sudden stop and the army retired hastily to Kumasi. The disaster of Osei Tutu's death was commemorated in the establishment of the great oath *Memeneda*.[66] The name of the place where he was killed, Koromante, also became an oath; this village was named after the

---

[63] Rattray says "after the battle of Feyiase". But I do not see why a battle, however victorious, should be the turning point. It seems to me that the institution of the Golden Stool, which united the whole nation by religious or spiritual bonds, is the crucial event.

[64] Rattray, *Ashanti Law and Constitution*, 74.

[65] The analogy with European feudalism is striking. One is constantly coming across cases of Ashanti constitutional law which might have come straight out of Bracton's notebook.

[66] The Akan institution of the oath (*ntam*) is of great importance. The oath is a word or a phrase, usually commemorative of some disaster, which has a taboo attached to it, and which cannot therefore be uttered without incurring a penalty. The oath has a guardian, who is responsible for exacting the penalty, and therefore the utterance of the tabooed phrase must be reported to him, in order that the circumstances may be investigated. The penalty attached to the oath is exacted, not necessarily from the person who actually utters it, but from the person whose misbehaviour leads to its utterance. Thus, the swearing of an oath becomes in practice a citation before the tribunal of the oath's guardian. Oaths may be trivial oaths sworn by children to each other, which constitute an appeal to the head of the household, or some other older person; or they may be of all grades of importance up to the oath which recalls some great national calamity, the penalty for which was death. An appeal from the judgment of one

better known Koromante (Kormantine) on the coast, by an Akim chief who had visited the coast and was struck with the similarity of the physical situation on a long ridge of hill.[67]

The Northern States: Moshi, Dagomba, Mamprusi, Gonja

Our previous ideas of the history of the present Northern Territories of the Gold Coast have been revolutionized by Rattray's researches.[68] The traditions of these peoples greatly resemble each other in recording a migration from some country farther to the north or north-east; and we have assumed in the past that these traditions were based on the historical fact that the modern tribe is descended from ancestors who arrived as immigrants into an uninhabited land and there settled and multiplied. It has been shown by Rattray, however, that the population of these districts consists of two sections, a large mass of very old-established inhabitants, and a small ruling class of more recent arrival. If we re-read the local traditions from this point of view we find that they do not contradict Rattray's statement. They usually trace the origin of the tribe to one man or to a small party of men, who by their military strength have developed into a military power.

It seems impossible now to discover anything about the early history of the aboriginal inhabitants—Vagala, Isala and others. Their traditions are lost; those they relate today are not their own, but the traditions of the conquering race that rules them.

Their culture and social structure however can be studied, for they exist still, modified of course by the foreign influences brought in by the conquerors. Over the whole of what are now the Northern Territories there lived 500 years or more ago a population with a uniform culture.

"These peoples, even when their language differed considerably, had an almost identical social and political organization; the outstanding feature of this was a grouping of totemic clans under Priest-Kings whose influence and authority were

court to a higher court may be made by swearing the oath of the chief who presides in the higher court. The oath *Memeneda* (meaning 'Saturday', the day on which Osei Tutu was killed) became known as the 'Great oath' of Ashanti—so great that its real name was never mentioned. In later times two other oaths were added to it, so that the great oath of Ashanti became a composite one.
[67] Akim Kotoku tradition.
[68] *Tribes of the Ashanti Hinterland.*

considerable, though both depended upon moral and spiritual and not physical punishments; these indigenous peoples inherited through the sister's son."[69]

"Upon these more or less autochthonous peoples, with their very primitive institutions, descended small bands of strangers within comparatively recent historical times. They were better armed, better clothed, familiar with the idea of kingship or chieftainship in our modern sense, in some cases conversant with the rudiments of Mohammedanism and accustomed (even if circumstances had not later compelled it) to a patri-lineal manner of reckoning descent. These strangers super-imposed upon the primitive tribes, among whom they settled, a new and unheard-of political conception, namely the idea of territorial and secular leadership in place of the immemorial institution of a ruler, who was the high priest of a totemic clan and dealt only in spiritual sanctions. These warrior bands—possibly refugees or off-shoots from one or other of the Negro kingdoms of the interior—were composed of males alone. The result was that in a few generations their descendants were speaking the language of the tribes among whom they settled, from among whom they were compelled to find wives, and whose manners and customs they came largely to adopt. While always endeavouring to keep for direct descendants all posts of secular authority based on the principles with which they were familiar, the tendency was nevertheless for them to become merged more and more with the people among whom they had settled, to whom, in the course of time, they gave the name by which they called themselves formerly or which they had adopted."[70]

From time to time there have grown up in this way powerful states and confederacies among the multitude of clans and tribes of the north. Much of the history of this country has been made by the members of one masterful family. Its legendary founder was a certain Tohajie, the Red Hunter, who is said to have come from somewhere east of the Gold Coast, eight days' caravan journey east of Bawku. Tohajie's grandson Bawa or Gbewa migrated west-ward and settled at Pusuga near Bawku, and began to build up a

[69] Rattray, *Tribes of the Ashanti Hinterland*, preface p. xiii.
[70] Ibid., p. xii.

kingdom for himself.[71] Gbewa had eight sons; his eldest son Zirile succeeded him, but on Zirile's death there was a dispute between his younger brothers as to who should succeed, and the family split up. The eldest surviving brother, Sitobo, founded the Dagomba kingdom, the third, Yantaure, founded the Moshi kingdom, and the youngest, Tohogo, founded the Mamprusi kingdom. The other brothers also became chiefs of various places, but these three states were destined to become the greatest states of the north. Moshi, Dagomba and Mamprusi have never forgotten their common origin, and have often formed a triple alliance.

It is not as easy in the case of these northern states as on the coast to decide when these things happened, for the beginnings of Dagomba-Moshi-Mamprusi history are beyond the ken of contemporary Europeans or even Ashanti. There have been twenty-four rulers of Mamprusi since Gbewa, thirty of Dagomba. The sixth Mamprusi chief and the twentieth Dagomba chief are stated to have been contemporaries of Osei Kojo the Asantehene, and must therefore have lived about 1770. The Dagomba list thus gives an average of seventeen years for each reign from 1770 to the present day, the Mamprusi list an average reign of nearly ten years. But if Sitobo and Tohogo were brothers, the Mamprusi list must be seriously incomplete. The Moshi capital was Wagadugu in the modern French colony of the Ivory Coast,[72] and we have no list of Moshi chiefs for comparison. There is no intrinsic improbability in the Dagomba list; accepting it therefore as a basis for calculation, we find that Sitobo lived approximately 500 years ago, say about 1430.[73] This may well have been the case; if so, the founders of these northern states were about a century earlier than those of the earliest Akan states.

Sitobo was the founder of this Dagomba state; but its military power dates from the time of his son Nyagse. Nyagse set out on a career of conquest. He made war on the Dagomba people, and wherever he went he killed the clan priests and appointed members of his own family in their places as territorial rulers. The clan

[71] Tamakloe, *Brief History of the Dagbamba People*, 9. For the rest of this section I am using this book, with chapters LIX. and LXI. of Rattray.
[72] Formerly known as the Upper Volta.
[73] Tamakloe places Gariba, the twentieth Dagomba chief, at 1700-20. This is fifty years too early, and his date for Nyagse, therefore, must be brought from 1416 to about 1460 or 1470. His precise chronology is too precise to be credible in a matter of oral tradition.

PLATE VII " . . . the water in the Oda river had risen eighteen inches over the bridge": African troops in the 1896 campaign crossing the Oda in similar circumstances

(from *The Relief of Kumasi* by Bibb, *Methuen*)

PLATE VIII   "This spectacularly situated castle": Kormantine   *(photo: P. Redmayne)*

priests are called *ten'dama* (singular *ten'dana*); they are the
guardians of the land and all the spiritual connections of the clan.
They make the necessary sacrifices, prevent the pollution of the
land by bloodshed, and purify the land if they have failed to
prevent bloodshed. In most parts of the Northern Territories the
ten'dama are still in existence today, though there is often a territorial chief as well, who describes his position by saying, "The
people belong to me, the land belongs to the *ten'dana*." In the
first rush of Nyagse's conquest, however, the *ten'dama* over a great
part of the Dagomba country were killed, and the Dagomba state
thus began as a military autocracy. There is no doubt, however,
that since the functions of the *ten'dana* were essential, a compromise must soon have been effected even in these divisions of the
Dagomba state. Elsewhere, the new military chiefs speedily evolved
a dual constitution, by which the religious position of the *ten'dana*
was recognized and he was accepted as an important counsellor of
the territorial chief.[74]

The Dagomba kingdom thus established continued its progress.
Nyagse's grandson marched westwards and conquered the king-
dom of Bona; but like the Ashanti, he paid little attention to his
conquest and allowed it to grow up again.[75] The first check to the
Dagomba power came in the reign of Dariziogo, the eleventh chief.
This check came from the rising power of the Gonja.

In chapter II, I have pointed out the difficulty in tracing Gonja
history, or rather their pre-history. The essential facts are these:
(*a*) The Gonja language is one dialect of a very widespread language
which is found in many other parts of the Gold Coast. (*b*) It is
closely connected with Akan, and appears to be a more archaic
member of the Akan family than Twi or Fante. (*c*) Nevertheless,
it is not the language of the mass of the people, but of the ruling
class. (*d*) The mass of the people in Gonja country speak Vagale.
(*e*) The Ashanti of today call the Gonja 'Nta-fo', which is the name

[74] Rattray, chap. XXI., and pp. xi., xiv.-xvi.; and Eyre-Smith, *Brief Review of
the History and Social Organization of the Peoples of the Northern Territories
of the Gold Coast*, 18ff. Cardinall, *Natives of the Northern Territories of the
Gold Coast*, chap. II. Dr. Field's *Social Organization* describes a similar dualism
in Ga country.
[75] Tamakloe, 19, 20. The kingdom of Bona or Bouna is north-west of Ashanti in
what is now the Ivory Coast. There seems to have been an ancient connection
between Bona and Ashanti, for it was customary for the two states to send
formal embassies to each other to notify the accession of a new chief; the
ambassadors were sacrificed.

E

given to the common ancestors of the Akan tribes. (*f*) The Gonja tradition, i.e. the tradition of the ruling class of the Gonja, is that they found the Ashanti living in the country when they arrived, and married the Ashanti women, and that is why their language is like the Ashanti language.

The only theory I can suggest to reconcile these facts is that the oldest inhabitants of the country were Gonja-speaking; that at a later date there occurred a gradual, and probably peaceable, infiltration by Vagale-speaking clans so that the two peoples lived side by side; and that when the recent invasion from the west took place, the small party of men happened to marry Gonja-speaking, not Vagale-speaking, women, so that the Gonja language became associated with the conquerors and became the language of the ruling class.[76]

This important invasion, which did for the Gonja what the invasion of Nyagse had done for the Dagomba,[77] was led by a man called Sumaila Ndewura Jakpa. His name, we are told, means the Spear-holder; Ndewura appears to be a Gonja name; *wura* is an Akan word meaning master, and many Gonja chiefs are called by the name of their chief town with *wura* as a suffix. Jakpa and his men swept over the country from west to east; like the Dagomba chief Nyagse before him, Jakpa appointed his own sons and other relatives chiefs in the conquered districts, and proceeded to organize them into a military empire. He captured the important salt-making centre of Daboia from the Dagomba, and then crossed to the east bank of the Volta and defeated the main Dagomba army under its chief, Dariziogo. He may be the founder of Salaga; he is certainly the founder of several less important towns. At his death the Gonja empire stretched from Bole in the west to Basari, far outside the modern Gold Coast in the east, a distance of some 200 miles. Jakpa's invasion occurred in the last decade of the sixteenth century.[78]

[76] I have suggested elsewhere (pp. 39, 40) that such infiltration of Vagale-speaking people as I have described may have taken place through Dagomba and Moshi pressure farther north on their main body. My theory is not nearly so simple as Rattray's theory that the Vagale-speakers were the oldest inhabitants and the Gonja-speakers were the invaders (Rattray, 516-17). Rattray's attractively simple theory, however, does not to my mind explain the antiquity and the wide connections of the Gonja tongue.
[77] Tamakloe says that Nyagse took the field against the Dagomba people; i.e. he welded the aboriginal tribes into a military state under his own rule. This is just what Jakpa did for the Gonja.
[78] Meyerowitz, *Akan Traditions of Origin*, 55-9.

From this time onwards there was rivalry between Gonja and Dagomba for a century, and for most of that time the Gonja were in a position of superiority to the Dagomba, if not actually their suzerains. During the long reign of the Dagomba chief Zangina, however, the Dagomba were at peace, and for some reason the Gonja chief Muhamman Wari Kumpati attacked the Dagomba in force. The Gonja were, however, decisively beaten by the Dagomba under the chief Asigeli, who succeeded the aged Zangina on his death.

This deliverance of the Dagomba may be dated soon after 1720; but it was short-lived. Fifty years later the Ashanti, who had already carried their frontier up to the Volta in Opoku Ware's time,[79] took the opportunity of a disputed succession in Dagomba to invade the country. Their army occupied the Dagomba capital Yendi without resistance, and demanded an idemnity of 2,000 slaves. The Dagomba chief, Gariba, was unable to raise such a large number, and the Ashanti thereupon commuted the fine for an annual payment of 200 slaves in perpetuity. From this time until 1874 this tribute continued, the Mamprusi and the Moshi sometimes helping the Dagomba to supply the full number. The majority of these slaves were retained in Ashanti as fighting men, not sold to Europeans. It may be that these janissaries were the 'Moors' whom Bowdich found possessing such influence in Kumasi.

What is the economic background of these rivalries? The answer may be summed up in three words: slaves, salt and guns. The Northern Territories consist of an undulating grassy plateau, dotted with small trees and thickets of bushes, with here and there a tall silk-cotton tree or a fan palm. Although there are plenty of cattle, it is not primarily a pastoral country, but an agricultural; unlike the southern parts of the Gold Coast, however, its fields are manured. The chief crops are yams and corn (maize), and there are two trees of great economic value, the shea butter tree and the dawa-dawa, both species of *Parkia*. There is very little fruit, and throughout the long and severe dry season there is an almost complete lack of green vegetables, not to mention great scarcity of

---

[79] Tamakloe, 33. The unsuccessful claimant to the chieftainship fled to Ashanti and asked the Asantehene to help him against his rival; thus the Dagomba, like the Irish in the twelfth century, invited the enemy into their country.

water. The country may be said to be semi-desert for one half the year and flooded the other half. The population naturally is thickest by the rivers and the perennial water-holes. A vanished earlier civilization has constructed in certain parts of the country underground water cisterns hewn out of the limestone rock,[80] but the present inhabitants know nothing of their origin, and they are silted up and useless, though they only need cleaning out to be once more valuable reservoirs.

These northern districts are a semi-arid area. The rainfall is adequate, but few of the streams are perennial, the water pouring away in deep and broad rivers which shrink to nothing in the dry season. Modern motor roads cross these 'drifts', as they are called locally, in fords; from November to April or May motors drive across a wide stretch of baked mud, from May to October they cross in ferries, and for days or even weeks at the height of the rainy season the river may be in such spate that the ferries are thrown out of action and the roads closed altogether to wheeled traffic.

The primitive agricultural society which is represented by the *ten'dama* was naturally self-sufficing in food. There were two commodities which it imported in pre-European days. These were salt and kola-nuts. There are salt-licks in the Daboia district in the Volta marshes; but this source of salt needed supplementing with sea-salt brought from the coast.[81] The kola-nut, the West African equivalent of betel, is a forest crop, and will not grow in the northern savannahs. Great quantities of kola were exported from Ashanti,[82] not only to the Moshi and Dagomba countries, but to the Sahara itself and the camel caravans. These two imports had to be paid for, and slaves were the export which was in greatest demand in the south.

The military predominance of the Mamprusi or the Dagomba chieftains over the aboriginal people was no doubt due to their better weapons. They may have triumphed by their horsemanship, or by the heavy swords and chain-mail which they inherited from the Crusades, or which had been manufactured by Arab armourers

[80] See an article by Captain Stewart in the *Gold Coast Farmer* for May 1936.
[81] The name Akim (Akyem) is derived from the Twi word for salt. The Akim controlled the chief salt-routes into the interior. To this day salt is scarce in the north, and poor people often use wood-ash instead.
[82] Rattray, *Ashanti Law and Constitution*, 109-11.

in imitation of the suits of mail stripped off dead Crusaders.[83] But cold steel and chain mail had to give place, in West Africa as in Europe, to firearms; and it was the Ashanti acquisition of firearms which ensured their victory over Gariba and his Dagomba. The Dagomba to this day call the Ashanti the Kambonse or gun-men. We have seen how the Denkyera were able, thanks to their plentiful supply of firearms from the Dutch, to hold down the infant power of Ashanti. Osei Tutu's victory at Feyiase would never have been possible had the Denkyera not allowed him to arm his troops with the new weapons. Seventy years later, the Ashanti triumphed by the same means over the Dagomba. Thus the wave of culture spread northward from the coast; and in due time, no doubt, we might have seen a successful Dagomba revolt against Ashanti and perhaps a Dagomba conquest of the Mamprusi or of peoples farther north. But before that could happen the muzzle-loading gun was itself conquered by breech-loading rifles and artillery, and Ashanti and Dagomba both came under British rule.

Ewe[84]

The Ewe-speaking peoples claim to have migrated from a place called Ketu, somewhere east of the Niger, to a town called Notsie[85] in French Togoland. Notsie was for the Ewe people what Asantemanso was for the Ashanti; the centre from which the tribes dispersed. Tradition says that while at Notsie they wore only skins and bark cloth, which suggests that the dispersal from Notsie took place early in the period of European connection with the Gold Coast. But as Notsie was well outside the Gold Coast as the term was understood in the seventeenth or eighteenth century, and was fifty miles inland, European cloth no doubt remained quite

[83] Such suits of chain-mail may still be seen, much the worse for wear, in ceremonial processions of northern chiefs at mid-Ramadan. Some may be authentic twelfth-century European work, most are probably Arab imitations. There is nothing impossible in the existence of medieval armour in West Africa; it is not so long since a silver cup with the royal arms of Richard Cœur de Lion was discovered in Ashanti, after 700 years of who knows what vicissitudes.

[84] Some Ewe traditions have been recorded in the Ewe language by the Bremen missionaries. I have to thank Mr. Ayivor of Achimota for making me a translation, on which I have based this narrative. It may be worth mentioning that the name Ewe is pronounced in two syllables; both vowels resemble the vowel of the English *get*, and the consonant resembles a soft Italian V.

[85] Spelt on the French maps Nouatya; it lies on the railwav line from Lome to Atakpame.

unknown there long after it was familiar in Ga or Fante country. With the information that we have, it is difficult to fix an approximate date for the dispersion from Notsie. It seems fairly certain that the Anlo or Awuna state was well established by the time of Ashangmo of Accra (1680). The kingdom of Dahomey is said to have been established by men from Notsie; and this kingdom had subdued its neighbours and risen to power by about 1720, so may perhaps be assumed to have begun a century or so earlier. Lastly, according to Ewe tradition, some of the Ga migrants were associated with the westward movement from Ketu, so that it may have begun as early as the fifteenth or the sixteenth century. On the whole we may conclude that the dispersal from Notsie must have taken place not later than the early years of the seventeenth century.[86]

The inhabitants of Notsie separated, according to tradition, in the time of an oppressive chief named Agokoli. They divided into three main groups, a northern, a middle, and a southern group. It seems probable that the course of their migrations was influenced largely by the hills and river valleys of western Togo. The Togo range is a continuation of the Akwapim hills, and runs north-north-east from the beautiful Volta gorge at Akwamu. Its sides are steep and rocky; in some places it forms a double chain with long longitudinal valleys between the two walls, down which flow tributaries of the Volta. The country south of the range is a coastal plain, about ninety miles wide in the longitude of the Volta mouth. Like the Accra plain, of which it is a continuation, it is a country of arid grassland, dotted here and there, especially near the river, with isolated kopjes.

The northern group of migrants seem to have marched roughly north-west from Notsie, and to have arrived at the hills somewhere near Palime; from this point they spread north and south into the hill country and occupied the long valleys. The most southerly division of this party, the Peki[87] people, pushed south-west until they formed a composite state with the Kyerepon people of the

---

[86] It is described in the tradition as a sudden event, but it is more likely to have been a process stretching over several years.
[87] The tribe and its country are named Krepi: Peki is the name of its capital town. For notes on the history of the Krepi, see a booklet by C. W. Welman, *The Native States of the Gold Coast, I, Peki*, published by the Gold Coast Government.

Anum hills overlooking the Volta gorge. The whole range from
Peki northwards as far as Akpafu was colonized by Ewe-speaking
immigrants, though here and there are still to be found islands
of Guan speakers, showing that the Ewe conquest was far from
complete.

The middle group, on meeting the hills, turned to the left and
settled at the foot of the range and on the groups of kopjes near
Ho. One division of this group diverged from its companions, went
farther to the south into the plains, and then (probably on coming
into contact with settlers from the southern group), turned northwards again and settled at Adaklu near Ho.

The southern group is the most important as far as Gold Coast
history is concerned. Although the 1914 frontier between the Gold
Coast and Togoland was ethnologically unsound, in that it divided
the Ewe people, like the Dagomba, between British and German
rule, it does seem to have corresponded fairly closely to the connections established in previous history. The British territory east
of the Volta consisted of the states of Akwamu and Krepi or Peki,
and of a broad stretch of the coastal plain corresponding to the
area occupied by the southernmost group of Ewe migrants from
Notsie. These territories are those which had constant dealings
with the states west of the Volta; the Krepi and Akwamu were in
increasingly close contact with Ashanti and Akim, and the Anlo
or Awuna of the south were from their earliest settlement in contact with the Ga tribes, especially the people of Ada. The remaining
Ewe tribes seem to have had little political dealings with these
westerly peoples, but to have looked eastwards to the powerful
states of Dahomey and Yoruba.

The southern group marched in two divisions, led respectively
by Amega Wenya and his nephew Sri. Throwing off colonies of
settlers as they went, they marched south-west to the lagoons and
creeks that lie east of the Volta mouth. Wenya's party came to
Atiteti on the north shore of the great Keta lagoon, and thence
crossed in canoes to the long sand-spit between the lagoon and the
sea and settled there. Wenya's two sons, Akaga and Awanyedo,
founded the town of Keta.[88] Sri's party continued its march on the

---

[88] The name means 'the head of the sand'. The name Peki means 'late-comers';
these people halted on the march long enough to raise a crop, and arrived after
their companions had settled. I shall call the Anlo state by that name, not the
form Awuna.

north of the lagoon and colonized the area between the lagoon and the Volta.[89] Eventually Sri and Wenya joined forces again and established the strong maritime state of Awuna or Anlo. The capital of the state was Awunaga or Anloga, a few miles south of Keta on the same great spit of sand. After some heavy fighting against its eastern neighbours, who were vassals of Dahomey, and later against the Accra settlers at Little Popo, the Anlo state established itself, and for the first half of the eighteenth century lived a fairly peaceful existence, broken only by petty bickering with its Ga neighbours at Ada over the fishing rights in the Volta. It was not until the intrusion of the Akwamu into the Krepi country and the organization of a strong and aggressive Akan state in Akwapim that the country east of the Volta became the scene of heavy fighting.

[89] The country on the left bank of the Volta between the lagoons and the hills is arid and thinly peopled; there were no strong tribes between the Anlo and the Krepi.

CHAPTER VII

BRITISH ASHANTI AND FANTE TILL 1816

OPOKU WARE was the grandson of Osei Tutu's sister, and had been named by Osei Tutu himself as his successor. He began his reign amid great difficulties. The Ashanti army had retired hurriedly after the disaster of Osei Tutu's death; and it is not surprising that Denkyera, Sefwi and Akwapim rose to help the Akim to crush the upstart Ashanti power for good and all. Opoku Ware, however, triumphed. In two campaigns he defeated the Akim, killing three paramount chiefs and capturing the Notes for the three forts at Accra. During one of the Akim campaigns the Sefwi made a sudden attack on Ashanti; they sacked Kumasi, killing Opoku Ware's own mother, and rifling the royal graves for gold. Opoku Ware hurried back from Akim and sent a force to follow up the victorious Sefwi as they were retiring. The commander of this expedition was Amankwa Tia the chief of Bantama, the first of several chiefs of that name to distinguish himself as an Ashanti general. Amankwa Tia caught the Sefwi army before it could recross the Tano river, completely defeated it, and killed the Sefwi-hene Ebirim Moro. The Sefwi territory between the Tano and the Bia was annexed to Ashanti and became known as Ahafo, the hunting preserve of the Asantehene.[1]

Having secured his position in this way, Opoku Ware took the offensive; in alliance with the Brong state of Nkoranza he attacked and subdued Tekyiman, and pushed beyond it to defeat the Gyaman people, whose chief Abo Kofi[2] had made himself a golden stool in imitation of the Stool of Ashanti.

Opoku Ware died in 1742, and was succeeded by his uncle, Kwasi Obodum, "the chief that never killed a man if he could help

[1] The boundary between the modern administrative districts of Sunyani and Ahafo Goaso perpetuates the memory of this annexation. The Ahafo Goaso of today represents the conquered territory, which was thoroughly devastated by Amankwa Tia, and has remained thinly populated until the present day. Claridge (I, 213) puts this Sefwi war later, in Osei Kojo's time. I prefer Fuller's chronology which is supported by Bekwai and Kokofu tradition. Bekwai says that Ebirim Moro was a woman chief.
[2] Usually called in Ashanti Abo Kobina; but Gyaman tradition, recorded by Tauxier (*Le Noir de Bondougou*) calls him Abo Kofi.

it, but always commuted the death penalty to a fine".[3] Kwasi
Obodum was already an elderly man; but in spite of this and of
his peace-loving disposition he found himself involved in a war
against the Akim, who were supported by the powerful state of
Dahomey. He defeated the Akim by the swiftness of his attack
before the Dahomey army could give them any effective help; but
the punitive expedition which he sent across the Volta into the
enemy's country was repulsed, and suffered heavy losses in a rearguard action while recrossing the river.[4]

Osei Kojo succeeded his uncle Kwasi Obodum in 1752, and continued the warlike policy which Opoku Ware had begun and
Kwasi Obodum had been forced to continue. Some Ashanti traders
had been killed in the Banda country north of Gyaman, and when
Osei Kojo threatened war, Banda was openly joined by Gyaman,
Denkyera, Wassaw and the distant state of Kong. All Banda and
much of Gyaman lay beyond the forest belt, and Banda and its
allies made the common mistake of supposing that a nation that
had specialized in one type of warfare would not be able to endure
warfare of an unfamiliar type. The Ashanti were specialists in
forest fighting; and therefore the Banda thought they would not
be able to stand up to a pitched battle in the open. Twice, indeed,
they repulsed the Ashanti attacks, but the third time the Ashanti
won a complete victory. Banda and Wassaw were added to the
Ashanti empire, and Denkyera and Gyaman were punished for
assisting them.[5] Kong, whose cavalry had been conspicuous in the
fighting, was prudently left alone; it was too remote to be safely
attacked. Meanwhile Dagomba, which had taken no part in the
Banda war, was weakened by a disputed succession; one of the
rivals invited Ashanti assistance, and the other rashly sneered at
the value of any help Ashanti could give. An Ashanti army moved
north across the Volta and easily defeated the Dagomba forces,
which had to stand against the Ashanti guns with nothing but
spears and arrows. An annual tribute in slaves and livestock was
imposed upon the Dagomba, which continued to be paid until 1874.

[3] So he was described to me by the Adansi when relating their history.
[4] This expedition into Dahomey, which Fuller says did not take place until later,
seems to be referred to Opoku Ware's time by the tradition of Kumawu (Rattray,
Ashanti Law and Constitution, 221), whose chief was killed in it. Claridge,
following Bowdich, places it in Kwasi Obodum's reign.
[5] Fuller, 34; Claridge, I, 211, 212.

Osei Kojo, like his predecessors, had to deal with Akim, Akwapim and Assin. These states bordering on Ashanti were regarded as belonging at least to its sphere of influence, if not actually to its empire. The Akim and the others constantly resisted the Ashanti claim and took every opportunity of asserting their independence. Osei Kojo's Akim war was probably the sixth in about seventy years, and on this occasion, as in 1745 in Kwasi Obodum's time, the Akim widened the area of the war by allying themselves with their western neighbours the Assin. This was a momentous step, for the Assin were in close contact with the Fante, and the question of the Fante neutrality became important. Osei Kojo thought it so important that he paid the Fante chiefs a cash subsidy in return for a promise not to assist the Assin in any way.[6] The Fante took the money, but broke their promise, which so exasperated Osei Kojo that he swore to be revenged. This must have happened about 1765, for in that year the Council of the British Company in Cape Coast considered the possibility that war might break out between Ashanti and Fante. This is the first mention of Ashanti in the British records.[7]

Osei Kojo was not able to keep his oath. He was old and infirm, and in the middle of his preparations for war he died in 1781. From 1765 to 1772 the British on the coast were apprehensive of an Ashanti war,[8] but Osei Kojo never found leisure to begin such a distant campaign. There was trouble within Ashanti, which actually led to sharp fighting between Mampon and Juaben,[9] and when that trouble was settled by the personal intervention of the Asantehene, there arose the threat of yet another war with Akim and Akwapim, which, however, came to nothing.

The policy of expansion paused at Osei Kojo's death. His successor was a boy, Osei Kwamina, who was still a minor, and for ten or twelve years the country was governed by a regent. No major wars were undertaken during his reign. When he assumed power in person he proved unwelcome to the council of chiefs, and was soon

---

[6] This is the Ashanti account; I have not heard what the Fante have to say about it; but there is one case on record dating from 1695 where the Fante betrayed the Dutch in this way—see Claridge, I, 150, and see also below, p. 150.

[7] Claridge, I, 213.

[8] Claridge, I, 213, following Cruikshank.

[9] Claridge, I, 213; see also Fuller, 35, and the Juaben and Mampon traditions; Rattray, *Ashanti Law and Constitution*, 172, 238, 239.

deposed.[10] He was followed by his younger brother Opoku Fofie, who died suddenly after a reign of only a few weeks. Opoku Fofie was succeeded in 1709 by a still younger brother, Osei Asibe Kwamina, one of the greatest but most unfortunate of his great line.[11]

In a century Ashanti had grown from a group of small allied states to a great empire. The territory of Ashanti had been at Osei Tutu's accession a block about thirty miles by forty. Osei Tutu had trebled its area by his conquest of Denkyera and the Doma country, without counting the thinly peopled Afram plains, which also were added to Ashanti in his reign. In Opoku Ware's time the upper valley of the Tano was added, and the frontiers of Ashanti at his death may be taken as being roughly the Bia river on the west, the Tain and Volta on the north and east, and the Pra and the Ofin on the south. Ashanti was now a fairly compact territory about 150 miles from east to west and averaging ninety miles from north to south. Outside this area came the ring of states—Banda, Gyaman, Dagomba, Akim, Assin and Denkyera,[12] over which Ashanti claimed and from time to time attempted to assert authority. The smallest of these, Assin, was a little smaller than the Ashanti over which Osei Tutu had been chosen to reign.

The Ashanti nation itself, thanks to the statesmanlike genius of Okomfo Anokye, had developed rapidly and successfully out of a group of small settlements connected by ties of kindred but not by any political links. Okomfo Anokye's statesmanship, which seemed miraculous to the Ashanti of his day, lay simply in this; that he persuaded the different Ashanti groups to lay aside their rivalries and to join as partners in a higher association. As new tribes and groups were conquered by the forces of the new federation they were admitted to membership on equal terms. Their customs were respected, their territory was left intact, their chiefs became members of the *Abrempon,* or council of chiefs of Ashanti.

This policy was brilliantly successful when applied to tribes like the Doma or the Kwahu, who lived within a few miles of Kumasi and who were closely akin to the Ashanti themselves. Osei Tutu is

[10] Claridge, I, 224; he soon afterwards was put to death at his own request.
[11] He is usually called Osei Bonsu; Bonsu means a whale, and he assumed this name in honour of his successful campaign on the coast. See below, p. 156.
[12] As a result of Osei Tutu's wars all Denkyera territory north of the Ofin was annexed by Ashanti, and the headquarters of the state of Denkyera was shifted south-east to the lower valley of the Pra. It was this 'New Denkyera' over which Ashanti was now claiming authority.

said to have decreed that such new recruits to the federation should cease, on pain of death, to relate their own traditional history; their history must begin anew from the date of their joining Ashanti. Whether this decree is genuine or not, it is a fact that it is extremely difficult to discover any coherent traditions dating from before his time in any Ashanti state. It seems as if in such cases there did grow up a real national spirit which centred in the Golden Stool.

As the Ashanti conquests spread outwards, however, this policy became less and less effective. Okomfo Anokye was working to build up a solid Ashanti state out of scattered fragments. He was encouraging and accelerating a process that was already at work; we have seen that Oti Akenten's reputation was attracting more and more Ashanti settlers to his fief of Kwaman. But a policy which was suitable for uniting Ashanti groups and for attracting to Ashanti small neighbouring tribes of similar origin and ways of living was not well adapted for bringing into the Ashanti state large nations with a long tradition of their own. Akim, Denkyera, Banda, Gyaman had all of them a strong national feeling, and were bitterly opposed to the idea of becoming part of an Ashanti federation. Ashanti statecraft, however, was unprogressive; Okomfo Anokye's policy was blindly continued in circumstances for which he had not intended it; and the results, both for Ashanti and for the neighbouring states, were deplorable.

The Okomfo Anokye tradition did not permit the Ashanti to develop a system of provincial administration. After a successful campaign the conquered territory was not garrisoned; a tribute was imposed on it, an Ashanti chief was appointed as governor, and the province became liable to provide a military contingent to the Ashanti army when called on. The native chief was left in authority, the Ashanti governor usually continuing to reside in Ashanti except for occasional visits. Every Ashanti chief who lived at a distance from Kumasi had his honorary representative at the Kumasi court, one of the court officials who acted as a sort of consul or ambassador, much as a Roman senator under Trajan might be the patron at court of some far away provincial tribe or city.[13]

[13] Claridge, I, 228, 229; Rattray, *Ashanti Law and Constitution*, 95; this aspect of the Ashanti constitution is described in chaps. XII. and XIII. The friend at court (called simply *Adamfo* or 'friend') was not in any sense the social superior of the chief whom he represented.

This system was extended to the newly-conquered provinces, and otherwise they were left to themselves. Sometimes the victors interfered sporadically in the internal government of the province in the hope of weakening it; thus, Opoku Ware tried to weaken the power of Gyaman[14] by killing Abo Kofi the Gyamanhene and placing on the stool a certain Kofi Sono from a rival family. No doubt he hoped that the Gyaman would waste their strength in civil war; but as a matter of fact the Gyaman soon made an agreement to take their chiefs alternately from the two rival families; so that Opoku Ware's plan failed.

The result of this policy, as far as the non-Ashanti states were concerned, was that they were left alone to bide their time and plan for their revenge. Their military strength was left almost undamaged, for the Ashanti hoped to use them as part of the Ashanti forces.[15] Ashanti thus became surrounded by a ring of bitter enemies, all of whom were eagerly watching for any sign of weakness that might encourage them to rise and overthrow the Ashanti suzerainty. This in turn induced the Ashanti government to be continually prepared for military adventure to demonstrate its military strength.

But the main cause of the expansionist policy of Ashanti was economic. Ashanti was an inland country, and European goods were only to be obtained from the coast at exorbitant prices owing to the middlemen activities of the coast tribes. Ashanti needed European goods, especially firearms,[16] and the imports from Europe had to be paid for by exports. In competition with other Gold Coast nations, Ashanti could export gold, but other districts were richer in alluvial gold, and the rich quartz reefs of Ashanti could only be scratched on the surface by African mining methods.

[14] The Gyaman were very deserving of special attention. They were rapidly building up a Brong state on much the same lines as the Ashanti state and were already beginning to incorporate the non-Akan peoples of the savannah country round Bondugu. There was every prospect of their becoming dangerous rivals of the Ashanti.

[15] Sometimes the Ashanti government was more subtle. The Akim Bosome tradition relates that in the early years of the nineteenth century the Akim Bosome were so often called on to provide contingents for the army that they suspected the Ashanti government of having a definite plan to kill them off. In 1874 the Asantehene Kofi Karikari certainly treated the Brong contingents from northern Ashanti in this way.

[16] It will be remembered that Osei Tutu's first step in preparing for his war against Ntim Gyakari was to import guns from the coast. Bekwai tradition says that at that time Bekwai had only thirty guns.

The one export commodity that Ashanti could produce in large quantities was slaves.

Ashanti thus became deliberately a slave-dealing state. Many slaves were bought in the markets of the north, especially Salaga, in peace time, and were marched to the coast and there sold at a profit, just as cattle are bought and sold today. But many were obtained by raiding and warfare, and the great slave market at Manso near Cape Coast was largely kept supplied from the proceeds of the Ashanti wars.[17]

While Ashanti had thus been expanding its territory and fighting against all its neighbours, the nations on the coast had also been developing. The most conspicuous fact in coast politics was the development of the Fante state. In Bosman's day, about the year 1700, the Fante country was remarkable for its disunity: "every part of Fantyn hath also its particular Chief, who will sometimes scarce own himself subject to the Braffo, who hath the ineffectual name only of Supreme Power." A century later these tiny Fante states had come together into a federation, under the nominal presidency of the chief of Abora; general concerns were discussed at a regular council; and by diplomacy and fighting the Fante federation had extended its rule from the Sweet river[18] near Elmina as far to the east as Beraku, a distance of some sixty miles. It may be conjectured that economic causes were as important in the growth of the Fante state as they were in that of Ashanti. The strip of coast from the Sweet river to Beraku contained British forts at Cape Coast, Anomabu, Tantamkweri and Winneba, and Dutch forts at Mori, Kormantine, Apam and Beraku. British and Dutch were often enemies, and the obvious policy for the Fante was to unite in order to make as much profit as possible from their dissensions. United, the Fante could control the trade routes and make it worth the Europeans' while to pay them regular subsidies for keeping the routes working;[19] not to mention the fact that they could trade more or less on their own terms.

There were, however, political reasons as well for the Fante to unite into a strong federation. They were feeling the pressure of

[17] The Banda war brought thousands of slaves into the market at Manso; Gold Coast slaves were commonly known in the trade as Kormantines and were highly valued.
[18] The Sweet river was the eastern frontier of Elmina.
[19] See above, p. 98.

states which were shrinking away from the growing Ashanti power. The chief of these states was Denkyera, which had been driven by the Ashanti from its original territory in the Ofin valley, and had settled in the lower part of the valley of the Pra. Although the Ashanti pressure on Akim did not constitute any great threat to the Fante states, it was clear that if that pressure were applied to Assin, Akim's western neighbour, the Fante would at once be affected. Then again, the long-continued wars against Elmina and the Dutch made some permanent military alliance necessary, especially if the campaign was to be conducted, as it actually was in 1694, in alliance with the people of Kommenda.

Meanwhile the Royal African Company, which was concerned with trade, not with politics, was feeling far from happy. Parliament had declared in 1698 that the West African trade was open to all on payment of a licence fee of ten per cent on exports and imports, and the proceeds of the sale of licences were to be used in maintaining the forts and establishments on the coast. But in the view of the Company, this arrangement was not a success. The two chief articles of export, gold and slaves, were exempted from duty, so that the revenue was far smaller than might have been expected. The Company also put forward the familiar argument that the competition of the ten per cent traders raised the prices of all African produce and depressed the prices of British exports, and generally ruined the trade. Naturally the ten per cent men took up the challenge; and the matter developed into a struggle between the London merchants, who were mostly members of the Company, and the merchants of Bristol and Liverpool, who were mostly non-members.[20] The non-members did not fail to point out that in the days of the Company's monopoly the price of Negroes, whatever it may have been on the Coast, rapidly doubled itself in the West Indies, and other prices rose similarly; so that the Company could ill afford to reproach the non-members for raising prices by their competition. At length, in 1750, Parliament, after having for twenty years voted an annual grant of £10,000 to the Royal African Company, passed an Act by which the Royal African Company surrendered its charter and property in return for compensation, and a new regulated company was formed called the African Com-

[20] Claridge, I, 207, 208; Lipson, II, 355-60; Martin, *The British West African Settlements, 1750-1821*, 7-9.

pany of Merchants. The new company was forbidden to engage in joint-stock enterprise, membership was opened to all British merchants on payment of a forty-shilling fee, and an annual grant of some £13,000 was paid by Parliament to maintain the forts.[21]

The payment of a regular Parliamentary grant brought the Government into close contact with the African Company. Parliament demanded from time to time an account of the administration of the West African settlements, and in 1772 and again in 1777 the Company's control of the forts was severely criticized. The idea was beginning to gain ground that the government of the settlements should be taken over by the Crown, and that the Company should confine itself to trade. When the French settlements on the Senegal were ceded to Britain by the Peace of Paris of 1763, they were erected into the Crown colony of Senegambia; but the Company was left in control of the Gold Coast settlements, and twenty years later, when the French had recovered the greater part of Senegambia, the remnant was handed over to the Company.[22]

Both the Seven Years' War and the War of American Independence brought about fighting on the Coast. In 1757 the French made an unsuccessful attempt to capture Cape Coast. A few years later the Dutch sent an expedition from Axim westward across the Ankoba into the Nzima country.[23] The Nzima people met them and defeated them, capturing their artillery and driving them back across the river. The Nzima then invited the British to come and build a fort in their country, and a fort was built at Beyin. In 1780 Britain, already at war with France and Spain as well as with the American Colonies, declared war on Holland. A few months later an ambitious plan for a combined attack by land and sea on

[21] The Royal African Company received over £100,000 in settlement of its debts by way of compensation from Parliament. Claridge gives figures showing that over a period of fourteen years the Company received about £110,000 in duties, half of which came from its own members, while the cost of maintaining the forts was £280,000. According to figures given by non-members (quoted in Lipson) the Company's own trade was only about one-fifth at the most of the total West African trade; some put the proportion as low as one-tenth. If so, there must have been a vast amount of evasion of the 10 per cent duty. The duty was abolished in 1730, and the annual grant from Parliament established in its place. The basic figure of the grant was £10,000 from 1750 to 1761, and £13,000 from 1761 to 1807; but supplementary grants for special expenditure were sometimes made; Martin, 17, 18.
[22] Martin, 16-21.
[23] Claridge, I, 215. The Nzima country was nicknamed Apollonia by the early missionaries and the name stuck. The new fort at Beyin was named Fort Apollonia.

Elmina failed miserably, the two British warships standing by idly watching while the troops were repulsed from the guns of Fort Conraadsburg on St. Jago hill. Next year, however, the same naval commander, Captain Shirley, took the Dutch forts at Mori, Apam, Kormantine and Beraku. A military expedition, assisted by a force of seamen, landed from H.M.S. *Argo,* took the Dutch fort at Kommenda. An expedition against the Dutch Fort Crèvecœur at Accra was indecisive. The fort was shelled by the ships and by the guns of the British Fort James and there was a good deal of land fighting between the British allies and the Dutch allies. Eventually the Dutch forces retired into the bush and left Fort Crèvecœur to its fate. The one Dutch success in the war was the capture of the British fort at Sekondi. By the Peace of Versailles of 1783 the *status quo* was restored, but the fort at Sekondi had been destroyed by the Dutch and was not rebuilt.

During the closing years of the eighteenth century the condition of the British settlements was unenviable. The wars with the Dutch and the French[24] had been expensive, and had weakened the position of the British, and indeed of all the Europeans, against the African states. The Europeans were entirely devoid of political authority and of political reputation in the eyes of the Africans whose tenants they were. In 1786 the British commander of Tantamkweri was kidnapped on the beach and stripped and flogged; the commandants of Sekondi and Mori were similarly treated; in 1812 the commandant of Winneba was killed, as the Dutch governor of Elmina had been shortly before.[25] The Europeans could seldom employ enough force to compel respect, and such outrages as these went unpunished.[26] Lacking force, the

[24] The French made some feeble attempts to re-establish themselves on the Gold coast in 1788 and 1794; Claridge, I, 225-7.
[25] Martin, 51, 52; Claridge, I, 267-72.
[26] Martin and Claridge give several instances of the humiliating position in which the Europeans lived. When the commandant of British Sekondi was assaulted in the evening as he was going to call on the commandant of the Dutch fort, the Council of Cape Coast shrugged its shoulders with the remark that he ought not to have been paying visits so late. The forts were dependent for wood and water on the villages nearby, and the villagers always kept the work of providing wood and water in their own hands, though, of course, the forts kept rain-water tanks as a reserve supply. In 1774 the Company's authorities at home sent out instructions that less was to be spent in subsidies and presents; but the Company's officials on the Coast replied "Owing to the weakness of the Company's position it is necessary to keep black men of power in our pay that we may live in peace with the natives, who would otherwise molest us, knowing we have not sufficient power to protect ourselves." The murder of the commandant at Winneba was to

Europeans had to use bribery. In short, the European traders were merely tolerated by the Africans because they were useful, but they were neither liked nor feared.

To the Europeans in the forts Ashanti was an Eldorado, though it was not known whether the gold which was supposed to be so abundant there was produced in Ashanti itself or imported from farther north still. Apart from gold, it was known to be an insatiable market for firearms and powder, and a great supplier of slaves. No European had visited the country, and both its fighting strength and its riches, great as they were in reality, were regarded with all the greater respect for being hidden in mystery.

In 1765 the Council of the British settlements began to be apprehensive of a war between Ashanti and Fante, and it seemed to them likely to be disastrous. They feared that if the Ashanti won, the European forts would be captured, while if the Fante won, the miltary power of Ashanti would be broken and its value as a source of slaves destroyed. But it was not until 1792 that the threatened war seemed likely at last to be coming upon them. In that year the Danish governor of Christiansborg applied to the Asantehene Osei Kwamina for a force of mercenaries to help him in his wars with the eastern tribes. The British were aghast at his rashness, and sent to Kumasi to urge the Asantehene to refuse the conquest. Osei Kwamina would not listen to them, and went on with his preparations; but before the Ashanti contingent reached the coast the Danish governor who had asked for it was dead, and his successor paid the Ashanti to go back home without fighting.[27]

Osei Tutu Kwamina Asibe, to give him his full name, became Asantehene in 1800. His reign began with the usual crop of wars, including not only one against Gyaman, but also a war against Gofan, a state lying north of Bondugu. The Gofan army attacked and conquered Banda, and then moved against Ashanti, but was defeated in two engagements by the Ashanti force under a general bearing the historic name of Amankwa Tia.

It was in 1805 that Ashanti was for the first time drawn into war

some extent punished; the town was destroyed by the guns of a warship and the fort was abandoned and blown up. This happened in 1812 when the people of the coast were thoroughly afraid of the Ashanti; so in order to have the fort rebuilt the people of Winneba consented to pay an indemnity. But this would not have been possible before the Ashanti terror.
[27] Claridge, I, 223, 224.

against the Fante and the British. The occasion of the quarrel was
a comparatively small dispute in Assin. Assin was ruled by three
chiefs: the eastern section, Assin Apimenem, was under Amo
Adae, and the western section, Assin Atadanso,[28] was under two
chiefs, Kwadwo Otibu and Kwaku Aputae. One of Amo Adae's
sub-chiefs died, and various gold ornaments were buried with him,
as is customary. The funeral was attended by a relative of Kwaku
Aputae, who afterwards came secretly and robbed the grave. The
crime was discovered, and Amo Adae sent to Kwaku Aputae to
demand compensation. Kwaku Aputae and his brother chief
refused to consider the case, dismissing the whole story as pure
invention. Amo Adae appealed to the Asantehene, who summoned
all three chiefs to appear before his court in Kumasi. Kwadwo
Otibu, being an old man, sent his excuses, but the other two went;
and after trying in vain to have the matter settled out of court, the
Asantehene gave judgment in favour of Amo Adae, and ordered
Kwaku Aputae to pay compensation to the plaintiff. Aputae was
detained in Kumasi until he had complied with the order of the
court, but he managed to escape and slipped away home to Assin.

The plaintiff, Amo Adae, having secured a judgment but having
failed to secure compensation, now took matters into his own
hands and invaded Assin Atadanso. The fighting was indecisive,
and the Asantehene made another attempt to settle the case. He
ordered the enemies to cease fighting and await further legal proceedings. Amo Adae obeyed, and withdrew north of the Pra to the
Moinsi hills near Obuasi. Kwaku Aputae, in obedience to the
Asantehene, retired from his position to allow Amo Adae to return
to Assin; but he treacherously fell upon him during his march and
utterly defeated him. This was bad enough; but in his exultation
at his victory he executed the messengers of the Asantehene, a
symbolic act which signified an insulting declaration of war.[29]

The Asantehene, whose forbearance had been remarkable considering the flagrant contempt of his court that Aputae had shown
throughout the proceedings,[30] could forbear no longer, and took

[28] Or Assin Atandaso.
[29] It was not uncommon for war to be declared by cutting off the little finger of
the enemy chief's representative, but to kill him was unusual.
[30] It is at least arguable that by submitting to the jurisdiction of the Asantehene's
court both parties had acknowledge themselves his subjects, in which case
Aputae's behaviour was still more audacious.

the field himself to punish Kwaku Aputae. Aputae managed somehow to induce the aged and reluctant Kwadwo Otibu to risk everything and come out openly on his side; and the two chiefs advanced
to meet the Ashanti army. At Kyikyiwere,[31] on the slopes of the
Moinsi hills, they met the Ashanti, and were completely defeated;
their army was driven across the Pra and scattered, and the two
chiefs fled through their own land of Assin and sought refuge in
Fante country. They came first to Asikuma, and hard on their
heels came messengers from the Asantehene demanding that they
be given up to him. They did not await the Asikuma reply to the
messengers, but fled again to Abora, the capital town, if so it could
be called, of the Fante confederation. There a council of Fante
chiefs and advisers met to consider what should be done with them.

Even to contemporaries the occasion seemed historic. Two
powers which had never before come into contact were now face
to face, and the whole balance of power on the Coast depended on
the result. Each had behind it a long period of steady expansion,
each was supreme in its own district. In deliberating whether or
not to surrender the Assin chiefs, the council at Abora well knew
that it was deliberating peace or war, and that war, if it came,
would be decisive, bringing utter destruction to the vanquished.

The council decided to shelter the two chiefs of Assin, and to
defy the Asantehene: a decision which to us, looking back on the
sequel of these events, seems sheer folly. As the event proved, the
Fante were quite unable to stand against the Ashanti attack, and
unable to give any effective shelter to their guests. But this could
hardly have been foretold. The Fante had plenty of military success in their history; and the Ashanti, powerful as they were, had
not shown themselves by any means invincible. Apart from the
repulse of Osei Tutu's last invasion of Akim—which might have
been regarded as a piece of sheer luck owing to the killing of Osei
Tutu himself—and from the Sefwi invasion which achieved a
momentary success owing to the absence of the army on the Akim
campaign, the Ashanti had many times been repulsed or defeated
in pitched battles. Kwasi Obodum had been repulsed in a bloody
and indecisive battle in Dahomey, which lasted all day and which
he did not think it prudent to renew next morning. His rearguard

---

[31] Pronounced, and often spelt, Chichiwere; a common place-name meaning
'consolation'.

was annihilated in the same campaign while his main body was retreating across the Volta. Osei Kojo sent two unsuccessful expeditions against Banda before the third expedition which conquered it. The constant campaigns against Akim, momentarily successful though they were in dispersing any military opposition, never succeeded in breaking the spirit of the Akim.[32] In deciding to take the risk of opposing the Ashanti army, therefore, the Fante council was not taking an unreasonable risk. The Ashanti might be defeated altogether. They might win the battle and impose a tribute; but it would surely be possible to let the tribute fall into arrears, for such a distant campaign was too expensive for the Ashanti to undertake often. The European forts might give the Fante some support; and even a heavy defeat need not necessarily therefore be fatal to the whole Fante state.

From the point of view of military prudence, then, the decision was not an obvious blunder. There were other considerations involved. There was clearly the question of chivalry; it was quite certain that if the Assin chiefs were given up they would be tortured and killed. Moreover, Assin was the nearest neighbour to the Fante confederation, and the Assin could not be expected to forgive such an unfriendly act as surrendering their chiefs to the enemy. To incur the enmity of a near neighbour in order to please a more distant state seemed unwise. Lastly, Ashanti had already grounds for quarrel with the Fante, for the Fante had helped the Assin against Osei Kojo,[33] and there may have been another incident of the same sort in Osei Kwamina's time.[34] Whether the Fante now provided the Asantehene with a further *casus belli* or not, they may well have felt that the Asantehene was certain to attempt to be revenged on them sooner or later, and they might as well face it now and get it over.

The Asantehene seems still to have behaved with remarkable caution or forbearance. The council refused his demand for the surrender of the fugitives. He suggested that Fante delegates should be

[32] These Ashanti defeats are recorded by Claridge and Fuller.
[33] See above, p. 139. Whatever the Fante version of the incident may be, they must have known that Osei Kojo had vowed vengeance on them.
[34] See Fuller, 39; but I suspect that this is the same incident as the one in Osei Kojo's time. I see no reason why the Ashanti should want to cross Fante country to invade Assin; but if they were invading Akim they might very well wish to send a flanking column that way. I think Fuller has probably written 'Osei Kwamina' by mistake for 'Osei Kojo'.

sent to his camp to discuss the whole matter, and when this also was refused he asked permission to follow the fugitive Assin chiefs with his army through Fante country. This last demand led to a declaration of war, his messengers being killed by the Fante; and at last he ordered his army to advance against the Fante positions.

The campaign was short and decisive. The Ashanti won victories in the border country, and again were willing to discuss terms of peace; but once again the Fante refused to listen to talk of peace, and the Asantehene swore the great oath that he would not return to Kumasi without the heads of his enemies. The Ashanti army approached the sea, and after one or two smaller successes utterly defeated the main Fante army in May 1806 at Abora, which was only four miles from Cape Coast.

The war had now come right up to the walls of the European forts, and the British authorities in particular had to make their decision. The two Assin chiefs had escaped from the defeat at Abora and reached Anomabu, and thence went to Cape Coast to visit the British governor; while the Ashanti advance guard occupied Kormantine, where the Dutch commander of Fort Amsterdam surrendered the fort without any attempt at resistance.

The British governor was Colonel Torrane, who in spite of his military title had no military experience. He had resigned from the Coast in 1797, and had since then kept himself in the Company's eye by explaining to the Committee in letters what was wrong on the West Coast and how everything might be put right. In October 1804 he was appointed to put it right; he was given the honorary rank of Colonel, provided with fresh instructions which made him almost independent of his council, and sent out to tighten up discipline and make the Company's service more respectable.[35] Coming out to the Coast on these terms, he could not hope for popularity; but everyone acknowledged his firmness and vigour. Moreover, he was not utterly preoccupied with 'respectability'; he was a man of ideas. He seems to have realized that friendship with Ashanti was vital for British trade; and he made a plantation of coffee near Cape Coast.[36] It is a pity that

[35] Martin, *British West African Settlements*, 147-50. 'Respectability' seems to have been a favourite word of Torrane's; for the sake of respectability the Company's officers ought to wear side-arms, and Cape Coast ought to have a chaplain.
[36] Claridge, I, 253-4.

he should have been led to spoil his reputation with an act which appears neither firm nor according to modern ideas respectable.

Torrane had to decide the British policy. There was no precedent to guide him, and his Dutch colleague or rival had bowed to the storm. The quarrel between the Ashanti and the Assin was no concern of the British; nor were the British in any way bound to aid the Fante, whom indeed they had little cause to love. The British were merely traders, with no authority whatever beyond the walls of their forts, and even the ground on which the forts stood was rented from the African states who held the Notes for it. Torrane could hardly have been blamed for holding entirely aloof from the whole quarrel, and making the best terms he could with the Ashanti. The Ashanti would find the Europeans just as useful as the Fante found them, and there was no reason to think that trade need suffer if the Fante states became provinces of the loosely-knit Ashanti empire.

On the other hand, to take such a course would have required a very cool head, a good deal of callousness to the suffering among the coast people, and a soundness of judgment which could hardly have been expected on the information at Torrane's disposal. On the origin of war, Torrane can hardly have had any information except that given him by the two Assin chiefs and by the Fante. Little was known about the Ashanti except that they were exceedingly strong from the military point of view, which the events of the last few months had amply confirmed. No European had visited Ashanti, and Torrane could know nothing of the solidity of their constitution and their very considerable degree of civilization in social and legal matters. They must have been represented to him as mere savages, formidable by reason of their military strength but nothing but an obstruction which must be cleared away before civilization and trade could develop. Torrane himself could see that the British had sound economic reasons for desiring friendship with Ashanti; but he had no means of knowing whether those economic reasons would appeal to the Ashanti also. For all he knew, the Ashanti army, having destroyed the Fante opposition, might then proceed to take all the European forts as it had already taken Fort Amsterdam, and exclude the European trade altogether from the Gold Coast. He could not know that Osei Bonsu the Asantehene was a good deal wiser and more virtuous than many of his contemporary European statesmen in the age of Metternich and Talleyrand.

Torrane made his decision. The Assin chiefs asked for his help; the chiefs of Cape Coast promised to protect them, and were confident that they could hold the town against the Ashanti force; and Torrane, who was inclined at first merely to offer his mediation, allowed himself to be committed to help the Assin and the Fante, "either by mediation or by force of arms".[37]

Events then moved rapidly. The main Ashanti army advanced from Abora, four miles north-west of Cape Coast, passing behind Cape Coast itself, and joining its advance guard at Kormantine. three miles from Anomabu. Anomabu itself was full of refugees, and the fighting force of the town was strengthened by the men who had rallied after their defeat at Abora. Early in June, Mr. White, the commandant of Fort William at Anomabu, sent to the Denkyerahene, who commanded the Ashanti advance guard at Kormantine, offering his mediation in the matter between the Ashanti and the people of Anomabu. This was refused,[38] and, his mediation having failed, White prepared to use armed force. On the 14th of June the people of Anomabu attacked a small Ashanti advanced post at Egya, a mile away; and on the next day this attacking force, which had gained a local success and had forgotten to secure its communications with the town, was attacked by the whole Ashanti army and driven back in full retreat upon its base. Next day the Ashanti assaulted the town. Two thousand non-combatants, as many as the place would hold, were admitted into the fort, and the rest crouched outside the walls in the hope that they would be safe under its guns. The garrison of the fort consisted only of five officers and twenty men; but White hoped that the Ashanti would be unable to stand up to the unaccustomed experience of artillery.[39]

In this hope he was disappointed. By eleven in the morning the

[37] Claridge, I, 241-54; Fuller, 40-6. Both these quote largely from Ellis's *History of the Gold Coast*, especially his vivid description of the attack on Fort William.
[38] The Denkyerahene demanded a preliminary payment of money before he would open negotiations. It is probable, as Claridge suggests, that he did not take White's offer seriously. White had asked him to state his case against the Fante; the Ashanti may well have regarded this as a device to gain time and, in any case, if the British wished to intervene in their dispute they must not come into court empty-handed!
[39] The fort mounted twelve guns, ranging from three-pounders to twenty-four-pounders.

Fante were driven back into the open space around the fort, and two guns were fired over the town in the hope of checking the pursuit. These shots had no effect, and the Ashanti pursued the Fante on to the beach and killed them as they were trying to escape by sea. The guns of the fort opened fire with grape, but could not save the Fante from slaughter; and the Ashanti, of course, promptly attacked the fort itself.

The garrison at once discovered a fatal weakness in the design of the building: the embrasures were so wide that it soon became impossible to work the guns in the face of the heavy Ashanti musketry fire. Seventeen of the garrison of twenty-five men were wounded in a few minutes; the guns guarding the western gate had to be abandoned, and this gate was defended only by musket fire. On the eastern side of the fort two 3-pounders did great execution, their embrasures being narrower than those of the bigger guns. Three assaults on the gate[40] were beaten off, and at dusk, after six hours' continuous firing, the Ashanti drew off. The attack was renewed, however, next morning, and the exhausted garrison could not hope to hold out much longer. Luckily a canoe managed to escape and carry word to the governor at Cape Coast, twelve miles away; and as the day wore on the Ashanti began to despair of ever taking the fort, before which they had already lost 2,000 men, and their attack slackened considerably.

In the cool of the evening on the second day, reinforcements arrived by sea from Cape Coast, and the Ashanti actually allowed a party of three officers and twelve men to land and enter the fort. The newcomers brought with them orders from Torrane to show a flag of truce and try to come to terms with the Ashanti, and messengers were sent to the Asantehene accordingly. They found the Asantehene ready to discuss peace; he explained that he had no wish to fight against the British, but that the British had begun the fight by firing on his men as they were pursuing the Anomabu people. A deputation of chiefs visited the governor in Cape Coast, but they were not authorized to conclude peace, and the

---

[40] It is uncertain which of the two gates was so fiercely attacked. Ellis says the eastern, Meredith (who was second-in-command to White at the time, and played a gallant part in the defence) says the western. Apart from any question of the value of Meredith's first-hand evidence, the western gate is the more probable, for the guns on this side were silenced, whereas the eastern guns were still being served.

Asantehene himself refused to leave Anomabu. Torrane, therefore, saw there was nothing for it but to go to Anomabu himself. He determined to take with him the two Assin chiefs and hand them over to the Asantehene. The chiefs of Cape Coast protested against this treachery; but Torrane won his point "either by mediation or by force of arms". He sent a strong force unexpectedly to the houses where the Assin people were living, and he seems to have induced the Cape Coast people to support him against the wishes of their own chiefs, by allowing them to enslave as many of the Assin people as they could catch. Kwadwo Otibu, who was old and blind, was taken, and duly handed over to the Asantehene, who had him tortured and killed; Kwaku Aputae contrived to escape. The just comment on this indefensible action was made by the Asantehene himself some years later. "From the hour Torrane delivered up Otibu," he said, "I took the English for my friends, because I saw their object was trade only, and they did not care for the people."

Undoubtedly Torrane was in a difficult position. He had expected to be able to give sufficient protection to the coast towns by the gunfire from his forts. Now Anomabu fort, in spite of its gallant resistance, had not only failed to protect the people of Anomabu, but had had to capitulate while it could still obtain favourable terms.[41] Torrane was not in a position to drive a hard bargain with the Asantehene, but he need not have gone out of his way to curry favour with the Ashanti by an act of treachery which had not even been demanded of him.

The meeting between Torrane and the Asantehene did not result in any formal treaty of peace. Kwaku Aputae had escaped, and had joined forces with the people of Asikuma; and the Asantehene was anxious to move against them. A temporary agreement was made, and the Asantehene promised to return and transform it into a regular peace treaty; but he did not. No written record was made of the armistice; but it is agreed that Torrane made some general acknowledgment that the whole Fante country belonged to Ashanti by right of conquest. The Ashanti title, in virtue of the Notes, to the land on which the European forts stood was also recognized, and Torrane reserved merely a vague judicial authority over the towns, such as Anomabu and Cape Coast, in which there

[41] It would undoubtedly have been taken by storm the following day; see the Ashanti plan for the attack in Claridge, I, 254.

were forts. Lastly, having already done his best to hand over to the Asantehene both Kwadwo Otibu and Kwaku Aputae, Torrane handed over also half the refugees who had sheltered within the walls of Anomabu during the siege. Osei Bonsu had originally demanded all of them, but in true Ashanti fashion Torrane "begged him for half".[42] Lest there should be any suspicion that he had sought this compromise from motives of humanity, he sold his share—1,000 people— as slaves to America. Having thus amply acknowledged the authority of the Ashanti and destroyed whatever reputation the British authorities might have acquired by the gallant defence of Anomabu and its refugees, Torrane said farewell to the Asantehene and returned to Cape Coast.[43]

The negotiations between Torrane and the Ashanti had taken the latter half of June 1806; on 3rd July the Ashanti army struck camp and began to move slowly eastward. The force led by Kwaku Aputae was soon destroyed, and the war then degenerated into guerrilla warfare, the Ashanti army moving slowly eastwards and ravaging the country as it went. More than a year later the Ashanti were still on the coast; but in October 1807 their camp at Winneba was attacked with smallpox and dysentery, and Osei Bonsu led the remnant of the army back to Ashanti.

This first Ashanti campaign in the coast districts had been a complete success, and the Asantehene had every justification for wading into the sea at Winneba as he did and taking when he came out the name of Bonsu or Whale, because not even in the sea had he found an enemy to withstand him. The invasion had completely altered the balance of power on the coast. The military reputation of the Fante as the strongest power in coast politics was destroyed,

---

[42] Part of the ritual enstoolment in Ashanti is that the linguist asks the chief-elect for a gift of money "in order that I may tell you something", i.e. the news that he has been chosen chief. When the sum is named, the chief-elect always replies *Mesere wo fa*, "I beg you to halve it", and the sum is halved. See Rattray, *Ashanti Law and Constitution*, 102.
[43] White's second-in-command, Meredith, seems to have opposed Torrane's treachery; and Mr. Swanzy, the commandant of James Fort, Accra, lost his life in protesting. He was dangerously ill, but he insisted on getting out of bed and into a canoe and going at once to Cape Coast. His threats of exposure in England so moved Torrane and his council that they promised to do what they could to redeem the wretched 1,000 Anomabu people. Nearly of all of them, however, were already at sea, and nothing could be done. Swanzy went back to Accra and died at once as a result of his strenuous double journey when already ill. Claridge, I, 253, gives yet another instance of Torrane's misbehaviour during these events.

now that it was seen that the Ashanti were determined to become a coast power. Elmina and Accra, who both had cause to fear the Fante, now took fresh courage from the knowledge that Ashanti help could be provided if the Ashanti thought it worth their while. Lastly, the British henceforth regarded Ashanti with dread as the power which could if it chose expel them from their forts and destroy their coast trade altogether.

As soon as the Ashanti were gone the Fante determined to reassert their power over the other coast tribes. In 1809 they sent an army against Accra and another against Elmina. Neither met with very much success; the army advancing against Accra was repulsed after a sharp engagement, and the army that was to take Elmina, after some indecisive fighting, settled down to a long blockade of the town. The Elmina people, however, contrived to send a message to Kumasi, and the Asantehene, after explaining to the Dutch and British governors at Elmina and Cape Coast that he had no quarrel with them and would treat them as neutrals as long as they behaved as such, launched another campaign. In 1811 he sent two armies down to the coast; one, a force of 25,000 men under Opoku Ferefere, was sent to reinforce the men of Accra, and a smaller force, only 4,000 strong, was sent to relieve Elmina.[44] The war, however, took an unexpected turn. Atta Wusu Yiakosan, the chief of Akim Abuakwa, had served with distinction in the Ashanti army of 1806, and had fought well at Anomabu. He was now called on again to lead an Akim contingent to join Appia Dankwa, the Ashanti general who was marching towards Elmina. He refused; called up his men; allied himself with his kinsman Kwao Saforo Twie the chief of Akwapim; and declared war on Ashanti.[45]

[44] Opoku Ferefere Obuabasa, 'the breaker of hands' (so he is remembered in Ashanti today in the Ahuren tradition), seems to have had the reputation of a fighting general, like Cutts, "the Salamander' of Blenheim. At the battles of the Tain river and Akantamasu he was in the hottest of the fighting and, on this occasion, when he had an independent command, he seems to have lost so heavily that I suspect he despised strategy and tactics and went straight into frontal attack.

[45] Kwao Saforo Twie (the last name means 'leopard') is often miscalled Kwao Asafoachi. This is a simple mis-hearing of his name; asafaochi is a Ga word meaning 'general' or 'warrior'. The chief was, of course, an Akan, but his name Kwao betrays some Ga connection. The Twi form is Yaw. This may have led to the mistake. I use the form of his name given me by his successor on the Stool of Akwapim. But Kwao may possibly be a mis-hearing of Koa; see below, p. 228, note 35.

This upset the Ashanti plan of campaign entirely. Appia Dankwa had to fight his way down to the coast with only his 4,000 Ashanti troops, unsupported by the Akim contingent he had been instructed to take with him.[46] Opoku Ferefere was ordered to diverge from his line of march and throw all his weight into an invasion of Akim. In February 1811 he crossed the Pra; the Akim and Akwapim fought a stubborn battle and caused such losses that Opoku had to send an appeal for reinforcements to the Accra people, who were expecting help from him. They came in overwhelming numbers, and the Akim-Akwapim contingent, threatened from both sides, broke up rather than face a battle. Atta Wusu and the Akim retreated south-west towards the Fante country, with the sound strategical purpose of attacking Appia Dankwa's small force before it could join with the Elmina men. Kwao Saforo Twie and the Akwapim retired into the mountain ridges and glens of their own country with the idea of wearing out the Ashanti with guerrilla fighting. At first they were so hotly pursued that they retired south-east right through Akwapim to the Krobo country, and then, leaving the hills altogether, to Ada at the mouth of the Volta. The Ashanti army followed them there early in March, but Kwao Saforo Twie was as elusive as De Wet, and slipped past them back to his own country. From April to August guerrilla warfare went on among the Akwapim hills; in August the Ashanti army laid siege to the Krobo hill, on which was an Akwapim garrison, but completely failed to capture it, and next month was recalled to Kumasi in defeat.

Meanwhile Appia Dankwa's small force had been checked by a Fante army in a battle at Apam. The battle was a tactical victory for the Ashanti, but the Ashanti losses were so heavy that Appia Dankwa dared not risk another battle against the superior force of Atta Wusu, who arrived a week later. He retired into Ashanti, losing heavily in a rearguard action as he went. Atta Wusu, having thus gained his object, which was to prevent Appia Dankwa from joining the Elmina army, returned to the coast. He destroyed the

[46] Atta Wusu, with help from the Akwapim contingent, was able to repulse an attack by a force of 25,000. We may suppose therefore that the Akim and Akwapim force must have been at least 15,000 strong. The Akim contingent was no doubt the stronger of the two, so we may suppose that Atta Wusu may have commanded 8,000-10,000 men, assuming that the figure of Opoku Ferefere's strength was not exaggerated, which it well may be.

Dutch Fort Leydsamheid at Apam, and occupied and plundered the British fort at Tantamkweri; and then he planned to lead an allied army of Akim and Fante into Akwapim to help Kwao Saforo Twie against Opoku Ferefere. But the plan was never carried out; he died of smallpox in October[47] when Opoku Ferefere was already on his homeward march.

The Asantehene could not be content with the complete failure of this double campaign. Three years later he sent another expedition against Akim and Akwapim; Appia Dankwa was again put in command of a small force, whose object this time was not to undertake an independent campaign against the Fante but to block the Akim line of retreat south-westward. The main army, commanded by Amankwa Abinowa, defeated the Akim-Akwapim force, but did not destroy it. Having cleared the road to the sea, Amankwa advanced to Accra, and lay there for a year waiting for the Akim to come in and submit. The chief result of his stay in Accra was to make the Accra thoroughly disgusted with their Ashanti allies, who pillaged them as if they had been enemies; from this time onwards the Accra-Ashanti alliance ceased to exist. After waiting a year in vain, Amankwa (who seems to have been of a very different temperament from his predecessor Opoku) moved back into Akwapim to try to force the enemy to action. While there he received news that his colleague Appia Dankwa was dead, and he was ordered to take over Appia Dankwa's force and unite it with his own. He left Akwapim, and joined Appia Dankwa's force at Asikuma. The united army then moved towards Anomabu and Cape Coast, having a vague idea that Kwao Saforo Twie and Kwadwo Kuma, the new chief of Akim Abuakwa, might be sheltering there. There was no fighting. The Fante retired before them, and the Ashanti commander accepted the assurances of the British and Dutch governors of Cape Coast and Elmina that the men he wanted were not there. From March to June 1816 the Ashanti were in the neighbourhood of Cape Coast; then they struck their camp and began to move aimlessly back towards Accra. Amankwa was luckier than he deserved to be. Kwadwo Kuma fell into the hands of a small raiding party and committed suicide; and soon afterwards, Kwao Saforo Twie was betrayed into the Ashanti hands

[47] He died at Kwanyako on a Wednesday; *Wukuda ne Kwanyako*, i.e. Kwanyako Wednesday is today the greatest oath of Akim Abuakwa.

and shot dead in the scuffle. Having by these two pieces of good fortune accomplished the object of a campaign which his military conduct had done little enough to win, Amankwa returned in triumph to Ashanti.

These three Ashanti invasions of 1806, 1811 and 1814 had reduced the coastal regions of the Gold Coast to chaos. The military power of the Fante was broken; Akim and Akwapim, in spite of their long and stubborn resistance, had been overrun and shattered; the British, and still more the Dutch, had been forced to recognize the Ashanti supremacy; and the Fante country was formally incorporated in the Ashanti empire by being placed under the rule of Ashanti governors.[48]

In the middle of all this political upheaval, a heavy blow was struck at the economic system of the country. In 1807 the British Government abolished the slave trade.

To describe the abolition in this way is not to defend the trade itself. We may be entirely convinced, with Clarkson and Wilberforce and the Abolitionists, that the slave trade was iniquitous. We may applaud the courage of Pitt and Fox in abolishing the trade in the middle of the Napoleonic war, in the face of protests by Nelson and the naval men that it would mean ruining the navy.[49] We may be thankful for the good fortune which enabled the abolition to be carried out before the great expansion of the Lancashire cotton industry on the basis of slave-grown cotton in America; had Lancashire mill-owners joined with Liverpool shipping companies in supporting the trade, abolition might have been delayed until the American Civil War. And yet the fact remains that the slave trade was the main export trade of the Gold Coast. There existed a vast organization of wholesale dealers, brokers, depots for the collection of slaves. The slave trade, like the cocoa trade of today, was a trade in which the small man could share. The purchasing power of the people depended on it. Petty chiefs could sell into slavery people who lost their cases in their courts and could not pay their fines. Ordinary citizens could sell their debtors, and could kidnap passing strangers and sell them.[50] Not

[48] Claridge, I, 279.
[49] Fisher, *History of Europe*, 1032.
[50] This practice was a development of the well-established system of panyarring, i.e. the seizure of any fellow-townsman of the debtor and holding him as security. The family of the man thus panyarred would naturally put pressure on the

only European fortunes, but African fortunes, were founded on the slave trade.

It is not surprising therefore that the abolition was not a popular move among the African merchants with whom the European officials came into contact. The Committee of the Company told the Government roundly that it could not expect these Africans to give up without a struggle "a trade not inconsistent with their prejudices, their laws, or their notions of morality and religion, and by which alone they had been hitherto accustomed to acquire wealth and to purchase all the foreign luxuries and conveniences of life". As for the Company's officials, they were compensated by increases in salary for the loss of their chances of private trading in slaves. The Company hopefully suggested that trade might develop in rice, maize, indigo, palm oil and timber to supplement the old-established trade in gold and ivory and to replace the slave trade.[51] But it was not to be expected that the organization of the slave trade could be adapted for a large-scale trade in agricultural produce. The purchasing power of the country declined greatly, and it began to be doubted whether the forts were worth maintaining. On the other hand, though the legal slave trade was dead, a good deal of surreptitious slave trading continued, British and American slave-shippers running cargoes under the Spanish flag. This trade could not be stopped by the forts, and there was no convenient naval base on the Gold Coast for the British patrol ships. It is not surprising that opinion in Britain began to turn in the direction of unifying the West Coast settlements and bringing the coast under proper control, so that the slave trade could be stamped out and a healthy agricultural and mineral trade encouraged.

original debtor to pay. There is a clear resemblance to the method employed by the medieval European gilds. During the slave trade, however, there was a strong temptation to panyar a man for a small debt and sell him into slavery without giving his family a chance to secure payment of the debt; thus making a handsome profit.
[51] Martin, 150-3.

F

CHAPTER VIII

TREATIES WITH ASHANTI, 1816-31

THE Ashanti invasions, which began in the year of Trafalgar and ended the year after Waterloo, had completely changed the situation on the Gold Coast. The Company's officials now had to adjust themselves to a new state of affairs, in which their chief trade had ceased to exist, and what may be called the Ashanti Question came more and more to occupy their attention. Both for commercial and also for political reasons it seemed urgent that relations with Ashanti should be put on a proper footing. For commercial reasons, because if the slave trade were to be replaced by general trade, the Ashanti market must be opened up; for political reasons, because it was intolerable that the coast should live under the perpetual threat of fresh invasions, and that the Ashanti should have a large vague unsettled claim to authority, tribute or compensation, out of which to draw a fresh *casus belli* whenever they chose.

Among political questions, the most urgent was the question of the relationship between the Ashanti, the Fante and the British. The elements of the situation were as follows. Elmina claimed a connection of some sort with Ashanti, and was traditionally at enmity with the Kommenda people and the Fante in general. The people of Cape Coast, originally Asebu rather than Fante, had been tending more and more to identify themselves with the Fante,[1] and from 1809 onwards had done so completely, both as regards enmity with Elmina and as regards their policy towards Ashanti. The British in Cape Coast and the Dutch in Elmina, traditional rivals, were tending on the other hand to draw together under the pressure of the Ashanti danger,[2] though the Dutch governors naturally took every opportunity of using the Ashanti-Elmina alliance to keep on good terms with Ashanti. The first Ashanti invasion had completely broken the Fante resistance and compelled the British to capitulate, while the invasion of 1814 had

[1] Claridge, I, 259.
[2] In 1816 two Dutch officers were sent from Elmina to join the British in Cape Coast in arranging peace with Amankwa; Claridge, I, 276, 277.

completed the process by organizing the Fante country as an Ashanti province.

The Ashanti point of view is plain enough. Fante, Assin, Akim and Akwapim were all parts of the Ashanti empire, rebellious provinces which needed frequent punishment. The British had hoped to save the Fante from subjugation, but had failed. and they were only allowed to remain in the country because it suited the convenience of the Ashanti that they should maintain their trading posts. They were merely traders; they "did not care for the people"; and what Ashanti might do to the Fante was none of their business. They paid rent to the Asantehene for their forts; and Torrane had admitted that they were nothing more than traders, and that the Asantehene was lord of the Fante country.

The Fante, on the other hand, though they could not deny that the war had gone badly, did not accept their position as provinces of the Ashanti empire. They knew that the Ashanti empire was a loose organization, and that states like Akim Abuakwa, much nearer Kumasi than themselves, lived an independent life, although the Asantehene reckoned them as part of his empire. In a very few years the tribute would fall into arrears, and it would not be worth the Asantehene's while to suspend trade and undertake a long and expensive campaign to recover the arrears. Even if he did, the Europeans, who were themselves thoroughly alarmed, might be able to give much more effective help than they had done hitherto. In any case, neither British nor Dutch had any control over them, and it was nothing to them if Torrane chose to regard them as Ashanti subjects.

For the British, matters were not so easy. The Company was finding, as the East India Company had already found, that the position of a merely commercial company in the face of a strong military power was intolerable. For the last fifty years the East India Company had been acquiring and extending political authority. The African Company had not yet reached the conclusion that political authority was essential, but events were already setting in that direction.

The Company's first object was steady trade and open trade routes. Quite apart from any humanitarian considerations, all wars henceforth were bad for business—now that there was no chance of selling prisoners as slaves. And of all wars, a war between Ashanti and Fante was the worst, because it upset both the Company's principal customers. Ashanti regarded Fante as a province of its empire, the Fante denied the claim; and this dispute and the old enmity between Elmina and the Fante were always liable to bring on fresh wars. In any such wars, the guns of the British forts were almost certain to be called on to protect Fante women and children, if not fighting men, from Ashanti attack; for no British officer could be expected to watch from his ramparts in cold aloofness slaughter like that at Anomabu. The Ashanti knew this, and they knew also that British forts were strong. They drew the logical conclusion that if the British meant to protect the Fante from punishment, they must be prepared to accept responsibility for their actions. The Governor at Cape Coast, in other words, must be prepared to answer for the Fante to the Asantehene; he must either allow the Asantehene to do his worst, or he must punish the Fante himself, or he must pay the Asantehene compensation on their behalf. It was the assumption of this responsibility that was the difficulty for all British governors down to the days of Wolseley.

To British eyes such a responsibility implies political authority. The dilemma is unescapable: either the Fante were British subjects, in which case the Governor could control them and must accept responsibility for their deeds; or they were independent, in which case the Governor could accept no such responsibility whatever. But in Ashanti eyes there is a third possibility. There is in Ashanti a status known as *Adamfo*; the word means simply 'friend', but in this connection must be translated 'friend-at-court'. If A is a prominent chief living at a distance from Kumasi, there will be a distinguished member of the Asantehene's entourage, permanently resident at court, who is A's *Adamfo*. If B is A's *Adamfo*, he has the duty of watching A's interests of every kind at court; and all communications between the Asantehene and A will be made through the *Adamfo*, B. The relationship between A and B is purely honorary, and implies no subordination of any kind. If A gets into trouble B must do his best to smooth things over; and if he fails he has the unpleasant choice of joining either his master the Asantehene or his friend A. The knowledge that he is putting his *Adamfo* in such a difficult position will naturally have some restraining force on A's action; he is restrained, that is, not by any authority of B's (for B has none), but by the force of the friendship between them. Now the Asantehene seems to have looked on the British Governor as in a position resembling that of an *Adamfo* (though a non-resident one) of the Fante; all communications were to go through him, and he should remonstrate and use his influence with them if they were in trouble at Kumasi. If he failed he must either join them in war against Ashanti or must abandon them to their fate. The Asantehene knew quite well that the Governor had no authority over the Kommenda men and the other Fante; but he could not understand why the Governor made no attempt to use any influence over them and yet objected to his dealing with them directly.[3]

In 1817 the Company sent instructions that a mission should be sent to Kumasi to conclude a treaty with the Ansantehene. The initiative had been taken by the Asantehene himself some years before; he had suggested that a British Resident should be appointed at Kumasi, but nothing had been done. After another ten years of war and disturbed trade, however, previous objections to the scheme on the grounds of economy were dropped, especially as the Dutch were suspected of having some such plan on foot, and as public interest in the exploration of Africa was awakening.[4]

The mission left Cape Coast on 22nd April, 1817. It was led by Frederick James, commandant of James Fort, Accra; the other Europeans were T. E. Bowdich and William Hutchison, writers in the Company's service, and Henry Tedlie, surgeon. Hutchison was to stay in Kumasi as the first British Resident. The fact that this was the first British expedition to Ashanti, and the full and vivid account of it that Bowdich has left in his book,[5] tend to give an exaggerated idea of the mission's importance. As things turned out, it accomplished little work of permanent value.

The mission reached Kumasi on 19th May, and was given a cordial welcome by the Asantehene and the Ashanti Government. After a promising beginning to the negotiations, there was a serious misunderstanding on the subject of the Notes for Cape Coast and Anomabu forts. The Notes for Elmina and for the three

[3] The position of *Adamfo* is described in Rattray, *Ashanti Law and Constitution*, 93-8, but purely from the constitutional point of view, without reference to the historical significance I ascribe to it here.
[4] Mungo Park's second expedition was in 1805; in 1816 Gray set out to follow in his track, and a Government expedition was sent to test a theory that Niger and Congo were one and the same.
[5] *Mission from Cape Coast Castle to Ashantee* (London, 1819).

forts at Accra had all been captured by the Asantehene,[6] and the original documents were kept at Kumasi. When the Ashanti came down to the coast in 1806, Torrane paid to the Asantehene the rents for Cape Coast and Anomabu, thus acknowledging that the land had been conquered by him from the local chiefs. It seems, however, that instead of receiving from the local chiefs the original Notes for these two forts, the Asantehene had received new Notes from Torrane's successor, the Governor now in office. These new Notes were for greatly reduced amounts, and the balance of the original sums was still paid to the local chiefs. It is unnecessary to discuss who was responsible for this arrangement; the evidence is conflicting. The Asantehene, however, naturally jumped to the conclusion that the Governor and the Fante chiefs were conspiring to cheat him; there was an uproar, and the situation was only saved by Bowdich's energy in taking the words out of his superior officer's mouth and assuring the Asantehene that the whole matter could be cleared up by referring to the Governor.[7] This was done; the Governor's explanation satisfied the Ashanti, and the rent was raised to the old figure. No other difficulty obstructed the negotiations, and a treaty was signed on 7th September.

The treaty consisted of ten clauses, and Juaben was treated as an independent power, "the Kings of Ashantee and Dwabin" being throughout mentioned side by side. It was declared in general terms that no disputes remained outstanding between the British and the Ashanti, and that trade should be encouraged and Ashanti traders visiting the coast should be protected. A British Resident should be appointed at Kumasi, and the Elmina people should not be allowed to attack Cape Coast.

Clauses 2, 4 and 8 need more detailed examination. Clause 2 declared that peace existed between Ashanti[8] and "all nations of Africa residing under the protection of the Company's Forts and

[6] See above, pp. 122, 137.
[7] From Bowdich's own account (Martin, 159) it seems that he rescued the mission "from the Consequences of Mr. James's imbecility". This phrase is quoted, not from Bowdich's well-known *Mission from Cape Coast Castle to Ashantee*, but from another work which I have not read. The same opinion, however, is plainly to be seen in the more decorous language of his official account (46-58), and is endorsed by Hutchison and Tedlie. Bowdich convinced the Governor and the Council at Cape Coast, who censured Mr. James and recalled him, leaving Bowdich as the head of the mission.
[8] In Bowdich's version of the treaty, 'Ashantee and Dwabin' are throughout mentioned together.

Settlements on the Gold Coast". It is to be presumed that the Ashanti meant by this phrase to cover all the Fante, in defence of whom the British might consider that their guns should open fire. It is certain, however, that neither the Governor at Cape Coast nor the Fante themselves would regard the British as having any authority or powers of protection outside the forts. Trouble was to arise from this clause.

Clause 4 laid down that if Ashanti was aggrieved by "the natives under British protection", the Asantehene would report the matter to the Governor, and would not go to war against them without "affording the Governor the opportunity of propitiating". This clause, together with clause 2, clearly puts on the Governor the responsibility of at least guiding the coast nations in their relations with Ashanti. It is surprising that the treaty was signed by two Cape Coast representatives; we should infer from this that they accepted the relationship which was being set up between them and the British Governor.

Clause 8 gave the Governor jurisdiction over Ashanti visitors who were "guilty of secondary offences", but the Governor in return undertook to send back to Ashanti any Ashanti visitor who had committed a "crime of magnitude", "to be dealt with according to the laws of his country". The treaty makers did not realize that the Ashanti and the British conceptions of the difference between 'secondary offences' and 'crimes of magnitude' were very different, and the interpretation of this clause was a fruitful source of disagreement.

Two copies of the treaty were made, one being kept by the Asantehene and the other being brought back to the coast by Bowdich. Unfortunately, not only did Bowdich's version of the treaty leave openings for disagreement, but the two copies were very far from identical. In the Asantehene's copy there was no mention of Juaben, perhaps a small matter; but there were so many discrepancies in the next that the idea which the Governor had of the treaty and the Asantehene's idea of it were very different.[9]

---

[9] The two versions of the treaty are given in Bowdich, 143-5, and Dupuis (Appendix II, pp. cxix.-cxx.). The Bowdich version is given also in Claridge, I, 298, 299. The discrepancies are not such as to affect the spirit of the treaty. The chief of them are (i) that in clause 4, the phrase by which the Asantehene promises to give the Governor "the opportunity of propitiating it, as far as he may with discretion" is absent from the Ashanti version, and the Asantehene

This vaguely-worded and double-faced treaty soon led to fresh quarrels. In 1818 the Ashanti were involved in another great war against Gyaman. The Gyamanhene was named Adinkera; Kwadwo Adinkera Kakiri was his full name. He perhaps thought that the Ashanti were too preoccupied in the south to notice him; at all events, he followed the example of his predecessor Abo Kofi and made himself a golden stool.[10] This naturally led to war, and the Ashanti prepared very thoroughly for a long and difficult campaign, even recruiting a force of Fante carriers from Saltpond.[11] The war was settled by two tremendous battles, the second of which was fought on the banks of the Tain river, and was notable for a feat of arms worthy of Froissart.[12]

The Gyaman army stood in front of the river Tain, and the Ashanti moved to attack it. After much fighting the Ashanti were still unable to force the enemy lines, and the chief of Kokofu sent back a message from the fighting line to the Asantehene in the rear that he was thirsty. The Asantehene sent him sixty calabashes of water for himself and his men, but he poured it out on the ground, and sent back an answer that no water could quench his thirst but the water of the river Tain. Now the river Tain flowed behind the enemy's army; so the Asantehene asked him how he hoped ever to satisfy his thirst, seeing that they had fought so long without getting any nearer the river. The chief of Kokofu, whose

merely promises not to go to war against the British protectorate "without endeavouring as far as possible to effect an amicable arrangement". (ii) In this same clause, Bowdich's version extends this assurance on the Asantehene's part by the phrase "even against the other towns of the Fantee territory". This phrase is omitted from the Ashanti version. Other discrepancies are of no great importance.

[10] I was long doubtful whether the golden stool episode really occurred twice, or whether the same story is told of two different men by a confusion in chronology. I think now that it really did occur twice. The evidence for Adinkera's golden stool is overwhelming. The story is related also of Abo Kofi by Fuller (29, 30), who may be taken as following Kumasi tradition; and I find corroboration in a statement of the Ahuren tradition that it was Opoku Ware's wife, Suku Abena, who was herself from Sikassiko on the Gyaman border, who had told him about the Gyaman golden stool and would give him no peace till he had undertaken to punish the Gyamanhene. This story is related of Adinkera, not of Abo Kofi; but this homely touch of detail is to my mind clear evidence that Opoku Ware had to deal with a Gyamanhene who had made himself a golden stool. I would not indeed rely upon it unsupported, for the Ahuren people might have erred in the name and said Opoku Ware for Osei Bonsu; but I think it may be accepted as corroborating Fuller.

[11] Kokofu tradition: Rattray, *Ashanti Law and Constitution*, 201.

[12] I take this account from Ahuren tradition, adding a few details from Akim Bosome.

name was Offe Akwesim, said that if the Asantehene gave him
permission he would go himself and drink of that water. "In that
case," replied the Asantehene, "you may go; but where am I to find
men to go with you?" Offe Akwesim replied that he was sure others
beside himself were thirsty for that water; and sure enough, when
the Asantehene called for volunteers, the chief of Akim Bosome,
Koragye Ampaw by name, came forward, and the two chiefs with
only 300 men went forward against the enemy. They broke
through the enemy, they reached the river bank, and Offe Akwesim
had his drink; and then they settled down for the rest of the day to
hold the place they had won.

The news reached the Asantehene that his men were standing
on the river bank; and he sent Opoku Ferefere to reinforce them.
Darkness fell, and both sides rested where they stood. Next
morning the battle began again; fresh Ashanti divisions reached
the river, and the men of Ahuren forced a passage across the
stream, wading waist deep. As they reached the farther bank
and were beginning the task of dislodging the enemy from two
small hills, news reached them that Adinkera was killed. His
own people, fearful that his head might be taken as a trophy
to Kumasi, beheaded him, hid his head inside the belly of one
of the dead men,[13] and covered it with a great pile of slain; but
a prisoner told the Ashanti where it was hidden. The chief of
Kokofu took in commemoration of this fight the 'strong name'
of *Okogyeasuo*: 'he who fights to get at the water'. The
Akim Bosome commemorated their heavy losses in the oath
Gyaman.

The Gyaman war had lasted several months, and the Ashanti
had forbidden any of their men to take war news down to the coast.
Naturally the wildest rumours ran about, and many people jumped
to the conclusion that if things were going well for the Ashanti

[13] Some versions say that it was hidden inside a woman's belly. The forlorn hope
on this occasion lost heavily. Ahuren says that it set out on its attack 300 strong,
and Akim Bosome says that 120 Akim Bosome men who took part in it were
killed; but we do not know the Kokofu losses. Kokofu tradition, itself, curiously
enough, does not mention the incident, though it mentions the battle and gives
the 'strong name' of Offe Akwesim which he acquired as a result of the battle.
Perhaps if Rattray had pressed harder he might have extracted the story. Kokofu
and Ahuren agree that it was Adinkera's son Apow, 'a redhaired man' Ahuren
adds, who was taken prisoner and gave away the secret. Adinkera's skull was
so shattered that it could not be preserved as a trophy; a gold cast was made
of it instead.

they would release information fast enough. It was soon widely
believed that Gyaman had been victorious, that the Ashanti power
was broken, and that Adinkera and his men were on the march to
occupy Kumasi. These rumours were denied by the Dutch and the
Elmina people, and by the Ashanti Residents who had been left in
charge in various Fante towns; but the denials carried no weight.
In many places the people broke into rejoicings, which the British
made no attempt to check. In the midst of the rejoicings, however,
Ashanti messengers arrived on the coast bringing the news of the
victory, and bearing with them jaw-bones of the enemy dead as
gifts from the conqueror. This was a universal custom between
friendly powers; it constituted a courteous invitation to join in the
rejoicing over the victory, and should have been acknowledged by
a message of thanks and congratulation and a small complimentary
gift. The Fante, however, could not believe their eyes; they rejected
the courtesy and at Kommenda the messengers were grossly
insulted.[14]

The Ashanti messengers from Kommenda came straight to Cape
Coast to complain to the Governor in accordance with Bowdich's
treaty. But Mr. Hope Smith declined to do anything in the matter,
and the messengers reluctantly and fearfully left Cape Coast to
carry the news of the treatment to Kumasi.[15] The Governor had
now put himself clearly in the wrong. Whatever the precise word-
ing of Bowdich's treaty, the spirit of it undoubtedly was that in
consideration of the Asantehene's refraining as far as possible from
making war on the coast, the British Governor should use his
influence with the coast people to avert as far as possible the
occasion of war. The Governor might say that he had no control
over the Kommenda people; but there was a British fort in Kommenda, with two 18-pounder guns and others. He might not have
real control, but he certainly had a good deal of influence. It has
been suggested[16] that it was unreasonable to expect the Governor to
use his 'authority and influence' to compel the Kommenda people

[14] Claridge, I, 301, 302, 313-17. The Kommenda people refused to give the Ashanti
messengers a drink or to let them enter the town, and hooted and pelted them.
It was subsequently suggested that the messengers demanded a heavy payment
of tribute; but this is most improbable, for various reasons.
[15] They had good reason to be fearful; they ran the risk of being tortured in
the belief that they were lying. One of them refused to carry such a message
to Kumasi at all.
[16] Ellis, History of the Gold Coast, 139.

to behave as vassals of Ashanti. But it does not appear that the Governor made any attempt to inquire into the complaint against the Kommenda. He seems merely to have washed his hands of the whole affair, not only at the beginning, but through all the subsequent negotiations.

In January 1819 there arrived at Cape Coast the first British official directly appointed by the Crown: Joseph Dupuis, who had been appointed consul at Kumasi. From the outset his mission was hindered by the jealousy between him and the Company's officials, from the Governor downwards. They were jealous of his royal commission, and he took no pains to conceal his scorn of "the servants of a mercantile board".[17]

In March the Asantehene formally complained to the Governor of the behaviour of the Kommenda people. The message was fair and reasonable in tone; and several people who were present in the hall of Cape Coast fort when it was being delivered gave it as their opinion that the official interpreter when translating it into English considerably altered the spirit of the message, turning it into one of defiance and adding at the end the threat (which was not in the original at all) that if the Governor did not compel the Kommenda people to give satisfaction the Asantehene would come down in forty days and punish them himself. The Governor, however, refused to do anything, and said that the Asantehene could come down whenever he liked. Meanwhile some steps were taken to put Cape Coast in a state of defence.

In June and September further protests were received from Kumasi. The messenger who came down to Cape Coast in September was a man of high rank, who brought with him the Asantehene's copy of the 1817 treaty to convince the Governor that he was justified in demanding that the Governor should use his influence on the Kommenda people. The ambassador's instructions were that if the Governor still refused to take any action, he was to leave the dishonoured treaty with him as a declaration of war; but before this could be done, Dupuis, who was present, announced

---

[17] Dupuis, *Journal of a Residence in Ashantee*, Introduction, p. xxxvii. This book contains a full account (pp. xv.-xxxvii.) of the negotiations between Hope Smith and the Asantehene, as well as of Dupuis's own mission to Kumasi. The text of Dupuis's treaty is given in Appendix III, pp. cxx.-cxxiii. The book is full of jealousy, both of Hope Smith and of Bowdich; but there is no reason to doubt its general accuracy. It is difficult to imagine any defence for Hope Smith's behaviour.

himself as an officer of the Crown who had been sent from England specially to visit Kumasi. This news was considered sufficient to suspend the declaration of war until the Asantehene had been consulted. This led to yet another postponement; but in January 1820 a new embassy came from Kumasi, headed by a nephew of the Asantehene called Adum. Adum recounted the whole affair from the beginning: he explained that under the terms of Bowdich's treaty the Asantehene considered that the Governor was bound to investigate his complaint against the Kommenda people and do him justice, but complained that the Governor not only refused to do this, but was preparing for war[18]: he accused both the Governor and the Cape Coast people of deliberately breaking the treaty: and he demanded an idemnity of 1,600 ounces of gold from Cape Coast and the same sum from the Governor. Mr. Hope Smith replied that this demand must be withdrawn before he would continue the negotiations; but Adum declared he could not withdraw it without the Asantehene's permission. It was agreed, however, that Dupuis should at last visit Kumasi as the representative of the Crown, and should try to settle the dispute directly with the Asantehene. He arrived in Kumasi at the end of February 1820, a year after his landing at Cape Coast.

In his negotiations with Dupuis, the Asantehene still showed himself anxious for peace and fair dealing. He complained that the old matter of the Notes was not yet properly settled. The specified sums were paid in kind at the coast, Ashanti carriers coming for the goods; and the Asantehene showed that the Governor was overcharging him for the goods he supplied, adding sometimes as much as fifty per cent to the regular price of the goods.[19] This matter being settled, Dupuis asked why the Asantehene had demanded a cash idemnity from the Governor for breaking the treaty. It turned out that Osei Bonsu was under the impression that the treaty provided for an idemnity to be paid by either party in default of specific performance. Not only did he and his chiefs say that Bowdich explained this to them when the treaty was first drawn up, but Dupuis's own servant, who had been Bowdich's servant,

[18] In April 1819 when the first messenger from Kumasi had returned with a defiant answer, a mud wall was hastily built all round Cape Coast as a defence against the expected attack.
[19] Claridge, I, 320; Dupuis, 123-6, 161-2; for £72 worth of rum he was charged £96, for sixty-six lead bars he was charged £8 5s. instead of £5 10s.

confirmed this.[20] At all events, the Asantehene withdrew this claim on the Governor, but he maintained his claim on the town of Cape Coast for their defiance of him, and refused to compromise on this point.

With very little trouble, a new treaty was made, dated 23rd March. It consisted of twelve clauses with three supplementary articles. There were the usual undertakings to preserve peace and further trade, and to protect traders and keep the paths clear. By clauses 2 and 11, the Asantehene and his chiefs acknowledged themselves as British subjects;[21] a declaration which might have had strange consequences if the treaty had ever been ratified. Clause 3 withdrew the Ashanti claim to an idemnity from the Governor, but the next clause reserved the Ashanti claims over Cape Coast, a subject which was further discussed in the supplementary articles. By clause 10 it was admitted that the Company's officials had been overcharging the Ashanti when paying the rent on the Notes; and Dupuis undertook to supervise the payments himself in future. The question of Cape Coast was more difficult.

The fifth clause of the treaty declared explicitly that the whole of the Fante country was part of the Ashanti empire; and the second supplementary article declared that the Asantehene was determined to "eradicate from his dominions the seeds of disobedience and insubordination", and that as disobedient and insubordinate subjects of his the Cape Coast people were excluded from the protection of the treaty. He undertook, however, to reduce them to submission without destroying Cape Coast town, or committing any acts of war in it, or permanently interfering with its trade. The fulfilment of this promise would have been a difficult piece of statecraft. But the treaty was never ratified. Dupuis arrived back in Cape Coast early in April. The Governor and his council refused to ratify the treaty, though the ratification of the treaty was not for them but for the Crown. They refused to recognize the Ashanti claim to sovereignty over the Fante country, though they

[20] This boy Kofi may have been terrified of contradicting the Asantehene; but Dupuis could probably have got a private hint from him of the truth. Possibly Bowdich did talk about indemnities by way of an oratorical amplification, to impress the Ashanti with the idea that the treaty was meant to be reciprocal.
[21] "The King of Ashantee, having taken his sacred oath of allegiance and fidelity to the Crown of Great Britain . . . " (clause 2). The same phrase is used in clause 11.

themselves were implicitly admitting it in paying rent to Ashanti
instead of to the local chiefs. The Ashanti ambassadors who
accompanied Dupuis to the coast with presents and a message to
deliver to King George in England were refused a passage in the
ship, in spite of Dupuis's own protests, and Adum himself was
refused admission to the fort of Cape Coast. Whatever their
opinion of Dupuis, and of his treaty, the Governor and his council
could hardly have behaved in a more discourteous way. All Dupuis
could do was to promise the Asantehene that he would appeal to
the Government in England and ask the Asantehene to await a
reply.

Nothing more was heard from him. The Cape Coast people paid
to Ashanti the indemnity that was demanded. The British built
another small fort to strengthen the defences of the town, and
maintained their attitude of silent scorn towards Ashanti. After
waiting for ten months in the hope of hearing from Dupuis in
England, Osei Bonsu ordered his traders to cease visiting Cape
Coast and other British forts, and to trade only with the Danes and
the Dutch. For some months Cape Coast was closely blockaded,
though the blockade was afterwards raised and some trade
resumed.

Under Torrane and Hope Smith the condition of the Company's
settlements on the Gold Coast had gone from bad to worse. The
new power of Ashanti, in spite of its manifest readiness to be
friendly, had been persistently snubbed. Political unrest had made
it impossible to do much towards opening up new lines of trade
to replace the slave trade. Critics in England murmured that the
slave trade itself had not been by any means completely put down,
and said that a committee of traders could not be expected to put
it down. The Company's staff on the coast had even failed in their
prime duty of keeping trade alive. The Company had often been
attacked before, but this time the attack was too strong for it. A
parliamentary committee was appointed in 1816 to examine the
condition of the West African settlements. Its report,[22] issued in
1817, found that the forts on the Gold Coast were not strong
enough to stand against attack, and were an inadequate base for

[22] Martin, 161-6. The first committee was appointed too late in the session to do
much; a fresh committee was appointed next session to continue the first
committee's work.

the suppression of the slave trade. The committee refrained from recommending that the Gold Coast forts should be abandoned altogether, merely because, inadequate as they were, they were better than no base at all. The report recommended that the Company should continue the administration, but that the Governor should be appointed by the Crown. In 1819 a Bill was introduced to give general effect to these recommendations, but it was dropped; two years later, however, in May 1821, a short Act was passed which abolished the Company entirely, and vested all its forts in the Crown. On 3rd July, 1821, the transfer was effected, and the Gold Coast settlements were placed under the Governor of Sierra Leone.[23]

The Governor of Sierra Leone and the Gold Coast, Sir Charles Macarthy, arrived and took over the governorship in April 1822. His two years' tenure of office was ruined by the fact that the old officers of the Company of Merchants refused to serve under him or to help him in any way, so that he was left without any experienced advice of any kind. He had met Dupuis in England, and had heard from him that the Ashanti could be made into valuable friends; but when he arrived on the coast everybody joined in decrying Dupuis and in representing the Ashanti as treacherous and tyrannical savages. He could hardly be blamed for abandoning Dupuis and concluding that it was useless to attempt to negotiate with the Ashanti. He began at once to prepare for war, and did not even send the customary courteous notification to Kumasi that he had assumed the governorship. Osei Bonsu, who had no doubt been waiting for Hope Smith to go in the hope that his successor might be more reasonable, could no longer restrain the impatience of his chiefs.

In May 1822 the occasion of the war arrived. An Ashanti trader at Anomabu fell foul of a policeman, and in the wrangle that ensued he abused the Governor; whereupon the policeman lost his

[23] The forts handed over to the Crown were eight in number: Apollonia, Anomabu, Accra, Cape Coast, Dixcove, Kommenda, Tantamkweri and Winneba. There were British settlements in one or two other places but no more forts. The first Crown Governor, Sir Charles Macarthy, abandoned all but the four forts at Accra, Anomabu, Cape Coast and Dixcove. In 1821 the Dutch had four forts: Axim, Elmina, Sekondi and Shama. They had abandoned five in 1816: Accra, Beraku, Butri, Kormantine and Mori, though Butri and Accra were reoccupied in 1830. Of the four Danish forts, three: Christiansborg, Keta and Teshi were still held in 1821; the fourth, Ningo, had been abandoned.

temper and abused the Asantehene.[24] In November the policeman
was kidnapped and taken to Dunkwa, fifteen miles inland, where
he was kept to await the Asantehene's pleasure. In February an
Ashanti party arrived from Kumasi and he was put to death.
Meanwhile, Sir Charles Macarthy had hastily arrived back on the
Gold Coast from Sierra Leone; and refusing an offer which one
of his officers made to go to Dunkwa or Kumasi to try to get the
prisoner released, he decided to punish those responsible for the
execution. A detachment of troops set out on a night march with the
object of surprising the Ashanti party in Dunkwa; but the detachment lost its way, was ambushed by the Ashanti, and had to retire.

The Governor now made active plans for war. He visited Accra
and succeeded in persuading the Accra people, who were still bitter
over the treatment they had had from Amankwa Abinowa in 1815,
to refuse to supply munitions to Ashanti. Having enrolled an
Accra militia to supplement the Cape Coast militia, and having
collected about 500 regular troops, Sir Charles returned to Sierra
Leone, thinking that there was no immediate danger.

In June 1823 the first news arrived of the Ashanti move. On
4th June their advance guard crossed the Pra, but it retired across
the river on the approach of a strong British and allied force. This
small success encouraged many of the Fante and other chiefs to
come in with their men; they saw that it was not to be a question
of waiting in Cape Coast to be attacked, but of advancing into the
bush against the Ashanti. In July and August there was some
desultory border fighting with varying results; but it was not until
December that the main Ashanti army invaded the Fante country

[24] This matter of 'abuse' is important, for it often leads to misunderstandings.
The matter is discussed by Rattray, *Ashanti Law and Constitution*, 309, 310,
326-9. The Gold Coast African is extremely sensitive to ridicule, and his training
makes him more so. The English proverb, "Hard words break no bones", is quite
contrary to Gold Coast feeling. Children are taught to be very careful to avoid
uttering any words that may imply ridicule or disrespect of others, and ridicule
is one of the strongest sanctions in Akan law. The word 'abuse' is used in Gold
Coast English to convey many ideas besides the correct English meaning; its
commonest meaning is perhaps 'jeering'. There are many Akan words signify-
ing different types of 'abuse', some of them untranslatable in English. This
explains why so often bitter hatred arises over a matter which seems to an
Englishman a childish trifle, the uttering of a jeering phrase. There have been
many examples in Gold Coast history of such misunderstandings: the case of
the Kommenda people and Osei Bonsu is one, the present case is another. An
Englishman is gradually hardened through his schooldays until he comes to
regard 'silly ass' as a term of endearment; and only if he is called a thief or a
liar does he lose his tolerant smile. An African's training is all the other way.

in force. Sir Charles arrived from Sierra Leone at the end of November, bringing with him small reinforcements of troops. Information on the Ashanti movements was very scanty, and the available troops were scattered in small parties on each of the roads by which the main invasion might be expected. The Accra militia, under Captain Blenkerne, was stationed at Accra, 1,600 strong. Most of the Fante levies were stationed at Fante Nyankumasi, between Manso and Dunkwa on the main road from Cape Coast to Prasu and Kumasi. Nearly all the disciplined troops were at Jukwa, a few miles north-west of Cape Coast, in a position where they could intercept any supplies going to the Ashanti from Elmina. These three posts were so placed as to block the three routes by which the Ashanti had previously approached the sea-coast.

This time the Ashanti took a different route Early in January 1824 they were reported as advancing in force on the right bank of the Pra through Wassaw. The Wassaw men had met them and had been defeated; and it seemed that the Ashanti plan must be to cross the Pra near its mouth and advance on Cape Coast from the west, passing Kommenda and Elmina. Their strength was unknown; but as they were advancing in no fewer than twelve parallel columns, it was evidently considerable. Once it was known that the weight of the Ashanti attack was coming from the west, it might have been wiser to concentrate the small British forces to meet it, bringing the Accra men by sea to Cape Coast. This was not done. Captain Blenkerne was ordered to advance towards Ashanti; Captain Laing, who had gained valuable experience in several successful skirmishes with the Ashanti, was sent away northwards with a force of Fante levies to make a diversion in Assin. The remainder of the troops, some 2,000 strong, were concentrated at Jukwa, and almost the whole of the force, under Major Chisholm, was sent forward from Jukwa to Ampensasu on the left bank of the Pra.

With the small remnant, just under 500 men, the Governor himself advanced westwards from Jukwa. On 13th January he crossed the Pra, and next day reached the village of Nsamankow. It was pouring with rain, the paths were almost impassable, and the troops had to spend the night in the open. Here he halted for five days, and sent orders to Major Chisholm at Ampensau, some thirty miles away, to bring up the rest of the troops at once. This letter took five days to reach Major Chisholm, and arrived far too late for him to do anything. Without waiting for him, however, the Governor pushed on another twenty miles with the quixotic idea of rallying the Wassaw and Denkyera, who were in full retreat after being defeated by the Ashanti. Near the little village of Bonsaso at two o'clock in the afternoon of 21st January he suddenly found himself face to face with the main Ashanti army.[25]

Neither party in the battle realized what was happening. The Ashanti thought that they had met another detachment of Wassaw or Denkyera men. The Governor thought he had met one of the twelve divisions of the Ashanti army. The Ashanti advanced with their war-horns blowing and their drums beating; in reply to this

[25] I have not had the chance of going over this ground; but the modern ordnance map shows the mistakes that the Governor made in his ignorance of the country. Ampensasu, where Major Chisholm was stationed, is on the left bank of the river Pra about thirty miles from its mouth. Below this point, the country east of the Pra is much more thickly settled than the country immediately west of the river; and the western bank of the river, having few villages, has naturally few good paths. There are three points from Ampensasu to the sea where important paths cross the Pra. A good path runs from the base at Jukwa to Ampensasu, crosses the river by a ferry, and forks beyond the river into two main branches, one turning NNW and the other running WSW; this latter branch passes Bonsaso, the scene of the battle, twenty miles beyond the Pra.

Downstream from Ampensasu there are no fewer than eleven ferries, one of which has been replaced in the last few years by the steel suspension-bridge which carries the main Cape Coast-Sekondi motor road. Nearly all these ferries, however, are unimportant, with no through path; they are either maintained by riverside hamlets for their own use, or are short cuts across a loop of the river. The only one that is important is the Deraboasi or Daboasi ferry, by which the Governor crossed; it is twenty miles below Ampensasu, close to the modern bridge. From Deraboasi there are two fairly good paths on the west bank of the river; one runs NW to Bonsaso, the other roughly west to Nsamankow. The Ampensasu and Daboasi ferries and the Beposo bridge are the only important crossing-places over the lower Pra.

If the Governor had known the country and had had better information on the direction of the Ashanti advance, he could have advanced direct from Deraboasi to Bonsaso, and ordered Major Chisholm to meet him there by the direct path from Ampensasu. This would have saved at least two days' marching for both divisions, and the army could have been concentrated at Bonsaso in time to meet the Ashanti attack. What the Governor did, however, was to go west to Nsamankow, and order Chisholm to follow him. For this purpose the direct path from Ampensasu was useless; indeed, the quickest way, if canoes had been available, would have been by water. We have seen, however, that Chisholm did not have the chance to act on his orders. Having sent off this dispatch, the Governor then moved twenty miles northward through the dripping forest by execrable paths or hunters' trails; so that if he had to retreat, the retreat to Deraboasi would have to be carried out over an unfamiliar path, and a path, moreover, which would not be the one by which his reinforcements would arrive. It was bad luck that with his tiny force he stumbled on the main Ashanti army, and that his ammunition supplies were not on the spot; but he should never have been at Bonsaso at all.

martial music, the Governor ordered the band of the Royal African Colonial Corps to play "God Save the King". Presently the Ashanti reached the bank of the Bonsa river and opened fire. The British fire prevented them from crossing the stream; but by four o'clock the British ammunition was exhausted. The officer in charge of the ammunition column had been ordered to have extra supplies ready for use; but he was evidently not used to trekking in the bush, for he had come on ahead of his carriers, and they had, of course, thrown down their loads and bolted.[26] It was soon over. The Ashanti forced the passage of the stream; the British force was almost surrounded; and only a few succeeded in escaping. The Governor was wounded and helpless, and killed himself to avoid capture; eight other European officers were killed and three wounded; and out of 250 men whose names were on the roll (apart, that is, from the Fante levies) no fewer than 178 were killed.

Major Chisholm received his orders on 22nd January, the day after the battle; and received at the same time a second dispatch sent off from Bonsaso just before the fighting began. He prepared to advance in support of the Governor by the direct path over the Ampensasu ferry; but the crossing took him the whole day, and before it was finished the arrival of a few survivors from the defeat told him that an advance would be useless.[27] He naturally concluded that the Ashanti would follow up their victory by marching as fast as they could on Cape Coast by way of the Deraboasi and Beposo ferries; so he retreated to Cape Coast to defend the town, and to his relief arrived in time. Captain Laing had also heard the news of Bonsaso, and returned from his reconnaissance into Assin to be available for the defence of Cape Coast.

It was the beginning of March, however, before the Ashanti made a move. They had indeed invaded the lower Pra valley to subdue Wassaw and Denkyera, and had been surprised to find themselves fighting the British.[28] In the middle of March they sent messengers to Elmina, asking the Dutch authorities there to

[26] This unlucky officer had managed to bring four kegs with him: but when they were opened during the action only one contained ammunition, the other three containing macaroni!
[27] There was only one canoe available. The survivors included Captain Ricketts, the Governor's chief of staff.
[28] Claridge, I, 364; Fuller, 71; modern Ashanti tradition, e.g. that of Asumegya, regards this as a war against Denkyera, and is at a loss to explain how it was that 'Mankata' (Macarthy) was killed in it.

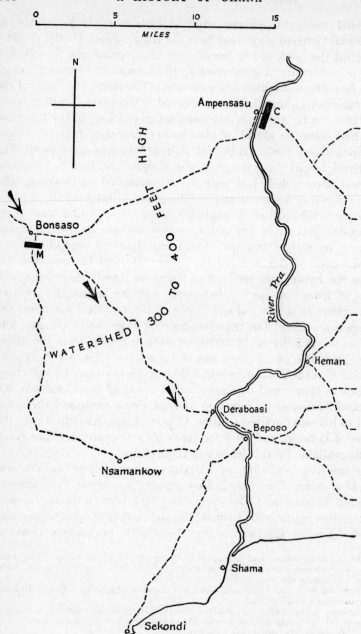

This map is based on the Gold Coast Survey.

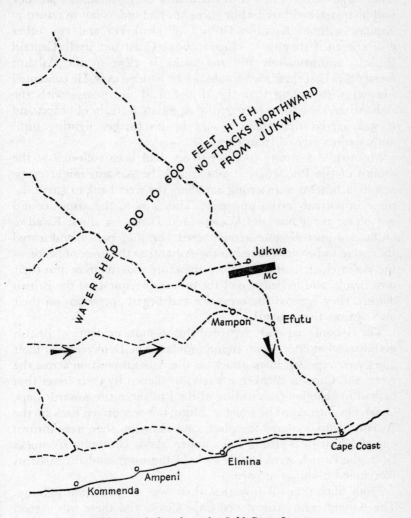

This map is based on the Gold Coast Survey.

FIG. 9. The Campaign of Nsamankow.

Dotted lines are paths. Arrows shows the line of the Ashanti advance.

MC = first troop concentration at Jukwa.

 C = Major Chisholm's position at Ampensasu.

 M = Sir Charles Macarthy's position at Bonsaso.

arrange a meeting with the British. Captain Ricketts went over from Cape Coast to talk with them, and they explained that they had no quarrel with the white men, but had orders not to return to Kumasi without Kwadwo Otibu[29] of Denkyera and two other chiefs, even if they took refuge in Cape Coast fort itself. Captain Ricketts unfortunately did not make it clear to the Ashanti messengers that these men would not be handed over. He contented himself with saying that the British had no quarrel with the Ashanti and would be prepared to negotiate a treaty of peace; and it was agreed that there should be no further fighting until ambassadors arrived from Kumasi.

Meanwhile a strong force of troops had been collected at the mouth of the Pra, where it was feared the Ashanti might cross; and detachments were strung out along the river bank to guard the more important ferries upstream. The news of the armistice did not please the Fante and Wassaw and Denkyera allies; Kwadwo Otibu and his colleagues remembered Torrane's policy, and feared they were to be surrendered to the Ashanti as the price of peace, as the Assin chiefs had been. They therefore took matters into their own hands, and in defiance of the orders or requests of the British officers, they ignored the armistice and began operations on their own against the Ashanti.

The Ashanti naturally regarded this as more evidence of British perfidy, and at once began counter-moves. The Denkyera and their allies were repulsed in an attack on the Ashanti position across the river, and Captain Blenkerne was so weakened by their losses that he had to abandon the crossing of the Pra and retire towards Cape Coast. On 10th April he stood at Efutu, but was driven back by the Ashanti, who occupied the place; and although they were thrown out of Efutu by a strong force under Major Chisholm six weeks later, the British were unable to hold the town, and the Ashanti reoccupied it almost at once.

From May 1824 till July 1826 there was no important fighting. The Ashanti army threatened Cape Coast, and there was a good deal of skirmishing. The Ashanti, however, did not risk an attack on the town; they lost heavily from smallpox and dysentery; and when they heard that the Danish Governor of Christiansborg was organizing an expedition into Akim to attack them on the flank,

[29] Not of course the Assin chief in 1805, but a namesake.

they abandoned their campaign and retreated with all speed to
Kumasi.[30] They returned without the head of the Denkyerahene;
but they had killed a British Governor and annihilated his force,
they had occupied the coast lands for several months and had
resisted every attempt to dislodge them, and when they decided to
retire they were allowed to do so unmolested. In spite of the
sudden collapse of their expedition they returned home with the
balance of victory decidedly in their favour.

The Asantehene, Osei Bonsu, had died on the same day as the
British Governor, Sir Charles Macarthy; and had been succeeded
by his brother Osei Yaw. The British authorities also were handicapped at this time by rapid changes in the command. Major
Chisholm died; a new governor, Major-General Turner, arrived in
the Gold Coast for the first time in March 1825 and left it in April,
having done little except make a defiant proclamation; he died
next year, and was succeeded by another Major-General, Sir Neil
Campbell. Captain Ricketts, however, was still available with his
experience of the country.

In January 1826 a new Ashanti army invaded the Fante country,
and after wandering unchecked up and down the land for seven
months decided to attack Accra and punish it for having abandoned
its ancient alliance with Ashanti. Early in August the Ashanti army
was concentrated near Dodowa, some twenty miles north of Accra.
A large allied army was collected to defend Accra, composed of
Accra and other Ga tribes, Fante, Denkyera, Akim, Akwamu, with
a small reserve of British troops, some sixty strong. Claridge puts the
allied strength at 11,000 and the Ashanti strength at slightly less.

The Dodowa countryside is part of the Accra plain; a rolling
grassy landscape between 100 and 200 feet above sea level, dotted
with isolated trees and small thickets. There are no permanent
streams, though in August the few rain-streams would probably be
in existence as strings of pools and mud-patches.[31] It is a

[30] August 1824.
[31] This would depend on the season. August is the 'small dry season', and as a
rule little or no rain falls in August on the Accra plains. If the so-called
'greater rains' of May to July were good, the streams would still be in this state.
It often happens, however, that the 'greater rains' are very poor, and the 'lesser
rains' of October give a much heavier fall. If this were the case in 1826 the
streams would be entirely dry. In any case, they would be no obstacle to troops.
The grass would be three feet high. Claridge mentions that the grass caught fire
during the battle, which suggests that the season must have been a dry one.

countryside suitable for pitched battles in the Marlborough tradition; there is no cover for large bodies of troops, and the physical features of the battlefield are too slight to have any effect on the fortunes of the fight. Some eight miles south of Dodowa, fifteen miles as the crow flies from Accra, stands the tiny hamlet of Katamanso, and here on 7th August was fought the 'soldiers' battle' which decided the fate of the Gold Coast.[32]

The allied line extended some four miles east and west, its centre resting on the hamlet, which occupies a tiny knoll with a thicket of trees. The centre was held by the militia of Accra, Cape Coast, Anomabu and Christiansborg, that is to say by the troops with some European discipline. The Akwamu were on the right, the Akim and the Denkyera on the left. The Ashanti advanced from the north, and a big tree standing in a copse near Dodowa is still pointed out as the place where their treasure was left during the battle.

Except that no cavalry were engaged, the battle is somewhat reminiscent of the battles of the Civil War. The Ashanti army came down at a slight angle, so that the allied left wing came first into action; very soon the right wing also was attacked, while the centre, which was slightly refused, was left for a little time untouched. Presently the British commander, Colonel Purdon, pushed his centre forward a little, and it at once came into the hottest of the fight. The Asantehene himself was in the centre, one division of which he commanded in person, and the other was commanded by the redoubtable Opoku Ferefere. These two divisions fought a fierce hand-to-hand fight with the allied centre, and all but broke it; the trained militia, however, stood firm and enabled the shaken ranks to rally again. Meanwhile the two allied wings had carried all before them,[33] and routed the Ashanti divisions opposed to them; eventually, with some difficulty, they were recalled to help the shaken centre, and attacked the successful Ashanti centre division from behind. At the same time the small party of British troops, which had been held in reserve in the rear,

[32] Claridge put the battlefield four miles from Dodowa; he is wrong. Local tradition is perfectly clear and vivid on the details of the battle.
[33] Kukurantumi tradition says that the Akim contingent of the left wing was less successful at first than the Denkyera contingent, being driven back "nearly to the sea" by the Ashanti attack.

advanced and opened fire with Congreve rockets: and under this double attack the Ashanti centre finally broke and fled.[34]

"One result of this victory," says Claridge, "was that the English for the first time became the owners of the land on which their forts and castles stood, and the payments of ground rent on the 'notes', which had been such a source of trouble in the past, at once ceased. These notes, having been claimed from the Fante chiefs by right of conquest, now reverted by the same right to the English, and the sites to which they referred became their absolute property."

In Akan tradition, this war, though known as the *Mankatasa* or

[34] Some picturesque details of the battle are recorded in tradition. Adansi tradition says that the Ashanti army included a reluctant contingent of Akim and Assin troops who took the first opportunity in the fight of deserting; large numbers of their countrymen, of course, were in the allied ranks. Much confusion was caused by the thick smoke; the two divisions of the Ashanti centre lost touch with each other. Each of them had a *perempe* drum; the drum in the Asantehene's division was being sounded when it was answered out of the darkness of dust and smoke ahead. The Asantehene thought that some of the enemy possessed a similar drum and were sounding it in defiance (Akwamu tradition relates that Ashanti originally got its *perempe* drums from Akwamu, so it was a natural mistake), and attacked the division ahead of him; and it was not till the evening that he found he had been fighting against Opoku Ferefere's division. The tradition of Kuntanase in Ashanti says that in the defeat the Golden Stool itself was lost. One of the Stool guards, who had lost his way in the flight, came on the Kuntanase men and gasped out the terrible news. The Kuntanase and Juaben contingents then joined together and determined to recover it; they did so, and caught up the main body on the bank of the Pra, bringing the Stool with them in triumph. They found the Asantehene, who was wounded, sitting 'expecting to die' because of the loss of the Stool; Juaben tradition, which confirms this story, explains that he was proposing to blow himself up with gunpowder, as many of his chiefs had already done, and Ashanti military honour required. The Juaben and Kuntanase chiefs naturally received a great ovation; Kuntanase remembers the words of the cheering: Osei! Antwi has received wounds; Antwi, we thank you for taking away our shame from us (*Osei e, yee yee; Antwi gye aboa, yeda w'ase o, wama yen amfere!*)! Antwi Panin, the chief of Kuntanase, had received thirty wounds in the battle; but his work was not over. The Pra was in flood and the army was finding it difficult to cross; so Antwi Panin was put in charge of the ferry operations, and got the army safely across. "Living near the lake," explain the Kuntanase elders, "of course he was quite used to water." It is pleasant to know that this stout fighting man recovered from his wounds and lived to a good old age.

Ahuren tradition records that the Ahuren contingent suffered heavy losses when attacked from behind by the Akwamu; the Ashanti army lost its commander-in-chief and thirty other divisional chiefs, and the Asantehene Osei Yaw himself received seven wounds.

The battle is usually called by the British the battle of Dodowa, but all Africans call it by the much more accurate name of Akantamasu or Katamanso, from the village in and round which the hottest of the action took place. Akantamasu is the Akan form of the name, Katamanso the Ga form. I shall call the battle by its Akan name henceforth.

Macarthy war, is regarded as being caused by the friction between Kwadwo Otibu the Denkyerahene and the Ashanti. The Denkyera had fought on the Ashanti side in the first war, but had broken away and asserted their independence. The Ashanti could never allow this without risking the loss of all their power in a war to the death against a hostile coalition; and such claims, whether made by Akim, Assin, Gyaman, Banda or Denkyera, were promptly answered with a punitive expedition. From the Ashanti point of view it was sheer bad luck that what was to them a purely internal matter brought them into accidental contact, not only with a coalition of coast peoples, but with the British.

Sir Neil Campbell, the new British Governor, landed in the Gold Coast a fortnight after the victory at Akantamasu, and proposed at once to offer peace to the Ashanti on condition of their promising to respect the territory of the British and their allies, and to give security for their behaviour. The Fante and Denkyera chiefs refused to agree; for it was the custom on the Gold Coast for the defeated party in war to make the first peace proposals, and for the British to make the first overtures to the Ashanti would completely destroy the moral effect of the victory. The Governor, however, insisted, and would not even summon the more distant allied chiefs, those of Akim, Akwapim and Akwamu, to help in the discussion. Three months were wasted in arguments between the Governor and the African leaders, and in November he returned to Sierra Leone, having accomplished nothing. For nearly a year Captain Ricketts, who was left in charge, was occupied in tedious discussions on points of diplomatic etiquette. Eventually the Lieutenant-Governor, Lieutenant-Colonel Lumley, arrived from Sierra Leone, and in December 1827 a meeting was held in Cape Coast with Ashanti representatives.

It seemed at first that peace would easily be made. The leader of the Ashanti embassy offered a complete apology and submission; and it was soon agreed that Ashanti should pay a sum of 4,000 ounces of gold as security, that they should send two hostages from the royal family to Cape Coast, and that the various allied states (Akim, Denkyera and the others) were to be regarded as independent. The peace conference failed, however, because the Fante insisted on blockading Elmina to revenge themselves for the help the Elmina people had always given to the Ashanti, and the people of Osu[35] refused to give up their Ashanti prisoners, including Akua Pusua, a wife of the Asantehene. The Ashanti, on the other hand, released their prisoners, and protested warmly against what they regarded as the allied treachery in attacking Elmina and in detaining the Ashanti prisoners in Osu. Nothing Ricketts could say would induce the Fante to give over their war with Elmina; and in September 1829 he himself left the Gold Coast.

For another eighteen months the coast was thus disorganized, with its trade almost at a standstill. Not until April 1831 did a new Governor, Captain George Maclean, succeed in prevailing on all the nations concerned to put an end to the chaos. A treaty was then signed, providing (a) that Ashanti should deposit 600 ounces of gold, and should hand over two young men of the royal family, as security; these securities were to be returned after six years: (b) trade should be unrestricted, and panyarring, denouncing and "swearing on or by any person or thing whatever" were forbidden[36]: (c) Denkyera, Assin, "and others formerly his subjects" were free from any allegiance to the Asantehene, but were prohibited from insulting him: (d) all quarrels were to be decided as already agreed by the parties. This seems to refer to the terms which had been agreed on in December 1827, but which had never been carried into effect because of the Elmina war and the difficulty over the Osu prisoners.[37] These provide that (i) any act of aggression committed by any party to the treaty should be referred to the Governor-in-Chief at Sierra Leone or to the Governor at Cape Coast, who should judge the matter with the assistance of two or more assessors chosen from 'adjacent' chiefs: (ii) any of the allies committing an act of aggression and refusing to accept the decision of the Governor was to expect no protection from the allies. The significance of these provisions is shown by Claridge: "This treaty mutually binds the three parties, British, Ashanti and Fante allies, by precise rules, and the superior authority of the former is

[35] Osu is the village in which Christiansborg stands, just east of Accra. The Osu people, having such an important prisoner, were naturally inclined to stand out of the peace negotiations and bargain for a higher price.
[36] This clause, of course, was never strictly obeyed, and could not be. It was intended not to stop the practice itself but the abuse of the practice, by which oaths were sworn for frivolous reasons as a pretext for extortion, plaintiff and court being in collusion to defraud the defendant.
[37] This is Claridge's highly probable conjecture. For these negotiations, see Claridge, I, 392-414

definitely acknowledged by the implied agreement of the other two
to accept the Governor as referee in any case of dispute. There was
also a tacit understanding that the allies would be afforded British
protection in the event of any further agression on the part of the
Ashanti."

The treaty was signed by the Governor, two Ashanti delegates,
six Fante chiefs, representatives of Assin, Tufel[38] and Denkyera,
and by some unnamed and unnumbered chiefs from Apollonia.
The preamble to the treaty allows for the subsequent adhesion to
the treaty of other signatories. The gold was duly returned to
Kumasi six years later, still in its original packages; a fact which
did something to increase the respect of the Ashanti for British
honour. The two hostages were sent to England to be educated,
and returned to Ashanti in 1841.[39]

The treaty of 1831 restored peace and settled the relations
between the British and the coast peoples on the one hand, and
Ashanti on the other, for forty years. In half that time, it is true,
peace was greatly endangered, but the treaty of 1831 was regarded
as containing the normal footing on which the affairs of the Gold
Coast should stand.

[38] Tufel or Twiforo or Twifu is a state occupying the Pra valley just below its
confluence with the Ofin; east of it is Assin, west and south of it is Denkyera,
north of it (across the Pra) is Ashanti.
[39] Claridge, I, 433.

CHAPTER IX

THE GROWTH OF BRITISH RULE, 1830-59

THE beginnings of Crown government in the Gold Coast had been singularly inauspicious. The first Governor had been killed at Nsamankow less than two years after arriving on the coast. The next two years were occupied with skirmishes and with the perpetual fear of more serious fighting. Then came the victory of Akantamasu, which not only removed the fear of an Ashanti conquest but raised hopes of a speedy and lasting peace. Akantamasu, however, was followed by interminable negotiations, continually endangered by the obstinacy of the Fante and the Osu people; and it was five years before peace was signed. It is not surprising that before peace was signed the Government had become heartily weary of such a liability as the Gold Coast.

In 1828 the Government decided to abandon the coast, now that it was possible to do so without appearing to be driven out by the Ashanti. A warship was sent to remove the merchants and their property, and Ricketts was ordered to demolish the forts and retire to Sierra Leone. The British merchants, however, protested strongly against cutting their losses just when they were expecting trade to revive; and their protests were supported by the Fante, who did not approve of being left to face either the Ashanti or the Elmina people without British support. The Government accepted the protest, and compromised by handing over the administration to a committee of three London merchants nominated by the Government. They were to maintain the forts at Cape Coast and Accra, appoint local officials, subject to the Government's confirmation, and administer the settlements and their trade on the coast. A Government grant of £4,000 a year was to be paid them for administrative expenses, and Cape Coast and Accra were to be maintained as free ports. The settlements were to be governed by a Governor and an elected Council; and their jurisdiction was expressly limited to "the forts, roadsteads or harbours thereunto adjoining, as well as the persons residing therein". The first[1]

---

[1] Pending Maclean's arrival, the senior merchant on the coast, John Jackson, was appointed an interim Governor; he might have had the post permanently, but he himself thought it better that the Governor should have no personal interests on the coast. Claridge, I, 402-5.

Governor appointed was Captain George Maclean, who arrived at Cape Coast in February 1830.

Maclean's first task was to conclude the peace negotiations, which were making no real progress whatever. The allies trusted that the Ashanti were so broken by their recent defeat that they would tolerate any insults; the Ashanti were brooding over what they considered British treachery in allowing the Fante and the Osu people to defy them when they themselves had loyally carried out the terms of the armistice. The blustering of Turner and the over-hastiness of Sir Neil Campbell had done nothing to diminish the low respect in which the Ashanti held British Governors ever since the time of Torrane and Hope Smith. Maclean, however, was both firm and dignified. He warned the Fante that if they persisted in obstructing the negotiations they would probably be left to make their own terms with Ashanti; and he hinted to the Ashanti that the British could if they chose follow up their victory at Akanta-masu by another campaign. Peace was signed.

Maclean then set himself to improve the economic position of the country. The chaos of the last twenty-five years had made it impossible to develop the rice, maize, indigo, palm oil and timber trades which the old Company had suggested as substitutes for the slave trade. The establishment of internal peace and security, and the development of trade went together; neither could succeed without the other. In ten years he more than trebled the country's trade, especially in palm oil; and cowrie shells were introduced as currency to replace tiny pinches of gold dust.[2]

With his tiny revenue of £4,000 a year and his tiny police force of 120 men, Maclean could have accomplished nothing had it not been for his own outstanding personality. He was absolutely fearless; he went alone, with no escort except a corporal's guard, into the camp of a chief whose name was a byword for ferocity and who had offered a reward for Maclean's head; and he returned with a treaty in his pocket containing the chief's complete submission. He was immensely patient, both in enduring calumny and mis-understandings, and in listening to both parties to a case who were stating their case with African eloquence. He was absolutely impar-tial: he was accused by his enemies of various misdemeanours, of harshness in his dealings with recalcitrant chiefs, and of

[2] Claridge, I, 419.

encouraging the slave trade;[3] but he was never accused of partiality. And perhaps most important of all, he was convinced that the Gold Coast people were worth all the trouble he could possibly take with them, and that they were capable of responding to friendship.

The careful limitations on Maclean's judicial authority were soon outgrown. His reputation as a judge spread outside his official court at Cape Coast from end to end of the country; and outside his legal jurisdiction there speedily grew up an extra-legal jurisdiction over African litigants of every rank and from every district between the Pra and the Volta. Chiefs brought their disputes to Maclean and begged him to decide between them; and unofficial though his position was, his judgments were hardly ever questioned.[4]

It was on this reputation for wisdom and uprightness that Maclean's political authority was based. From asking his advice on a dispute that had already arisen, it was a small step to consulting him on disputes that threatened to arise. Thus he was able to add executive to his judicial functions. He scattered the greater part of his small police force as resident constables at the courts of all the prominent chiefs, with instructions to keep him informed on everything that was going on. He let it be known that to interfere with travellers and with trade—in the local phraseology, to 'close the paths'—was a serious offence. The force behind Maclean was the force of public opinion. His government could have been overthrown by a united effort; but the people were not united. Everyone knew that the alternative to Maclean's government would be chaos again; and the people had had enough of that in the last twenty-five years. A chief who was inclined to resist Maclean's authority was always opposed and blockaded by his neighbours, and often disowned by his own people; in the end he always had to submit and pay a sum of gold as security, to be kept

[3] These charges were refuted by a select committee of the House of Commons which entirely vindicated Maclean. A charge of partiality, however, would have needed no refutation; it was never made.
[4] " . . . a kind of irregular jurisdiction has grown up, extending itself far beyond the limits of the Forts by the voluntary submission of the Natives themselves, whether chiefs or traders, to British equity; and its decisions, owing to the moral influence, partly of our acknowledged power, and partly of the respect which has been inspired by the fairness with which it has been exercised by Captain Maclean and the Magistrates at the other Forts, have generally, we might almost say uniformly, been carried into effect without the interposition of force." (Report of the Select Committee.)

safely as long as he behaved well, but to be forfeited if ever he gave trouble. Only once in his reign of thirteen years did Maclean need to use force.[5]

Striking though this gradual development of authority was, the strength of Maclean's authority must not be exaggerated. Its origin was purely judicial, and Maclean's revenue was too small to allow him to step far outside the purely judicial sphere of government. None of the revenue was locally raised, except a small customs duty of half per cent on imports, and certain harbour dues.[6] The Government had set its face firmly against any extension of British territory, and Maclean had no powers at all over chiefs and people outside the walls of the forts. His influence was great, but his legal authority was nil. He held a *de facto* power to hear causes, but he had no power of any kind to carry out public works, introduce any social services, or enforce obedience on a chief and people who were strong enough to defy the general opinion of the country. Nevertheless, his personal influence was so strong that from this time onwards we must recognize that a considerable area of country had accepted a position in a British sphere of influence. The area over which Maclean's influence was felt was bounded on the east by the Volta, and on the west by the Pra, and reached inland as far as the Ashanti border. Not every tribe in this area accepted Maclean's influence. Most of the Accra plains were under Danish influence, and Elmina, Axim and other towns were under Dutch influence. On the other hand, certain areas to the west of the Pra, including Wassaw, Apollonia and Dixcove, were in the British sphere. Roughly speaking, however, we may regard the British sphere as reaching from the Pra to the Volta, a distance of about 100 miles, and from the sea-shore inland to an average depth of about forty miles. For convenience I shall refer to this British sphere of influence as the 'Protectorate'; it must be borne in mind, however, that no legal protectorate was ever proclaimed over it, and that until 1874 its inhabitants were entirely independent of the British Crown. The position of the country was anomalous in that its independent peoples were voluntarily submitting to a restriction on their independence in the one particular of judicial matters, and in no other particular. Provided this anomaly is borne in mind,

[5] Claridge, I, 414-19, 447-9.
[6] Claridge, I, 416, 417.

there is no particular harm in the use of the inaccurate term 'Protectorate'; the inverted commas will serve as a reminder of its inaccuracy.

The limitations on Maclean's authority were imperfectly understood in England. Maclean himself was unlucky enough to attract public attention in England through his marriage with the popular poetess 'L.E.L.', and through her sudden death very soon after her arrival on the Gold Coast. A section of his wife's admirers made up their minds that he had murdered her, and determined to hunt him down. The coroner's jury having returned a verdict of death from misadventure,[7] they set themselves to discredit Maclean's government in every way they could. He was accused of over-harshness in putting down human sacrifice and of slackness in putting down slavery. Their agitation succeeded in securing the appointment of a Select Committee of the House of Commons to report on the state of the West African settlements. The Committee's report, however, praised Maclean's administration highly, and recommended that the Crown should resume control of the Gold Coast, separating the judicial work which had been such an outstanding feature of Maclean's governorship from the political authority of the King's representative. In 1843, therefore, the Crown once more took control of the Gold Coast settlements; Commander Hill, R.N., being appointed Governor, and Maclean being appointed to the congenial post of Judicial Assessor. His duties were to sit in court with the Fante chiefs and try cases where Africans alone were concerned, in accordance with the Fante customary law and the principles of British equity. The Government confirmed Maclean's view, for which he had been so much attacked in England, that in such matters as domestic slavery in the 'Protectorate' he had no authority to prohibit the system, but only personal influence to be employed to soften its abuses.

The report of the Select Committee had recommended that the relation of the peoples of the 'Protectorate' to the Crown should be "not the allegiance of subjects, to which we have no right to pretend, and which it would entail an inconvenient responsibility to possess, but the deference of weaker powers to a stronger and

---

[7] Claridge, 426-31. The only doubt is whether the verdict should not have been one of death from natural causes. There is no shadow of blame attaching to Maclean himself.

more enlightened neighbour, whose protection and counsel they seek, and to whom they are bound by certain definite obligations". To carry out this recommendation, and define the exceedingly uncertain and indefinite obligations then existing, Commander Hill's first important act was to negotiate the celebrated agreement with a number of Fante and other chiefs which is commonly known as the Bond of 1844. This document, which is regarded by modern Gold Coast politicians as their Magna Carta, is so short that its text may be quoted in full.

"1. Whereas power and jurisdiction have been exercised for and on behalf of Her Majesty the Queen of Great Britain and Ireland, within divers countries and places adjacent to Her Majesty's forts and settlements on the Gold Coast; we, chiefs of countries and places so referred to, adjacent to the said forts and settlements, do hereby acknowledge that power and jurisdiction, and declare that the first objects of law are the protection of individuals and property.

"2. Human sacrifices, and other barbarous customs, such as panyarring, are abominations, and contrary to law.

"3. Murders, robberies, and other crimes and offences, will be tried and inquired of before the Queen's judicial officers and the chiefs of the districts, moulding the customs of the country to the general principles of British law.

"Done at Cape Coast Castle before his Excellency the Lieutenant Governor, on this 6th day of March, in the year of our Lord, 1844."

The document is signed by the Governor and by eight chiefs, including those of Denkyera, Anomabu, Cape Coast and Assin.

The effect of the Bond was to legalize and define the jurisdiction which had grown up in the 'Protectorate' under Maclean's influence. It will be observed that the language of the preamble clearly implies that the power and jurisdiction are to be exercised in the future as they have been in the past, and in no other way. There is no intention to grant to the Crown any territorial sovereignty or suzerainty, nor is there granted any authority beyond that of enforcing compliance with the orders of the court. Whatever may be said of the contention so often put forward on the Gold Coast today that the Bond of 1844 is still the only legal basis for British rule, it is certain that the Bond cannot be

construed, and at the time was not construed, as granting any
authority beyond this.

In January 1850 the Gold Coast was separated from Sierra Leone
and constituted a separate government, with its own executive and
legislative councils. From the constitutional lawyer's point of view,
this step was made possible by the British Settlements Act of 1843.
The irregular jurisdiction exercised in the 'Protectorate' depended
on the Foreign Jurisdiction Act, also of 1843, which "empowered
the Crown to exercise any jurisdiction it might have in a foreign
country in as full a manner as if that country had been acquired
by conquest or cession".[8]

A few weeks later negotiations were completed with the Danes
for the purchase of their forts and settlements by the British. The
Danish forts were all on the arid coastal strip east of Accra. There
was no possibility of their developing a trade in tropical crops[9]
such as cocoa, coffee, cotton, sugar or rubber; they were twenty
miles from the southern edge of the forest country, and right off
the main gold routes. The slave trade had been their great standby;
and now that the slave trade was ended their forts were a liability.
In March 1850 they sold all their forts to the British for £10,000,
and the British flag was hoisted on the two sound forts of
Christiansborg (Asu) and Keta, and the more or less ruined forts at
Teshi, Ningo and Ada. The Danes had a vague protectorate over
Akwapim and a still vaguer one over Akim, similar to the British
'Protectorate' of Maclean's making. This Danish influence now
passed to the British Government, the chiefs and people concerned
giving their consent.

The acquisition of the Danish possessions seemed likely to help
the British Government in raising a local revenue, a matter which
was increasingly occupying the Government's attention. British
authority was spreading as more chiefs adhered to the Bond; and
there was growing up among the people a desire for more Govern-

[8] Wight, *Development of the Legislative Council*, 58-9, 62-3. The members of
both councils were nominated by the Governor: the first legislative council
consisted of the Judicial Assessor, the Collector of Customs, and two merchants,
under the Governor's presidency (Crooks, 323).
[9] This coastal plain grows little but cassava. In recent years plantations of
coconut palms have been made along the coast, and a small copra industry is
developing. The district could grow sisal, but a recent Government experimental
sisal plantation failed to secure the interest of the local farmers and was
abandoned. The district is becoming increasingly important for the cattle
industry.

ment activity such as medical and educational services and roads. The grant from the Crown was quite inadequate for this, and the Government was anxious to supplement it by a locally raised revenue. The Government hoped to be able to levy customs duties on imports; but although the Danish forts were now in British hands, their trade was only small compared with that of the forts farther west, and on this part of the coast the British and Dutch forts were so intermingled that it was impossible for either to levy duties without the co-operation of the other. This co-operation was for some reason[10] never obtained, and without it nothing could have been done to check wholesale smuggling.

The plan for customs duties was therefore given up and a new plan was tried. In April 1852 a large assembly of chiefs and elders met at Cape Coast in the presence of the Governor, and apparently at his invitation, to consult with the Governor and the council on means of raising revenue. The meeting was attended by a large number of Fante chiefs and others from the 'Protectorate'; it was supplemented soon afterwards by a similar meeting at Christiansborg, attended by chiefs from Accra, Akim, Akwapim and even beyond the Volta; who associated themselves with the decisions of the Cape Coast assembly.[11]

The meeting resolved itself a legislative assembly, "with full powers to enact such laws as it shall deem fit", and went on to declare that "its enactment, sanctioned and approved of by the Governor, shall immediately become the law of the country, subject to the approval of Her Majesty the Queen, and be held binding upon the whole of the population being under the protection of the British Government".

The meeting then declared that in consideration of the advantages derived from "the protection afforded them by Her Majesty's Government" it was reasonable and necessary that the people should pay taxes; and it voted a poll tax of one shilling a head for every man, woman and child in the 'Protectorate'. The tax was to be collected by officers appointed by the Governor, not (as might have been expected) by the stool authorities. Its proceeds were to be used in paying stipends to the chiefs, and providing for "the public good in the education of the people, in the general improvement

[10] There was usually, but not always, considerable rivalry and commercial jealousy between the British and the Dutch.
[11] Claridge, I, 478-80.

and extension of the judicial system, in affording greater facilities of internal communication, increased medical aid" and other measures of improvement and utility.[12]

This series of resolutions was approved and confirmed by the Governor, and was adopted under the name of the Poll Tax Ordinance as a legal ordinance of the settlements. The Governor clearly contemplated that this assembly of chiefs should be a permanent part of the constitutional machinery of the Gold Coast. It appeared to him and his advisers that the rights and authority of the chiefs were being steadily encroached upon by the lower classes, and that the Government was tacitly acquiescing in this social revolution. It was desirable, therefore, to take some bold step to check this tendency, and the constitution of a legislative assembly of chiefs and the institution of a regular system of stipends would establish the chiefs' authority firmly.[13]

On this matter the Governor, like so many other Governors, was misinformed. The self-styled legislative assembly was an assembly of men who had no constitutional authority to levy a tax on their people, even for the recognized purposes, without the express consent of their people. The poll tax was a novelty, and the people had not had enough opportunity of discussing the proposal in their villages and giving their opinion on it. Moreover, the tax was not collected by the chiefs or stool authorities, but by specially appointed agents, who were not in any way under the control of the people. A poll tax could have been collected satisfactorily if several months had been allowed for discussion beforehand and if the collection had been left in the proper hands. Levied as it was it caused great dissatisfaction. Not content with this, the Government committed another blunder in spending the money. The intention of the assembly had been that all the money collected, apart from the expenses of collection, should be directly spent on work in the country. The Government naturally regarded central administrative expenses as a necessary part of the cost of maintaining services in the country districts. This point of view, however, was not shared by the people, and when the Government spent part of the proceeds of the tax on salaries of headquarters' officials they

---

[12] The texts of the Bond of 1844 and of the Poll Tax Ordinance are given in Crooks, 296, 297 and 325-8.
[13] Claridge, I, 481-3, 495-6.

regarded it as a breach of the agreement on which the Ordinance was based. The natural result was that more and more difficulty was encountered in collecting the tax, and very soon both the tax and the assembly which had decreed it vanished for ever. The Government had expected the tax to produce £20,000 a year; but the actual proceeds fell off steadily from £7,500 in 1853 to £1,500 in 1861, after which the tax was abandoned.[14] In 1854, and again in 1857, difficulties over the collection of the tax led to rioting, and in the former year matters at Christiansborg and the neighbouring villages became so serious that the guns of the castle, assisted by H.M.S. *Scourge*, bombarded the town, and loss of life occurred both among the townsfolk and among the castle garrison.

Ephemeral though the legislative assembly and the poll tax were, they have considerable historical importance. Though no legal protectorate had been proclaimed, the Government and the assembly had acquiesced in the phrase "population being under the protection of the British Government". The chiefs of the 'Protectorate', if not the majority of their people, had admitted that it was reasonable to pay taxes to support the Government in return for the performance by the Government of certain duties. The frontiers of the 'Protectorate' might not be fixed, but there was now in existence a British Government, responsible for providing schools, law courts, roads and hospitals, as well as other unspecified "measures of improvement and utility", and entitled to collect a revenue to maintain the services it provided. No mention had been made of military matters; but it was certain that no future Governor could plead to the Asantehene that he had no control over any of the tribes in the 'Protectorate', or could permit the Ashanti to attack Assin or Denkyera without coming to their aid. In this respect the Ordinance of 1852 supplements the Treaty of 1831; the independent states referred to in the treaty as being free from their old allegiance to Ashanti had now transferred a good part of their allegiance to the British Government.

In 1853, the year after the Poll Tax Ordinance, the first Supreme Court Ordinance was passed by the Governor and Legislative Council.[15] By this ordinance regular courts were established within

[14] Claridge, I, 495.
[15] That is, the legislative council of the settlements, as established in 1850; not the short-lived 'legislative assembly' of the 'Protectorate' which passed the Poll Tax Ordinance.

the settlements to deal with civil and criminal cases arising within their boundaries. Appeals from the judgment of the Judicial Assessor in cases arising in the 'Protectorate' were to be heard before the Governor and Legislative Council sitting with the Judicial Assessor. The distinction was thus carefully maintained between the jurisdiction on British territory and the jurisdiction over the 'Protectorate'. In 1856, however, an Order in Council extended British jurisdiction[16] to the 'Protectorate' in certain cases, such as bankruptcy, in which the Judicial Assessor had been accustomed to dispense with the usual panel of chiefs. The offices of Judicial Assessor and Chief Justice were held by the same man.

This organization and consolidation of the British power naturally resulted in attracting more nations into the 'Protectorate'. Assin and Denkyera were among the original signatories of the Bond of 1844, and within a few years the Akim Abuakwa, many divisions of the Akim Kotoku,[17] the Wassaw, the Agona and others of the nations between the sea and the upper Pra had adhered to the Bond. The acquisition of the Danish settlements brought more nations under British influence. In 1850 the British Governor, Sir William Winniett, accompanied the Danish Governor, Mr. Carstensen, on a tour through the Danish protectorate, and Akwapim, Krobo and Krepi (the last state being east of the Volta) became members of the British 'Protectorate', though it was not till 1886 that the Akwamu entered it.

Ashanti, therefore, was now almost completely cut off from the sea by territory under British protection. The whole of the left bank of the Pra was protected territory, and no European settlement could be reached from Ashanti without passing through protected territory, except Assini in the far west and Keta in the

[16] The practice in the 'Protectorate' in and after Maclean's time (he died in 1847) was for the Judicial Assessor to be assisted on the bench by a panel of chiefs in order that due regard might be had to native customary law. Where native customary law was silent, the Judicial Assessor sat alone. The effect of the Order in Council was to enable magistrates who had been appointed to act within the settlements to have jurisdiction also in the 'Protectorate' in such cases.

[17] Akim Kotoku tradition. The Kotoku complain that as the paramount chief himself did not enter into relations with the British (which he could not do, as he was living then at Dampon on the Ashanti border under close surveillance by the Ashanti authorities), the British assumed that all his sub-chiefs who made treaties with them were subjects of Akim Abuakwa. In this way, they say, the Kotoku state lost the allegiance of many of its divisions.

far east.[18] On the other hand, Ashanti had some outposts in the 'Protectorate' in the form of allies. The most important of these was Elmina, which still maintained, beneath the protection of the Dutch guns, its proud connection with Ashanti and its implacable enmity to the Fante states. East of the Volta were two more Ashanti allies; they were, first, the Akwamu, who were perpetually at feud with the Krepi, the Krobo and the Akwapim, and, second, the Awuna or Anlo of the Keta district, who were at feud with the Ada and other Ga tribes west of the Volta. Both these two nations looked to Ashanti for help against their enemies; they were both (like the Elmina people) far enough away from Ashanti not to feel much fear of being reduced to permanent vassalage.

The Bond and the Poll Tax Ordinance marked a turning point in the relations between the British and the Gold Coast peoples, not merely in constitutional matters but in economic and social developments. Torrane had experimented with coffee growing, and the experiment was revived in Maclean's time,[19] though without permanent success. In 1850 an experimental cotton plantation was made, but this also was a failure. In both cases the difficulty was the supply of labour. The farmers would not engage themselves in plantation labour, though they were quite willing to employ pawns;[20] and when the Government discouraged the system of pawn labour, they abandoned the whole scheme. The time was not yet ripe for the development of large-scale agriculture for the growing of export crops; in 1846 the four staple crops were maize, yams, cassava and plantains, though the palm-oil industry was slowly growing. In 1846 the revenue amounted to £4,876, an increase of £355 over the previous year; £4,000 of this sum was the Government grant.[21]

Education had begun in the Gold Coast as long ago as 1752, when the Rev. Thomas Thompson, one of the early missionaries of the Society for the Propagation of the Gospel, arrived from America.[22]

[18] In 1843 the French established forts at Assini and Grand Bassam, the beginnings of the modern French colony of the Ivory Coast (Crooks, 291, 292).
[19] Crooks, 306; Claridge, I, 478.
[20] A pawn is a person pledged into a state of semi-servitude as security for a debt; see Rattray, *Ashanti Law and Constitution*, 47-55. Pawns are not slaves, though the Government condemned the system as too much like slavery.
[21] Crooks, 310.
[22] His own account of his stay has been reprinted in facsimile by the S.P.G.: *Two Missionary Voyages by Thomas Thompson, A.M.* Claridge wrongly gives the date of his arrival as 1751.

He settled at Cape Coast, and visited the other British settlements at Anomabu, Tantamkweri, Winneba and Accra. He did not regard himself merely as a chaplain for the officials and other Europeans there, but set himself from the first to work also among the townsfolk. He was an enlightened and broad-minded man; he set himself to study the Fante language, which few of his contemporaries cared to do; and he was prepared to inquire into the real meaning of African customs which seemed to him at first sight ridiculous or sinful. On the subject of language study he says, "I could never be informed of any one ever having entered into the Grounds of this Language, which is the rather to be admired at, as there have been, and are Gentlemen at the Coast now, of Education and Ingenuity;[23] but they seem not to regard it any otherwise than as Currency of a bad Allay, which they do not hoard, nor refine, and only want it to pass again. Yet most of the Words in it are very well compounded of Vowels and Consonants, and I am sure, much better framed for the ease of Delivery, and freedom of Elocution, than some of our northern Languages. The People value themselves upon their speaking, and some do not mistake their Talent." He goes on to lament, as many have done since his time, the difficulty of learning the language from inexperienced teachers who are themselves not accustomed to thinking of their speech in terms of formal grammar: "instead of giving a Word by itself, they would either join with it a Pronoun, or an Epithet, or else a Participle, or give the Plural Number for the Singular, and sometimes join a Substantive and Verb together instead of speaking the one singly by itself. . . . This is a specimen of the Misery of learning Languages without either the Help of Books, or the Instruction of a proper Master." He seems, however, to have had a good ear, and to have acquired a fair working knowledge of Fante.

Mr. Thompson stayed nearly four years on the Coast, from May 1752 to February 1756, after which his health compelled him to retire to England, where he settled down into the comfort of a Kentish vicarage.[24] His work on the Gold Coast had not been very

[23] This testimony from a man who was himself a gentleman and a scholar may warn us against generalizing too rashly on the roughness or worse of the British on the Coast in that day. He distinctly says, moreover, that in his time relations between the British and the Cape Coast populace were cordial. This should be set against the general impression derived from Bosman and Cruikshank given on p. 90.
[24] See the biographical introduction to the Thompson reprint, pp. xiii., xiv.

fruitful of conversions. He records having baptized eight men, and having been disappointed in his hopes of baptizing others. His first convert moreover disappointed him sadly after his baptism; having "made an extraordinary progress in the Christian Knowledge", and having acquitted himself to the amazement of several gentlemen in an oral examination "upon many Points of Doctrine, besides the several Articles of the Creed", he was a sad backslider: "He was indeed the best taught," says Mr. Thompson mournfully, "of any of his Colour that I ever had, and he made the worst Use of his Instruction." Thompson, however, never lost faith in the possibility of bringing Africa to Christianity; "I consider them as being a more civilized People than the Nations in general, and as far as they are removed from Barbarity and Savageness, they are certainly more capable, and the fitter to be dealt with in the Way of Christian Instruction."

The education of the children had been an important part of Mr. Thompson's plan of campaign; but in this also he was disappointed. He suggested to the Cape Coast chiefs that they should provide a schoolroom; they agreed at once—but did nothing. He then hired a room at his own expense, "and several of the young Blacks came to me; but Children growing weary of what is no longer a Novelty, and the Parents neglecting to keep them to it, and make them come duly, my Hopes were quickly at an End of doing any Good this Way". He arranged therefore with his Society to send over a few boys to England for education; it seems that they were not the first, for he mentions two young men at Cape Coast who had been educated at London.[25] Three lads were sent to England, and "were placed out to School at Islington, under the Care of one Mr. Hickman". One of these boys, Philip Quacoe, was afterwards ordained in the Church of England, and returned to

[25] These were probably the two who were sent to England in 1735 by the Governor and Council, and returned two years later; their names (in modern spelling) were John Acquah and George Sackey. They seem to have had an enjoyable time, marred only by their both catching smallpox. They "waited upon my Lord Halifax," who "expressed himself well pleased with seeing them". They received an excellent outfit, with silver lace, buttons, and buckles not lacking; in the interests of their schooling they were shown the Town; and it is not surprising that when Lord Halifax good-naturedly desired that they might stay a longer time in England, "the Black Boys also earnestly requested" it. But it was not to be; however, "the Committee in order to entertain the Two Black Gentlemen before their departure for Africa have agreed to give them a Dinner at the King's Arms, Cornhill" (Crooks, 28-30).

his native country as a "Missionary, Schoolmaster and Catechist to the Negroes". He served there from 1765 to 1816, when he was relieved by an English chaplain sent out by the African Committee.[26]

In 1788 we hear of a school at Cape Coast for twelve children; the chaplain (that is the Rev. Philip Quacoe) was in charge. The Committee of the Company made grants for school books and, of course, also paid the chaplain's salary of £140 a year;[27] the S.P.G. seems to have made grants for other expenses, and the fines levied on the Company's officials for non-attendance at chapel were applied to the upkeep of the school. In 1816 the school was being carried on in the house belonging to Mr. White, the defender of Anomabu. The Committee suggested to the newly-appointed chaplain that it would be as well for him to familiarize himself with the Madras system so that he could bring the Cape Coast school into line with modern theories; it may well have become a little old-fashioned during the fifty-one years' rule of its headmaster Philip Quacoe. It is clear that under the new regime the school flourished; in 1820, only four years later, the staff had increased to an establishment of five schoolmasters and four assistant teachers, though there were only two European schoolmasters and three African assistant teachers actually appointed, together with a lady as teacher of needlework. In 1830 the school contained seventy boys. In 1843 the Select Committee recommended in somewhat vague terms that "schools of a higher class than any of which are there at present" should be encouraged; and three years later we hear for the first time the complaint that "at present, there is no employment for educated boys, except as teachers in schools, and clerks in government and mercantile establishments, and hence the results of education, pleasing as they may be, are not so healthy, vigorous and permanent as they would be if they were associated with various branches of useful mechanical knowledge".[28] The controversy over African education had begun.

Other mission work in the Gold Coast began with the arrival of the Methodists in 1833 and the Basel mission in 1827. A small knot

[26] Claridge, I, 280; this was the Rev. William Philip; Crooks, 113-14.
[27] £80 as chaplain, and £60 as writer; Crooks, 78.
[28] Crooks, 145, 152, 281, 308, 113-15. I have to thank Mr. F. L. Bartels for pointing out that similar castle schools were run by the Dutch and the Danes, and that some of the men they trained were outstandingly successful.

of Christians existed as a result of the Rev. Philip Quacoe's work and influence and of the Bible study which was carried on among the scholars of the school at Cape Coast. One of these men, William de Graft, later settled for a time at Dixcove as a trader, and asked one of the ship captains to bring out from England a case of Bibles. The captain did more; he mentioned the matter to the committee of the Wesleyan Methodist missionary society, and offered to take out a missionary at his own expense. In this way the Rev. Joseph Dunwell came to the Gold Coast as the first Methodist missionary.

The early days of the mission were hard. Dunwell died in six months, and for a time the young mission was left again to African leadership. In September 1836 two new missionaries, Mr. and Mrs. Wrigley, arrived and were followed in January by Mr. and Mrs. Harrop; but both the newcomers and Mrs. Wrigley died early in February, and Wrigley himself lived only a few months more.

In his agony Wrigley sent a last appeal for help. "Come out to this hell," he wrote, "if it is only to die here!" In January 1838 there landed at Cape Coast the man who was to do more than any other to establish the Methodist Church firmly. Thomas Birch Freeman was the son of an African father and an English mother, and was impelled to offer himself for missionary work in the Gold Coast by the news of the death of Mrs. Wrigley and the Harrops. Before he landed, Wrigley too was already dead. Freeman suffered the same heavy blow; a month after their arrival Mrs. Freeman died. But Freeman himself worked in the Gold Coast till his death in 1890, beating Philip Quacoe's record by one year. In 1839 he visited Kumasi and founded a mission station there, which lasted with varying fortunes till 1872.

The first missionaries of the Basel mission landed at Accra in 1827, eight years before Dunwell's landing at Cape Coast. A party of four Danish missionaries came to Accra and began work under the shadow of the castle of Christiansborg at Osu. Three of them died within a few weeks, but a fourth man, Henke, worked at the Danish government school till he died in 1831. A few weeks after his death three more missionaries arrived, but again in a few weeks there was only one man, Riis, alive. Riis carried on the work at Christiansborg until 1835, and then moved to Akropong in Akwapim, where the chief Ado Dankwa allowed him to open a mission station. In 1847 the Basel mission founded a station at Aburi in Akwapim, and a new mission society, the Bremen mission, began working east of the Volta. The Basel and Bremen missions expanded their work within the Danish sphere of influence, working in the Ga, Twi and Ewe languages. The Methodists, on the other hand, developed mainly in Fante country. The Basel and Bremen missions from the first made great efforts at language study, and translated the Bible into the three languages they used. In this respect the Methodists were less forward; Freeman himself, throughout his half century of untiring effort, never preached a sermon in Fante. The Basel and Bremen missions worked largely through schools, and in technical education especially the Basel mission made itself a great name. The Methodists relied more on direct evangelization; in 1887 there were three times as many local preachers as school teachers.

During these years from Maclean's time onwards there was thus a growing educated community and a growing body of Christian influence. The legislative assembly of 1852 even passed an education ordinance,[29] though without staff or funds it could have little effect. The missionaries were establishing a network of Christian congregations all over the country, and they produced large numbers of men and women of fine character. In the towns there came into being a group of people with a very high degree of culture. As we shall see, a generation after Maclean's time a British Governor reported that the educated Africans compared favourably with the European residents on the Coast. The country might have had a happier history during the century after Maclean if the Europeans had felt at ease in the society of educated Africans and able to meet them on equal terms.

On the other hand, the introduction of Christianity and of western education brought fresh problems. Christianity and education went together, and there were inevitably many who acquired only a thin veneer. There was a good deal of trouble from semi-educated men whose scanty stock of learning led them to arrogance or downright rascality. In the early days, there was much antagonism—even sometimes rioting—between professing Christians and those who still followed the old ways. The Basel

[29] I have to thank Mr. F. L. Bartels again for drawing my attention to this ordinance, which I had overlooked.

mission, and to some extent other missions as well, adopted a policy of separating their converts entirely from the old life for fear lest the social and artistic attractions of the old life should lead them to forget their new religion: a policy which may have been inevitable from the point of view of the Christian evangelist, but which led to a most unfortunate cleavage in the life of the community.

Moreover, we have seen that complaints were soon raised that the education supplied was of the wrong type, better at turning out clerks than carpenters. The first demand for education came from the Government and the commercial firms who wanted clerks, and it was natural that the educational system should at first be designed to supply them. Naturally therefore, education and the clerical professions became associated in African minds, more especially as the Europeans did not engage in handicrafts or manual labour. The work of the Basel missionaries founded a healthy tradition of honest craftsmanship; but in spite of a century of educational effort, the great majority of school pupils regarded a black-coated job as the only desirable end of education. It is only in the last few years, with the increasing demand for technicians and the consequent development of technical education, that this prejudice has begun to diminish.

CHAPTER X

ASHANTI AND OTHER NATIVE STATES DURING THE TIME OF OSEI YAW AKOTO AND KWAKU DUA, 1824-67

THE Asantehene Osei Bonsu was succeeded by his brother, Osei Yaw Akoto. The first seven years of his reign were taken up with the Fante war, and it was not till the peace of 1831 that he was able to devote much attention to home affairs. The chief event that is remembered of this period is that the old feud between Kumasi and Juaben broke out into open war. The two states had been on bad terms at intervals ever since the battle of Feyiase; on that occasion the Juaben men had actually captured Ntim Gyakari, and had taken the gold bangle on his arm, which had intercepted the first blow struck at him, and the gold *wari* pieces with which he was playing. According to Ahuren tradition, Kumasi fought no fewer than seven wars with Juaben to make the Juaben men give up these relics. Juaben, moreover (perhaps on the strength of this exploit), was always inclined to claim equality with Kumasi, and had actually persuaded Bowdich and Dupuis into regarding it as an independent state.

The occasion of this present war was twofold. Kwasi Boaten the Juabenhene had helped to recapture the Golden Stool at the disaster of Akantamasu; but he had not recaptured a box of gold dust which had been with it, and on his return he was accused of having appropriated it. On top of this quarrel there ensued another; a Juaben man who was in trouble with the Juabenhene fled to Kumasi, and the Juabenhene sent to demand his head. The Asantehene refused to have the man executed without going into the case, and summoned the Juabenhene to Kumasi. The pride of Juaben was aroused, hot words passed, and the matter reached such a stage that war was the only solution.[1] The Juaben found themselves at war not only with Kumasi but with the whole of

---

[1] The Kumasi tradition (Fuller, 82-3) says that Juaben refused to come to Kumasi, and not only insulted the Kumasi messenger but went so far as to abuse the Asantehene. The Juaben version (Rattray, *Ashanti Law and Constitution*, 172-3) is that the Juabenhene executed the man himself, after having at the Asantehene's request promised to spare his life.

Ashanti, and were completely defeated. The whole tribe left Ashanti and went to Kibi, the capital of Akim Abuakwa,[2] where they placed themselves under the protection of Ofori Atta Panin the Abuakwahene. In spite of Osei Yaw's efforts to get them back, they stayed in Akim all the rest of his lifetime, and only returned when requested to do so by the new Asantehene, Kwaku Dua I. Kwaku Dua succeeded in 1838, and next year the Juaben people began their homeward journey, having demanded and received from the Asantehene the heads of several of the prominent Kumasi chiefs who had fought against them. Their chief Kwasi Boaten died on the way back; his successor Kofi Boaten died after a short reign of eighty days; and the ceremonies connected with this double funeral delayed the tribe's return. It was 1841 before the Juaben people arrived back in Kumasi, under the leadership of Ama Sewa the Queen Mother; she actually became Juabenhene and rebuilt the town of Juaben, and reigned for eight years before being succeeded by her daughter.[3]

Osei Yaw Akoto died in 1838 and was succeeded by his nephew Kwaku Dua I.

Kwaku Dua began his reign well by settling the Juaben quarrel and by clearing up old disputes with Nkoranza and Gyaman. He allowed Mr. Freeman, the pioneer Wesleyan missionary, to visit Kumasi, though with much trepidation and careful precautions against any ill effects from the white man's magic. This first visit was made in 1839, and no particular disaster having occurred, Kwaku Dua gave Freeman permission for a second visit two years later. On this occasion Freeman was accompanied not only by a second missionary, Brooking, but by John Ansa and Nkwantabissa, the two Ashanti hostages who had been delivered to Maclean in 1831. They were closely related to Kwaku Dua, and it may have been partly due to them that the Asantehene granted the mission a piece of land for a mission station. Freeman soon returned to the coast, but Brooking was left in charge. Next year, 1842, he was joined by another missionary named Rowland, but Rowland died in a few weeks, and it was a year before Brooking saw another white face, when Freeman brought with him on his third visit to Kumasi a missionary named Chapman.

[2] The paramount stool of Akim Abuakwa, after several previous seats, finally settled at Kibi in the fastnesses of the Atewa hills, probably about 1815.
[3] Rattray, *Ashanti Law*, etc., 173-4.

Kwaku Dua was a peaceable man, like his uncle Osei Bonsu; but like Osei Bonsu he was fated to spend most of his reign in war or the threat of war.

The fundamental cause of the trouble was that the Ashanti could not reconcile themselves to the loss of Assin, Akim and Denkyera, which they had for so long regarded as provinces of their empire.[4] This part of the treaty of 1831 was most unpalatable to them, and disposed them to look for opportunities of taking their revenge. While these states were independent, the Ashanti felt that their own access to the European settlements was only by permission of their former subjects, who were none too friendly towards them, and who, with the Fante, would lose no chance of making Ashanti traders feel friendless and forlorn. Moreover, the defeat at Akantamasu rankled badly; and apart from the shame of it, the defeat had led to the loss of the rent for the British and Danish forts. Lastly, the British had stopped the slave trade, which the Ashanti, like many others, still regarded as the most fruitful and profitable trade of the country. It was likely, therefore, that any misunderstandings with the British authorities would lead to trouble.

Such misunderstandings unfortunately were not long in occurring. In December 1844 a party of Ashanti traders was returning to Kumasi from the coast, and on the way through Assin a woman in the party was suddenly attacked by a man who rushed out of the bush, knocked her down, and ran back into the bush with her load. The man was caught and handed over to the chief of the Assin, Kwadwo Otibu,[5] but as the woman attacked had died of her injuries, he declared that the matter was too serious for him to deal with, and sent the criminal to the Governor at Cape Coast. The Ashanti party went on its way to Kumasi, and naturally reported what had happened to the Asantehene. Feeling in Kumasi ran high against the Assin, but it was expected that the matter

[4] The Assin were originally living north of the Pra and were related to the Adansi; they had crossed the Pra in order to escape from Ashanti rule, though some stragglers of the nation were still on the Ashanti side of the river. The Akim Kotoku served Ashanti till 1824, when they revolted, betrayed an Ashanti army under Kwaku Biri into the hands of the Akim Abuakwa, and moved from Dampon to a new home at Gyadam. The Akim Abuakwa finally threw off Ashanti influence in 1811. The Denkyera contingent did good service for the Ashanti in the first Fante war.

[5] A namesake of his predecessor, the accomplice of Kwaku Aputae, in 1805; and also of the fighting Denkyerahene of Akantamasu.

would soon be settled by the Governor either sending the criminal to Kumasi for execution or executing him in British territory. Time went on, however, and nothing was heard from the Governor; and the Asantehene called a council to decide what he should do.[6] Many of the chiefs clamoured for war, saying that the Governor had broken the treaty of 1831. Luckily there was in Kumasi a Wesleyan missionary, Chapman by name; he was invited to attend the council in order that he might report its proceedings to the Governor at Cape Coast; and his words led the Governor to realize that the matter was serious. In the end he very properly gave way, and sent the murderer back to Assin under escort, where he was executed in the presence of the Asantehene's messengers.

This affair had been entirely the fault of the British. In the next trouble the Ashanti were to blame. This same Kwadwo Otibu of Assin was dissatisfied with his position in the 'Protectorate', and intrigued with the Asantehene to bring his state again under Ashanti suzerainty. He went the length of accepting from Kumasi a gift of 400 ounces of gold, well knowing that its acceptance in such circumstances was an admission of his vassalage to Ashanti. Needless to say, his action was not taken with his people's approval, and was therefore quite unconstitutional.[7] The matter came to the Governor's knowledge, and he sent a soldier to Otibu to summon him to Cape Coast for investigation. This soldier was detained by Otibu, and a detachment of troops was then sent to arrest the chief. He was tried at Cape Coast, found guilty, and sentenced to deposition and imprisonment for life. After sentence had been passed, however, the Fante and Assin chiefs pleaded for mercy, and he was restored to his stool on giving pledges for his future behaviour.

Unfortunately for Otibu, the matter could not end there. He had accepted the Asantehene's money, and had to go through with his bargain. After his recent narrow escape he dared not openly appeal for Ashanti assistance; and he planned with the Asantehene

[6] Claridge and Fuller say that Commander Hill had committed a gross breach of courtesy in omitting to inform the Asantehene that he had assumed the Governorship in February that year. Crooks, however (p. 298), prints his letter to the Asantehene of 28th February. It seems that he did inform the Asantehene and sent the customary presents, though his letter was perhaps unduly curt in tone, and the tone of the Asantehene's reply shows that he felt it so.
[7] This incident is described in Claridge, I, 486-93; documents are printed by Crooks on 328-30 and 332-4.

that matters should be so arranged that he should appear to be the victim of force. The plan was that an Ashanti party should be sent through the Assin country to attend the funeral celebrations of the Denkyerahene, who had recently died. On its way back to Ashanti the party was to kidnap Otibu and as many of his chiefs and people as it could take, and rush them north over the Pra into Ashanti territory.

In March 1853 the Ashanti party, some 300 strong, arrived in Assin under the command of a chief named Akyeampon. Otibu took care to keep out of the way on their southward march; but the chief at Fosu took on himself the responsibility of stopping them, saying that he could not allow so large an armed party to pass without the Governor's permission. When the messenger from Fosu reached Cape Coast, the Governor at once sent up a British officer with a small detachment of troops, and Akyeampon was told that he could not be allowed to take his men to Denkyera. Meanwhile the chief of Fosu and his colleagues suspected the truth, and arrested Otibu and his accomplice Gabiri. Before sending them to Cape Coast, the Assin chiefs confronted them with Akyeampon, who lost his temper and revealed the whole plot. The two chiefs were at once sent down to Cape Coast, but even although the whole scheme was now exposed, Akyeampon seems to have clung to the hope that he could do by force what he had failed to do by cunning. He made excuses for postponing his return across the Pra, and more and more reinforcements came to join him until his force swelled to 6,000 men. Against this force Ensign Brownell, the British officer who had been sent to investigate, had only forty men, though he was afterwards reinforced by Ensign Hill with forty-six more.

Matters began to look serious. The Fante people began to arrest every Ashanti trader they could lay hands on, and in a short time 400 were in custody. The Government levied a Fante army, and sent for detachments of troops from Sierra Leone and elsewhere. Ensign Brownell with immovable countenance delivered an ultimatum to Akyeampon, demanding that the Ashanti should recross the Pra within twenty-four hours under pain of war; and orders from Kumasi very opportunely reached Akyeampon ordering him to withdraw. The incident thus ended peaceably. The Ashanti army recrossed the Pra on 10th April, nearly three weeks after their arrival at Fosu; on the 18th the wretched Otibu and Gabiri were beheaded in the allied camp at Dunkwa.

Though this unpleasant incident was thus closed, nothing had been settled about the underlying causes of ill feeling between Ashanti and the British. The Asantehene himself had no wish for war, but he, like all his chiefs, felt that Assin and the other states would still have been serving him if it had not been for his defeat at Akantamasu. The British felt that his dissatisfaction at the treaty of 1831 was the real trouble, and at the end of 1853 a messenger was sent to Kumasi to ask the Asantehene whether he would rather keep to the old treaty or make a new one. Kwaku Dua in his reply laid all the blame for the recent incident upon the two Assin chiefs, ignoring the fact that Akyeampon had blurted out the whole truth to Ensign Brownell; however, he disclaimed any desire to make a new treaty.

The years 1854 to 1862 were years of peace in Ashanti, though eventful years in the history of Akim. It will be better to postpone mention of Akim events and to pass straight to the next step in the quarrel between Ashanti and the British.

This occurred in 1862. In the autumn of that year an old Ashanti man named Kwasi Gyani found a gold nugget, and kept it for himself instead of surrendering it to the Asantehene as the law required.[8] He was accused of the offence, and swore the Asantehene's oath that he was innocent; but instead of going to Kumasi to stand his trial he fled to Cape Coast. At the same time there was in Cape Coast on the same errand a slave boy who had escaped from his Ashanti master and begged the Governor not to send him back.

The Governor, Richard Pine, was in a dilemma. In December a formal embassy arrived from Kumasi to demand the surrender of Kwasi Gyani. Among the ambassadors was the bearer of the Golden Axe, a symbolic weapon which was regarded by the Ashanti as having magic power to cut a way through all difficulties and misunderstandings.[9] The slave boy had complicated matters

[8] The Asantehene, like other Akan chiefs, claimed a proportion of the revenue from all gold workings in his country; and in addition, all nuggets above a certain weight were his property, that is to say they were a windfall for the State, not for the finder.
[9] It was not, as was supposed by some British both then and in 1881, a threat of war; Fuller, 151-6.

by swearing the great oath of Ashanti that he would not return there: which made it certain that he would be killed if ever he set foot on Ashanti soil. The old man for his part pleaded that he was innocent of concealing the nugget, and said that the whole case against him was trumped up in order that his wealth might be confiscated by the Ashanti state.

The Governor was greatly embarrassed. His dispatch to the Secretary of State[10] shows clearly that he fully appreciated all the facts of the situation, except perhaps one. He writes:

"there is not a tittle of evidence except the remotest hearsay in support of the allegation, and the accused solemnly denies the charge. He is a man of property, and declares that the King desires only to entrap him, take his head, and afterwards possession of his property.

"The King's messengers offer to swear that the accused will be fairly tried, and even if found guilty, will not lose a hair of his head.

"The old man imploringly cries to me, 'Kill me if you like; that will be better than giving my head to the King.' And no one can assure me that I may rely upon the King's word; yet all would be delighted for me to restore to him his subjects.

"Gladly would I try an experiment, and send back these subjects of Ashantee, for if confidence were once created between this Government and Ashantee, the greatest obstacle in the way of amicable relations between us would be removed; and if against the old man there were the slightest shadow of a *prima facie* case of criminality, my course would be clear; but as it is, I dare not deliver him up, much less the runaway boy. Their blood would be upon my head. And yet I feel that I am estranging, if not exasperating, the most powerful King on this coast, and upon whom, according to his ideas, I am committing a gross injustice."

The one fact which Mr. Pine did not know was that he might rely on the word of the Asantehene. On this point, however, Maclean and Cruikshank are agreed; in their time runaways from Ashanti had been several times given up, on condition that the Ashanti messengers who had come for them swore the great oath

[10] Crooks, 348, 349.

that their lives should be spared, and Cruikshank adds, "There is no instance known of this oath given under such circumstances being violated."[11]

The Government decided not to return the fugitives. In February 1863 a fresh embassy arrived from Kumasi to protest against this decision, and again, as in 1819, the embassy solemnly accused the Government of violating a treaty. No record exists of the text of such a clause; but there seems no doubt that there did exist, either in writing or merely by word of mouth, an understanding to the effect that fugitives should be restored to their own country.[12] Mr. Pine's difficulty was that Kwasi Gyani's offence was according to European eyes insufficiently established, and only a technical one: but it was a serious offence in Ashanti law, and the question of his innocence or guilt had yet to be established. The whole question, for a Governor who had to consider questions of humanity as well as those of policy, was a most difficult one to decide; the audience in the hall at Cape Coast were deeply divided; but it seems that the final decision was the wrong one, and, as Mr. Pine's dispatch quoted above shows, the deciding factor in his mind was that he could not reply on the Ashanti promises.

The Asantehene, as Mr. Pine realized, felt that the British were "committing a gross injustice"; and even if he himself had been inclined to let it pass, he could not have persuaded his council. War was at once determined on; but it could not be at once begun. The Ashanti began buying munitions at Elmina, while the Fante people naturally set themselves to intercept these convoys, even though the countries were not yet at war. Long ago, the Denkyera had allowed Osei Tutu's supply columns to pass through their territory when he was preparing for war against Ntim Gyakari, and the Fante can hardly be blamed for avoiding the Denkyera mistake; nevertheless their interception of these convoys in what was technically a time of peace was another incentive to war. It was March 1863 before the Ashanti invasion took place. It was planned in the usual three columns: a small western column to contain the Wassaw and Denkyera on the west bank of the Pra, a stronger one

[11] On the subject of oaths, see above, p. 125, note 66; and Rattray, *Religion and Art in Ashanti*, chap. XXII. To us with our fuller knowledge of Akan customs than was then available to Europeans, it is inconceivable that the Asantehene should ever violate the great oath.
[12] See the discussion of the evidence in Claridge, I, 505-8.

to advance straight down the main road from Prasu towards Cape Coast, and a third advancing through Akim. On this occasion, the easternmost column was the strongest. This was apparently because the Ashanti had a subsidiary objective in the capture of the Akim Kotokuhene, Agyeman. Agyeman had sheltered the two fugitives on their way to the coast, and had returned an insulting answer when called on to surrender them.[13]

On the British and allied side, the problem was the constant one of finding regular troops to stiffen the Fante and other African levies, and of finding supplies of powder and lead for the lavish expenditure of ammunition which was characteristic of African warfare. A company of the 2nd West India Regiment, which happened to call at Cape Coast on its way home to the West Indies from a spell of duty at Lagos, was detained to strengthen the garrison, and even with this reinforcement, the troops available only amounted to 400 men. Some 15,000 levies were raised, and these allied troops formed two camps, one at Asikuma and the other at Manso. Small naval detachments were landed to garrison the forts, and all the available troops, commanded by Major Cochrane, took up a position at Mankesim.

Meanwhile, the eastern Ashanti column advanced across Akim without opposition, and at the beginning of May fell upon the allied camp at Asikuma and destroyed it. Some of the allies rallied at Bobikuma, some fourteen miles away, and there they were joined by Major Cochrane and his 400 men. The allies were in good spirits, for had made a stubborn resistance at Asikuma, and were encouraged by Major Cochrane's presence to hope for another Akantamasu. The British commander, however, amazed them all by issuing prompt orders for a retreat. The main body retired a few miles to another village, a rearguard left behind at Bobikuma

[13] This story was related two years afterwards by Colonel Conran, who did not arrive in the Gold Coast till August of that year, so is not a first-hand witness. There is, however, no reason to doubt it, though the story is not confirmed by Kotoku tradition. According to Mr. Pine (Crooks, 356), the Ashanti general told him that Agyeman had "insulted and wronged" his father, and that although he had no quarrel with the white men or the Fante, Agyeman's head he must have. The tradition of Ashanti Mampon (Rattray, *Ashanti Law and Constitution*, 240) records a campaign at this time against a chief called Agyeman Nkonto of Akim. The name Nkonto is clearly a nickname given by the Ashanti, for it is an abusive epithet combining the ideas of 'liar' and 'insulter'. Perhaps 'foul-mouthed' would be the nearest English equivalent. This nickname is further evidence of the truth of the story.

was attacked in force and routed, and Major Cochrane himself retired to the seaside village of Mumford.

The moral consequences of this were, of course, disastrous to the allies. The Governor himself went to Ajumako, where a small British detachment had refused to join in the retreat. About 8,000 men gathered round him, and hard things were said about Major Cochrane's behaviour. The Ashanti luckily had not followed up their successes at Asikuma and Bobikuma, so there was still available for service the whole of the Manso contingent, as well as the remains of the army which had been twice defeated. The Ashanti were encamped at Akim Soadru on the Birrim, and even after the mauling the allies had received, they were prepared to advance again against the Ashanti if the Governor or Captain Williams, the commander of the Ajumako detachment, would lead them. At the beginning of June Major Cochrane arrived in the camp, but his force was left behind; and before they could be found and brought into the camp, the Ashanti, realizing that the rainy season was beginning in full severity and remembering the disease and suffering it had brought their armies on previous occasions, struck their camp and returned to Ashanti in triumph. They had not secured the three men they came for, but they had stayed in the 'Protectorate' as long as they wished, had defeated every allied force they met, and returned home at their own time and without opposition.

The Governor saw clearly that this state of things could not be allowed to continue indefinitely. No British or allied troops had ever ventured beyond the Pra, and the force of disciplined troops on the Gold Coast was so small that it could not hope even to defend the settlements without the help of large African levies.[14] These African levies in turn were useless without enormous supplies of powder and lead,[15] far more than could normally be carried in store. The result was that the settlements were always weak against sudden attack; and although, as in this case, there was usually some weeks' warning given not merely by diplomatic negotiations but by

[14] The local forces consisted of the Gold Coast Corps and the militia. The Gold Coast Corps replaced the old Royal African Colonial Corps, which had begun as a European force and had gradually been Africanized as the white troops rapidly died. The Royal African Colonial Corps ceased to exist in 1840. The strength of the Gold Coast Corps was 129 in 1844 and 338 in 1851; the militia, consisting of volunteers from the merchants and their staff, were sixty-two strong in 1844 (Crooks, 269, 292-4, 302-4, 316-19, 345-7, 351-2).

[15] Brackenbury and Huyshe, *Fanti and Ashanti*, 78-9.

the Ashanti purchases of ammunition, the exact moment and route of the attack could never be foretold. The forest of the Pra screened all the Ashanti dispositions from view until the moment they entered the 'Protectorate', and once the Ashanti had retired again across the river they were safe from pursuit. The remedy was plain: the Ashanti must be followed into their own country, and there dealt such a blow that they would give up the idea that the 'Protectorate' was at their disposal whenever they chose to attack it. Mr. Pine therefore proposed to the British Government that he should be allowed to organize an expedition into Ashanti.

The question then remained, what was to be done with Ashanti when the British flag had been carried to Kumasi? Claridge thinks there could be no intermediate stage between annexation and a continuance of the *status quo*; and the *status quo* implied that the Ashanti were liable at any time to make war in great force because of some incident like those of the Kommenda people and Kwasi Gyani, or to reassert a claim to Assin or Denkyera. But it should not have been impossible to make a fresh treaty, profiting by the experience of 1817 and 1831 and by a fuller understanding of Ashanti law and custom. The Asantehene had already made it clear that he would welcome a British Resident,[16] and there seems no reason why British influence should not have gradually developed in Kumasi until Ashanti and the 'Protectorate' were able to live at peace. This natural development never took place partly through a false economy, which continually grudged the staff and the money which would have been necessary to maintain a permanent Resident in Kumasi[17]: partly through the British persistence in regarding Ashanti as a savage and despotic state which could not be trusted: and partly through what Sir Hugh Clifford calls the British Government's "characteristic vacillating caution,"[18] which caused it to hesitate long between the contradictory aims of keeping the Asantehene strong so that he could control his people and keeping him weak so that he could not become a nuisance.

[16] Crooks, 337-8; a Resident was actually appointed in 1854. There had been Hutchison and Dupuis forty years before; but the appointment had lapsed.

[17] One of Mr. Pine's difficulties in 1862 was that he had at the moment no European civilian staff whatever, but was left to run the country single-handed, with the assistance of the military and naval officers who happened to be available. Long after this time, in the 'eighties, the Government was embarrassed over and over again in its dealings with Ashanti and other states by having nobody available to send to them.

[18] In his preface to Claridge, pp. vii., viii.

The Government in London refused permission for an advance into Ashanti; but refused it in a hesitating way which suggested that the Government might easily be persuaded to change its mind. The Secretary of State admitted that Major Cochrane's feebleness must have been a great setback to the confidence felt by the people in the British Government; but, he wrote, " . . . the proposal of a regular invasion to be made upon that nation (the Ashanti) and of a march upon their capital, is too serious to admit of my encouraging it. I will merely say at present that I should feel very averse to its adoption, except in case of overruling necessity, and also after the report of some more competent military commander than anyone from whom there has yet been an opportunity of obtaining an opinion at the Gold Coast." [19]

Meanwhile, information received from stray reports led the Governor to fear that another Ashanti invasion was to be expected during the next dry season, and the British authorities on the coast again formed the plan of going into the bush to meet it. Small Ashanti parties were still south of the Pra, and partly to clear them out of the 'Protectorate', and partly to impress the Ashanti by a bolder advance than had ever been made before, it was decided to make a British post on the bank of the Pra at Prasu. The Government in London wavered. It did not send out a 'competent military commander' to investigate the situation and report; but it sent out reinforcements of troops under Lieutenant-Colonel Conran. These men were from the 4th West India Regiment, and with detachments from the 2nd and 3rd battalions which had been brought from Sierra Leone and the Gambia, they brought the strength of the troops to 700 men. Still further reinforcements were promised. The 4th West India arrived in August, and stayed in Cape Coast till the end of the rains; and in January 1864 they all moved up to Prasu and began to occupy themselves in constructing defences.

The British Government now changed its mind, and gave permission for the advance into Ashanti; but the permission was given in such terms that only the boldest and most enterprising officer would be likely to avail himself of it. The Secretary of State's dispatch of 21st December, 1863 hoped that it would not be necessary to enter Ashanti in order to punish the Ashanti forces; but it

[19] Crooks, 360; dispatch of 22nd August, 1863.

was desirable to remove the bad impression given by their unrestricted roaming about the 'Protectorate' the previous season,
and to deter them from trying to repeat their performance; and
the Governor was not to regard himself as absolutely prohibited
from entering Ashanti in any circumstances, if such an advance
would secure the peace of the 'Protectorate' and would be safer,
and less costly, and more decisive than waiting for an Ashanti
attack.[20]

Mr. Pine was prepared to make the attempt, and waited only for
the promised reinforcements; he had told the Government that he
would need 2,000 troops, and he was waiting to receive them.
Meanwhile the dry season went on, and soon the necessary work at
Prasu was finished. By the middle of March the troops had nothing
to do but wait; the rain began early, and the men began to go
down with fever and dysentery; and by the end of the month
conditions in the camp were so bad that the Cape Coast authorities
ordered half the troops back to the sea-coast to recuperate. As soon
as they had reached the coast the long-expected reinforcement
arrived, nearly 700 men from the 1st and 4th West India.[21] The
new arrivals were sent straight up to garrison the camp, in the belief
that being fresh to the country they would stand 'the climate'
better; but in a very short time they also succumbed to the malaria
and yellow fever and dysentery amid the misery and boredom of an
isolated camp in the midst of the dark dripping forest. The men
began to die; the Government became alarmed; and the troops
were withdrawn. The epitaph of the expedition was supplied in a
succinct comment by Kwaku Dua; "The white man brings his
cannon to the bush, but the bush is stronger than the cannon."[22]
Downing Street expressed itself more diffusely: "It may be hoped
that the display of force made during the last few months will not
have been without its due effect, both on the Ashantee enemy and
on the friendly Native Chiefs, and that the cessation of the rains
may not bring with it the necessity for a renewal of warlike

[20] Claridge, I, 525.
[21] Claridge, I, 527; Crooks, 360, 361. The total force collected on the Gold Coast
amounted to sixty-four officers and 1,745 men; by 1st May, 1864 thirteen officers
and forty-five men had died, twenty-two officers and eighty-two men were ill, a
total casualty list of over half the officers and seven per cent of the men. It must
be remembered that nearly all these casualties would have occurred in six weeks,
after the middle of March; and the rainy season might be expected to last until
October. These returns are given in Crooks, 364-5.
[22] Claridge, I, 529; Crooks, 362.

preparations on your part to defend yourself or the friendly Native population from wanton attack." From the Asantehene's remark we may infer that the hopes of Downing Street were not fulfilled.

Nobody on the Gold Coast expected the hopes of Downing Street to be fulfilled. It was only through the personal influence of Kwaku Dua that the Ashanti refrained from invading the 'Protectorate' again at the end of 1864. There were sundry negotiations for peace, and a proper embassy was sent down from Kumasi at the end of 1865 to conclude a treaty. The chance, however, was thrown away by Colonel Conran, who issued as Governor a bombastic proclamation that Ashanti had sued for peace and that he was prepared to grant it. The Asantehene was furious at the suggestion that he had sued for peace, and at once broke off the negotiations, declaring that he would talk no more of peace till Kwasi Gyani was given up to him. He did not again, however, invade the 'Protectorate', preferring to act against the British indirectly by giving assistance to the Anlo, who were engrossed in one of their frequent quarrels with the people of Ada and other coast towns, and had been brought into war with the British. In April 1867 he died, like Osei Bonsu a wise and peaceful ruler who had spent nearly the whole of his reign in war through what he regarded as British perfidy.

Akim

After the allied victory over the Akwamu at the Nsaki river in 1733, the history of Akim and Akwapim consists of constant wars against the Ashanti in an attempt to break away from the Ashanti empire; these attempts were generally unsuccessful, and Akim contingents regularly served in the Ashanti army.

It was the Akim Abuakwa that were conspicuous in this long resistance. The Akim Bosome served Ashanti faithfully right up to the Adinkera war of 1818, and it was their warrior chief Koragye Ampaw, who distinguished himself so much at the battle of the Tain river, that brought them down to their present home on the Birrim.[23] As for the Akim Kotoku, they were clinging to the hills of northern Akim and Ashanti-Akim, nearer the centre of the Ashanti

[23] Bosome tradition.

power; and although they frequently joined Akim Abuakwa in its wars against Ashanti, they seldom shared in its periods of independence.

The Akim Abuakwa were often at war with Ashanti during the eighteenth century; there were at least six wars from 1700 to the death of Osei Kojo in 1781. The Ashanti did not succeed in forcing the Akim to pay tribute; but it is significant that in the first Fante war the Akim Abuakwa supplied a contingent to the Ashanti army, led by their paramount chief Atta Wusu Yiakosan in person. We have seen how in 1811 Atta Wusu revolted against a fresh call to service and fought a successful campaign against Ashanti until his death of smallpox; and how the Ashanti general Amankwa Abinowa, more by luck than judgment, defeated his successor Kwadwo Kuma.

At the time of Akantamasu, Akim Abuakwa was ruled by a woman, Dokuwa. She and her principal chiefs joined the alliance against Ashanti, and an Akim Abuakwa contingent fought on the allied left wing at Akantamasu. The victory at Akantamasu meant, of course, the end of all Ashanti suzerainty over Akim Abuakwa, and the prestige of queen Dokuwa rose high. It was at this time that many of the outlying Akim settlements commended themselves to the paramount stool of Akim Abuakwa, so that the Abuakwa state became consolidated.

Meanwhile in 1824 the Akim Kotoku, who had been settled for more than fifty years at Dampon on the right bank of the upper Pra, seized the opportunity of breaking away from Ashanti. They warned Dokuwa that an Ashanti force under Kwaku Biri was about to advance through Akim towards Accra. Dokuwa sent an urgent appeal to Ado Dankwa the Akwapimhene to join the Akim forces, and a combined army met Kwaku Biri at Asene on the north bank of the Pra.[24] The battle lasted two days; on the first day the main Akim division was driven back by the Ashanti attack, but when the battle was renewed the next morning the situation was saved by the Akwapim contingent, who worked round the flank of the Ashanti and took them in the rear. The Ashanti force was crushed, its general being killed; and thenceforth Akim Kotoku, like Akim

---

[24] That is Asene Krofoso, near Obogu and the Kotoku capital of Dampon; not the better-known Asene near Oda on the Birrim. The old road from Kumasi to Accra passed east of the lake, but instead of going through the Birrim gap went round the western end of the Atewa hills in which Kibi stands.

Abuakwa, was free from Ashanti rule.[25] The Kotoku signalized their victory by moving from Dampon to a new capital, Gyadam in the Birrim gap.

In 1860 the Abuakwa and the Kotoku quarrelled; "over some disputed gold nuggets", according to one tradition.[26] This probably means that the Abuakwahene Atta Obiwom was claiming some sort of suzerainty over the Kotoku and demanding a share of mining profits. The Kotoku at Gyadam were after all dwelling on land which had been ceded to them by the Abuakwa; and there is no commoner source of dispute today than a situation such as this. It is possible for a tribe to live on land belonging to one stool, and to owe allegiance to a different stool, and it is easy to see the confusion which may arise. Moreover, the Kotoku were a powerful tribe, but they had been a good deal scattered in the wars; and various splinters of the tribe had found it convenient to commend themselves to the British and had been arbitrarily attached by the British to the Abuakwa stool.[27] This led to a good deal of ill feeling between the two stools, and the Kotokuhene Agyeman seems to have been a man of overbearing character, likely to inflame any bad feeling rather than to soothe it. The upshot was that the Akim Abuakwa attacked Gyadam, and after a two days' battle the Kotoku abandoned the town, and migrated forty miles south-west to a point on the Birrim near its junction with the Pra. Here they bought land from some of the neighbouring Abuakwa divisions and from the Akim Bosome, and built themselves a new town, which was named Nsuaem (i.e. 'a slice'—because it was a slice cut off other people's land) but later renamed Oda in memory of their former capital north of the Pra.[28] All this fighting and migration left the Akim country in a state of considerable confusion; Abuakwa and Kotoku villages were mixed up with each

[25] Kukurantumi tradition. The Akwapim seem to have been successful with their flanking tactics; for another instance see the battle of Datsutagba, below, p. 228. According to Begoro tradition, the allied army was commanded by the Begoro chief, Awua Panin. Ado Dankwa, the Akwapimhene, grumbled a good deal at Dokuwa's choice of a commander, saying that Awua was a braggart who would never do anything. But, Begoro adds, they won the battle nevertheless; though from the Kukurantumi account Ado Dankwa himself was mainly responsible for the victory, so that his opinion of Awua Panin may have been just. But the allied army was almost certainly commanded, not by Awua Panin of Begoro, but by Kofi Aberante Panin of Kukurantumi.
[26] This is mentioned in the neutral tradition of Akim Bosome.
[27] Kotoku tradition. See p. 199, note, 17, above.
[28] From official records and Bosome tradition.

other, and there were a good many anomalies such as people living on Abuakwa land but owing political allegiance to Kotoku and vice versa.

The Ewe States—Anlo and Krepi

The history of the Anlo during the century from 1750 to the middle of the nineteenth century was troubled by frequent wars with Ada and other western neighbours. The primitive troubles over fishing rights in the Volta were aggravated by disputes caused by slave-raids and slave-trading. In 1750 a great war broke out between the Anlo and the Ada. The Ada were assisted by Akwapim and Akim Abuakwa, and a large allied army, under the command of Twum Ampoforo Apraku the Abuakwahene and Sekyiama Tenten the Akwapimhene, attacked Anlo.[29] The Anlo were defeated in a battle at Nonobe, and had to abandon their capital town of Anloga to the enemy; but they were fortunate in capturing both the leaders of the enemy force. They then discovered a successful general called Anyamakpa, who wiped out the shame of their defeat by a series of victories which forced the enemy to evacuate Anlo territory and scatter in confusion. It was not till 1767 that peace was made; Twum Ampoforo was restored to his people, but the Krepi shot Sekyiama Tenten instead of surrendering him according to the treaty.[30]

In 1776 the Anlo resumed the war, and the lower part of the Volta valley was again devastated in several years of fighting, in which on the whole the Anlo had the advantage. In 1783 a Danish trader was attacked and robbed by an Anlo party, and the Danish governor of Christiansborg determined to crush the Anlo once and for all. The war that followed is known to the Anlo people as the Sagbadre war, Sagbadre or 'swallow' being the local nickname of the Danish trader who was the occasion of the Danish intervention. The Danish authorities raised a force in Accra, Ada, Akwapim and Krobo, and the Anlo country was overrun and completely conquered. The treaty of peace was signed in June 1784; the Anlo agreed to allow a Danish fort to be built at Keta, and promised to keep the roads open for trade. Fort Prinzenstein was completed

[29] Claridge, I, 222; Anlo and Akwapim tradition confirm his account and add details.
[30] Akwapim tradition; this is the only evidence that the Krepi were engaged in the war.

and occupied that same year, Fort Konigstein at Ada being built at the same time. Three years later the Danes built Fort Augustaborg at Teshi to guard their land communications with Christiansborg; they had already for fifty years possessed a fort, Fort Friedensborg, at Ningo.[31]

Very soon after the establishment of these new forts the Danish Government, in 1792, prohibited the slave trade, and thereby brought itself into a very difficult situation; for the Anlo and other neighbouring peoples persisted in carrying on the trade, and the Danes had not sufficient force to stop it.

In 1839 a Portuguese slave trader who was operating in the district round the mouth of the Volta was attacked by the Danish authorities, but was released on undertaking to abandon the trade. Three years later, however, he was at it again, and this time was lucky to escape from the party sent after him. In 1844 the Danish sergeant who was in command at Fort Prinzenstein found the indefatigable Portuguese openly defying the Danish authority by marching a gang of slaves past the fort. He sent out a party of troops, who stopped the slave gang and brought the slaves into the fort. The owner promptly went to the Keta men and persuaded them to help him; they forced their way into the fort, recaptured the slaves and took them home in triumph.

The Danish commander sent for the chief of Keta to come to the fort and explain this riot. The chief refused to come, and the sergeant sent a party of men to fetch him, who killed the chief and burnt his house. The Keta men naturally at once attacked the fort; the sergeant sent to Christiansborg for reinforcements, and meanwhile did what he ought to have done sooner: he asked the Anlo chief to mediate between himself and the Keta men. The Anlo chief and his counsellors came, and advised the Keta men to be content with taking money compensation for the death of their chief; but finding the Keta men obdurate they went home again and left the war to continue. Eventually the sergeant was killed in a sortie, and the Keta men were content.[32]

[31] Claridge, I, 222, and Ewe tradition.
[32] Claridge, I, 457, 458, and Ewe tradition. It is important to bear in mind that relations between Keta and the Anlo at this time seem to have been like those between Cape Coast and the Fante. Keta was akin to the Anlo, but was actually independent, though tending more and more to identify itself with the Anlo. In between the killing of the Danish sergeant and the Anyako war, Ewe tradition records another curious little war. The sergeant's successor in command of the

Meanwhile the promised reinforcements arrived from Christians-borg, and set themselves to repair the fort, which was almost incapable of defence. Hitherto the Danes had been quarrelling not with the Anlo nation, but with the town of Keta itself. There was, therefore, no reason why other Anlo towns should not trade with the Danes; and a party from the important town of Anyako, on the north bank of the lagoon, came to sell shells for making lime. A quarrel broke out between them and the troops, several of the Anyako men, including their chief Dzokoto, were wounded, and the Anyako men promptly blockaded the fort. The Keta people, of course, joined them, and the Danish garrison, seeing that the situation was grave, sent a messenger to make his way to Christians-borg and ask for reinforcements.

The messenger got through the blockading force and reached Christiansborg safely. The Governor, Mr. Schmidt, at once set out himself with 120 men, and he and his force were allowed to enter the fort. There was little or no fighting, but the blockade was strictly maintained, and the Alata or Lagos quarter of the town was burnt by the besiegers because its inhabitants were found to be secretly selling food to the garrison. Meanwhile the guns of the fort bombarded the town, and what with the bombardment and the fire the whole town of Keta was destroyed. The garrison, how-ever, were in dire straits for food when a French warship, the *Abeille,* happened to arrive. The governor attempted to escape to her, but was wounded and had to turn back; the next man, how-ever, was luckier, and swam out to the ship safely. The French then opened fire on the town to cover a landing party, and took the governor back to Christiansborg; there he collected a large force of Accra and other troops, and made great preparations for a punitive expedition. A Danish warship was sent to accompany

fort asked the Anlo to help him against the Keta townsfolk. For some reason the Anlo did not wish to refuse, but they made a private arrangement with the Keta men to load the guns on both sides with powder only, and at the end of this bloodless warfare both sides were to share the Danish subsidy. The plan failed through the treachery or the carelessness of some of the Keta men, who fired with ball and killed some Anlo men and took a few prisoners. The Anlo then called in the help of the Akwamu and utterly defeated the Keta men and forced them to abandon the town, which they themselves later occupied. This ingenious, though unsuccessful, scheme for profiting from the white man recalls the so-called Kotoku-Twerebo war (powder-bag and flint war) of 1777, in which an exactly similar arrangement was made between the native allies of the Dutch and Danes of Accra. This war, like the Anlo-Keta war, ended in bloodshed. The Anlo-Keta war is not recorded by Claridge, but it must have occurred about 1845.

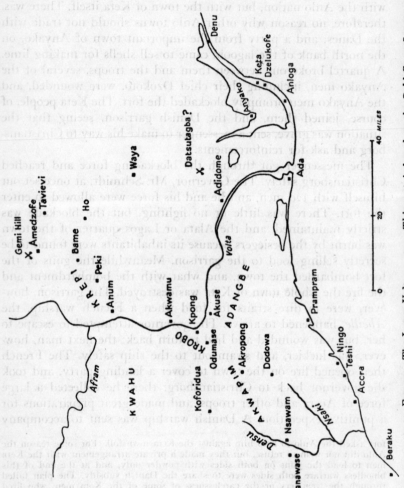

FIG. 10. The Lower Volta. This map is based on the Gold Coast Survey

the land forces, and the Anlo people submitted without further fighting. The Danish Government imposed heavy fines on the people, and compelled the slave-traders who had been the occasion of the trouble to abandon the district.

This series of operations lasted till 1847; the people made no attempt to rebuild the town of Keta as long as Danish rule lasted. It was not till the British took over from the Danes in 1850 that a man named Lagbo ventured to rebuild the town, and it was reoccupied by the Anlo.[33]

The slave trade continued to disturb the Ada-Keta district under British rule. The ringleader in this traffic during the sixties was a man called Geraldo de Lema. He had been the slave of a Brazilian slave-dealer of that name whose headquarters were close to Keta. On his master's death in 1862, Geraldo took possession of his master's name, property and wife, and carried on the business.

In 1865 Geraldo de Lema got into trouble at Ada, and the people drove him out of the town and took his slaves away from him. He went to the Anlo, and induced them to take up his quarrel for the sake of working off old scores against their traditional rivals of Ada. His army was unable to cross the Volta to attack the town, for the boats of two British warships held the estuary. He and his men thereupon marched north and plundered and burnt the town of Kpong on the west bank of the Volta. This attack on the British 'Protectorate' naturally brought the Government into the matter. The Anlo having refused an offer to settle the matter peacefully,[34] a large force of Accra and Akwapim troops was raised, and advanced to the district at the Volta mouth with the intention of invading the Anlo territory beyond the river.

On 17th March, 1866 the two armies came in sight of each other on opposite banks of the river near Adidome. The British commander bombarded the Anlo camp, which the Anlo at once abandoned; and he thereupon proposed to cross the river and follow them. This, however, was impossible as the council of chiefs disagreed among themselves and the majority refused to undertake an advance into the enemy's country. A fortnight was wasted in these wranglings, and the senior British officer, Captain Humphrey of the 4th West India regiment, retired in disgust with

[33] Ewe tradition and Claridge, I, 458.
[34] Anlo tradition.

his detachment of regular troops, leaving the allies to run the campaign as they chose.

Eventually the British District Commissioner, who stayed with the force, persuaded the leaders to cross the river, and on 3rd April the whole army advanced into the forest of fan-palms which lay on the opposite bank. They marched with little precaution, and on the 12th were suddenly attacked on three sides by the Anlo. The carriers were stampeded, and their flight threw the fighting column into utter confusion; baggage was abandoned, and guns and rockets could not be got into action for the crush. For a time it looked as though the allied force would be utterly defeated. Two things saved it. One was that the Anlo ran out of ammunition and had to do the best they could with small stones. The other was that the Akwapimhene Koa Adade, who was in the rear of the column, led his men to the flank of the battle, circled round, and brought a surprise attack against the Anlo rear. This made the fight more even, and after two hours more the Anlo gave way and retired.[35]

This Pyrrhic victory of Datsutagba, as the Ewe people call it, ended the campaign. Had the Government followed it up by offering again the peace terms that it had offered four months before, it is likely that the Anlo might have accepted them. It was not, however, till October that the Government made any move; and by then the Anlo had accepted an offer of alliance from the Asantehene Kwaku Dua, and an Ashanti army, under a general called Nantwi, had entered the Krepi country in earnest of the promised Ashanti assistance.[36]

The Krepi state was traditionally hostile to the Akwamu, and hence to the Anlo, who were Akwamu allies. Krepi was in a weak position, for its natural allies, Accra, Ada and Akwapim, were all far away on the other side of the Volta, and thus it could never expect from them any direct help against its near enemies.

Krepi seems to have arisen as a composite state formed by a

[35] Anlo tradition, and Claridge, I, 549-51; also Ellis, 237-42. The name of the Akwapimhene was not Kwow Dadi, as given by Ellis and Claridge, but Kao Adade, meaning Adade's slave; Adade being a god to whom he had been dedicated, presumably by his mother in thankfulness for his birth (Akwapim tradition).
[36] Nantwi appears to have been soon superseded by another general, Adu Bofo, who is much better known. Akwamu and Anlo tradition both mention him, however.

fusion of the Kyerepon people of the Anum hills with the Ewe-speaking invaders from Notsie. When the Akwamu were driven to cross the Volta and enter this hill country, it seems that they acquired some sort of power over the reluctant Ewe and Kyerepon tribes, and under the weight of Akwamu rule the Krepi state tended to split into its two main component parts, the Ewe-speaking and the Kyerepon-speaking sections.

It was in 1829 that the first attempt was made by the Krepi to break away from Akwamu; in that year one important Ewe-speaking town rebelled, but an overwhelming force came against it and the rebellion was easily crushed. The great Akwamuhene, Akoto Kwaafo (c. 1830-70) contrived somehow to enlist the help in this campaign of Accra and of some Akwapim and Akim stools, states which were by no means frequent allies of the Akwamu. Peki itself, and even some of the Kyerepon towns of Krepi, remained faithful to Akwamu, and the war was soon over.

Four years later, however, Peki and other Krepi towns succeeded in breaking away from Akwamu. They had been called up for service in the Akwamu army in a long and dreary war which flickered up and down the plains for three years. The chief of Peki, Kwadjo Dei I, accusing his overlord of deliberately prolonging not only the war but also the peace negotiations, seized the opportunity of deserting after a decisive victory in the field. Akoto at once broke off the campaign and followed Kwadjo Dei towards Peki; he was repulsed at Bame and retired to Waya to collect an army. Once again he succeeded in gathering under him a strangely mixed collection of allies, including not only the Anlo but also their old rivals the Ada and a number of Adangbe and Ewe-speaking states. Meanwhile Kwadjo Dei had succeeded in inducing the Kyerepon section of Krepi to join him in renouncing his allegiance. From his base at Waya, south-east of Ho, Akoto advanced again to Bame, drove back the Krepi force, and entered Peki in triumph; but there he was furiously counter-attacked by the Krepi. For a time the battle went decidedly against the Krepi; but then the chief magician of the Akwamu and their allies was killed, and they lost their nerve and broke. This battle at Peki founded Krepi independence.[37]

[37] This account of the wars of 1829 and 1833 is mainly based on Welman, 10-12; the incident of the magician's death is added from Anlo tradition.

The Akwamu, however, were far from giving up hope of recovering the Krepi allegiance. They still retained the character they had had when at Nyanawase,[38] of turbulent neighbours to all around them. They made a habit of waylaying Akim Kotoku traders and robbing them, and eventually they became such a nuisance that the Kotoku men complained to their government, and a member of the Kotoku royal family named Dompre went by the Akwamu road to investigate. Finding from his own experience that the complaints were true, he returned to Akim, brought an army together and attacked Akwamu. Dompre and his force proved such a stubborn foe to the Akwamu that the Krepi people, feeling no doubt like a certain medieval Pope, "Truly the Scots are a cure for the English," threw in their lot with him in the hope of finally crushing the Akwamu who had oppressed them so long.[39] Dompre thus took command of a mixed force, and returned again and again to the attack. He was by no means always successful, but no defeats seemed to prevent him from reappearing from a different direction to fight again. The Akwamu themselves say that it was Dompre's activity that forced them to ask for help from Ashanti. This was the opportunity which the war party in Kumasi seized for sending Nantwi and his army into the Krepi country. His presence there would serve several purposes. It would encourage the Anlo to resist the Ada and the British, and thus keep the south-eastern country a constant source of anxiety to the British Government. It would strengthen the Akwamu against Krepi and Akim; and Akwamu would be a useful ally against Akim and Akwapim, which were certain to be involved in any fresh war with the British. In general, the presence of a strong Ashanti force east of the Volta would be a constant threat to the whole of the eastern frontier of the 'Protectorate', and the alliance with Akwamu meant that the crossing of the river was permanently secured.

When Kwaku Dua died in April 1867 almost the whole of what is now the Colony was on the edge of war. Nantwi with his army was in the Krepi country. The Anlo were in a state of almost

[38] See above, p. 111.
[39] Akwamu tradition. Dompre's exploits have made such a deep impression on Akwamu tradition that the length of his career is almost certainly greatly exaggerated. There was a small Akwamu-Krepi war in or about 1845. Dompre's activity, however, was probably confined to the third and greatest of these wars, the war of 1867 and following years. Dompre himself was a native of Nsawam.

chronic war with their neighbours, and were still technically at least at war with the British. Peace had never been made between Ashanti and the British Government since the Bobikuma and Prasu fiascos. The Fante coast was in a turmoil over the affairs of the exchange between British and Dutch, and the beginnings of the Fante confederation. The moment was one of the most critical in Gold Coast history.

CHAPTER XI

BRITISH, DUTCH AND FANTE, 1863-74

THE campaign of 1863 and 1864 had been such a failure from the British point of view that both Downing Street and the Fante began to give up hope that British rule could ever give the coast proper protection against the Ashanti. Trade was almost at a standstill; the Ashanti were boasting with reason that 'the bush was stronger than the cannon'; the British and the Ashanti were still at war, and there seemed no prospect of reaching any compromise on the questions over which the war had started.

In October 1864 the British Government appointed Colonel Ord, R.E., to visit the four West African colonies.[1] He was instructed to investigate the efficiency of the colonial Governments and the state of their finances, to consider the possibility of closer co-operation between the four colonies and of improving their sea communications, and to consider also the influence of the colonial governments on the African peoples, and their future relationships.[2]

On Colonel Ord's return a Select Committee of the House of Commons was set up to consider his report. He had recommended that the settlements should be maintained and that they should be federated under a Governor-in-chief, who should be stationed at Sierra Leone. With steamship communication it would be possible, as it had not been formerly, for the Governor-in-chief to maintain close enough control over his lieutenants to make such a centralized system workable.

The Select Committee, after considering Colonel Ord's report and hearing evidence from him and from other people concerned, recommended to the Government that Colonel Ord's scheme of federation should be adopted; that it was "not possible to withdraw the British Government, wholly or immediately, from any settlements or engagements on the West African Coast"; but that "all farther extension of territory or assumption of Government,

[1] The island of Lagos had been ceded to Britain in August 1861 and made an independent colony.
[2] Colonel Ord was Governor of Bermuda, and had formerly been in the Gold Coast service, and so was an experienced administrator. His instructions are given in Crooks, 366-8.

or new treaties offering any protection to native tribes, would be inexpedient"; and that the Government should aim at gradually withdrawing from all four colonies, except probably Sierra Leone.[3] These recommendations were adopted by the British Government. They were clearly a compromise between the cautious policy which appealed to many people in England, and perhaps to most members of the Government, and the policy, which commended itself more to the officials on the coast, of maintaining the British position against the Ashanti pressure. The general opinion in England was that the West African colonies were not worth keeping; they were unhealthy, poverty-stricken and perpetually troubled with barbarian raids.[4] The men on the spot saw them in a different light; they saw the advances which were being made in civilization, and they looked forward to a future in which trade and education would penetrate to the interior. Of those who thought in this way, many, like Governor Richard Pine, realized that it was impossible to stand still; that the more the area of the 'Protectorate' developed in European civilization the more would border tribes be attracted into it, and that there could therefore be no limit set to the expansion of British influence, if not of British dominion.

Whether the compromise recommended by the Committee was workable or not, it was never given a fair chance. On the coast itself events moved so rapidly that the compromise policy seemed unworkable and was abandoned. At a later period it was tried in the British dealings with Ashanti; but it was applied so hesitatingly and with so little realization of the real position that it proved disastrous.

On the Gold Coast the text of the resolutions had an unfortunate effect. There were plenty of people who could read them, but few who could properly understand them.[5] There were two passages that caused particular misunderstanding. One was the qualifying phrase 'more and more' in the third resolution:

[3] Crooks, 369-70.
[4] In 1860 the revenue of the Gold Coast, apart from the Parliamentary grant and the poll tax, was £3,947, a decrease of £338 from the previous year; the expenditure was £9,558, an increase of £1,990. The Parliamentary grant was £4,000; the dwindling revenue from the poll tax was barely adequate to balance the budget, and after 1861 the poll tax was abandoned (Crooks, 342, 343).
[5] Semi-educated Africans in the Gold Coast often find difficulty in grasping the full meaning of English subordinate clauses and qualifying phrases. In their own languages, ideas which are thus expressed in English are often expressed by co-ordinated principal clauses.

"That . . . the object of our policy should be to encourage in the natives the exercise of those qualities which may make it possible for us more and more to transfer to them the administration of all the Governments . . ."

The other was the warning given in the fourth resolution that although the 'policy of non-extension' would apply to all new settlements, there might be cases, in dealing with existing settlements, in which the 'policy of non-extension' might not properly apply.

These important qualifications to the general tendency of the resolutions to look forward to the withdrawal of British authority were overlooked or ignored by many African readers. It was commonly supposed in the Gold Coast that the British Government intended to withdraw in the very near future; although one would think that the first resolution was explicit enough on this point:

"That it is not possible to withdraw the British Government, wholly or immediately, from any settlements or engagements on the West African Coast."

This plain statement, unfortunately, was largely neutralized by an announcement of the local authorities that in any subsequent Ashanti invasion, British troops would only be used to defend British settlements, and that the people of the 'Protectorate' must defend themselves.[6]

It is not to be wondered at that the chiefs and people of the 'Protectorate' began to think of organizing themselves in preparation for the withdrawal of the British. There was a good deal of unrest and uneasiness, but only in Cape Coast was there serious trouble. The 'king' of Cape Coast, John Aggrey, proceeded to act as if he thought the British Government on the point of departure. He incited another chief to make open war on a neighbour, and to defy the Government's order to surrender the prisoners he took. He refused to allow any appeals from his judicial sentences to the British courts; and finally he announced that he was raising an army to defend his country. In December 1886 he was arrested, deposed, and exiled; though three years later he was allowed to return to Cape Coast as a private citizen.

The Aggrey case is of no great importance in itself; but I have briefly mentioned it because it is typical of the misunderstandings

[6] Claridge, I, 537.

which were common throughout the period of British rule between the British authorities and one section or another of the Gold Coast people. These affairs followed a regular course. There was nearly always some vacillation or change of policy on the part of the Government, which could be represented by a hostile or prejudiced critic as a broken promise. This was fastened upon by some African leader, who saw in it evidence of a deep-laid plot against the liberties of the subject. A popular agitation followed, or what was represented as such, though the humble farmer or fisherman might know little of the matter in dispute. The Government made little or no effort to explain itself or to counter the hostile propaganda, but carried out its intentions in spite of the outcry. This in turn became fresh evidence of the Government's indifference to the wishes of the people, and the presumption of the Government's evil intentions was strengthened for the next occasion. A great deal of political energy was thus allowed to go to waste, which might have been utilized for constructive work. It was not always entirely the Government's fault. Staff was always short, and officials were moved about far too often. But the real trouble was that the Government as a whole followed no consistent policy. On the one hand, it was committed to a policy of educational expansion and a gradual advance towards self-government. On the other hand, most British officials feared and distrusted educated African leaders, and were all too ready to label them 'agitators' and have nothing to do with them. As literacy advanced, an African Press developed, often scurrilous and irresponsible; it would have been surprising if the untrained and underpaid journalists who ran it had produced anything better. Yet for all its deficiencies, it was a genuine African voice, and inevitably carried an appeal which no Government gazette could hope to rival. It was natural that some of the early manifestations of growing nationalism should be crude and immature. If the Government had recognized this earlier, had set itself more earnestly to explain itself to the people, and had made more effort to enlist the co-operation of educated Africans in state affairs, the country might have been spared some unfortunate misunderstandings. These educated men, looked up to with reverence by the ordinary citizen who had not visited England, yet often repulsed from the service of the African tribal states, turned naturally to politics to become the champions of their fellow-Africans. In politics, however, they found themselves compelled to remain in permanent opposition. Until 1943, when two Africans were first appointed to the Governor's executive council, such men were excluded from office and from any controlling influence on Government policy.

In 1867 the British and Dutch Governments arranged to exchange some of their forts in order to divide the coastline into a Dutch and a British stretch, and to get rid of the inconvenience of having Dutch and British forts mixed together. At some places, such as Accra, there were two forts in the one town. More than once the British had suggested to the Dutch that a uniform customs tariff should be adopted; but the Dutch had refused the suggestion, and as long as the two tariffs were different it was quite impossible to stop the wholesale smuggling.

The treaty was signed on 5th March, 1867.[1] The frontier was fixed at the Sweet River just to the east of Elmina; the British ceded to the Dutch four forts—Beyin, Dixcove, Sekondi and Kommenda—west of the river, and received in exchange the four Dutch forts — Mori, Kormantine, Apam and Accra — to the east. The British ceded to the Dutch also their 'rights of sovereignty and jurisdiction' over Wassaw, Denkyera and Appollonia.

Never was there a greater political mistake. It does not seem that the African peoples concerned were consulted until several months after the whole matter had been settled between the two governments. The cession of the actual forts, of course, was a simple matter. But the cession of the vague rights which were claimed over the African states raised very difficult problems. The Denkyera and Wassaw had been allies of the British against the Ashanti, whereas the Dutch had been steadily neutral; and it was to be expected that these states would be left defenceless by the Dutch against Ashanti vengeance. At various points along the coast there had grown up feuds between the townsfolk living under rival British and Dutch forts, and these feuds would not lapse because the white men chose to come to an agreement between themselves. Moreover, convenient though the Sweet River was as a frontier, it cut right through Cape Coast territory and severed Cape Coast from much of its food supply.

The transfer was to take effect on 1st January, 1868, and in the

[1] Claridge, I, 557ff.

early days of January the four eastern Dutch forts were duly handed over to the British without any trouble. But when the joint Anglo-Dutch commission moved beyond Elmina and tried to transfer the four British forts, trouble began at once. The Kommenda people refused to accept the Dutch flag, and the Commission left them to think it over while they went farther west to try the three remaining forts. At Dixcove and Sekondi the people did not dare to resist, as the guns of the forts commanded the towns; it is clear from later events, however, that at Dixcove at any rate there was as much opposition to the transfer as at Kommenda. At Beyin the people abandoned the town and prepared to resist the transfer of the country by arms.[8]

At the end of January the Commission returned to Kommenda. The chief of Kommenda had in the meantime changed his mind, and agreed to accept the Dutch flag; but he was promptly disowned by his people, and the attempts of the European seamen and others to hoist the Dutch flag in the face of the townsfolk were unsuccessful. In the end the Commission gave up the attempt, and after bombarding the town of Kommenda from their Dutch warship they returned to Elmina.

This was the beginning of a long war between the Kommenda and the Dutch, which flickered on and on, and which the Dutch were quite unable to bring to an end. The Kommenda plundered the Elmina villages: the Dutch made unsuccessful attempts to recapture the town of Kommenda itself, both by land and by naval expeditions; and eventually the Kommenda men became so emboldened by success that they carried a guerrilla warfare right up to the outskirts of Elmina itself.

Meanwhile, a widespread movement was started to help the Kommenda in their resistance, and to help also any other tribe that should be forced to accept Dutch authority against its will. A meeting was held at Mankesim, at which the Fante chiefs and people agreed to help Kommenda against Elmina, and in a short time a Fante army appeared before Elmina and blockaded the town. The states represented at Mankesim included some of the principal Fante states, and also Assin, Wassaw and Denkyera; and

[8] They applied to the British for ammunition to use in the campaign; the British, of course, refused to give them any, but some of the Fante states gave them some. Claridge, I, 565.

this group became known as the Fante Confederation. Cape Coast did not join, but Anomabu did.

The British Government was naturally aghast at the storm the transfer of the forts had raised; and the institution of the Fante Confederation was the crowning blow. The British did all they could to cut off supplies from the Fante army and to persuade the Confederation to dissolve. The Fante reply was simple and crushing. The British had every right to hand over their forts to the Dutch (though even here the Kommenda people had been their landlords and so might have been consulted) but they had no right to expect their allies to accept Dutch rule against their will. In fact, once again the Europeans, both British and Dutch, were faced with the ancient anomaly of their position on the Gold Coast: they had gradually assumed, and continually exercised, so many rights of jurisdiction that they had come to believe that they also held rights of sovereignty. The two phrases are coupled in the treaty of 1867: a fact which shows the confusion in the minds of the authorities. Ever since 1805 the British had steadily maintained to the Asantehene that the Kommenda and others were not their subjects and so were not under their control. Now, however, they expected the Kommenda to acquiesce when the 'Protectorate' which had been exercised over them by the British was transferred to the Dutch. They should not have been surprised at the result.

In April 1868 the people of Cape Coast itself, who had hitherto kept out of the war, were infuriated by an Elmina attack on one of their villages, and a Cape Coast contingent at once marched out to join the blockading army. The British Administrator,[9] Mr. H. T. Ussher, took action against the two Cape Coast chiefs, Kwaku Atta[10] and Kofi Amoa, who commanded the contingent; he declared them outlawed, pulled down their houses, and confiscated their property. Nothing he could do, however, had any effect on the determination of the allies. Mr. Freeman, the Wesleyan missionary, visited the allied camp to persuade them to abandon the war, but for some time he had no success. Eventually, however, after a heavy but indecisive battle outside Elmina, a great

[9] The Gold Coast was at this time under the Governor-in-chief at Sierra Leone; the officer in charge of the Gold Coast was styled the Administrator.
[10] So Claridge calls him; Ellis calls him Kwasi Atta.

part of the Fante force agreed to raise the blockade and leave their quarrel with the Elmina to Mr. Ussher to settle.

A peace conference was then held at Elmina. The terms of peace suggested were that fighting should cease and freedom of trade and intercourse should be resumed between Elmina and the Fante states; and that in return the alliance between Elmina and Ashanti should be suspended for six months. The Elmina representatives naturally accepted these terms; but the Fante Confederation just as naturally refused them. The Ashanti alliance, together with the guns of the Dutch forts, was the chief strength of Elmina; and the Ashanti, unlike the Dutch guns, could reach any tribe that offended their Elmina friends. The fear of an Ashanti invasion was always at the back of the Fante minds; and to suspend the Elmina-Ashanti alliance for six months simply meant that the Ashanti would be free to come down as soon as they could prepare their army. The Fante Confederation therefore refused to consider peace unless the Elmina gave up their Ashanti alliance altogether. This, of course, the Elmina would not do, and the deadlock was complete. The çlose blockade of Elmina was not renewed, but no trade was possible between Elmina and the other towns, and the Elmina farms had been so devastated during the rainy season that the town was very short of food.

This deadlock continued throughout the rainy season of 1868. In October of that year the Governor-in-chief, Sir Arthur Kennedy, arrived from Sierra Leone and tried to induce the Elmina people to give up their Ashanti alliance. He pointed out that Elmina was without a friend on the coast, and would always be friendless as long as the alliance with Ashanti was maintained. The Elmina people, however, after apparently wavering for some time,[11] finally announced that they were determined not to cut their connection with Ashanti. Sir Arthur Kennedy was bitterly disappointed, and on reaching Cape Coast he informed the Fante chiefs that they could do what they liked against Elmina. Thus, as Ellis comments, "in November it became lawful to do that for which in April Kwasi Atta had been outlawed and his property confiscated and destroyed".

---

[11] Ellis and Claridge suspect that their final decision was influenced by the Dutch, who saw in Ashanti their sole source both of trade and of recruits for their army in the East Indies.

In thus persisting in their loyalty, the Elmina people were not by any means quixotic. They were in close touch with Ashanti and had good reason to hope for Ashanti help. For the time being Ashanti could do nothing. Kwaku Dua died in April 1867. For some months after his death there was a good deal of disorder in Ashanti. During the killing of royal attendants in Kumasi to attend the dead Asantehene in the next world, one of the royal family,[12] included in the slaughter the nephew of a distinguished general, Asamoa Nkwanta. Furious at the insult, Asamoa Nkwanta prepared to lead an armed insurrection against Kumasi. After several weeks of negotiations this was avoided, and Asamoa Nkwanta agreed to accept in satisfaction of the feud the death of a near relative of the man who had slain his nephew.[13] He still refused for some months more to enter the palace or to have anything to do with court circles: and his influence in the army was so strong that a serious war would have been most unwise.

This affair in Kumasi delayed the accession of Kwaku Dua's successor. In July, however, Kofi Karikari was enstooled.[14] He was the son of the daughter of Kwaku Dua's sister. Some say that at his accession he promised "My business shall be war"; and although the story may not be true it is certain that for the whole of his reign his business had to be war, whether he wished it or not.

The accession of Kofi Karikari was notified to Elmina in the usual way by the dispatch of a special envoy who was sacrificed in the town, and the Elmina people returned the courtesy by sending a considerable embassy to Kumasi to represent them at the funeral

[12] One of the sons of the dead Asantehene, not strictly in the matrilineal Akan society one of the royal family at all. Fuller points out that it is wrong to say, as Ellis and Claridge say, that custom allows any passer-by to be killed. The men killed are all royal attendants, a fact which makes Asamoa Nkwanta's resentment understandable. There was not even a technical justification for his nephew's death.

[13] Claridge says the killer himself and his two sisters; Fuller, who should be more reliable on such a point, says that the killer himself escaped and was replaced by his uncle.

[14] Rattray would have us call him Kakari; but Karikari is the more familiar form to English ears, and just as accurate, though the second syllable is certainly slurred. Contemporary English writers commonly called him Kalkallee, while the public rejoiced over the name of 'King Coffee'. Kofi is one of seven names which record the day of the week on which a man is born: beginning with Sunday they are, Kwasi, Kwadwo (Kojo), Kwabena (Kobina), Kwaku, Yaw, Kofi, Kwamena. The corresponding names for women are, Akosua, Adwoa (Ejua), Abena, Akua (Ekua), Yaa, Afua (Efua), Amma. Every Akan person bears one of these names.

and installation ceremonies. When the blockade of Elmina began, the Ashanti government did not yet feel secure enough to attempt an invasion in force, but it offered Elmina a small contingent to help in the defence of the town. This offer, however, was declined by the Dutch governor, Colonel Boers.

Towards the end of 1868, however, conditions in Ashanti were so much improved that the Asantehene and his council decided to act in force, so as to relieve Elmina, settle with Krepi and its allies, and conclude the long war with the British which had begun over Kwasi Gyani in 1863 and had never been formally closed. Nantwi's army in the Krepi country was brought up to 30,000 men and placed under the command of a more enterprising general called Adu Bofo. A second general called Akyeampon was sent with a small force, only a few hundreds strong, to organize and take command of the Elmina army. The Asantehene himself, with the main force, was to cross the Pra when all was ready for the triple attack.

The triple attack, however, was delayed. Akyeampon with his small force left Kumasi at the end of 1868. The roads through Fante, Denkyera and Wassaw were all closed by the Fante Confederation, and he was forced to make a long detour to the west in order to outflank their territory and reach the sea-coast through neutral territory. At Krinjabo, at the head of the great lagoon at the mouth of the Tano, in what is now the Ivory Coast, he was detained for several months by the local chiefs. Eventually, after negotiations with Kumasi, they allowed him to proceed, and he reached the sea at Assini. He then turned east, and marched along the coast to Axim, where he arrived in October 1869.

Meanwhile on the other side of the country his colleague Adu Bofo had his hands full. He invaded Krepi in the last few weeks of 1868, but both he and his Akwamu allies found that under Dompre's leadership the Krepi were capable of an exceedingly stubborn resistance. Dompre was defeated more than once, but he returned again and again to the fight, and pressed his attacks hard against the Akwamu capital. But the result of the war could not be in doubt. The Ashanti and the Akwamu, with the assistance of the Anlo and some other southern Ewe tribes, had an overwhelming advantage in numbers, and unless Dompre could obtain help from the traditional enemies of Akwamu on the west bank of the Volta, the war could only end in the utter destruction of the Krepi state.

Dompre's appeals for help to Akwapim, Accra and his own native Akim raised such excitement and tension in the British 'Protectorate' that the acting Administrator, Mr. W. H. Simpson, decided to cross the river himself to try to smooth affairs over. His chief, Sir Arthur Kennedy, had recently visited the Anlo to make peace between them and the Ada people; in November 1868 he had crossed the Volta bar in a Government steamer, and the Anlo were so taken aback at this novel threat that they agreed to make peace and to refer all future disputes to the Governor's arbitration.[15] Mr. Simpson, as the Secretary of State, wrote tartly, "appeared to have considered himself bound or at liberty to follow up what he supposed to be your policy, by proceeding to the scene of the dispute and endeavouring to repeat or supplement your work".

Mr. Simpson's diplomacy was unsuccessful. He went to Odumase, a few miles on the safe side of the Volta, and thence invited the Akwamuhene to visit him. The Akwamuhene refused, and Mr. Simpson crossed the river to visit Akwamu. The Akwamu seemed disposed to yield to his persuasions, and he flattered himself that he would succeed in detaching them from the Ashanti alliance; but Adu Bofo heard of the negotiations and hurried to the spot, and the Akwamu promptly changed their minds and detained Mr. Simpson as a prisoner. As he was an ambassador, however, the Ashanti general would not hear of his being killed, and did not wish to keep him as a prisoner for fear of provoking a war with the British before the Ashanti were prepared. After five uncomfortable days, therefore, Mr. Simpson was released, much to the disgust of the Akwamu.

This was in March and April 1869. After Mr. Simpson's release fighting continued on the east bank of the river; and early in June the Ashanti attacked and took possession of the two towns of Anum and Ho, at each of which there was a German mission station. At Anum there were two missionaries, Messrs. Ramseyar and Kühne, Ramseyar having with him his wife and baby son.

[15] "A treaty," wrote the Secretary of State, "which, I collect, they disregarded as soon as you had left the river." Crooks, 386; the whole dispatch, from which I have quoted also above, is a scathing rebuke of poor Simpson for his imprudence; not so much for venturing into the enemy camp (which might have succeeded), but for entering into all sorts of commitments on behalf of the British Government.

This little party waited in the mission station till the Ashanti took possession of it, and were then arrested and sent to Kumasi. The missionaries at Ho had been more prudent, and abandoned the station before the Ashanti arrived; but a Frenchman, M. Bonnat, the trading manager of the station,[16] had stayed with the idea of selling powder and lead to the Ashanti. His enterprise was ill-timed; for the Ashanti burnt the mission buildings, helped themselves to his stores without paying for them, and took him also prisoner to Kumasi. The unfortunate missionaries had an unpleasant journey to Kumasi, a march of about two months. The commander of their escort was a bully, and although the rank and file treated them with as much consideration as they could, the prisoners suffered greatly through the privations of the hard march. The child died before they reached Kumasi. The Asantehene treated them with every kindness once they arrived, allowing them to move about freely in the town and giving them an ample subsistence allowance.

The capture of these European prisoners placed the Asantehene in a strong bargaining position, and he took full advantage of it. We need not trace in detail the long and unsuccessful negotiations that went on from the time of their capture in the middle of 1869 until the outbreak of war in November 1872. These negotiations became tangled up with the discussions about the position of Elmina and the ancient rent which was payable to the Ashanti in respect of Elmina castle. The British Government was in a very difficult position with regard to the captive missionaries. They were not British subjects, nor had they been taken on British territory; the campaign in the course of which they were taken was being fought between the Ashanti and various tribes who were neither British subjects nor allies of the British, and was a campaign which the British Government — as poor Mr. Simpson found — was at great pains to keep away from. It was difficult, therefore, for the Governor to take any official action in the matter; and there could, of course, be no question of any attempt to rescue them by force. The only hope lay in diplomacy.

The question of Elmina was exceedingly complicated. Everyone

[16] The Basel and Bremen missions always included a trading concern, the profits of which helped to finance the mission's religious work. Not every mission station by any means had a store attached, but there were stores at both Anum and Ho. Kühne was the trading manager at Anum.

knew that the Asantehene regarded it as to all intents and purposes part of his kingdom; his language varied between describing the Elmina people as his 'friends and relations'[17] and saying that "the Dutch delivered the Elmina to him as his own".[18] Dutch authority in Elmina had so diminished that the Netherlands Government, disappointed at the failure of the exchange scheme with Britain, was making up its mind to abandon the Gold Coast altogether. The wars and the general unrest had throttled their trade. They were utterly unable to put a stop to the guerrilla warfare of the Kommenda men. Akyeampon, whose march from Axim along the coast to Elmina had been accompanied by killings and other barbarities under the very eyes of the Dutch authorities,[19] was in Elmina with an Ashanti force. His presence was naturally a great encouragement to the Elmina people, and the Dutch authorities in the castle had no control over them whatever.[20] It was known, moreover, that another contingent, 5,000 strong, was on its way to reinforce him.

The Netherlands Government therefore decided to give up its Gold Coast possessions, and in November 1869 negotiations began between the two governments for the cession of the Dutch forts to the British. The British Government was very willing to acquire them, if it could be sure that the acquisition would not bring fresh troubles. This caution was stronger in London than in Cape Coast. In Cape Coast it was felt that if the British controlled the whole coastline from Beyin to Keta it would be fairly easy to stop the incessant bickering between Elmina and the Fante towns, to impose a uniform customs tariff, and to stop smuggling; the old alliance between the British and the western tribes could be

[17] In a letter of 19th August, 1871; Claridge, I, 612.
[18] In a letter of 24th November, 1870; Fuller, 105-6.
[19] This strong phrase is justified by the facts. At Axim, Sekondi and Elmina, Akyeampon put to death sundry Fante whom he found in the towns right in front of the forts; and the Dutch commandant at Axim had great difficulty in persuading him not to kill two Englishmen whom he found there. Ellis, 257.
[20] In March 1870 an Englishman, Mr. Finlason, was visiting a friend in Elmina who was actually a member of the Dutch legislative council. He was arrested by Akyeampon and the Elmina men, and was on the point of being put to death when he was rescued by a strong party of Dutch troops and was escorted to a ship to return to Cape Coast; Ellis, 258-9. No doubt technically Elmina was not Dutch territory and the people were not Dutch subjects; but it was disheartening for the Dutch that after nearly 250 years of their government such disorder should be taking place under the very guns of their headquarers fort. The Dutch, as a matter of fact, had always endeavoured to control Elmina much more closely than the British controlled Cape Coast.

resumed, and Ashanti intrigue on the coast would be much easier to control. Moreover, if Elmina castle and its ring of satellite forts were in British hands the Ashanti control of Elmina town would be greatly weakened. The Ashanti difficulty was seen, but was not regarded as very serious.

In London, and in Sierra Leone, on the other hand, the Ashanti difficulty seemed so great that the Government was determined not to take over Elmina unless the Dutch authorities could satisfy it that they had a good title, and that the Ashanti claims to anything more than friendship and alliance were unfounded.

In the face of historical facts the Dutch Government found it difficult to give such an assurance. The Dutch had always paid rent for the ground on which the castle stood. The Note for this payment had passed from Caramansa's successors to the Denkyerahene, and had been taken from Ntim Gyakari by Osei Tutu. Ever since 1702 the rent of twenty ounces of gold or £80 a year[21] had been paid to the Asantehene. The Elmina people themselves paid a regular tribute to Ashanti, and had always received in return, not merely the customary courtesies such as regular embassies to announce accessions and attend funerals, but also considerable military assistance against the Fante. We may consider that this assistance was given as much in Ashanti's own interests as in the interests of the Elmina people; but this is merely to admit that the alliance benefited both parties. But most conclusive is the fact that the British themselves, in Bowdich's treaty, had recognized the right of the Asantehene to control the Elmina people, and had secured a guarantee from him that Elmina should not make war on Cape Coast. I have pointed out elsewhere that in Ashanti eyes the giving of such a promise need not necessarily imply political authority over Elmina; but there is no doubt that the British in 1817 regarded the Asantehene as having the sort of authority over Elmina which they themselves disclaimed over Kommenda. Nothing that had happened since 1817 had tended in any way to change the situation. On the contrary; after the battle of Akantamasu the Asantehene had made it quite plain to Captain

[21] The Dutch governor, Colonel Nagtglas, gives this figure in a letter to the British governor in December 1870 (Crooks, 392). Other sources mention twenty-four ounces a year (a figure which is mentioned also by Colonel Nagtglas in this same letter), and say that the rate was originally half this but was doubled in Osei Tutu's time.

Ricketts that he regarded it as treachery on the part of the British and Fante to go on blockading Elmina during an armistice which he had understood to include all his subjects, among whom he counted the Elmina people.[22]

Nevertheless, Colonel Nagtglas assured the British authorities that the Ashanti had no claims, either to Elmina town or to the castle. He represented the annual payment as a stipend or subsistence payment, which had formerly been made to the Denkyera in return for services in keeping the trade routes open. As for the town and people of Elmina, he declared roundly that the Asantehene had no recognized claim upon them.[23] The British authorities accepted these assurances: a fact which is probably significant of the way in which public affairs on the coast suffered from the lack of continuity in administration. One would have expected that the trouble which Bowdich had had over the pay Notes for the British forts would have been enough to make them extremely suspicious of this annual "present paid entirely to encourage the trade". Mr. Ussher indeed, the Administrator, does seem to have had his suspicions, and he specifically referred to the previous dispute of Bowdich's day. The Government in London, however, were satisfied that no serious trouble need be feared, and the agreement for the cession of the Dutch possessions to the British was signed at The Hague in February 1871, though its ratification was postponed until the Elmina business should be finally disposed of.

Meanwhile the Asantehene heard of the matter, and in November he wrote to Mr. Ussher to remind him that Elmina was his 'by right', and to hope that Elmina was not included in the proposed cession. The Dutch Government then sent a messenger to Kumasi to induce the Asantehene to withdraw his claim, and to threaten him that if he persisted in it they would stop the payment of his subsidy. If the Dutch Government expected Kofi Karikari to withdraw what he considered a just claim, under a threat that they would cease to pay him what he considered was justly due to him, they must have understood Ashanti as little as their British rivals. The messenger they chose was an African clerk named Plange. Mr. Plange arrived in Kumasi at the end of June 1871, and left it

---

[22] Ellis, 191-2.
[23] His letter, which is a reply to a letter from Mr. Ussher enclosing a copy of the Asantehene's protest, is in Crooks, 391-3.

on 4th September, returning with a document in his own hand-writing purporting to be a 'Certificate of Apology' from the Asantehene to the British Government. The gist of the document was that the Asantehene's protest of the previous November, in which he had claimed that "the Dutch delivered the Elmina to him as his own" and that it was consequently his 'by right' was "a vague, formal, or nominal expression, the sentiments of which I therefore must now write that the whole is a mistake". The annual payment made by the Dutch was now admitted to be only "board wages or salary, and not tribute by right of arms".

This document, if genuine, was the very thing the two Governments wanted, for it removed all scruples. The Dutch Governor certainly believed it genuine, for he at once wrote to Kumasi acknowledging it, and summarizing its contents. But it seems much too good to be true. The captive missionaries were in Kumasi for the whole of Mr. Plange's visit, and it was the Asantehene's custom to get them to explain every letter passing between him and the coast. The date of this document is 19th August, so that the Asantehene, even if he had omitted his customary precaution beforehand, had a fortnight in which to discuss it with the missionaries afterwards. But they knew nothing of it, and when Plange left Kumasi on 4th September they believed that he had completely failed in his mission. The document was accepted as genuine not only by the Dutch and British Governments, but also by the Elmina chiefs, whose interest would have been to prove it a forgery; but a forgery it almost certainly must have been. The Asantehene's subsequent references to Elmina were quite inconsistent with this alleged certificate; and in any case, the whole question speedily became a purely academic one, as he went to war to establish his claims by force.[24]

On the strength of this document the treaty for the cession of the Dutch settlements was ratified. The ratifications were exchanged in February 1872, and the actual transfer took place at Elmina on 6th April. The Dutch authorities had at last managed to get Akyeampon out of the town, and the Elmina people, seeing that the transfer was inevitable, had deposed their chief Kobina Edjan, who with a section of the elders had stubbornly refused to

[24] The document is printed in full in Crooks, 399-401, also in Ellis, Claridge and Fuller, all of whom regard it as a forgery.

agree to the British flag. The ceremony was entirely peaceful. The British flag was hoisted alongside the Dutch flag, and both flags remained flying from the same flagstaff until sunset. The heads of the several companies of Elmina warriors formally accepted the transfer, the Dutch Governor and his staff were ceremoniously escorted to their waiting warship and left the coast amid the booming of saluting British guns. During the next few days the other Dutch forts were handed over, and Dutch rule thus ceased on the Gold Coast after lasting for 274 years.[25]

The Government in London had issued the strictest instructions to the new Governor-in-chief, Mr. Pope Hennessy, that he was not to effect the transfer if there seemed the slightest chance of trouble from the Elmina people or the Fante.[26] Mr. Hennessy seems to have been a man who relied on his own opinion and was not too ready to accept advice;[27] but there seemed even to experienced local advisers every prospect that the Elmina question might now be regarded as settled. Both Mr. Hennessy and the outgoing Dutch Governor wrote to Kumasi to inform the Asantehene of the transfer of Elmina, and Mr. Hennessy promised to double the annual payment that the Dutch had been making for so long. He reopened the roads to Ashanti, which had been closed to trade for several years. A message came down from the Asantehene in reply, to the effect that the only question still outstanding was the ransom to be paid for the captive missionaries. As for Elmina itself, all the company heads present in the great hall of Elmina castle had publicly stated that they approved of the transfer to the British; and Kobina Edjan had been deposed, and his deposition confirmed by the Dutch Governor before the transfer was carried into effect.

Below the surface, however, things were not so easy. The deposition of Kobina Edjan had not been by any means unanimous. Several companies had not attended the meeting at which it was agreed to depose him, and had no intention of withdrawing their support. The deposition in fact was quite unconstitutional, and trouble was to be expected from Kobina Edjan and his party. The

[25] Reckoning from the Dutch settlement at Butri and other places in 1598. The treaty (Crooks, 393-6) provided that the buildings of the Dutch forts should be ceded free, but that the stores should be bought by the British at an agreed valuation. The sum eventually agreed on was £3,790 1s. 6½d.
[26] His instructions are printed in Crooks, 404-6.
[27] Ellis, 276-8, gives several instances of his acting against the advice of the local officials, and the results were unfortunate.

expected trouble came on 26th April in the form of a serious riot, in which a Dutch officer was killed;[28] and although accounts disagree as to the immediate occasion of the riot, Mr. Hennessy soon realized that the underlying source of the trouble was the unconstitutional situation in Elmina at the time, and he set matters straight on 9th May by recognizing Kobina Edjan as chief of Elmina. This action was sound as far as it went. But Mr. Hennessy made no inquiries into Kobina Edjan's political position, and did not apparently realize that he was just as strongly opposed as ever to accepting British rule and becoming in British eyes at best a small Ashanti enclave in Fante country, at the worst, one of many Fante chiefs. The truth was that Kobina Edjan and his party, while not daring to oppose the British by force of arms, were waiting only until the assistance they had been promised should arrive from Ashanti. When that arrived their true attitude was made plain.

As regards the relations between the British and the Ashanti, Mr. Hennessy had not, as he hoped, disposed of all possibility of war. There were other matters besides that of the captive missionaries. The British and the Ashanti were still technically at war, and had been so ever since the affair of Kwasi Gyani in 1863. The Ashanti were quite determined not to give up their claim to Elmina, especially as they had been threatened. They felt confident that the British could do nothing against them, for was not the bush proved to be stronger than the cannon? On the other hand, they wanted to teach the Fante a lesson for closing the roads to Ashanti trade and for blockading the Ashanti town of Elmina; and Adu Bofo had won merely Pyrrhic victories in Krepi. For the time being they could do little until they had laid in a stock of warlike materials, and Mr. Hennessy's kindly thought in reopening the roads was just what they needed to make this possible. Whatever the Asantehene himself might feel, his great council was determined upon war: war for which, both against the Fante and the British, they felt they had a just cause.

Note.—These confused negotiations will become plainer if the essential dates are tabulated:

1870 November 24   ...   Asantehene protests against the proposed cession of Elmina, which he claims is his.

December 15   ...   Mr. Ussher refers his letter to Colonel Nagtglas.

December 20   ...   Colonel Nagtglas replies repudiating the claim.

[28] He had come to arrange some financial details of the transfer. The causes of the riot are discussed by Claridge, I, 631-5.

1871	February 25	...	Treaty for the cession signed at The Hague.
	April 14	...	Dutch arrest Akyeampon at Elmina.
	August 19	...	The dubious 'Certificate of Apology'.
1872	February 17	...	Ratification of the treaty.
	February 20	...	Asantehene writes to say that Adu Bofo demands 1,800 oz. ransom for the missionaries, and peace cannot be made until the money is paid to Adu Bofo.
	February 24	...	Kobina Edjan deposed.
	April 3	...	Deposition carried out and confirmed by Dutch.
	April 6	...	Formal transfer of Elmina to British.
	April 20	...	Dutch and British Governors both write to Kumasi: Hennessy promises to double the stipend and to reopen the roads forthwith.
	April 22	...	Hennessy writes to ask for the liberation of the missionaries (without ransom).
	April 26	...	Riot at Elmina.
	May 9	...	Hennessy reinstates Kobina Edjan.
	May 31	...	Prince Ansah informs Hennessy that the Asantehene considers the question of the missionaries the only matter outstanding.
	May 31	...	Hennessy writes to Kumasi declining to ransom the missionaries, but offering to pay Adu Bofo's expenses; later he suggests a maximum of £1,000.
	September 2	...	The Ashanti great council refuses to take less than £2,000 and threatens war.
	October 13	...	Ashanti ambassador in Cape Coast accepts £1,000; money is paid at Cape Coast to Mr. Grant in trust for the Asantehene, and Asantehene is informed.
	October 28	...	Akyeampon arrives in Cape Coast under arrest.
	November 9	...	Asantehene writes to demand payment before he will release the missionaries.
	November 26	...	This demand is refused.
	December 9	...	The Ashanti army leaves Kumasi for the front.
	December 12	...	Akyeampon is released from Cape Coast to return home.
1873	January 29	...	First fighting between Ashanti and Assin.

It would seem, indeed, that Ashanti was almost determined on war as early as February 1872, and perhaps even earlier. It must be remembered that Akyeampon's mission in Elmina was to organize the Elmina forces and to stiffen them with his own contingent of Ashanti troops, so that they might be capable of acting as the centre column of a triple attack on the Fante country and the British. The triple attack was delayed by the unexpected difficulty met with by Adu Bofo in his Krepi campaign. Instead of overcoming all opposition and standing ready on the left bank of the Volta, the Ashanti left wing was only able to win a series of barren and extremely costly victories, and was so weakened that it had no hope of playing any great part in the general plan of campaign. But the triple attack was merely delayed, not abandoned. It is possible that if the British authorities had promptly paid the ransom demanded the attack might have been further delayed until a fresh pretext could be found. But it is certain that Mr. Hennessy's policy of generous concession was construed as a confession of weakness; and a fresh pretext would have soon been forthcoming. It seems that the Asantehene himself was prepared to maintain peace; but his council of chiefs was almost unanimous in demanding war.[29]

For the time being, however, Mr. Hennessy at least had no thought of war. For some time his attention, and the attention of the Gold Coast Administrators under him, was taken up by the proceedings of the Fante Confederation.

The Fante Confederation had begun with the meeting held at Mankesim which decided to support the Kommenda in resisting the Dutch flag. In July 1868, after raising the blockade of Elmina, the Fante chiefs met again at Mankesim and decided to make the Confederation a permanent political unit. Mr. Ussher was at that time the Administrator. The Confederation had begun as an organization for the purpose of doing what the British Government had forbidden, namely, supporting the Kommenda against the Elmina and the Dutch. The members of the Confederation were not British subjects, and the Government at Cape Coast had no control over them. When the Cape Coast men had joined in the confederate army, however, the Administrator took the strong step of outlawing the two Cape Coast chiefs who led the contingent, pulling down their houses, and confiscating their property; thus implying that the Cape Coast people were British subjects, a very dubious implication. All the origins and early activity of the Fante Confederation were thus thoroughly associated in the minds of the British authorities with resistance to their wishes. It is not surprising, therefore, that Mr. Ussher expressed himself angrily to the assembly at Mankesim. "Your conduct," he wrote, "has been such that I can no longer have relations with you. . . . As you voluntarily throw off your allegiance you must not be surprised that I accept your act, and treat you, until you come to your senses, as apart from Great Britain. . . . In case of a war with Ashanti, as you will have provoked it, you will bear the brunt thereof, without help from the Government.[30]

Again we see the fatal uncertainty as to the status of the Fante

[29] See the account of Kumasi events in Fuller, 109-14.
[30] Crooks, 424-8; Claridge, I, 616.

tribes. Mr. Ussher assumes that they owed allegiance to Britain, and had thrown it off. But it was not correct to regard them as owing allegiance. The Select Committee of 1843 had specifically rejected the use of the word 'Allegiance',[31] and although it is true that the Poll Tax Ordinance of 1852 had imposed on the British Government at Cape Coast the duty of carrying out various "measures of improvement and utility", there was no mention of political allegiance. In any case, the Government's power to carry out the desired measures vanished when the Poll Tax ceased. Nothing since 1852 had introduced the idea of political allegiance; and although for the British officials to regard the "power and jurisdiction" of the Bond of 1844, and the "protection afforded by Her Majesty's Government" of the Poll Tax Ordinance, as amounting together to political authority was no doubt easy, it was incorrect.

Further, Mr. Ussher implies that to punish the Fante for acting against the wishes of the British, the British would give them no help in the war which he foresaw against Ashanti; it is to be inferred that if the Fante had been careful to follow those wishes, they would have received British help. But in 1865 the British had proclaimed that they would not in future fight an Ashanti invading force unless the forts were directly attacked. In that same year the Secretary of State had plainly warned the Administrator, Colonel Conran, that he was not to give the impression that British jurisdiction extended over Gold Coast territory outside the forts themselves. It seems then that the Fante states had ample grounds for regarding themselves as free to combine, and to act in combination as they pleased in matters not directly affecting the British forts; and Mr. Ussher had no grounds for regarding them as rebels against British authority.[32]

Having written this uncompromising letter to the Fante Confederation in July, Mr. Ussher went on leave in August; and was succeeded during his absence by the unlucky Mr. Simpson, whose diplomacy at Akwamu was to be so unsuccessful a few months later. Mr. Simpson at first naturally maintained Mr. Ussher's

[31] See above, pp. 193, 194; the relevant passages from the report are printed in Crooks, 278-81.
[32] Claridge, I, 537; Crooks, 374. It is, of course, possible to argue that the particular question at issue in 1868 did directly affect the British forts. But it was not the hoisting of the Dutch flag over Kommenda fort that caused the trouble, so much as the transference to the Dutch of a non-existent "sovereignty and jurisdiction" over the Kommenda people.

policy of treating the Confederation as a disloyal assembly. This policy, however, soon became impossible. In May 1869, just after Mr. Simpson's return from his ill-starred trip to Akwamu, the Kommenda captured four Dutch seamen, who had been part of a boat's crew sent inshore to discover a landing-place for the Dutch troops who were to capture Kommenda. The Kommenda men sent the news to the Fante Confederation, and Colonel Nagtglas asked Mr. Simpson to use his influence with the Confederation to get the men released. Simpson had, of course, no influence to use, but he had to do what he could; so he entered into negotiations with the Confederation, and by implication, if not openly, recognized it as a power.[33] Subsequently he went further; not only did he visit its officers at Mankesim, but he invited them to return his visit at Cape Coast and to discuss with him the constitution of the Confederation.

When Mr. Ussher returned from leave, he acquiesced in this change of policy, and continued the discussions that Mr. Simpson had begun. Throughout 1870, and for the first half of 1871, relations between the Fante Confederation and the British authorities seem to have been friendly. The Confederation at this time was regarded as still little more than a military alliance, and its assembly at Mankesim was a convenient institution through which the British could discuss affairs with the Fante chiefs.

All this time, however, constitutional discussions were going on; and on 16th October, 1871, they resulted in the production of a full-fledged written constitution for the Confederation.[34]

This document, called the Mankesim Constitution, consists of forty-seven articles. The preamble declares that the "Kings and Chiefs of Fantee" who were responsible for the constitution

"are of opinion that unity and concord among ourselves would conduce to our mutual well-being, and promote and advance the social and political condition of our peoples and subjects, who are in a state of degradation, without the means of education and of carrying on proper industry. . . . "

[33] It would seem from the memorandum submitted by Mr. Hennessy in April 1872 by a deputation representing the Confederation (printed in Crooks, 424-8) that Simpson had taken the step of visiting Mankesim even before the affair of the Dutch seamen.
[34] The Constitution is printed verbatim in Sarbah, *Fanti National Constitution*, 199ff: and in Casely Hayford, *Gold Coast Native Institutions*, 327-40.

The objects of the Confederation which it was hoped would thus advance the social and political condition of the Gold Coast people were thus defined:

"(1) To promote friendly intercourse between all the Kings and Chiefs of Fanti, and to unite them for offensive and defensive purposes against their common enemy.[35]

"(2) To direct the labours of the Confederation towards the improvement of the country at large.

"(3) To make good and substantial roads throughout all the interior districts included in the Confederation.

"(4) To erect school-houses and establish schools for the education of all children within the Confederation, and to obtain the service of efficient schoolmasters.

"(5) To promote agricultural and industrial pursuits, and to endeavour to introduce such new plants as may hereafter become sources of profitable commerce to the country.

"(6) To develop and facilitate the working of the mineral and other resources of the country."

These six clauses constitute article 8 of the Constitution, and certain other articles, 21 to 27, amplify article 8 in some respects. Articles 26 and 27 propose the building of main roads, "fifteen feet broad, with good deep gutters on either side", and provide for the financing of the road scheme. Articles 21 to 25 lay down an educational scheme: schools are to be established in certain named districts, and great stress is laid on the training of craftsmen— "carpenters, masons, sawyers, joiners, agriculturists, smiths, architects, builders, etc." Girls' schools are also to be established, and schoolmistresses engaged to staff them. This educational scheme is to be financed by the Confederation's central funds, local chiefs of course supplying materials and labour. In districts where Wesleyan schools already exist, the local chiefs are to insist on the daily attendance of all children between the ages of eight and fourteen.

Of the remaining articles of the Constitution, certain have considerable political importance. Articles 5, 6 and 10 between them lay down that whereas the president of the Confederation is to be "elected from the body of kings, and be proclaimed king-president" of the Confederation, the officials are to be men of education and

[35] I.e. The Ashanti.

position; and that the Representative Assembly of the Confederation is to be composed of two representatives of each "king and
principal chief", one being educated, the other being a chief or
headman. Great care is thus taken to secure the co-operation of the
traditional authorities and the new class of educated men. The
representative assembly is to have legislative powers, and is also to
be an executive body for the purpose of carrying out the wishes
of the British Government; and it is to levy taxes on the member
states of the Confederation.[36]

Articles 29, 36 and 37 provide for the appointment of provincial
assessors. Their duties are to hold courts, with the assistance of the
local chief, accounting for court revenue and expenditure to the
central treasury; to supervise the construction and upkeep of
the roads, and to inspect the schools; and to maintain police
services and to execute writs and summonses, both from the
Confederation's courts and from the British courts on the coast.

The remaining articles of the Constitution deal with internal
administration and procedure, and need not concern us.

Had the Mankesim Constitution been carried into effect it would
have substituted for the mosaic of small independent Fante states
a strong Confederation, making its own laws and providing its own
public works, education and judiciary. It would have made use
both of the services of educated Fante men, and also of British
technical staff, and would have acted in the 'Protectorate' as the
agent of the British Government. In an explanatory memorial to
Mr. Hennessy,[37] the agents of the Confederation emphasized that
the Confederation could not work without "the recognition,
countenance and support and hearty co-operation of Her Majesty's
Government and its friendly aid and advice". The whole tendency
of the British at that time was to withdraw from the affairs of the
'Protectorate' except so far as judicial work was concerned. The
Confederation would open up the 'Protectorate' and introduce
improvements which there seemed no chance of the British
Government's introducing for a long time to come.

The Constitution, however, never was carried into effect. At the
end of November 1871 a deputation of the Confederation's officials
waited on the acting administrator, Mr. Salmon, and handed him

[36] See also articles 12, 42, 44.
[37] Quoted in Claridge, I, 620-1.

a copy of the Constitution with other documents, requesting him to forward them to the Governor-in-chief at Sierra Leone for the information of the Secretary of State. Much was made by the local British authorities of the fact that the documents were submitted merely for the Secretary of State's information, not for his approval; but it seems foolish to boggle at a word, when the intention of the Confederation's officials manifestly was to invite the Secretary of State's comments. In any case, the correct word 'approval' was duly substituted in later communications.

Mr. Salmon, to quote Claridge, "seems to have regarded the whole of these proceedings as a personal insult and to have entirely lost his temper". He decided that the Confederation was "a dangerous conspiracy", and reported it in these words to his chief. He arrested the three officials who had brought him the documents, on a charge of treason, and lodged them in gaol; he issued warrants for the arrest of the other officials, those who had not ventured to Cape Coast, and some of them were actually arrested. A few days later, however, all were released on bail.

The Secretary of State took a less serious view of the matter. In his dispatch of 16th January, 1872,[38] he gave instructions that the parties concerned were to be freed from their bail, and any proceedings which the Administrator might contemplate taking against them were to be stayed. On the other hand, he made it plain that in his view the Mankesim Constitution was going too far, or at least too fast. "There is hardly room for question," he wrote, "that some of the Articles in the Constitution of the Confederation were practically inconsistent with the jurisdiction of the British Government in the protected territory. I think that the Administrator might have confined himself to issuing a proclamation warning British subjects from taking office under the Confederation, and stating that those who did so would be held responsible for their acts. He would have been quite right also in declining to recognize in any way the 'Constitution' until the Articles had been approved by Her Majesty's Government. . . . Her Majesty's Government have no wish to discourage any legitimate efforts on the part of the Fantee Kings and chiefs to establish for themselves an improved form of government, which indeed it is much to be desired that they should succeed in doing; but it is

[38] Crooks, 402, 403.

necessary that all parties concerned should understand that as long as they live under the protection of Great Britain, the protecting Government must be consulted as to any new institutions which may be proposed. . . . "

Mr. Salmon accordingly issued a proclamation, and on his return from leave Mr. Ussher issued another; but both were regarded by the Secretary of State as too strongly worded. When the Governor-in-chief, Mr. Hennessy, came to the Gold Coast in April 1872 he found time, among all his preoccupations with Elmina affairs, to receive a deputation and a memorandum from the Confederation. He submitted the whole scheme formally to the Secretary of State for approval; and in March 1873 the Secretary of State replied[39] that he had made up his mind on the subject of the Fante Confederation, but that the moment was inopportune for discussing it, and he proposed to await a more favourable opportunity. The favourable opportunity never came, and the Fante Confederation as an effective body ceased to exist.

The question arises whether the Mankesim Constitution was a practicable scheme, or merely an ingenious paper draft which would never have worked. Claridge raises the subsidiary question whether its promoters were acting in good faith, and concludes, without citing any evidence to this effect, that "the whole Constitution seems to have been framed by a few educated and semi-educated men, primarily no doubt for the good of their country, but secondarily for the benefit of themselves; and it was alleged that many of the Chiefs whose marks were appended to the documents had no knowledge of their contents and had not even been present at the meetings".[40] This question need not detain us long. Relations between the British authorities and Gold Coast organizations are too often embittered by accusations on both sides of bad faith; and to suppose that the framers of the Mankesim Constitution were thinking of feathering their own nests is no more necessary than to suppose, as some African writers have done, that "notwithstanding all protestations to the contrary, the intention of the British Government was not to allow the people self-government at all, but to govern the country as a Crown Colony. And, of course, the Constitution went diametrically against that

[39] Crooks, 437.
[40] Claridge, I, 619.

I

policy."[41] Even if there were some self-seeking men among the constitution-makers, they would not have remained long in office. It is no easier in the Gold Coast than elsewhere to fool all the people all the time.

It is a much more important question whether the Mankesim Constitution could ever have worked. Claridge thinks that it could not have worked, for two reasons: one, that the Confederation did not include the whole of 'the country' (by which he presumably means that it was a Fante affair only), and the other, that the people would never have agreed to pay taxes to the Confederation authorities. He suggests also that it shows how impractical the founders of the Confederation were that in their memorandum to Mr. Hennessy, though not in the Constitution itself, they propose that the chiefs should give up their rights of jurisdiction to the Confederation, and receive in return fixed stipends. He points out that any attempt to limit the judicial authority of chiefs always meets with opposition from "the very same class of people" as those who framed this scheme. He does not suggest that the scheme might have failed because the Fante people were without administrative experience; and we may take it perhaps that he had no fears on this ground.[42]

Let us take Claridge's points one by one. It is true that the thirty-three chiefs who signed the scheme were all Fante. There was, however, in existence at the same time a body calling itself the Accra Native Confederation, with very similar aims and a similar, though less detailed, organization.[43] Further, in previous joint activities, such as those resulting in the 1844 Bond and the 1852 Poll Tax, and the various treaties with regard to Ashanti, the Fante chiefs had been associated with Assin, Wassaw, Denkyera and others; Assin, Wassaw and Denkyera had actually been members of the original military Fante Confederation of 1867. There seems no ground for fearing that the Fante Confederation would not have spread so as to include the whole of the 'Protectorate'.

It is true also that in recent years the Gold Coast people have

[41] Casely Hayford, *Gold Coast Native Institutions*, 189.
[42] Mr. Hennessy reported in a dispatch to the Secretary of State that in his judgment "the educated natives have contrasted favourably as a body with the European residents", and he describes the Treasurer of the Confederation as "certainly not the inferior of any European on the Gold Coast in character, ability, or mercantile position". Casely Hayford, 191.
[43] Claridge, I, 615-16.

shown themselves strongly opposed to the idea of direct taxation. But those who oppose direct taxation so strongly have been careful to explain that they do not disapprove of taxation, even of direct taxation as such, but of taxation levied by the central Government, over the levying and the spending of which they have had no effective control. There is little or no opposition either to municipal rates, which are levied and spent by town councils containing a strong African element, or to taxes levied by state councils in accordance with traditional custom. The opposition to Native Administration Treasuries established at the suggestion of the British Government dies down as it becomes realized that such Treasuries are really controlled by the Native Administration, and are not just a cunning scheme for enabling the Government to levy through the District Commissioner taxes which it would not dare to levy in other ways. What reason is there for fearing that the Fante Confederation would prove unable to levy taxes? The Mankesim Constitution takes such care to associate the traditional rulers with the educated class in all the work of government, that it should have found no more difficulty in raising money than the average Native Administration Treasury of today.

There is more weight in Claridge's point that the chiefs would not have acquiesced in the loss of their judicial powers, even in return for compensation. In this he is very likely right. But it is far from certain that this was intended. The Constitution does not say that the chiefs are to lose their judicial powers. Article 36, subsection 1 of the Constitution provides that the provincial assessors, who are the Confederation's judicial officers, are to hold courts "with the assistance of the king or principal chief". It is unlikely that the memorialists of 1872 can have intended to override this section. What they probably meant was that the chiefs were to give up their rights of independent jurisdiction; they were to sit on the bench to assist the provincial assessors, as they had long been in the habit of doing on the bench of the British Judicial Assessor in Cape Coast. In this way the traditional judiciary was preserved, and in my opinion it could have worked satisfactorily in these circumstances.

One very great merit of the Constitution, without which it almost certainly would not have worked, is the care taken to associate educated men with the traditional chiefs, all of whom at that time would be uneducated. One great source of trouble in the Gold Coast of today is the cleavage which exists between these two classes. In most states, the elders fear that an educated chief, or educated advisers, would undermine the traditional constitution; they would use their familiarity with the English language and with European ways to deal direct with the Government without consulting those who have traditionally the right to be consulted. Educated men on the other hand have little inducement to offer their services to the state organization, where they are thus regarded; and there is thus an unfortunate separation between these two classes of men who could help one another so much. Both the Government and many of the leaders of African opinion realize the evils of this separation, but suspicion and prejudice cannot be overcome quickly. In the Mankesim Constitution this separation would never have come into being.

It seems then that the British Government lost a great opportunity when it first opposed, and later neglected to support, the Fante Confederation. The Confederation might well have proved the foundation of a flourishing system of indirect rule; and whatever its shortcomings and dangers, it might seem better to use and to improve a scheme produced by the people themselves than to impose a fresh scheme from above.

Why then did the British Government not support the scheme? The dispatch which the Earl of Kimberley, then Secretary of State for the Colonies, promised "when a more favourable juncture of affairs presents itself" was actually written, though never sent. It says that for the reasons given in the dispatch of 16th January, 1872, the Government cannot accept any scheme which contemplates an intermediary agency between the chiefs and the local Government; the only confederation which can be accepted is a purely military confederation for defence against the Ashanti. The only practicable alternatives are to annex the country — which cannot be contemplated; or to withdraw all jurisdiction from the 'Protectorate', and leave the chiefs to govern the country themselves. We are thus driven to fall back on the dispatch of 16th January, 1872. In it, Lord Kimberley criticizes the haste which led the promoters of the scheme to act upon it as a settled institution before submitting it to Mr. Salmon at all; but his main criticism is that "some of the Articles in the Constitution of the Confederation were practically inconsistent with the jurisdiction of the British Government in the protected territory". What was this jurisdiction? In 1865 his predecessor, Mr. Cardwell, had written to Colonel Conran,[44] "The extension of British territory . . . cannot receive my sanction . . . (I) wish you to avoid introducing any expressions which bear the appearance of extending jurisdiction over territory at the Gold Coast." In 1869 Earl Granville had written to Sir Arthur Kennedy, with reference to Mr. Simpson's somewhat reckless promises of assistance to Fante, Akim, Krepi and others, that the wars in which British allies engaged themselves "are their wars, and not the wars of this country; that they must rely on themselves for success in those wars, and that the British Government is unable to make itself responsible for their defence in case they should prove unable to defend themselves".[45] The only jurisdiction of the British in Fante country outside the forts was the judicial authority of the British courts, which was exercised in accordance with the Bond of 1844. Political authority there was none.

Nevertheless, in spite of the recommendations of the Committee of 1865, and in spite of the care shown by successive Secretaries of State to avoid any appearance of extending British jurisdiction, there was an obstinate tendency to stiffen British influence into an illegitimate British jurisdiction. In 1867 the British and Dutch exchanged their 'rights of sovereignty and jurisdiction' over the Kommenda and others. The whole position was so anomalous—a mass of tribes, responsible for their own defence, owning their own land, independent of British authority, and yet subject in many respects to British law, and indissolubly linked with the British settlements both in commerce and in their preoccupation with the danger from the common enemy—that it seems to have been beyond the grasp of Downing Street's comprehension. In truth, there was no middle course for the British between abandoning all political authority on the coast and assuming full rights of sovereignty. If British jurisdiction did not exist, it seemed that it would have to be brought into existence. It may have been so, but if so it was an unfortunate necessity.

Then came the Ashanti war, in which all British ideas about leaving the Fante and other tribes to defend themselves had to be

[44] Crooks, 374. The abortive dispatch is in the Record Office, C.O. 96/104.
[45] Crooks, 385-8.

abandoned; and after the war the Government decided to grasp the nettle and to annex the 'Protectorate'.

The Earl of Carnarvon put forward this new policy on the ground that it was impossible to return to the old uncertainty. The minutes in the Colonial Office file are more revealing than the official dispatch:

" . . . I do not however think that we could make any good use of such an organization as the erstwhile proposed Fantee Confederation. It is difficult to see how any half measures with regard to the Government of the Protectorate can be made to suffice. Unless we directly govern, up to the Prah, we can have no guarantee against wars and disturbances. I am not at all sure that the annexation of the whole Protectorate (which I look upon with horror) is not the only cheap and safe alternative to retirement from all the coast except perhaps one or two naval depots. R.G.W.H., Ap. 17.

"Complete annexation or total abandonment are I fear the only alternatives. The former is too ghastly a scheme to contemplate, the latter too charming to be capable of execution. All these halting tentative half measures such as Protectorates, etc., etc., may do for a time and I suppose something of the kind will have to be attempted until the vulgar prejudice which is nowadays dignified by the name of 'Public Opinion' veers round to a common sense and unsentimental view of this question. J.L., April 20.

"A very evil choice to have to make . . . 21 Apl. (Carnarvon)." [46]

A very evil choice indeed; but it was made.

On 24th July, 1874, a new charter was issued, separating the Gold Coast and Lagos from Sierra Leone, and erecting them both into a separate colony called the Gold Coast Colony. In August of the same year an Order in Council empowered the Legislative Council of the new colony to legislate for the colony by ordinance, subject, of course, to the royal right of disallowance. By a royal proclamation[47] the power and jurisdiction of the Crown were defined as

[46] Record Office, C.O. 96/114.
[47] Printed in Sarbah, *Fanti Customary Laws*, 293-5. Claridge says that this proclamation was published on the 12th of September; but there is some doubt as to whether it ever was published locally at all, extraordinary as the oversight may seem.

including the preservation of peace and the enactment and administration of laws (due regard being paid to native customary law), the abolition of slave trading and of "immoral, barbarous, and cruel customs", public works, public health, education, police and prisons, the establishment of municipalities, the settlement of disputes between chiefs, and taxation.

The creation of the Gold Coast Colony has always been a sore point with many Gold Coast Africans. Logically they have a strong case. They point out that right up to the outbreak of the Ashanti war the British had been disclaiming any jurisdiction over the interior of the country; that the first mention of any such jurisdiction occurs in Lord Kimberley's dispatch condemning the Fante Confederation: that their Confederation was apparently not reconsidered after the war: but that by an arbitrary act of power the Imperial Government assumed complete rights of jurisdiction over the whole country, which they were not asked to cede, and would never have consented to cede. In short, they say, the Gold Coast was treated as a conquered country, although it had not been conquered.

The explanation of this arbitrary act is given in Lord Carnarvon's dispatch of 20th August, 1874, to Governor Strahan, enclosing the draft of the proclamation.[48] He points out that the Bond of 1844 was the only document which attempted to define the Queen's jurisdiction in the Gold Coast in other than strictly political matters. But that Bond no longer truly expressed the facts of the case. It was silent on the matters of civil justice, public health, municipalities, education, roads, and the levying of customs duties. "On all these matters, the Legislature or Government of the settlement has, with or without the co-operation of the native rulers, exercised authority to an extent which, strictly speaking, could only be justified on the assumption (the justice of which I am satisfied is not open to question) that these matters have by usage and by the sufferance and tacit assent of the natives fallen within the province of the Queen's authority."[49]

[48] Sarbah, 288-92.
[49] The Bond of 1844 provided for criminal jurisdiction, but not for civil; this had been provided by the Supreme Court Ordinance of 1853 and the Order in Council in 1856. Municipal corporations had been set up in 1857, but they were a failure, and lapsed in 1860. Agricultural plantations had been established both by Torrane and by Maclean. Education was, of course, of long standing in

It being thus desirable to define the Queen's authority more accurately, the alternatives were to negotiate a fresh Bond with the chiefs or to issue a royal proclamation. In 1844 a negotiated Bond was the only possible method. In 1874 the power of the Government had so increased that a royal proclamation was possible. It seemed more desirable to assume authority by royal proclamation, as the Government would be placed in a difficult position if any considerable body of chiefs refused to accede to a proposed treaty, or if a chief who had not been directly invited to accede made difficulties on the ground that his assent was as necessary as that of others who had been directly invited. For these reasons, a royal proclamation was decided on.

We may concede the objectors their case. If rights of sovereignty did not exist on 23rd July they could not be brought into existence by the issue of a charter on 24th July. Under the Foreign Jurisdiction Act the annexation was perfectly legal and proper from the British point of view; but it might well be replied that no Act of the British Parliament could confer on Britain rights over non-British people. And yet it is hard to see any practical alternative. A reversion to the old chaos was unthinkable. In my view, co-operation with the Fante Confederation would have been the best solution; but if the Secretary of State felt unwilling to run the risk of this untried expedient, there was no other way but the way he chose. He was unquestionably right in rejecting the alternative of a freshly negotiated Bond.

Cape Coast, apart from the mission schools in other places. The construction of roads had begun in 1843, and had been fitfully continued, largely for military purposes, on various occasions since then. Customs duties were the main item of revenue. Public expenditure, including health expenditure, was of course greater during the period of the Poll Tax.

CHAPTER XII

ASHANTI FROM 1869 TO 1902

I PROPOSE to tell in one chapter of moderate length the events of thirty-odd of the most eventful years of Ashanti history: years which begin with Ashanti at the height of its military power and which end with the loss of Ashanti independence and its reduction to the position of a British colony. This period includes two major wars, the wars of 1874 and of 1900, called by the Ashanti themselves the Sagrenti and the Yaa Asantewa wars after the two great leaders, one a British general and the other an Ashanti queen. These two wars between them occupy over a fifth of Claridge's book, and the events of this chapter take nearly the whole of his second volume. This very fullness of detail with which Claridge relates the story of the campaigning and the diplomacy makes it unnecessary for me to follow his example, particularly as in this period the fate of the Gold Coast and of Ashanti itself was determined not by accidents of detail but by the interplay of powerful political forces.[1]

Let us take up the story at the capture of the German missionaries in June 1869. Adu Bofo's military position was, of course, in no way improved by their capture; and Dompre's incessant activity was rapidly wearing out the Ashanti army. His small force was as elusive as a Boer commando. Ashanti convoys of provisions and ammunition were cut off, and the occasional victories Adu Bofo gained over detachments of Dompre's forces seemed to bring him no nearer an end of the campaign. In October 1869 he at last induced Dompre to stand and fight a pitched battle. The Krepi men took up a position on the steep rocky Gemi hill, near the town of Amedzofe, and rolled rocks down on to the clambering Ashanti and Akwamu to their complete discomfiture. The news of this defeat caused the Akim, Akwapim, Krobo and others to come to the help of the Krepi, and the Asantehene actually sent orders to Adu Bofo to abandon the campaign. Adu Bofo himself was so dejected that he gave the allies hostages for

---

[1] The details of the fighting may be read in Claridge, II, chaps. I-VIII and XXII-VI; dispatches are printed in Crooks, chaps. XX-III.

the safety of the missionaries, including one of his own sons; and this step had a success which he probably anticipated, for the allies, thinking that the missionaries would soon be released, withdrew their army, and Adu Bofo was able to remain in Krepi. During the next few months he went on with the war, ignoring in his improved circumstances his orders of recall; and things went much better with him. In November or December 1870 he had a great stroke of luck; Dompre was ambushed on one of his raids, and was killed by the Akwamu. This enabled him to withdraw from Krepi without too much discredit, and he returned to Kumasi having lost 136 chiefs and nearly half his troops, and having so greatly depleted the Ashanti stock of ammunition that there could be no thought of beginning another major campaign until it had been replenished.

Mr. Hennessy hoped to avert war by generosity. He released the hostages and reopened the roads, thus allowing the Ashanti to obtain fresh supplies of ammunition. He employed as his messenger to Kumasi Mr. Plange, whose previous embassy to Kumasi on behalf of the Dutch had rendered him a very suspicious character in Ashanti eyes. The Asantehene refused to surrender the missionaries until Adu Bofo had been paid his price for them, and Adu Bofo fixed the price at 1,800 ounces of gold, about £6,500. The haggling that ensued was probably not meant seriously by the Asantehene; at all events nothing came of it, and the Ashanti army left Kumasi for the front on 9th December, 1872.

The Ashanti plan of campaign followed their traditional three-fold type. Adu Bofo with four or five thousand men was to contain the Denkyera and Wassaw, a small force was sent on the other flank to contain the Akim, while the main army marched in the centre straight down towards Cape Coast. Asamoa Nkwanta still remained in retirement, and the supreme command was given to Amankwa Tia, chief of Bantama.[2] The appointment was not a good one. The general bore an honoured name; but he was not popular with his men, who despised him for his indecision and his drunkenness.

The flanking parties disappeared in the forest. The left division

[2] Amankwa Tia was a traditional name for the chief of Bantama, which was the Scone, Rheims or Westminster of Ashanti. One Amankwa Tia had commanded the punitive expedition against Sefwi in Opoku Ware's time; another had distinguished himself in victory against Gofan in 1803.

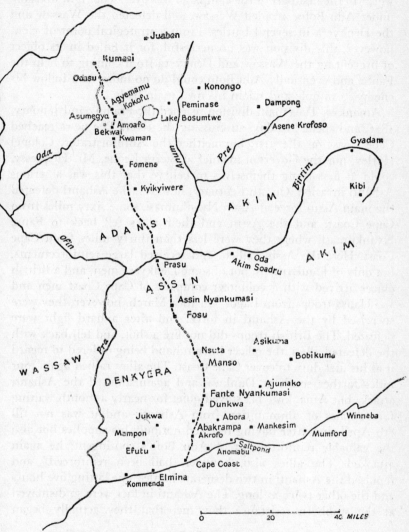

FIG. 11. The Ashanti Wars.
The dotted line marks the old track from Cape Coast to Kumasi.

did little; it started late, and was soon recalled and sent on a futile plundering expedition which kept it out of all chance of any useful work till the first part of the campaign was over. The right division, under Adu Bofo, invaded Wassaw, and defeated the Wassaw and the Denkyera in several battles. From a strategical point of view, however, this division was unsuccessful, for it failed in its object of preventing the Wassaw and Denkyera from coming to help the Fante, and eventually Adu Bofo could do no more than follow his enemy's example and rejoin his own main body.

Amankwa Tia's main division reached the Pra on 22nd January, 1873, and spent five days in crossing the river. The news reached Cape Coast on the 31st, but neither the Administrator, Colonel Harley, nor the Governor-in-chief at Sierra Leone, Mr. Hennessy, could at first bring themselves to believe that this was a serious Ashanti invasion. On 9th February, however, the Ashanti defeated the main Assin force at Assin Nyankumasi, some sixty miles from Cape Coast, and the Assin and their allies fell back to Fante Nyankumasi, where they were less than thirty miles from Cape Coast. Here the Assin rallied, and received large reinforcements, not only of Fante troops, but of some Denkyera men; and a British officer arrived with a volunteer company of Cape Coast men and 100 Hausa troops from Lagos. On 10th March, however, they were surprised by the Ashanti in force, and after a hard fight were defeated. The British troops did not fire a shot, and fell back with the defeated allies, the officer in command being ordered to regard it as his first duty to cover Cape Coast. The allies rallied again four miles farther south at Dunkwa, and again awaited the Ashanti attack; but Amankwa Tia stayed quiet for nearly a month waiting for supplies of ammunition from Ashanti; and it was not till 8th April that after having received not only his supplies but also the valuable reinforcement of Adu Bofo's contingent, he again attacked. The allies also, however, had been reinforced,[3] and repulsed the Ashanti in two desperate battles, one lasting five hours and the other twice as long. The Ashanti in fact were so dismayed at the stubborn resistance they met that they actually began

---

[3] A new detachment of the 2nd West India Regiment arrived from Sierra Leone, but was held in reserve. Ellis estimates the numbers engaged at Dunkwa as 25,000 allies for the first battle, and more than twice that number for the second; the Ashanti force as 15,000-18,000 on both occasions. The total allied casualties in the first battle were under 900.

destroying some of their baggage in preparation for a retreat. The
allies did not know this, and although in the evening they declared
stoutly that they would renew the battle next day, in the cold grey
dawn they thought better of it and retreated towards Cape Coast.
The volunteers and the Hausa troops covered the retreat, and the
allied army rapidly dispersed.

While this fighting was going on a letter came to Colonel Harley
from the Asantehene. It gave as the reasons of the invasion the old
claim, not only to Elmina but also to Denkyera, Assin and Akim;
and accused the Administrator of having threatened to visit
Kumasi and take away power from the Asantehene. It looked as
though Mr. Plange's tongue had been running away with him.
This letter, of course, put the Ashanti in the wrong. The claim to
Elmina was a fair *casus belli*, and another one was ready to hand
in the Kwasi Gyani affair of 1862, which had never been settled.
The Asantehene, however, made no mention of Kwasi Gyani, and
he made no mention of the captive missionaries, which he had
spoken of previously as being the only obstacle to peace. Instead
of this, he raked up the old claim to Denkyera, Assin and Akim,
which he had explicitly abandoned in the treaty of 1831.

Amankwa Tia was unable to follow up the disintegrating allied
army. His own men were short of food and beginning to suffer
greatly from disease. The rainy season, which had just begun, was
an unusually heavy one. The mud houses in Cape Coast tumbled
in wholesale, and even some of the Castle ramparts gave way,
taking the platforms and guns with them. The Ashanti troops,
camping in the open or in grass huts and always wet and cold, were
in much worse plight than the townsfolk in Cape Coast. Amankwa
Tia contented himself with forming a camp at Dunkwa on the site
of his victory, where he stayed for a whole month. In the latter part
of May a large army of Fante and Denkyera collected at Jukwa,
seventeen miles N.N.W. of Cape Coast; and on 5th June the
Ashanti army, having abandoned the direct Cape Coast road and
moved south-west across country, attacked and destroyed it.

Their defeat at Jukwa was a terrible blow to the allies. The town
was the Denkyera capital, and it was thought very important that
it should be held. Great efforts had been made to get together an
adequate force to defend it, and some of the Fante chiefs had
brought their contingents to the battle in spite of great terror lest

their own towns should be attacked while left undefended.[4] On the other hand, the allies felt that Colonel Harley was giving them very little effective help, even considering the small forces that he had; an opinion which was shared by many unofficial Europeans. It was suspected also that he was underestimating the seriousness of the situation in his reports to London. The defeat at Jukwa, however, convinced both Colonel Harley and the Imperial Government that drastic measures were needed. The whole countryside was in panic; fifteen to twenty thousand refugees thronged the streets of Cape Coast; and Colonel Harley found Cape Coast undefended by any organized force save 260 men of the Hausa police and the West India regiment, and about the same number of Cape Coast Volunteers.

The Elmina men naturally felt that their deliverance was at hand. Not only was Amankwa Tia with the main Ashanti force encamped at villages only a few miles outside the town, but their ancient ally Akyeampon, with a fresh force, was advancing from the west. Kobina Edjan, however, unwisely showed his hand too soon, and before the Ashanti could rescue him he was promptly arrested and deported to Sierra Leone. This kept the Elmina quiet for a few weeks longer, until the news of Jukwa. Then they rose: but they were already too late. The first British reinforcements, a force of 110 marines, landed on 9th June, four days after the battle of Jukwa. Four days later Elmina was surrounded, martial law was proclaimed and the inhabitants ordered to give up their arms. They ignored the command, and the town was bombarded and destroyed. The fighting men abandoned the town, and retired into the bush, where they were reinforced by a strong Ashanti detachment. The seamen and marines were on their way back to the ships when the Ashanti and the Elmina men attacked them; and a running fight ensued over the grassy plain that skirts the sea, till eventually the Ashanti retired in good order into the scrub a mile or two inland, and the action was broken off.

Conditions were now very bad for both sides. Cape Coast was

[4] Their fears were very natural; for some of them, whose towns lay directly between the Ashanti and Cape Coast, had to make a flank march across the Ashanti front, and if the enemy had chosen to go straight ahead instead of striking away to his right to go to Jukwa, nothing could have saved their homes from destruction. This battle of Jukwa is universally remembered in traditional stool histories: it is a chronological landmark like Akantamasu.

quite unable to feed the refugee population, especially as the outlying villages and plantations were held by the Ashanti; and the
incessant heavy rain increased the misery of the shelterless crowds.
The Ashanti army, on the other hand, was now reasonably well
fed, but was suffering heavily from smallpox and dysentery. The
warlike enthusiasm of the chiefs was quenched, and they compelled
Amankwa Tia to send to Kumasi asking permission to return, without which no Ashanti army may break off a campaign. The
Asantehene, however, who had never been anxious for the war,
refused permission: he replied, "You wished for war, and you
have it; you swore you would not return till you could bring me
the walls of Cape Coast, and now you want me to recall you
because many Chiefs have fallen and you are suffering. It was not
I; it was you who wished it."[5]

In July and August more small reinforcements arrived from
England, bringing the available disciplined troops to about 600
men. And now the British Government was converted to Mr. Pine's
opinion that only a determined attack into the Ashanti country
could put a stop to these repeated invasions of the 'Protectorate'.
It sent out, as the 'more competent military commander' whom it
had considered sending in 1863, Major-General Sir Garnet Wolseley. He arrived on 2nd October, 1873, and was sworn in as Civil
Administrator, the Government having determined to "unite the
chief civil and military command" in his hands. His instructions
were to rally the allied forces, to send an ultimatum to the Asantehene requiring him to withdraw his army and to give compensation
and security for his future behaviour, and if necessary to use force
to compel the Asantehene to make peace. Sir Garnet's name
became in African speech 'Sagrenti', and the campaign which he
directed is commonly known on the Gold Coast as the Sagrenti
war.[6]

Sir Garnet's first business was to raise troops. Recruiting officers
were sent to Lagos, Sierra Leone and the Gambia, and bounties
were promised to the Fante and Assin chiefs if they would provide
contingents. These efforts were largely useless. The chiefs had no
faith in British help, which had been no use to them in 1863, and
had helped them very little in the present campaign. Moreover,

[5] Fuller, 118; the authority is the memoirs of Ramseyar and Kühne.
[6] Often also the Toto war: this name imitates the sound of the British guns.

they knew that the Ashanti army was in a bad way, and would soon be returning home. They had fought hard in five battles, and had suffered five defeats; and now they felt it better to stay quiet and be hungry at home than to go to face another defeat in the bush.[7] The result was that the only troops that could be raised were two regiments of foot, known as Russell's and Woods' regiments, and an irregular force, amounting altogether to some 2,500 men, half of whom were natives of the Gold Coast. These men, together with the marines and bluejackets of the Navy, and the Hausa and West Indian troops, made up a force of between three and four thousand men, a force too small for the work of pursuing into its own country an undefeated enemy army of fifteen thousand or more. The General, therefore, sent to England for the two battalions of British infantry which were being held in readiness, and a few days later requested that a third battalion might be sent in addition.

Meanwhile it was necessary to do something to relieve the pressure on Cape Coast and to demonstrate that the British were prepared to take the offensive; and a surprise expedition was accordingly sent by sea to Elmina. The Ashanti were taken by surprise at daybreak, and after a short action they abandoned several villages with large stores of powder and provisions; the villages were burnt and the troops returned to Elmina and re-embarked. This successful operation was useful in inconveniencing the enemy, but it had little of the hoped-for effect in stimulating recruiting.

At the same time, Sir Garnet sent to the Asantehene the ultimatum he had been instructed to send, three copies being dispatched by different messengers. They were, however, intercepted by Amankwa Tia, who took on himself to send a reply as follows:

SIR,

I have received those two[8] letters which you sent to me in order to send them to the King of Ashantee. For what purpose I came here is that: Assin, Dankra, Akyem,

[7] There were thus reasons for their apathy, which greatly annoyed the British. It is not fair to attribute it to cowardice, though from the experience of the latter part of the campaign it would certainly seem that the morale of the allies had been badly shaken by their defeats.
[8] The third copy reached Kumasi on 20th November.

Wassaw. Those four nations belong to the King of Ashantee, and they refused to serve the King, and they escaped away unto you. If the King sends his servants to or to buy something at Cape Coast they catch them and plundered their good to. And those nations ordered the King of Ashantee that he may come and fight with them. Therefore I said that they are not a friends with the King. On account of that I shall come down here to catch those four chieves who ordered the King of Ashantee to come to fight with them.

And they fought with me six times, and I drove them away, and they escaped to be under you. But the King did not send me into Cape Coast, and when you deliver Assin, Dankra, Akyem, and Wassaw unto me, I shall bring unto the King there is no any quarrel with you.

I send my love to you.

I am your,
AMANKWATIA.

Still no mention of Elmina or Kwasi Gyani, much less of the European prisoners; but the letter is honest in revealing the underlying Ashanti resentment at the treaty of 1831, and their irritation at having no trading post of their own by the sea.[9]

This letter was written on 20th October; but Amankwa Tia had already begun his retreat four days before. He intended to retire by the way he had come, leaving his main camps at Efutu and Mampon and marching through Jukwa to join the main Kumasi road at Dunkwa. This plan, however, could not be carried out, for the British had established a post at Dunkwa. Amankwa Tia then decided to divide his force into two columns, one striking the road farther south at Akrofo, and the other marching on Dunkwa. His idea was that the British garrison at Dunkwa would march south to relieve the smaller post at Akrofo, and that the northern Ashanti column, having halted unobserved in the bush three miles west of Dunkwa, would then seize Dunkwa and command the main north road. The British, however, did not co-operate. The Dunkwa garrison found out that the northern

[9] It is possible that some chiefs of these four nations may have sent insulting messages to Kumasi, and that Ashanti traders may have been mishandled on the road. Such incidents did occur.

Ashanti column was at Iskabio, three miles away; and instead of withdrawing southward it suddenly attacked the Iskabio position, and fought two actions with the Ashanti there. The British commander was disgusted with the conduct of his allied irregulars, which prevented him from making any real impression on the Ashanti position; but at all events he had done enough to convince Amankwa Tia that nothing but a very strong attack farther south had any chance of drawing off this obstinate garrison.

He made his attack on the afternoon of 5th November, and chose for his purpose not Akrofo but Abakrampa, five miles farther north, and some fifteen miles from Cape Coast. The town was strongly held by a mixed force of bluejackets, West India, Hausa and men of Russell's regiment, and about 500 allies, and was well prepared for defence, the bush being cleared, buildings loopholed and trenches dug. The attack was kept up with the greatest vigour from four in the afternoon till midnight, but was repulsed. Next day the Ashanti resumed the attack at eleven in the morning and continued it till sunset; but had no better success. That evening a fresh naval brigade force arrived without being opposed, and next day it was found that the Ashanti had abandoned their position and retired northward. Amankwa Tia found to his dismay that the Dunkwa garrison was still in position, and that British posts had been established as far north as Manso, nearly forty miles north of Cape Coast. He ordered paths to be cut through the bush parallel with the main road and three or four miles west of it. This was a slow matter, and the allied vanguard pressed hard on his heels until he turned on them. After this, he was allowed to retreat in peace, and on the 24th and following days his army, moving in three columns, struck the main road at Nsuta and beyond, his vanguard being sixty miles at least from Cape Coast, and only some twenty miles from the Pra.

On 26th November Colonel Wood, in command of the British van of nearly 300 trained African troops, reached Nsuta, where he found camp fires still burning; and next day he pushed on to Fosu to harass the Ashanti rear. The Ashanti, however, specialized in rearguard actions, and Asamoa Nkwanta had emerged from his Achilles-like seclusion to take command of this force. The Hausa and Sierra Leone troops advanced in open order into the bush against heavy fire, but were in danger of being outflanked and had to retire. The Hausa men were covering the retirement of the rest, when they were seized with a sudden panic and bolted, throwing the whole force into confusion. The retreat became a rout, much ammunition and baggage were lost, and Colonel Wood had to give up any idea of harassing the Ashanti army as it recrossed the Pra. Asamoa Nkwanta received for this action the title of Srafo Kra, the warrior's soul.

The last of the Ashanti crossed the Pra on 30th November; they were short of canoes, and lost many drowned. On 22nd December the army returned to Kumasi, having lost 20,000 men out of its original strength of 40,000. It returned in mourning. Its failure was causing much searching of heart in Kumasi, and while Amankwa Tia was cutting his way through the bush near Manso, one of Sir Garnet's letters at last reached the Asantehene. This drew from the Asantehene the reply that he had sent his army to attack Kwaku Fram the Denkyerahene, who, Plange had told him, was to be given Elmina. Now he understood that Kwaku Fram was dead, so as far as he was concerned the war was over; but he thought it unfair that the British should attack his army at Fosu when they could see that it was already retiring as fast as it could. The Ashanti did not yet realize that the war was only just beginning.

The European troops arrived in December—battalions of the 2nd Rifle Brigade, the 23rd Royal Welsh Fusiliers and the 42nd Highlanders (the Black Watch), with detachments of Engineers, Artillery and auxiliary services. The 1st West India regiment also arrived from Jamaica. The strength of this European contingent was just over 2,500. The troops were sent away to cruise until the road should be ready as far as Prasu, so that they should not be landed till fighting was about to begin.

The plan of campaign was one that should appeal to the Ashanti; for it resembled their own favourite converging attack. Captain Glover, with a small body of Hausa troops, was to raise an allied force in Accra and the south-east, and advance towards Juaben. Captain Butler was to raise a force of Akim and advance more or less parallel with Captain Glover towards Kumasi. Captain Dalrymple was to advance with a force of Wassaw and Denkyera men and attack Ashanti from the south-west. The main column, under Sir Garnet Wolseley himself, was to advance straight up the main Cape Coast-Kumasi road through Prasu. All four columns were to be ready on the Pra or the Ofin, the Ashanti frontier, on 15th January.

On 7th January, 1874, an advanced party occupied Asaman, the first village north of the Pra, to serve as a bridgehead for the bridge constructed by the engineers. Sir Garnet sent a further ultimatum to Kumasi, warning the Asantehene that he was about to begin his advance, and offering the following armistice terms: all prisoners in Ashanti to be delivered, an indemnity of 50,000 ounces of gold to be paid, Sir Garnet, with an escort of 500 men, to visit Kumasi and sign a formal treaty after hostages had been given for his safety.

The Ashanti had no thought of accepting these terms, but the army had dispersed, and time had to be gained in order for it to reassemble. It was hard to believe that the white men would venture to enter Ashanti; but the situation was certainly serious, for on the day on which the General's letter was written, a big sacred tree, planted in Kumasi by Okomfo Anokye, fell down.[10] (There could hardly be a worse omen.) Kofi Karikari therefore temporized; he released Kühne and asked him to intercede with the General, but said nothing about complying with the armistice terms.

The country between the Pra and the Moinsi hills, though Ashanti territory, was unoccupied, since its Assin inhabitants had abandoned it years before. After occupying and fortifying the crest of the hills, the advance guard pushed on to Kwisa and Fomena, the Adansi capital, which were both found deserted. Kwadwo Oben,[11] the Adansihene, had determined to resist, and sent a message to Kumasi to say that the British were advancing, but that he had some powder to burn on them even if the Kumasi men had none. This taunt arrived while the Council in Kumasi was debating whether to release all the prisoners; it was in consequence of this that only Kühne was released. On the 23rd, however, another letter came from Kumasi, brought by the remaining missionaries; Kofi Karikari this time promised to make Amankwa Tia personally responsible for the idemnity, on the ground that he had been sent to make war on the Denkyera, and had exceeded his instructions

[10] Fuller points out that it was not, as Claridge says, the *Kumnini* tree, which never grows very large, but an enormous *Owawa* (Triplochiton Scleroxylon) one of the biggest of forest trees.
[11] Not Kobina Obin, as Claridge calls him. Fuller's version of the name is confirmed by Adansi tradition.

in attacking Elmina. Sir Garnet in his reply insisted on the release of all the Fante prisoners, the payment of half the idemnity as a first instalment, and the delivery of the queen-mother, the heir to the Asantehene, and the heirs to the stools of four of the principal divisions. Though he could not be expected to know it, these terms were such as the Asantehene could not possibly accept. The six hostages demanded were together more important than the Asantehene himself, and the Ashanti would never deliver them until all power of resistance was broken. Moreover, it was quite impossible for the treasury to raise such a large capital sum as 50,000 ounces of gold. The Akan financial system requires that money coming into the treasury shall flow out again at once, and large reserves did not exist. There could, therefore, be no reply but war.

The Ashanti determined to await the attack of Amoafo, a mile east of Bekwai. Amankwa Tia was superseded, and the command of the defence was given to Kwabena Dwumo, chief of Mampon; while the stout old warrior Asamoa Nkwanta, Srafo Kra, was sent to take charge of the Adansi forces, who were to delay the British as much as possible. The Ashanti plan for the defence was that the Adansi and other advanced troops should offer just enough resistance to entice the British well into the country in the hope of an easy victory; that the defensive position at Amoafo should occupy the whole attention of the invader for some days at least; and that while the British were busy here, the Juaben men should make a great detour to the east, break down the bridge at Prasu, and hold the crossing of the Pra, cutting the British off from the sea.

On 31st January the invading army came into touch with the Ashanti near Amoafo. The Kumasi road was here running parallel with the ridge of hills surrounding the lake, and was rising and falling over the lateral spurs of the ridge and the small valleys between them. South of Amoafo the road dipped over a spur, descended into a swampy valley some fifty feet deep, crossed the stream and bore to the right to climb the next spur. The whole landscape was thickly forested. The Ashanti held both spurs and the saddle of hill joining them, so that they flanked the advance of the British as they came down the first hill, and enclosed them in a semi-circle when they were in the valley.

Sir Garnet's plan of attack was to advance along the main road with a centre column, while two flanking columns moved diagonally to right and left, and a rear column extended to keep in touch with the flanks. If the Ashanti tried their usual flanking tactics, which he could not prevent with an inferior force, the right and left columns were to face outwards and the advance was to continue in square.

The centre column had little difficulty till it reached the stream; but when it tried to climb the farther hill it could make little progress against the Ashanti fire. Infantry reinforcements having failed to carry the position, the two guns were brought up; and a series of short artillery bombardments and quick rushes enabled the Black Watch, after four hours' fighting, to carry the town of Amoafo. Meanwhile the left column, consisting of the Naval Brigade and Russell's regiment, cleared the left flank and rejoined the centre body at noon, just as the Black Watch entered Amoafo. The right column had similar work to do, but they were attacking the main Ashanti force, and it was not for another hour and a half that they were able to silence the Ashanti fire. As firing ceased on the front and the flanks, it broke out in the British rear, where the Ashanti attacked the advanced base at Kwaman, two miles behind. This attack was kept up till dark, but was repulsed.[12]

The battle of Amoafo was won mainly by superior weapons. The British rifles were, of course, superior to the Ashanti muzzle-loading guns, and the continual advance of the Black Watch gave the Ashanti too little time to reload. Even so, seven companies of the Black Watch and a company of the Royal Welsh Fusiliers could make little impression on the Ashanti position until the two seven-pounder guns were brought into action. Against these, of course, the Ashanti could make no reply; and the victory of Amoafo was largely due to the guns, as that of Akantamasu had been largely due to the rockets. The Ashanti loss was unknown; 150 of their dead were buried by the British, and many more were carried off by the Ashanti themselves. The British lost one officer and three

[12] Amankwa Tia was killed at Amoafo; tradition says that he was engaged in an altercation with the commander who had superseded him and, as he was tearing his cloth in fury, a bullet killed him. Fuller says that he had sworn not to return alive anyway, so furious was he at being superseded. Ellis and Claridge say that Kwabena Dwumo of Mampon, the commander-in-chief, was also killed; but Mampon tradition denies this, and says that he was engaged in the civil wars of 1875.

men killed, and 21 officers and 173 men wounded. The heaviest losses were among the Black Watch, who had two men killed and nine officers and 104 men wounded.

The next day, 1st February, was spent in bringing up supplies, and in attacking and destroying Bekwai, which lay a mile to the west of the road and was too dangerous a place to leave available to the Ashanti as a base for attack on the British communications. On the 2nd the troops advanced from Amoafo, and in the afternoon of the 3rd arrived at the Oda river. The General was now beginning to be anxious over his timetable. The advance was slow owing to the difficulty of bringing up supplies through hostile country and guarding the line of communications against attack. On the other hand, he wanted to finish the campaign and be out of the country again before the rains began in earnest, by the end of March at the very latest, and if possible sooner. He decided, therefore, to form an advanced base and to make a quick dash for Kumasi, which was only fifteen miles away, in the hope that such a quick stroke might end the fighting and bring the Ashanti to ask for peace.

By daybreak on the 4th, the engineers had finished the bridge across the Oda, which was fifty feet wide and waist deep. At six o'clock the advance began, and after two hours' hard fighting the advance guard of the Rifle Brigade reached the village of Odasu, seven miles from Kumasi. The main body was heavily attacked on both flanks as it followed, and as the Naval Brigade which formed the rearguard marched along escorting the baggage to Odasu, the Ashanti closed in on the deserted camp with songs and cheers, thinking that the British force was lost now that its retreat was cut off.

The whole force was now concentrated in Odasu village, and for an hour the Ashanti kept up a vigorous attack. The Rifle Brigade held the perimeter of the place, and as there seemed no chance that the fighting would die down for some hours, Sir Garnet decided that the Black Watch must break out at all costs, disregarding any flank attack, and must carry Kumasi at a rush. There was no alternative, for the men had only four days' supplies with them to carry them to Kumasi and back to their advanced base at Agyemamu, eight miles behind their present position at Odasu.

Asamoa Nkwanta had laid the plans for the defence of Odasu,

and the Asantehene himself was present. The plan was a miniature of the general Ashanti strategy of the campaign. A large force was held in reserve to the flank of the road, with orders to close in and cut the British communications if they succeeded in forcing their way into the village. This was done, but the advance of the Black Watch, so gallantly carried out, was contrary to all Ashanti notions of war, according to which an army was in mortal danger if threatened on the flank, and ruined if threatened in the rear. The Black Watch carried out their orders;[13] they rushed straight forward, pipes playing, officers to the front; they broke through all opposition, and without needing the assistance of the guns or the Rifle Brigade, they reached Kumasi at half-past five, having been marching and fighting for nearly twelve hours after a night spent in grass huts under a torrential rainstorm. Sir Garnet arrived soon after six, and forming up in the main street of Kumasi, the troops gave three cheers for the Queen.

Kumasi was reached; but the war was not won. The Asantehene was out of reach, no hostages had been given, no indemnity paid, and no treaty signed. Sir Garnet sent another letter, demanding that either the Asantehene or the queen mother of the stool heir should appear to negotiate, and that if these people were out of the question as hostages, others of high rank should be sent. The messengers were told that if the peace treaty could be made on the next day, not only would the ambassadors be safe, but the town would be unharmed; if treachery were attempted, however, the town would be destroyed and its inhabitants slaughtered. These messages were of little effect, as during the night all the towns-people left Kumasi with their belongings, so that the place was completely deserted in the morning; while the Fante prisoners who were released amused themselves by looting and by setting fire to the town. The Asantehene, therefore, had little incentive to trust Sir Garnet's word.[14]

The General's anxiety was increasing; for he had over sixty wounded to carry back, he had to get back to Agyemamu before his supplies failed, and all the afternoon it rained in torrents, and

[13] Sir Archibald Alison's 'purple patch' of description, quoted by Ellis and Claridge and Fuller, makes gallant reading.
[14] It goes without saying that the General did his best to preserve order. The troops were kept up all night putting out fires, and one Fante was hanged and several flogged for looting.

news came that the water in the Oda river had risen eighteen inches over the bridge. He could wait no longer than one day; and as nobody came to him, he had the town fired and the palace blown up. On the morning of 6th February he began his march back to the coast.

The other three columns had been less fortunate. Captain Dalrymple failed to raise more than fifty men from Wassaw and the neighbouring districts, and his men refused to cross the Ofin river into Ashanti. He rejoined the General on the homeward march. Captain Butler was ready to cross the Pra as ordered on 15th January, but his Akim levies were unwilling to enter the enemy country. It was not till the 25th that he was able to cross the river with about 1,400 men and advance towards Kokofu, an important town six miles north of Amoafo. When within a few miles of Amoafo he received orders from the General to co-operate in the battle by attacking the Ashanti left flank; but on the day before the battle his Akim troops deserted. Captain Butler himself rejoined the General at Agyemamu on the return march.

Captain Glover had similar difficulties. He began his work with a small force of Hausa troops from Lagos, and enlarged it by enlisting numbers of men called Odonkos. These were men from what are now the Northern Territories, who had been brought down into the coast districts as slaves. As they used a corrupt form of Hausa as a *lingua franca*, Captain Glover and his staff thought they were a tribe akin to the Hausa, and enlisted all that came to them. This caused trouble when the masters came to reclaim their slaves, for Glover's officers replied shortly that slavery could not exist on British soil, which they imagined the 'Protectorate' to be. This led to rioting and a good deal of distrust, and conservative tribesmen were disinclined to co-operate with men who showed such shameful disregard of the rights of property.

Captain Glover had promised the General to cross the Pra on 15th January with 15,000 troops: but he soon saw that he had no chance of keeping his promise. He did indeed gather nearly 12,000 men, but they refused to consider moving against the Ashanti until they had settled with the Anlo, who were Ashanti allies and who were profiting by the general confusion to feather their own nest at the expense of their neighbours. In this they could not be blamed, for the war between the Anlo and the Akwamu allies against the

Krepi had been going on for several years, and from the point of view of the Krepi and their allies, the Ashanti campaign was a sideshow. Glover, therefore, asked for permission to reduce the Anlo before entering Ashanti, but the General sent him peremptory orders to cross the Pra on 15th January at all costs. The allied chiefs refused to follow him, and he invaded Ashanti, therefore, on the appointed day with nobody but his semi-trained force of 750 Hausa and Odonko, though he received small reinforcements of Akim Bosome and others as he marched. By the end of January he reached Konongo, but could not advance farther, as the Juaben men held the line of the river Anum in force. Here he waited for orders from the General, but the message which was sent to him miscarried. Sir Garnet wished him to stay where he was, containing the Juaben force, until 14th February, and then to retire on the Pra. Not receiving these orders, Captain Glover waited only to receive reinforcements and supplies, and on the 8th he advanced to attack the Juaben position. To his surprise he found it abandoned, the Juaben having heard of the fall of Kumasi; and Captain Glover, knowing nothing of what had happened, pushed on through Kumasi and followed the General down to Prasu and Cape Coast.

These auxiliary columns had nevertheless rendered the General great service. Captain Glover had completely held the Juaben contingent, and prevented it from swinging round to attack Prasu. Captain Butler had similarly drawn off the Kokofu contingent, and even Captain Dalrymple, the unluckiest of the three, was believed by the General to have drawn off the Bekwai contingent. In this he was wrong, for the Bekwai men fought both at Amoafo and Odasu; but it may well be that part of the Bekwai force had to remain to guard the frontier against Captain Dalrymple.

The advance of Captain Glover's column against Juaben was the final blow to the Ashanti. The fall of Kumasi had shaken the Ashanti state to its foundations, and many of the great feudatories were thinking of breaking away. Juaben had actually surrendered without consulting the Asantehene, and the Ashanti could not be sure that the British might not return and join with Captain Glover's force. On 13th February envoys from the Asantehene overtook the General at Fomena and promised that the Asantehene would accept his conditions. They produced 1,040 ounces of gold.

saying that it was impossible to collect more for the moment; and they took back with them a draft treaty for signature. Sir Garnet continued his homeward march; he reached Cape Coast on 19th February, and all the European troops were at sea by the end of the month, the General himself sailing on 4th March.

The treaty, which was signed by the Asantehene and nine Kumasi representatives, and by single representatives of Juaben, Bekwai, Kokofu, Kuntanase, Nsuta, Mampon and five minor states, was executed at Cape Coast on 14th March; it is, however, called the Treaty of Fomena, the place where the draft was first given to the Ashanti representatives. The treaty consists, apart from purely formal matters, of seven clauses: II, an idemnity of 50,000 ounces of gold; III, the Asantehene renounces all allegiance from Denkyera, Assin, Akim and (a newcomer to this list) Adansi; IV, he renounces also Elmina and its allied tribes, and all payments from the Government in respect of any of the forts; V, he will withdraw his troops from the south-west; VI, the trade routes shall be kept open; VII, the road from Kumasi to the Pra is to be kept clear; VIII, the Asantehene will do his best to stop human sacrifice.

The treaty of Fomena replaced the treaty of 1831 as the basis of relations between the British and Ashanti. The indemnity was fixed at an impossibly high figure; if paid at all, it could only be paid in instalments spread over many years. It would be impossible for the Asantehene to put a rapid stop to human sacrifice without destroying the whole Ashanti religion, and when that was destroyed the sanctity of the Golden Stool would be destroyed also, and with it the Asantehene's authority. Ashanti could, no doubt, be gradually transformed into an up-to-date state on Western lines; but it could only be by a long, gradual and difficult process, which would leave something very different from the Ashanti of 1874.

The mention of Adansi was ominous. The Adansi had been prominent in counselling resistance, and Asamoa Nkwanta himself had been in charge of their force. They had made a heavy attack on their capital town, Fomena, when it was occupied as an advanced base and convalescent camp. They now, however, applied to be taken under British protection, saying that they had always been opposed to the war and had taken no part in the fighting; and they said that they would be forced to emigrate from Ashanti, whether they received British protection or not, as the Asantehene would take vengeance on them for their disloyalty. Sir Garnet did not wish to encourage the Adansi to secede from Ashanti, but he felt that if the Wassaw and Denkyera, who would be their new neighbours, felt ready to have them it was not for him to interfere. He told the Adansi, therefore, that they must make their own arrangements with these tribes, but that he would see that the Ashanti gave them no trouble; and their claim to independence was inserted in the treaty. It was unfortunate that in clause III of the treaty, the Adansi and the others are described as "allies of Her Majesty", when nothing was done to define their alliance. Further, the Adansi told Sir Garnet that they wanted to emigrate; but after the treaty was signed they stayed north of the Pra in their own country, and made a nuisance of themselves by claiming to be under British protection no matter where they were or how they behaved.

For the time being, Ashanti had fallen to pieces. Most of the important states, including Mampon, Nsuta, Bekwai, Kokofu, Juaben and even Okomfo Anokye's town of Agona, refused to obey the central government; and all the outlying provinces such as Kwahu, Gyaman, Sefwi, Banda, and the northern tribes, openly declared their independence. The Asantehene, Kofi Karikari, was not the man to reassert his authority. He asked the Governor to send up an officer to mediate between him and the Juaben chief Asafo Agyei, and with some reluctance the Governor did so; but the only terms on which Juaben would accept peace were complete independence. In August or September 1874 Kofi Karikari was deposed. He had some of the gold treasures brought out of the tombs of the royal family, and his mother recognized some of her own mother's trinkets, which she knew had been buried. There was a terrible scandal, and Kofi Karikari was deposed, being succeeded by his younger brother Mensa Bonsu.

Mensa Bonsu set himself to rebuild Kumasi and to reassert the authority of the Golden Stool over the rebellious provinces. He tried his hand on Juaben, but Juaben would have none of him, and the Juaben men went to the length of killing all the Kumasi traders they could find. Juaben and many of the other states had already applied for British protection, but the Government was determined not to increase its responsibilities in this way, and rejected all the requests. When Asafo Agyei of Juaben carried his defiance of the Asantehene to such acts of war, Mensa Bonsu naturally sounded the British Government's views. The Government had already refused to take Juaben under its protection; would it now allow Juaben to close the roads and evade its share of the indemnity demanded by the Treaty of Fomena? The Government still declined to interfere in any way; so the Asantehene set himself to make the Juaben question into a test case for the rest of the Ashanti states. All of them, faced with the alternatives of rallying round Kumasi or around Juaben, supported Kumasi, though few of them gave Kumasi more than moral support. In October 1875 the Asantehene attacked Juaben with an army composed mainly of Kumasi men but with a few troops from Kokofu and Asumegya and Bekwai. At first the Juaben troops held their own, and some of the Kumasi generals, including the famous Asamoa Nkwanta, blew themselves up in despair; but on 3rd November the Juaben ammunition was exhausted, and the Juaben broke and fled. Hundreds of Juaben prisoners fell into Kumasi hands, and were sent through Sefwi to be sold as slaves in the hinterland of French territory in exchange for arms and ammunition. The Juaben survivors fled to Kibi, as their fathers had done forty years before; they saved their Stools, and settled down as a body on land near Koforidua, where they established the state of New Juaben. Asafo Agyei sent to Sefwi and persuaded the Sefwihene to hold the Juaben prisoners until he should have a chance to redeem them; this he eventually did, and they were able to return home. In 1877 Asafo Agyei was found to be plotting with some chiefs of the Colony to win back his Ashanti land by force, and after having neglected a warning from the Government that this must cease, he was exiled to Lagos.

This Juaben war had greatly strengthened Mensa Bonsu's position. No other state had supported Juaben in its revolt, the Government clearly would do nothing to interfere with him, and the flight of the Juaben had allowed the direct rule of Kumasi to be extended over some of their towns such as Asokore and Effiduase. It was natural that Mensa Bonsu should decide that he had nothing more to fear from the British, especially as the rapid retreat of Sir Garnet Wolseley's force after the burning of Kumasi seemed to the Ashanti a confession of fear. The Government seemed to them like Macbeth fleeing from the crime he has committed:

> "I'll go no more:
> I am afraid to think what I have done;
> Look on 't again I dare not."

The Government's actions indeed were feeble. It sent Dr. Gouldsbury to Kibi when the war was threatened, with instructions to warn the Akim to take no part in it, and then to go on to Juaben and Kumasi and try to stop the war. Dr. Gouldsbury went to Akim, and was met there by the news that the fighting had begun; he reached Juaben to find it in Kumasi hands, and then went on to Kumasi, where he could, of course, do nothing. Captain Lees, who had been sent up the previous year to mediate between Kumasi and Juaben, had been treated with every mark of honour. Dr. Gouldsbury was treated as a nobody; and Captain Baker of the Constabulary, who arrived about the same time with an escort to receive another instalment of the war indemnity, was hooted and pelted in the streets of Kumasi. This treatment so alarmed the Government that it never sent again, and only 4,000 out of the 50,000 ounces of gold demanded by the treaty of Fomena were ever paid. "Thus," says Ellis, "within less than two years after the burning of Kumasi the Ashanti had, thanks to the Government policy of non-intervention, recovered the whole of their lost territory except Kwahu and Adansi, and escaped the payment of the greater part of the indemnity."

The policy of the Gold Coast Government towards Ashanti from 1874 to 1890 was utterly timorous and vacillating, and the fruits of the campaign of 1874 were completely lost in an incredibly short time. Sir Garnet Wolseley won the war; the Gold Coast Government lost the peace.

In criticizing the Gold Coast Governments of an earlier day we must always be careful not to blame them for mistakes made through unavoidable ignorance. It is very easy for us, having the benefit of later investigations into Ashanti laws and customs, to fall into the error of blaming Governments who had to govern before the days of Rattray. It would, for example, be unfair to blame Governor Pine in 1862 severely because he was not familiar with the nature of the Ashanti 'great oath', and so did not realize that he would be completely safe in trusting a promise confirmed by it. The only blame that he can fairly take is that which he may incur through ignoring the experience of Cruikshank and Maclean on the point.

But in criticizing the policy of the Government in the period from 1874 to 1900 we need not be restrained by such scruples. The mistakes it made were not made through lack of knowledge. It must have known from past experience that trouble would arise if refugees were allowed to come and claim British protection. It must have known that if Ashanti fell into anarchy refugees certainly would come and claim British protection. Its mistakes were made because it had not made up its mind clearly what it wanted and was not prepared to face the consequences of its own actions.

The two bases of its policy were a misunderstanding of the position of the Asantehene, and a determination never again to be involved in an Ashanti war. The Government did not realize the nature of the Ashanti state. It did not realize that it was originally a confederation of independent tribes, who were held together not by common subjection to a tyrant, but by free association for common purposes. The origin of the state had been military, and it was military defeat that had now shaken it apart. The member-states, Mampon, Bekwai, Juaben and the rest, were small and fairly evenly matched. If Ashanti ceased to exist as a unit, there would be rivalries and jealousy among the member-states, leading almost certainly to civil war and the utter extinction of trade.

The Government was in an unpleasant dilemma. It hoped for a revival of trade in Ashanti and the hinterland, and trade could only revive if peace were kept. Peace would certainly not be kept for long if Ashanti split up. On the other hand, if the Asantehene succeeded in regaining his authority over the Ashanti tribes, he would build up again the Ashanti military power. The Government, therefore, wanted the Asantehene to be strong enough to keep all Ashanti in order, but to be weak enough not to be a danger to the Colony. Two contradictory aims naturally led to chaos.

Further, the Government had already compromised itself. The treaty of Fomena imposed an indemnity on Ashanti, and treated Ashanti as a unified sovereign state. Captain Lees had brought about an agreement between Kumasi and Juaben, and Mensa Bonsu naturally, if not justifiably, considered that the Government should insist that an agreement thus made should be kept.

Dr. Gouldsbury's ineffective mission showed that the Government was not indifferent to what went on in Ashanti, but the Ashanti naturally despised a Government that expressed wishes without being able to enforce them. There were, in fact, two possible courses open to the Government. One was to declare openly that the war of 1874 had taught the Ashanti not to interfere with the Colony, and that it in return had no intention of interfering with Ashanti. This would have involved closing the Pra to refugees, and explaining that individuals or whole tribes (such as Adansi and Juaben) must stay north of the border and settle their affairs with the Asantehene by themselves. The other course was to declare that the treaty of Fomena had been made with the Asantehene on the understanding that the Asantehene would have the power to keep it, and that the interests of the Colony required that the Government should uphold the Asantehene's authority. This would have brought the whole of Ashanti in effect under the British protection, and would no doubt have involved for some years at least the maintenance of a British force of some sort to enforce the Government's decisions. Either of these policies would have been understood by the Ashanti; either would have raised problems, but could have been worked.[15] The policy actually adopted by the Government was not intelligible to the Ashanti, or to anyone else. It maintained the claims of the treaty of Fomena against the Asantehene, while on the other hand it allowed any rebellious tribe to cast off its allegiance to Ashanti on the sole condition that it crossed the Pra and refrained while in the Colony from intriguing or raiding on Ashanti soil. In effect, therefore, it did a great deal to weaken the Asantehene, while holding him entirely responsible for the evils which he could only hope to remove if he remained strong.

Mensa Bonsu remained on the stool from 1874 to 1883. The whole of this time was spent in efforts to restore Ashanti to its former position. In 1878 he sent to Gyaman to say that the Queen of England had given the whole of Gyaman to him. The Gyaman sent to the Governor at Cape Coast to ask if this was so, and a British officer was sent up to Bondugu to deny Mensa's claim. He was instructed also to offer the Gyaman British protection if they

---

[15] The policy of non-intervention, superficially more attractive, would probably have been much more difficult in the long run.

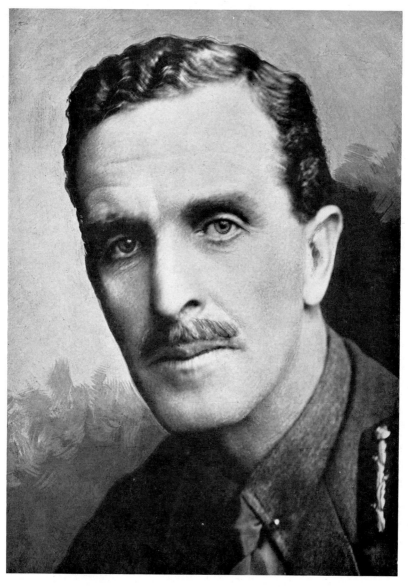

PLATE IX   SIR GORDON GUGGISBERG   (*Elliott & Fry*)

PLATE X   DR. KWAME NKRUMAH

wished for it. The Gyamanhene, Kwadwo Agyeman, was inclined to accept the offer, but most of his chiefs thought differently, and the offer was declined.

The Asantehene also tried to regain the allegiance of Adansi. Kwadwo Oben died in 1875, and there was a dispute over the succession, while one of the parties wished to bring Adansi back to its allegiance to Ashanti and the other wished it to remain independent. The parties nearly came to blows over the question, and sent to ask the Governor to arbitrate. He sent up an officer, Captain Moloney, who stayed some months in Adansi and succeeded in getting the dispute settled. Early in 1876 one Nkansa Berofon was appointed to the stool, and recognized by Captain Moloney on behalf of the Government; and Adansi decided to remain independent of Ashanti. Nkansa Berofon, however, was hardly the man for such a delicate position; his rule was unpopular, and quite apart from any question of Ashanti prestige, the Asantehene had many provocations from him.

Early in 1879 the Asantehene seemed to be having success in his efforts to win over the Adansi, and Nkansa Berofon took alarm and appealed to the Government for help. The independence of Adansi was by now almost the last relic of the fruits of the war, and the Government decided that it must be preserved. It sent up another officer, Captain Hay, to Kumasi to demand that the Ashanti agents be recalled from Fomena and that the Asantehene respect the treaty of Fomena. This step succeeded, and for the time being Mensa Bonsu left Adansi alone. For this success the acting Governor was censured by the Secretary of State; he was told that the question of enforcing the third clause of the treaty of Fomena was a matter of external policy which should have been discussed with the Imperial Government beforehand. The situation was similar to that of the 'sixties: the Imperial Government had for the time being adopted a settled policy of not interfering with Ashanti and of avoiding further responsibilities, while the officials on the Gold Coast were tending towards a more forward policy. There is little doubt that in dealing with Mensa Bonsu the officials on the spot were right and the Imperial Government was wrong. In theory, either policy was workable; but it was quite plain that the Asantehene was working hard to build up again the fighting power of Ashanti, and to allow him to ignore clause after clause

K

at his pleasure of a treaty which had been imposed on him only six years before was the shortest way to another Ashanti war.

There was indeed already a war party in Kumasi. The Asantehene and the queen mother were for peace, for they felt that a policy of peaceful intrigue would pay Ashanti better. The war party, however, was growing stronger. Feeling that Ashanti had been beaten largely by superior weapons, they had for some years been buying Snider breech-loading rifles, especially since the removal of the embargo by the British authorities in 1878 enabled them to import them openly through Cape Coast—to the great disgust and bewilderment of the Fante and the Assin. They had formed a corps of Hausa troops, and had the services of a German adventurer as an instructor for the force. This war party was making Mensa Bonsu's position very difficult. The deposed Asantehene, Kofi Karikari, had not committed suicide, as strict etiquette recommended, and the war party was beginning to regard Mensa Bonsu as pusillanimous and to think of Kofi Karikari as a national hero who stood up to the British and braved hard fate. This war party in Kumasi was supported by Kokofu, and Bekwai too was very restive at Mensa's tolerating Adansi independence, though Bekwai did not for the moment abandon its allegiance to the Asantehene.

In January, 1881, there came an incident which brought all this tension to breaking-point. A man called Owusu Tasiamandi arrived at Elmina to claim the protection of the Governor. He was a member of the royal family of Gyaman, and was a possible heir to the Gyaman stool. On his father's side he was closely connected with the royal family of Ashanti, and it was probably for this reason, rather than for any crime that he had committed, that the Asantehene was anxious that he should not be allowed to get to Gyaman, where at the time there was a member of the royal family, named Kokobo, who was intriguing with Ashanti support to have Kwadwo Agyeman deposed. Owusu Tasiamandi's arrival in Gyaman might well have been fatal to Kokobo's plans, as he would have provided the opposition party with a leader who would replace Agyeman without submitting to Ashanti.

The day after he arrived in Elmina, an embassy arrived from Kumasi to demand his surrender. The messengers brought with them two symbols which caused much misunderstanding. These were the golden axe and a golden facsimile of the mud nest of a mason wasp. These were interpreted by the British as a threat of war if the embassy's demands were not granted; but it seems certain that this was a misrepresentation. The golden axe symbolized determination to cut through all difficulties until a solution was reached; it may have had also some magical significance. The wasp's nest, according to Claridge, also did not mean war, but merely that the matter in hand was one which might lead to war if a satisfactory solution could not be found. Both these symbols thus implied, not that Ashanti threatened immediate war, but that the matter in hand was of the highest importance, so high that war was conceivable. The distinction may seem a fine one, but is very real.

The Governor, Mr. W. Brandford Griffith, naturally replied that Owusu had committed no crime[16] and was now under British protection, so that there could be no talk of sending him back to Ashanti. The embassy then asked that in any case he might be prevented from going to Gyaman, whither he had asked to be sent under escort. The reply was that he could go where he pleased. This seems to have led to some heated talk, and the Governor received the impression that the Ashanti would invade Assin if their demands were not granted.[17] It was well known that there was a strong war party in Ashanti, so that this possibly was not to be dismissed; and something like panic seems to have broken out. Trenches were dug, sandbags piled, armed police concentrated, preparations made for calling up levies, stores sent up to Prasu, and even a battalion of the West India regiment obtained from the West Indies. The Asantehene, of course, heard of these preparations, and sent no fewer than four separate embassies to explain that he did not intend war, and to ask why the British were preparing to attack him.

A newly-appointed Governor, Sir Samuel Rowe, arrived in the Colony in March 1881. He ignored or gave evasive answers to the two Ashanti embassies he found awaiting his arrival, and continued large scale military preparations. Eventually, the Asante-

[16] There was some talk of his having acted high-handedly in arresting a man accused of theft; but the charge does not seem to have been pressed, and he was clearly regarded as a political prisoner.
[17] It is uncertain what was said at the interview; but there is no doubt that the Governor received this impression.

hene, to the fury of many of his counsellors, decided to submit to the humiliation of asking for peace as if he had been defeated in a war. He voluntarily surrendered the golden axe, assured the Governor that he had never had the slightest intention of making war, and promised to pay an indemnity of 2,000 ounces of gold; and the Governor accepted his surrender. There seems no reason whatever to doubt that the Asantehene's astonishment at hearing of the vast preparations being made against invasion was perfectly genuine. The affair should never have been allowed to grow to such a pitch of excitement; Maclean would have disposed of the whole misunderstanding in one interview. Owusu Tasiamandi, the unfortunate cause of all the trouble, committed suicide. The only permanent result of the affair was that Mensa Bonsu's position was made still more difficult, and friendship with Britain was associated in the minds of the Ashanti war party with national humiliation.[18]

The Government's policy of non-intervention was clearly not succeeding. It had brought the Gold Coast to the edge of another Ashanti war only seven years after the last one. Trade was small, and unlikely to increase. The Government decided to take the opportunity of sending an officer not only to Kumasi but beyond, to try to open up new trade routes. In October 1881, Captain Lonsdale was sent to Kumasi with gifts to the Asantehene and the notables on the occasion of the final closing of the Owusu Tasiamandi episode; and he was instructed to visit also Salaga and other places and try to open up new trade routes. Captain Lonsdale stayed a month in Kumasi, and had great difficulty in escaping to the north unaccompanied by an Ashanti embassy. The Ashanti naturally wished to remain the sole middlemen for the northern trade, and foresaw that if the routes were once opened it would be hard to stop Fante and others using them. Trade was interrupted because the Brong people of northern Ashanti had closed the roads between Kumasi and Salaga. The Brong had a grievance against Ashanti; for Kofi Karikari had sent to Krachi to inquire of the Dente oracle whether his war against the British would be successful, and on receiving an unpalatable answer had lost his temper with the priests of Dente. Dente was the most famous god of the

[18] The Asantehene was handicapped by his name Bonsu. As this so clearly recalled Osei Tutu Kwamina, Mensa was expected to emulate the deed of that great warrior, and his people's disappointment was all the greater as he seemed determined to avoid war. Names mean a great deal in the Gold Coast.

Brong people, and his priests exercised a sort of theocracy over all the Brong; so Kofi Karikari had extended his anger to cover the Brong nation as a whole, and had forced the Brong troops in his army to fight in the hottest places throughout the war. After the war the Brong had promptly rebelled and would have offered their allegiance to the British if the British had shown any sign of being willing to accept it. As they could not do this, they at least closed the roads to all Ashanti traders, so that the trade of Salaga was largely diverted to Kintampo. Some of it, however, still came from the north via Salaga and Krachi to Accra. Captain Lonsdale was instructed to do what he could to encourage this latter route. He visited Salaga and Yendi, the capital of the Dagomba, and returned to Accra through Krachi and the Krepi country. At the same time the Government opened negotiations with Sefwi and Gyaman, hoping to open a new western trade route through those districts.

Next year, 1882, there was more trouble between Ashanti and Gyaman, and Captain Lonsdale was sent up to try to mediate. The Banda people had recently been attacked by a neighbouring tribe—not Ashanti—and had accepted protection from Gyaman and been given Gyaman land to live on. They were now repenting of their bargain and were proposing to transfer their allegiance to Ashanti, but apparently without giving up the Gyaman land they had been granted. This, of course, led to trouble between Banda and Gyaman, and the war party in Ashanti saw an excellent chance of bringing both Gyaman and Banda under Ashanti rule. The Asantehene, however, disapproved of the war policy, and sent to ask the Governor's advice. Captain Lonsdale succeeded in postponing the fighting and getting the matter left to the Governor's arbitration; he then returned to the coast through Sefwi, where the Sefwihene and his chiefs swore allegiance to the British.

This latest instance of his subservience to the British made his chiefs utterly disgusted with Mensa Bonsu. He was unpopular for other reasons; he was avaricious and lustful, and the whole country was full of men sulking because he had intrigued with their wives or had fined them exorbitant amounts for small offences.[19] In February 1883 Mensa Bonsu was deposed.

[19] An instance is recorded in Ahuren tradition. A chief named Amofa swore that he would never enter Kumasi again. When his sub-chiefs asked him why not, he

There ensued a year of anarchy. There were three claimants to the stool: Mensa Bonsu himself, his elder brother Kofi Karikari, both of whom were personally unpopular, and a third candidate who was supported by most of the people: Kwaku Dua, son of Yaa Kyia, the sister of the other two men. Mensa Bonsu's chance was small; he was supported only by Kokofu and a few of the Bekwai men. Kofi Karikari had a fair amount of support, but lost his chance by being unlucky enough to be captured in a skirmish by his opponents. Kwaku Dua was by far the strongest candidate: he had been nominated as Asantehene by Kwaku Dua I, and it was only because he was a child that his two uncles had preceded him on the stool. In April 1884 he was enstooled; but in June of the same year he died of smallpox.

Of the remaining two candidates, there could be no doubt that Kofi Karikari was preferred. He was brought to Kumasi, but died a week later, probably from dysentery caught during his wanderings in the bush after his defeat.[20]

His death threw all Ashanti into utter confusion. Every chief did that which was right in his own eyes. Manso Nkwanta fought against Kumasi and defeated it, so that the Kumasi chiefs lost much of the prestige that they had through being the guardians of the Golden Stool. The town of Kumasi was deserted again, and all trade ceased.

After several months of anarchy it seemed as though nothing could restore Ashanti to its old power. But in October 1884 the queen mother, Yaa Kyia, made a desperate appeal to the Ashanti chiefs to save the nation by coming to Kumasi and choosing a new Asantehene. The chiefs agreed, but they made the stipulation that a British officer should witness the enstoolment and should confirm it on behalf of the Government. This request had already been made in connection with the enstoolment of Kwaku Dua II, but the Governor then had no officer whom he could spare to visit Kumasi, and the chiefs would not wait indefinitely. But the

replied that his son had been fined eight peredwans (about £64) for swearing the oath *Aheneakoraa* in Kumasi, and that this was an unreasonable and unheard-of sum; three peredwans would have been fair. The tradition says that Amofa received wide support, and this case began the open opposition to Mensa Bonsu. See also Claridge, II, 262.

[20] Fuller says that he was secretly put to death. But as he was of royal blood it is very doubtful whether this could possibly happen. Claridge's suggestion of dysentery is much more probable.

situation now was more serious, and the approval of the British
Government seemed more necessary. The candidate chosen by Yaa
Kyia was Kwasi Kyisi, who was, like Yaa Kyia herself, a grandchild
of Efua Sapon, sister of Kwaku Dua I.[21] The queen mother sent an
embassy down to the Governor, informing him that she proposed
to enstool Kwasi Kyisi, and asking him to send up an officer to
confirm the choice.

The Governor had nobody to send, and from October 1884 to
February 1886 the Ashanti messengers waited at Accra[22] in vain.

In this confusion the Adansi saw their opportunity. They had
not left their country to come and live south of the Pra, but they
had always encouraged the belief in Ashanti that they were under
British protection, and the events of 1879 had, of course, deepened
this impression. They now profited by the absence of all authority
in Ashanti to set up as a robber state on a considerable scale, and
early in 1886 they massacred the whole of a party of 150 Ashanti
traders who were returning from the coast. This matter was taken
up by Karikari, chief of Bekwai, who called out his troops to attack
Adansi, and began reprisals by killing sixty-five Adansi traders
who were returning from Gyaman through Bekwai territory. The
Adansi promptly applied for British protection on the strength of
the treaty of Fomena.

The independence of Adansi was certainly specified in the treaty
of Fomena, and the Adansi were described therein as British allies,
a title which they had done nothing to earn before or afterwards.
The Adansi had asked for protection on the ground that they
would not otherwise be able to remain north of the Pra; but it
would have been much better to have promised them the protection they asked for on condition that they moved into the Colony,
especially as they had arranged with the Wassaw people to do so,
and the Wassaw people sent to ask the Government in 1874 to
compel the Adansi to keep to the arrangement. This had not been
done; but the Government in these years seems to have attached an
almost superstitious importance to keeping Adansi free from any
Ashanti control. The Governor, Mr. Brandford Griffith, therefore

[21] See the genealogical table on p. 420. Claridge calls Kwasi Kyisi, Yaa Kyia's
sister's son; but this is not the case, and his own genealogical table does not
support him. Yaa Kyia was not strictly entitled to nominate the Asantehene;
but in practice any nominee of hers would almost certainly be chosen.
[22] The seat of government was moved from Cape Coast to Accra in 1876.

found himself able to spare an officer to visit Prasu for the sake of the Adansi, though he had not been able to spare anybody to visit Kumasi for the sake of general security in Ashanti.

The British officer, Mr. Firminger of the constabulary, visited Prasu in March 1886. He found that some skirmishing had already begun between the Bekwai and the Adansi, and that the Adansi were in fear of being attacked at any moment by the main Bekwai army. Mr. Firminger sent to Bekwai asking the chief[23] to state his grievances against Adansi and to refrain from fighting until Mr. Firminger had had a chance of settling them. The chief replied that more than two years ago he had sent in a complaint to Sir Samuel Rowe, but that he had never had a satisfactory reply; he would wait, however, until 20th March to give the Governor time to act on the old complaint or to send up an officer to arbitrate. Firminger sent this message on to Accra, but nothing was heard by 20th March; and Firminger did not think of letting the Bekwaihene know that he had sent it on and was not himself authorized to act as arbitrator. Had he done this, there is no doubt that the Bekwaihene would have extended the time of his ultimatum. It is not to be wondered at that the Bekwaihene, knowing that Ashanti messengers from Yaa Kyia had been waiting at Accra for over a year without a reply, should think it necessary to fix a time limit.

The time limit expired on the 20th, but it was not till the 23rd that the Bekwai men moved. On that day a skirmish occurred between a Bekwai reconnoitring force and an Adansi picket, and the Bekwai men retired after inflicting and receiving casualties. The Adansi regarded this as a great victory, and instead of asking for British protection, Nkansa Berofon quite changed his tone, and declared that he would invade Bekwai territory. He even went to the length of intercepting a messenger whom Mr. Firminger had sent to Bekwai, and sending him back under escort, with a message that the white man was too late and that he would follow the Bekwai wherever they went. He made an alliance with Dadiase, which though a subordinate of Kokofu was a strong little state, and was aspiring to become independent and to play a great part in politics. This alliance drew off a great part of the Bekwai men to watch against a flank attack from Dadiase; and towards the

[23] Karikari died on 1st February of this year and was succeeded by Yaw Gyanfi.

end of April the Adansi, supported by a Dadiase contingent, advanced on Bekwai and drove back the defending force in a series of hard-fought battles.

These Adansi successes, however, rallied all Ashanti to the support of Bekwai; for all Ashanti were anxious to see Adansi disciplined. They persuaded Dadiase to forsake the alliance; they sent a strong army to help Bekwai; they defeated the Adansi in a general engagement; and in June 1886 they drove the whole Adansi nation, over 12,000 strong, to cross the Pra to seek safety under the British flag. The Government rejected the advice given by Inspector Dudley of the constabulary, who was responsible for supervising the settlement of the Adansi, to plant them at a safe distance from the Pra. It settled them in the Assin and Akim districts on the south bank of the river, with the result that they made themselves a thorough nuisance by their old habits of robbing, and were so successful in this occupation that the Akim Bosome and the Denkyera became their partners in the business. They used British territory freely as a base for raids against Bekwai, and all the Government could think of as a remedy was to organize a regular convoy system for traders crossing the Pra. It was not until the middle of 1887 that the Government was convinced by experience, and shifted the refugees, much to their disgust, to a district where they could do little harm.

Meanwhile the Gold Coast Government was attacked from a quarter which could not be ignored. In 1883 and 1887 the Manchester Chamber of Commerce addressed the Secretary of State complaining of the 'apathy and inactivity' of the Gold Coast authorities. They pointed out that the annual imports of Manchester cotton into the Gold Coast, after rising from £300,000 twenty years before to £591,000 in 1884 had relapsed to £318,000 in 1886. They gave it as their opinion that this fall was due to the fact that there was no proper law and order on the frontier, that there were still no proper roads or railways in spite of the increase in Government revenue, and that trade was being diverted into neighbouring countries. In July 1885, they pointed out, the Secretary of State had written to the Governor asking for information about Ashanti and asking for the Governor's opinion on the policy which should be adopted on Ashanti affairs; this letter had received no answer at all until April 1886, and even then the question of policy was ignored, the Governor saying that he had no officer who could be spared for negotiations with Ashanti. The Secretary of State rejected their request that a permanent British Resident should be stationed at Kumasi, but no Secretary of State can remain utterly indifferent to communications of this kind, and there is little doubt that the Manchester Chamber of Commerce helped to bring about a change of policy with regard to Ashanti.

In Ashanti itself there was still confusion, in spite of the efforts of Bekwai and of Yaa Kyia herself to get something settled. In August 1886 the Government at last sent up a representative, an African interpreter named Badger. Mr. Badger visited Bekwai, Kokofu and Kumasi, and delivered a message from the Governor asking if the chiefs still wanted a European officer to be sent, and promising if so to send one within two months. He found that Kwasi Kyisi had died, and that there were two claimants, Kwaku Dua (commonly known by his nickname of Prempeh, i.e. 'tubby'), son of Yaa Kyia and brother of the late Kwaku Dua II, and Yaw Twereboanna (i.e. 'the gun-flint that never sleeps'), another grandchild of Efua Sapon. Each of the two claimants was supported by a strong party of influential men and women; but Yaw Gyanfi of Bekwai was authorized to count the votes and send down to Accra the name of the claimant with a majority. A section of Twereboanna's supporters, however, headed by the notorious Akyeampon of Elmina fame, refused to accept this innovation,[24] and civil war broke out again. From January 1887 till October 1887 campaigning went on, Bekwai and Kokofu doing most of the actual fighting. At last, owing partly to the mediation of two British officers, Captain Lonsdale and Mr. Barnett, the war burnt itself out; Prempeh's party obtained a decided majority, and in March 1888 he was enstooled in the style of Kwaku Dua III.

Prempeh was a youth of sixteen, and was very much in the hands of his mother Yaa Kyia and the Kumasi chiefs. As soon as the British representative had left Kumasi his troubles began. Kokofu again rebelled, and was joined by a contingent of Adansi and Dadiase men from the Colony; but the rebels were defeated by

[24] Majority voting is not the African way. The debate in an African council continues until the minority has actively joined the majority. Passive acquiescence is not enough; the political sense of Africans demands that a decision shall be truly unanimous.

Kumasi, Bekwai and Juaben,[25] and were driven across the Pra. This time the Government made a feeble effort to move them away from the river, but most of them seem to have stayed in the villages along the south bank, though some were moved to Akroso near Nsaba.

The civil war spread. Owusu Sekyere of Mampon, who ought to have been present at the enstoolment of the Asantehene but had held aloof, attacked the territory which was loyal to Prempeh, though his representatives at Kumasi had promised that he would never make trouble because he had not been present. He was defeated, and fled north to Atebubu. There he persuaded the Nkoranza to join with him, but the allies soon quarrelled, and Nkoranza declared for Prempeh and defeated a Mampon force. The chief of Nkoranza, however, claimed from Prempeh as a reward various privileges which Mampon had long possessed, and when he did not receive all he claimed he broke with Prempeh and declared his independence. Meanwhile Mampon, more to annoy Prempeh than for any other reason, sent to Accra and asked to be allowed to settle in the Colony, and the Government was prepared to have him. The Government's non-intervention policy, in fact, had now been completely abandoned. Sefwi had accepted British protection in February 1887, a British mission visited Bondugu in January 1888 on an unsuccessful attempt to bring that country under British protection,[26] and a year later Mr. Badger was sent to Atebubu to offer protection to the chief of Nsuta,[27] in the belief that he had asked for it. British protection, in fact, was being offered to all and sundry, and, in effect, the British Government was extending a general invitation to all who cared to desert the Asantehene and come into British territory or accept British

[25] At the time of the Juaben defeat in 1875, the heir to the Juaben stool, Yaw Sapon, was taken prisoner. He was then a boy; and when he grew to be a man, Mensa Bonsu released him, saying that he would not take his land away from him. Yaw Sapon collected some of his people and prepared to return to Juaben, sending before him a man to light a fire among the ruins of the town "that the spirits might light their pipes, and to give them water to drink" (Rattray, *Ashanti Law and Constitution*, 176). There were thus two Juabens, one in Ashanti and the New Juaben at Koforidua.

[26] Kwadwo Agyeman, the Gyamanhene, asked for it, and through his chiefs were at first opposed to him on the subject, they came round. But an Anglo-French treaty had meanwhile allotted Gyaman to France.

[27] Nsuta had supported Twereboanna and had been driven north to Atebubu. The request for British protection, however, did not come from the Nsutahene, but from two of his subordinate chiefs, and Nsuta preferred to come to terms with Prempeh.

protection. The young Asantehene's position was difficult enough without this.

The Government's decision to accept Owusu Sekyere and his people was communicated to the Asantehene in a letter taken to Kumasi by Mr. Badger in December 1889. The Governor asked the Asantehene not to persecute the tribes that seceded from his kingdom, but to turn his attention to improving trade. The Adansi, he was told, would be allowed to return north of the Pra if he would guarantee not to molest them. The reply which the Asantehene gave Mr. Badger to bring back was to the effect that his position was an impossible one when every tribe that wished coud secede from Ashanti and obtain British protection; he did not wish Mampon to do this, and he believed that Sefwi and others would as soon return to their Ashanti allegiance as remain under the British flag, since they had sought British protection during the troubles when there was no security in Ashanti. As for trade, "When all my subjects have come to the Protectorate, where is then trade? for once they have crossed to you, they shall fear to cross over and pass on my land to the interior to trade." Nothing more was heard of Owusu Sekyere's receiving British protection, and on the general principles of the case the Asantehene's letter was unanswerable. The Government had never taken effective steps to keep the Adansi and other refugees under control, and at that very moment Bekwai territory was being raided by refugees from their bases south of the Pra.

This letter was followed in July by an embassy from Kumasi which came to make a formal request that the various refugee tribes should be restored to Ashanti, and promised that if they returned they should be well treated. The Asantehene repeated his argument that a strong, united and peaceful Ashanti would be able to trade, whereas an Ashanti split into a number of small independent states and constantly threatened with internal war and actually suffering from border raids could not possibly hope to develop commerce. The Governor replied that he would put no pressure on any of the refugees to return, but would allow them to go if they wished.

At last, however, the Government had realized that the position could not continue, and that its policy must be changed. From 1874 to 1890 it had maintained its attitude of distrust and non-intervention as consistently as it could; it had taken its stand on the treaty of Fomena and had interfered in Ashanti affairs as little as it could, but always in the direction of helping those opposed to the central power. Its distrust of Ashanti was stronger than its desire to establish a strong power with which trade could be carried on. Circumstances had now changed. The British were no longer, as they had been since 1872, the only colonizing power in this part of West Africa. The French had settled on the Ivory Coast long since, and they were now fast pushing inland. In 1888 they had made a treaty with Gyaman, and were pushing farther north. In 1885 the Germans had settled in Togoland, and next year annexed lands directly north of Keta. The British Government had then rapidly made a series of treaties with Akwamu, Krepi and other eastern states, and was wide awake to the necessity of pushing the British flag northward for fear that French and Germans should swing round and enclose the Gold Coast completely. It was now feeling, in fact, that if Ashanti did not become British it might soon become French or German. But that was a consideration which it could hardly explain to the Ashanti themselves.

In December 1890 a strong British mission was sent to Kumasi to offer the Asantehene British protection, and to urge him to accept the offer by "a curious mixture of professions of friendship and thinly veiled threats."[28] The Governor, it seems, expected the Ashanti to accept this offer and the draft treaty which accompanied it, presumably because so many of the Ashanti chiefs had already asked for protection and because in 1884 the nation seemed unable to help itself without Government assistance. But the circumstances were now quite different. There was an Asantehene on the stool, and all the leaders of the opposition to him were in exile; he was steadfastly maintaining the only possible policy for an Asantehene, that of working to restore the power of the central government; and he had already won successes in his attempts. The Asantehene considered the offer of protection, and declined it; and the Secretary of State censured the Governor for offering a treaty to Ashanti without consulting him.

The Asantehene meanwhile went on with his plans for recovering his revolted subjects. In August 1892 he attacked Nkoranza, which had declared itself independent three years before. The

[28] Claridge, II, 353.

Nkoranza were heavily defeated; they applied for British protection, and when that was refused they applied to the priests of Krachi Dente, from whom they got some magic gunpowder and other charms. With this help they reversed the luck of battle; but in June 1893 the Asantehene brought against them an overwhelming force supplied from the whole of Ashanti, and Nkoranza was utterly destroyed.

This alarmed the chief of Atebubu, who was already under British protection, and he sent to ask the Government to keep the Asantehene from attacking him also. The Government sent a warning letter to the Asantehene, and a force of 300 police under Colonel Sir Francis Scott was sent to Atebubu. The Asantehene replied that he had never had any intention of attacking Atebubu; this was probably not strictly true, but it was certain that he had so far committed no hostile acts whatever, whereas the chief of Atebubu had put himself in the wrong by actually helping Nkoranza against the Asantehene's troops. There was nothing to be done, and although Sir Francis Scott was anxious to march swiftly on Kumasi and was confident that there would be little effective opposition, the Governor would not risk it without the support of British troops, which the Secretary of State would not give him.

The Secretary of State, Lord Ripon, however, suggested as a compromise that the Asantehene should be asked to accept a British Resident in Kumasi, and that he should promise not to make war on tribes living outside a fixed frontier. In return, he and the principal Ashanti chiefs should receive stipends. This proposal was accordingly made by the acting Governor, Mr. Hodgson; but again the letter contained a threat, this time the threat that Twereboanna might agree to the proposal if Prempeh would not.

The Ashanti deliberated long over this proposal. They were unwilling to accept it; they distrusted professions of friendship which were accompanied by threats; they realized that the annexation of Ashanti was now the British aim, and that it would be a great economic advantage to the British Government; and they suspected that the British, who could not or would not keep the Adansi and other refugees in order, were not sincere in professing that they were acting at great inconvenience to themselves in the sole interests of Ashanti. On the other hand, they did not wish to provoke another war. They eventually decided to appeal from the Governor to the Secretary of State, and raised a poll tax of ten shillings a head to pay the expenses of sending an embassy to England. The Governor naturally protested, and produced a cable from the Secretary of State warning the embassy that the Queen would only communicate with the Asantehene through the Governor of the Gold Coast. The embassy, however, insisted on going to England, and sailed on 28th March, 1895.

In April 1895, only ten days after the Ashanti embassy had sailed, Mr. William Maxwell arrived to take over the Governorship from Sir Brandford Griffith. He brought instructions from the Secretary of State to send an ultimatum to the Asantehene, requiring him to receive a British Resident forthwith. The Asantehene was to be reminded that he had not kept open the road beyond the Pra, had hindered trade, and had encouraged human sacrifices, and had not paid the indemnity for the war of 1874. He was to be formally notified that the British would grant protection to all that asked for it; and was to return an answer by 31st October.

The Asantehene replied, a week beyond the time limit, that he had sent an embassy to England and could make no promises until he heard from it. But the Government had now made up its mind to allow no further delay. A military expedition was prepared to enforce submission, and when the Ashanti envoys returned empty-handed in December they found preparations well advanced. They were horrified at the prospect, and used their authority from the Asantehene to accept the proposal of a Resident, and asked that one should be appointed and sent up to Kumasi with them at once. They were told that if the Asantehene were sincere, he must show his sincerity by meeting the Governor at Prasu, making a fresh treaty, and paying a fresh indemnity to cover the expenses of the expedition.

The expeditionary force was made up of a Special Service Corps of infantry, the 2nd West Yorkshire regiment, a detachment of the 2nd West India regiment, and departmental units; this force totalled about 1,300, and was supplemented by 1,000 Hausa troops and a mixed force of 800 levies from the colony. Sir Francis Scott was in command of the force, and Major Robert Baden-Powell[29] was in command of the local troops, whose duty was to scout ahead of the force.

[29] The future Chief Scout.

The vanguard reached Prasu on 3rd January, 1896. The Asante-hene had summoned a general council to decide what was to be done, but the chief of Bekwai refused to attend, and sent to the British asking for protection. Major Baden-Powell was sent with a flying column to occupy Bekwai, and the flag was hoisted there without fighting on 5th January. At Asumegya the advancing force was met by messengers asking it to halt, and saying that the Asantehene "agreed to come under the white man's rule"; but the political officer, Captain Donald Stewart, replied that the troops would enter Kumasi and the Asantehene must make his submission to the Governor there.

On 17th January the troops occupied Kumasi, and early in the morning of the 20th the ceremony was held. The Governor, Sir Francis Scott, and other officers sat on a dais at one side of a square. Opposite them sat the Asantehene Prempeh, the queen-mother and the principal chiefs of Ashanti; but their attendants were excluded from the square by the troops. All round were the red coats and the shining bayonets of the troops, and beyond the dark crowds of spectators was the wall of forest. The Governor reminded the Asantehene that the expeditionary force had come to Kumasi because he had not answered the ultimatum and had sent his dele-gates to England after being warned that their journey would be in vain; that he had not observed the treaty of Fomena with reference to the indemnity, human sacrifice, and the road north of the Pra; but that the Government would not depose him provided he made his submission on the spot and paid an indemnity of 50,000 ounces of gold.[30] The Governor added that he was waiting to receive the submission at once.

Prempeh made no answer. Slowly and reluctantly he slipped off his golden circlet and his sandals,[31] and with his mother he walked across the square, prostrated himself, and embraced the feet of the Governor, Sir Francis Scott, and Colonel Kempster the second-in-command of the expeditionary force.

[30] Fuller divides the sum by ten; but Claridge (II, 420) makes the larger figure much more likely. The figure was supposed to bear some relation to the cost of the expedition, and £200,000 meets this requirement better than £20,000.
[31] Slipping off one's sandals is a recognized piece of deference to a superior. In some cases the relationship is so nicely defined that the correct thing to do is to slip the feet out of the sandals only at the last moment, and then to stand upon the sandals but not in them. The Asantehene would never before have slipped out of his sandals except at religious ceremonies.

As soon as he regained his seat, he rose and said, "I now claim the protection of the Queen of England." He was reminded that he had yet to pay the indemnity. He replied that he could not pay anything like 50,000 ounces, but offered 680 ounces down and the balance in instalments. The Governor said that if he could afford to send an embassy to England he must be able to pay more than that; and if he could not, he must give ample security for the balance. "The King, the Queen-mother, the King's father, his two uncles, his brother, the two war chiefs, and the Kings of Mampon, Ejisu, and Ofinsu, will be taken as prisoners to the coast. They will be treated with due respect." [32]

The Ashanti were thunderstruck; they had expected that they would have to pay an indemnity and receive a British Resident, but the idea of losing their king was utterly new to them. But they could do nothing but protest, and their protests were disregarded. The Asantehene and the other prisoners were at once arrested and the meeting closed; the troops took possession of the palace and of the royal mausoleum at Bantama in the hope of finding gold for the indemnity, but found nothing. [33] The engineers blew up the sacred trees and some of the temples; and the troops left with the prisoners on the 22nd, carriers being provided to carry the Asantehene and the other prisoners in litters.

The Government had made up its mind to regard Prempeh as Kumasihene merely, and not Asantehene. This decision had been taken the year before, and some bickering had taken place between the Governor and the Ashanti embassy because the embassy was addressed as the "messengers from the King of Kumasi". It is to be presumed that the real reason for this was that the Government had decided to dissolve the Ashanti state by offering protection to its various members; and in 1896 separate treaties were made with Bekwai, Agona, Ofinsu, Ejisu, Nsuta, Mampon, Kumawu, Bompata, Abodom and Kokofu, so that as far as the Government was concerned Ashanti as a unit had ceased to exist. The arguments by

[32] Quoted in Claridge, II. 413-14, and in Fuller. It is doubtful if anybody expected that "to the coast" would mean as far as the Seychelles. Small points like this all contribute to a general impression of bad faith.
[33] The mausoleum was also the State treasury where the reserves were stored; that is to say, the gold that was buried in the brass coffins there with the mighty dead could be used in desperate emergencies with the consent of the Council. Kofi Karikari was deposed for breaking into this reserve frivolously for his own convenience.

which the Government attempted to justify its action to the Ashanti, however, were undignified as well as frivolous,[34] and can have deceived nobody. The Government for its own convenience wanted to call Prempeh chief of Kumasi only; but when it came to a question of paying an indemnity or clearing the road as far as the Pra (only the first ten or twelve miles of which, out of seventy or eighty, were in Kumasi territory) it was more convenient to blame him for not discharging the responsibilities of Asantehene, and the Government followed its own convenience.

The prisoners were taken first to Elmina, and later to the Seychelles. Major Piggott was appointed the first Resident of Kumasi, and ruled as lightly as possible over an almost deserted town and a people who were furious at what they considered an act of treachery and who were preparing to fight to revenge it.

It is hard to acquit the Government of sharp practice. It had not given the Asantehene a fair chance. It had not taken effective steps to prevent the Adansi and other refugees from using the Colony as a base of operations against Ashanti territory. In 1890 it had offered him British protection, and had warned him that if he did not accept the offer the friendship of the Government might be withdrawn. In March 1894 it had invited him to accept a British Resident in Kumasi, and hinted that if he refused it might set up Twereboanna instead of Prempeh. All this time it was accepting the offers made by his subjects to transfer their allegiance. And now in 1896 it demanded submission and an indemnity, and accused the man whom it called chief of Kumasi of having neglected to fulfil the terms of the treaty of Fomena which were binding on the ruler of all Ashanti. Prempeh made his submission on the spot, and promised to pay the indemnity in instalments; but he was immediately deposed, although the Governor had just said that he would not be deposed if he accepted those two conditions. To the Ashanti the conclusion was irresistible that Prempeh was deposed merely in order to extort money, to make him increase his offer of a first instalment of 680 ounces.

Of course, this is not the whole truth. The fact is that the Government, having first tried to keep out of Ashanti affairs, had decided to change its policy and bring Ashanti into the Empire. Its reasons for doing so were strong enough: this step would enable

[34] They are set out in Claridge, II, 389, 300.

it to deal more satisfactorily with the innumerable disputes between rival stools, it would abolish most, if not all, of the disorder and insecurity that hindered trade on the border, and it would forestall France and Germany. But these reasons could not be openly avowed, and so other reasons had to be found. Nevertheless, it was most unfortunate that the Government was made to appear as deporting all the leaders of the country merely as security for money, after having repeatedly promised that it would be content if the money were paid. The question then arises whether the Governor really believed that the Asantehene could pay such a large sum. He said that if the Asantehene could pay for an embassy to England he must be able to afford it. But the expenses of the embassy were raised by a poll tax; and the cost of an embassy was a very different matter from £200,000. The Governor must have known that the later instalments of the Fomena indemnity were paid mostly in trinkets; he must have realized that if the deportation of the Asantehene and the queen-mother and the others did not produce the money—as it did not—it could only mean that the money did not exist. In fact, the Governor did not expect that the Ashanti could pay the money, and he only made the demand as a pretext for deporting the Asantehene. This strong statement is justified by Sir Frederic Hodgson's letter[35] of 29th January, 1901: "The Kumasis and the Kings of those of the confederated tribes who supported Prempeh found that they had entirely miscalculated events, and that the British Government not only intended to remain, but made demands which were unexpected, and which without previous preparation they could not comply with." It is a pity that a British Government found it necessary to behave in this way.

After a few uneasy years, it was in 1900 that the inevitable revolt occurred. In December 1899 an Ashanti boy offered to tell the authorities in Accra where the Golden Stool was hidden, and Sir Frederic Hodgson, now Governor, decided to search for it. Needless to say, the search party did not find the Stool; but the Governor was contemplating a visit to Kumasi, and the Ashanti formed the idea that he was coming to search for it in person.

[35] Quoted in Claridge, II, 439. Sir Frederic Hodgson was Colonial Secretary of the Gold Coast in 1896, and had acted as Governor on various occasions from 1889 onwards. Rattray (*Ashanti*, 291) says that the Ashanti on this occasion had agreed not to fight for fear of losing the Golden Stool.

On 28th March, 1900 the Governor held a meeting of chiefs in Kumasi. He informed the people that neither Prempeh nor Twereboanna would ever return to Kumasi; that authority over Ashanti was vested in the Resident; and that the Government claimed the right to call people up for public works such as road construction or for transport. He reminded them that the indemnity had not been paid; and said that although he had no intention of enforcing payment of the whole sum, he did require an annual payment of 8,000 pereguans (£64,000) as interest. And then he went on to demand the surrender of the Golden Stool. He said:

> "What must I do to the man, whoever he is, who has failed to give to the Queen, who is the paramount power in this country, the stool to which she is entitled? Where is the Golden Stool? Why am I not sitting on the Golden Stool at this moment? I am the representative of the paramount power; why have you relegated me to this chair? Why did you not take the opportunity of my coming to Kumasi to bring the Golden Stool, and give it to me to sit upon? However, you may be quite sure that although the Government has not yet received the Golden Stool at your hands, it will rule over you with the same impartiality and with the same firmness as if you had produced it." [36]

This demand was a terrible blunder. The Golden Stool was never sat upon in any circumstances, even by the Asantehene himself on the most solemn occasion. It contained the soul of all Ashanti; and the Ashanti could no more produce it to be sat upon by a foreigner than a Christian bishop in the Dark Ages could be expected to invite a barbarian conqueror to feast off the communion plate at the high altar of his cathedral.

The Ashanti heard the speech in silence, and the meeting broke up quietly; but every man went home to prepare for war. That night the Kumasi chiefs held a secret meeting and swore to endure British rule no longer. Three days later fighting began.

The war which followed is known as the Yaa Asantewa war, since Yaa Asantewa, the queen-mother of Ejisu, was the inspiring

---

[36] Lady Hodgson says that the Governor did not insist that he should actually sit on the Stool. But he wanted it handed over to the British as a trophy and in Ashanti eyes the sacrilege would be as bad.

force of the Ashanti. Many of the great Ashanti states remained neutral or helped the British, and most of the opposition was from the Kumasi people and their neighbours.[37] The Governor tried to negotiate with the enemy leaders. Their terms were that Prempeh should be brought back, and should arrange for the collection of any payment to the Government: that they should be allowed to buy and sell slaves: that they should no longer be required to provide carriers or build houses and supply thatch; and that all strangers should be expelled from Kumasi. The Governor refused all these terms except the one about building, concerning which he said that he was willing to consider modifying the regulations so as to cause less hardship. The negotiations broke down, the Governor wired for troops, the insurgents closed round Kumasi, and the siege of the fort began.

By 25th April the telegraph wires were cut and Kumasi was completely surrounded. During the short period of British rule a fort had been constructed, and all the Europeans and the troops took refuge in this, while thousands of refugees crowded beneath the walls, like the Fante at Anomabu nearly a hundred years before. Before the fort was completely cut off, a detachment of police arrived from Accra, and during the next few days two more detachments fought their way in from Accra, and from the north, bringing the total population of the fort up to twenty-nine Europeans (including the Governor, Lady Hodgson, and three ladies from the Basel Mission, twelve officers, six doctors and six other civilians) and 750 troops. The besieged were terribly short of food and of ammunition, but luckily not of water.

By the second week in June people were dying of starvation and disease at the rate of thirty a day, and Dr. Chalmers reported to the Governor that the death-rate had risen "from .75 per 1,000 per diem (i.e. 273.75 per 1,000 per annum) to 10.6 per 1,000 per diem (i.e. 3,869.0 per 1,000 per annum); or in other words, the population would have ceased to exist in about ninety-four days from 18th June at the rate of mortality on that day." The gloomy jesting of Dr. Chalmers and his decimal points could not hide the fact that the position was desperate; and a sortie seemed the only hope. At dawn of 23rd June the sortie was made; three officers and 150 men were left to hold the fort, and all the rest managed

[37] See p. 311, note 39.

to escape. Arrangements were made to move down the Cape Coast road in the certainty that information would leak out to the besiegers. The column formed up as if to march out by that road, but when all were ready it turned about and slipped out westward. An enemy stockade opened fire, but it was lightly held and was rushed; and although all through the first day's march the column was fired on from time to time, the Ashanti commander who was detailed to bring it to a halt contented himself with snapping up the abandoned loads. On the third day the column entered friendly territory; but it had lost a fifth of its fighting men and probably a greater proportion still of its carriers and camp-followers. The Governor and Lady Hodgson reached Cape Coast on 10th July.

Meanwhile 1,400 troops from other parts of West and Central Africa had been ordered to the Gold Coast, and Colonel Willcocks, C.M.G., D.S.O., was placed in command of the expeditionary force. No European troops were employed, all being Africans except a small detachment of Sikhs. Colonel Willcocks landed at Cape Coast on 26th May, and on 1st July he was able to advance from Prasu into enemy country. On the 10th he received the first news from Kumasi; a Hausa soldier crawled into his camp with the following message:

"From O.C. Kumasi to O.C. Troops, Esumeja. His Excellency and main troops left for Cape Coast seventeen days ago. Relief most urgently wanted here. Remaining small garrison diminishing, disease, etc. Reduced rations for only few days more. F. E. Bishop, Captain, G.C.C."

The force marched out of Bekwai on 13th July, and spent nineteen and a half hours in a drenching rainstorm in marching fifteen miles to Peki. Next day it had some fighting to do, and reached a point only five miles from Kumasi. On the 15th the column had to fight its way slowly forward under constant flank attacks, and it was not till four in the evening that it came upon the main stockades which formed the beseigers' lines round Kumasi. There was no time to lose; the guns opened fire on the stockades till the infantry had cut their way to the flanks and deployed; and suddenly the bugles sounded the 'cease fire' and the troops rushed the stockades with the bayonet. At six o'clock the commander of the fort, Captain Bishop, "saw the heads of the advance-guards

emerge from the bush, with a fox-terrier trotting gaily in front".
The advancing troops could not tell till the last moment whether
they were in time. "Everywhere was desolation. The only living
things visble were the vultures that rose lazily from the decom-
posing corpses lying on the path or in the long grass beside it, while
over all hung a depressing silence and a sickening stench. On
reaching the top of the slope, however, just after six o'clock, the
fort burst into view and all doubts were set at rest by the notes of
a bugle blowing the 'general salute'." [38]

From the middle of July until the end of September the troops
were busy in attacking and destroying stockades, and there was
much fierce fighting. By October this part of the war was finished,
and the main Ashanti force had split up into small parties which
kept up a guerrilla warfare. This change was helped by a demon-
stration of the power of the 75-millimetre guns which was given
in Kumasi in the middle of September; a specially-built stockade
was demolished by these guns in most impressive style, and stockades rapidly went out of fashion. Colonel Willcocks was able to
leave Kumasi on 3rd December, by which time the war was almost
over; Yaa Asantewa herself and most of the remaining insurgent
leaders were captured soon afterwards. [39]

In March 1901, nearly a year after the outbreak of the war, the
new Governor, Major Nathan, visited Kumasi. Sixteen of the
leaders of the rising were deported to the Seychelles to join the
Asantehene, and thirty-one others were imprisoned for a time in
Elmina castle. The people were disarmed, only licensed hunters
being allowed to carry guns, and all damage had to be made good
and the necessary military posts to be constructed. No extra
indemnity was imposed, but the original indemnity was maintained; and the insurgent leaders who had been imprisoned or
deported were replaced by Government nominees, elected it is true
by their people as far as possible in accordance with native custom,
but naturally not carrying among their people the same authority
as 'the king over the water'. In actual practice, the tribute was

[38] Fuller, 203-8; Claridge, II, 526-31.
[39] The Kumasi people were aided in the rising by Ejisu, Ofinsu, Atwuma, Ahafo,
Bekyem, Nkwanta, Adansi and part of Kokofu; of the remaining states, Bekwai,
Mampon, Juaben, Nsuta, Kumawu, Atebubu, Tekyiman, Wenkyi, Berekum, Wam,
Nkoranza, Gyaman and Mansu Nkwanta took no part in the rising, and some of
them actively helped the British (Fuller, 190).

collected in 1901, and partly collected in 1902; but after that it was found that the development of trade enabled it to be replaced more easily and fruitfully by indirect taxation, and the tribute was dropped.

On 1st January, 1902 three Orders in Council were published, one for the Colony, one for Ashanti, and one for the Northern Territories. Ashanti was formally annexed, and placed under the authority of a Chief Commissioner, who was responsible to the Governor of the Gold Coast. Ashanti became a Crown Colony, and Gold Coast laws were made to apply to it with certain modifications. The first battalion of the newly-formed Gold Coast Regiment of the West African Frontier Force was stationed in Ashanti to garrison the new colony, and Ashanti entered upon a new chapter of its history.

CHAPTER XIII

POLITICAL HISTORY, 1874-1938

THE return of Adu Bofo to Kumasi after the death of Dompre and his bitter campaign in the Krepi country caused the centre of interest in the Sagrenti war to shift to the main Cape Coast-Kumasi road. The war in the east, however, was far from over, as poor Captain Glover found when he tried to raise a force from the eastern districts to advance on Kumasi.

Captain Glover had already begun his trans-Volta campaign against the Anlo when he received Sir Garnet's peremptory orders to march at once for the Pra and be ready to cross it on 15th January, 1874. He broke up his camp on 29th December, leaving Mr. Goldsworthy and Lieutenant Moore, R.N., with nearly 12,000 levies, to continue the Anlo campaign. Fighting went on with varying results for the next three months; the Anlo and the Akwamu fought hard, hoping to receive before long assistance from Ashanti. After the treaty of Fomena had been signed, however, Ashanti envoys arrived at Keta with the news that they could give the Anlo no more help and that the Anlo must make the best terms for themselves they could. In June a treaty was signed at Dzelukofe near Keta: the Volta was to be open to trade, and Keta, Dzelukofe and other towns on the coast were to become British territory on the same terms as the lands west of the Volta. The eastern frontier was extended to Adafia or Adafienu, eighteen miles east of Keta, and the whole Anlo country was thus brought under British rule. A similar peace treaty had been signed a week earlier with the Akwamu at Odumase.

In 1877 and 1878 there was serious trouble in the Keta district. Geraldo de Lema, having been forced to abandon the slave trade, had transferred his attention to smuggling, and being a man who always worked on the grand scale, had enlisted almost the whole Anlo people in his activities. The European traders had established stores at Denu, a mile outside the frontier, and landed goods there duty free. When buying produce at Keta they paid in orders on their Denu stores, and Geraldo de Lema's combine made a living by smuggling the goods from Denu to the head of the Keta lagoon, only twelve or fifteen miles overland, and thence by canoe through the creeks.

In January 1878 Lieutenant A. B. Ellis[1] was appointed District Commissioner of the Keta district, and set himself to stop the smuggling, in which he was far too successful to please Geraldo de Lema and the Anlo chiefs. They discussed whether to revolt against the Government or to murder the too efficient D.C.,[2] and decided to begin at any rate with the murder. In October he was waylaid by a party of men with cutlasses, but he was armed, and though wounded made his escape to Keta. A few days later Keta fort was attacked, and for a few days there was desultory fighting. It was eventually arranged that the Anlo should withdraw their forces, but nothing was done to punish either them or Geraldo de Lema. Next year the frontier was moved eastward to Aflao to lengthen the overland journey of the smugglers on their way to the lagoon, and supplementary treaties were made both with the Keta people and also with the people of Agbosome, an important inland town near the head of the lagoon.

Geraldo de Lema was incorrigible. In 1884 he tried to persuade the Anlo to kill the D.C., Captain Campbell. They would not do this; but the Anyako people living on the north bank of the lagoon agreed to cut off Keta's food supply. The D.C. determined to arrest him, and with the help of two loyal chiefs, Tamaklo and Akolatsi, succeeded in doing so; but he then unwisely sent him by land to Accra with an escort of only five police, though the road lay for twenty-five miles through village after village of the prisoner's friends. A few miles along the road the party was stopped and Geraldo de Lema was released. Captain Campbell at once set off with thirty-eight police and with Tamaklo and Akolatsi and some sixty of their men. He found the party still in the village where it had been stopped, and the rescuers were taken by surprise at the sudden arrival of the D.C. and his party. The prisoner and his escort were started off again on their journey to Accra, which they reached in safety; and the D.C. and his men started back next day for Keta. They had barely started when they were attacked by a

[1] Afterwards Colonel Sir A. B. Ellis, the historian.
[2] I shall use the convenient and familiar abbreviation D.C. for District Commissioner, the title corresponding to District Officer in some other African colonies.

band of some 3,000 Anlo; they returned the enemy's fire and pushed on. The men had only twenty rounds of ammunition each, and after an hour this was exhausted; but they fixed bayonets and drove off the enemy in a series of bayonet charges, finally reaching Keta with a loss of three police killed and twelve wounded. The D.C. himself was wounded five times, and the loyal Anlo contingent suffered several casualties.

A punitive expedition was, of course, arranged; four armed boats' crews were provided by H.M.S. *Frolic,* and a force of 120 police was taken to attack Anyako. The gunfire from the guns mounted in the boats drove the Anyako people in dismay to abandon their town, which they had regarded as safe from attack. The town and a small village nearby were burned and the force returned to Keta. Next day the ship shelled some of the mainland villages, and the Anlo capital, Anloga, was attacked and burnt. The whole nation then surrendered and peace was made. Geraldo de Lema was sentenced in Accra to a long term of imprisonment.

In 1885 the coast immediately east of Aflao was occupied by Germany, and an international boundary commission defined the boundary inland for two and a half miles. Germany did not intend, however, to be content with a strip of sea-coast; and in 1886 she annexed Agotime and other districts which lay immediately behind Keta. The British Government was thus forced to extend its territory inland, and a series of treaties was rapidly concluded by which Akwamu, Krepi and neighbouring states became British.

During the 'eighties there were several such affairs in different parts of the colony, minor quarrels which needed just the right amount of tact and the right amount of firmness to prevent them from growing into major incidents. Some of them were well handled, others less so; but all but one of them were settled somehow with little or no loss of life. The one great exception is the Tavievi war of 1888-9; there were actually two Tavievi wars, but the second war is the only one that concerned the British Government.

The Tavievi country lies some fifteen miles north-east of the Krepi country, and resembles it in being a long narrow mountain valley, difficult of entry. It is about eight miles long and nearly two wide, and the paths leading into it are steep. The first Tavievi war took place in 1875. The Tavievi people had helped Adu Bofo

against Krepi, and after their Ashanti allies had retired they had
to face Krepi vengeance. After some fighting, a meeting was
arranged to make peace at Siafi, just beyond the southern end of
the Tavievi valley; and there the unarmed Tavievi delegates were
massacred by the Krepi people.

In April 1888 the Tavievi came to take their revenge. They
attacked Siafi and took it, and took a bloody revenge for the loss
they had suffered there thirteen years before. By this time Krepi
had become part of the Colony, and Kwadjo Dei VI, chief of Krepi,
reported the attack to the Government and asked for ammunition
to fight the Tavievi with. Captain Dalrymple, who after the
Ashanti war had remained in the Gold Coast as a police officer,
was sent with another officer and a small force of police to settle
the matter, and if possible to induce the Tavievi also to become
British. Captain Dalrymple sent the Krepi men home, while he
himself went into the Tavievi country to hold an inquiry. On 11th
May Captain Dalrymple held his inquiry at the Tavievi capital,
and arrested the head chief and some of his subordinates in the
middle of their people. He and his colleague, with their small escort
of sixty-three armed police, then set out to take the prisoners back
to Accra. Two miles from the town they were ambushed and
attacked; Captain Dalrymple was shot dead and most of the
prisoners escaped, while the second British officer made his way
out of the valley and reached safety. There were nine casualties
among the police.

The Government ordered the commanders of police detachments
at Oda and at Keta to concentrate at Kpong and to move to Ho
in readiness for a campaign against the Tavievi; their united
strength would have amounted to nearly 300 men with three guns.
There was, however, trouble in western Akim, and the Oda detachment could not leave, so Mr. Akers with 120 men was left to deal
with the Tavievi alone. He entered the valley at three in the
morning and was apparently not noticed till he got within a short
distance of the chief town, which he occupied at the cost of one
policeman killed and two scouts wounded. The Krepi sent a strong
force to help him hold the valley, and the Tavievi were harassed
till they evacuated the valley and fled to the hills.

Mr. Akers was in the Tavievi country from 28th May to 2nd
June, when he left the valley in obedience to orders which reached

him from Accra to reinforce his colleagues in western Akim. He left fifty police to occupy the valley, and ordered them and Kwadjo Dei and his Krepi men not to take the offensive until he returned. Nevertheless, Kwadjo Dei could not resist the temptation to attack the Tavievi who were gathering in the hills, and on 4th June he was defeated, and his men fled to Siafi. Captain Dalrymple's colleague, who had all this time been remaining at Ho, a few miles outside the mouth of the valley, then took upon himself to order the detachment of constabulary to evacuate the valley and retire to Ho. Mr. Akers' work was thus completely thrown away. Luckily, it was found that the position in Akim was better than had been feared, so he was able to return by forced marches to Tavievi. On 18th June he attacked the enemy and completely defeated them, and followed up his victory with four days' guerrilla warfare against scattered bodies of Tavievi fighting men. On 23rd June the fighting ceased and the Tavievi surrendered. Various Tavievi chiefs agreed to serve Krepi and come under the British flag; they surrendered their head chief and others who had been concerned in the murder of Captain Dalrymple; they agreed to pay a fine of £300, give up their guns and ammunition, and keep the trade routes clear. After £41 2s. 3d. had been paid the balance of the fine was remitted by the Governor. The unfortunate Mr. Akers was subsequently tried and found guilty, on a complaint laid by Kwadjo Dei, of flogging without trial fifty Krepi men for looting; he pleaded that strong measures were needed to prevent wholesale plundering, but it was held that his measures were unnecessarily strong. The murderers of Captain Dalrymple were acquitted by an Accra jury, largely it seems to express the jury's detestation of Mr. Akers; but the Government had an ordinance passed to legalize their imprisonment nevertheless. The ordinance was repealed seven years later. The Tavievi campaign had caused great suffering to the people of the valley, and many women and children had died of starvation and exposure.[3]

After the annexation of Ashanti, the British hoped that they would be able to treat the country beyond it as an area of free trade in which they need not accept any political responsibilities. But

---

[3] For the Tavievi campaign see Claridge, II, 315-23; Welman, *Peki*, 15-20. Mr. Akers received much condemnation from African opinion, not only for flogging the Krepi men, but because it was felt that he had been unnecessarily savage in his treatment of the Tavievi.

the competition of France and Germany forced them to push north to safeguard Ashanti trade, as they had already been forced to push into Ashanti to safeguard the trade of the colony. The process was hastened by the activities of two notorious slave dealers, Samori and Babatu. These men raided up and down the Sudan, maintaining large armies well supplied with modern weapons. They agreed not to poach on each other's preserves, Samori raiding in the western Sudan and Babatu farther east; their boundary fell more or less along the line of the present western frontier of the Northern Territories.

The French had attacked Samori on various occasions during the 'eighties, and their slow advance into the interior of the Sudan from their bases on the Senegal and in Algeria had by 1890 made it much more convenient for Samori to confine his activities to the territory on the right bank of the Niger from Sierra Leone to Ashanti. In 1893 a French force from the Senegal came into contact with a British force from Sierra Leone, and a sharp engagement followed, each party thinking the other to be Samori's men. This enabled Samori to escape from both of them, and he was next heard of in 1896 in the Gyaman country, where the traces of his devastation are plain to this day in burnt and ruined villages. In February 1896 a small British expedition visited Bondugu, but could not get in touch with Samori, and returned after making treaties with some of the local Akan tribes.

A few months later another expedition was sent to this district to occupy Bona and Bole, while officers from the newly-annexed Ashanti were sent straight up north to make treaties with the tribes there. The Bole expedition was commanded by Lieutenant Henderson, and included a police officer and a doctor, and an African surveyor, Mr. Ferguson. They were too late at Bona, which had already been burnt by Samori, but they occupied Bole and built a small fort there, having already taken Wa, where they built a fort and hoisted the British flag. Mr. Henderson then moved to Dawkta, between Wa and Bona, and warned the local commander of Samori's troops to cease raiding a district where he proposed to hoist the British flag. Samori's general in reply said that he had no wish to fight the British, but that he intended to take Dawkta, and advised the British to retire. Mr. Henderson refused to go, and was attacked for forty-eight hours by 8,000 men. He then declined a second invitation to retire, but two days later found his position so difficult that he determined to cut his way through the enemy to Wa. This he succeeded in doing with small loss; but the next day he was again attacked in Wa itself, and the water supply failed, so that the position was hopeless. Mr. Henderson determined to try to secure favourable terms, and set out himself for the enemy camp, instructing his second-in-command to evacuate the fort and retire without him if he did not return that night. The enemy commander insisted on unconditional surrender, which Mr. Henderson would not hear of, and he was detained as a prisoner while his men slipped out of Wa that night and made their way to safety. Mr. Henderson was well treated by the chivalrous commander, who admired him for visiting the enemy camp alone; and after being kept a short time as an honoured guest he was released. Mr. Ferguson, who had been wounded, was unable to march, and was abandoned by his carriers to the enemy, who shot him.[4]

After being chivvied for two more years by French and British forces, Samori himself was captured by the French in 1899. This co-operation and competition with the French led the British Government to organize its northern zone into a political division called the Northern Territories. The Anglo-French boundary was defined by three boundary commissions, in 1889, 1893 and 1898. Samori's colleague Babatu was hunted down about the same time, and on his death many of his men came in to join the newly-established Gold Coast Regiment, one battalion of which was stationed at Gambaga. In 1907 this battalion was disbanded and replaced by the Northern Territories Constabulary, a semi-military force which has recently been assimilated to the Gold Coast police.

The eastern boundary had been defined by an Anglo-German boundary commission in 1886 for a distance of two-and-a-half miles from the sea, the British Government apparently not comprehending the 'grab for Africa' that was beginning. Next year, however, the German Government occupied certain territories

[4] Claridge, II, 425-30. Ferguson was a remarkable man, well deserving to be remembered for the sake of his own work. He spent a long time in trekking up and down all over the present Northern Territories and much of the adjoining French country, methodically making surveys and concluding treaties with the local chiefs. The faithfulness and accuracy of his work, at first somewhat decried, has since been fully recognized. He took his life in his hand, for there was no telling when he might fall in with one of Samori's or Babatu's parties. He died with a gallantry befitting his life.

inland, and the British annexed Krepi and other districts; and a new agreement was drawn up at Berlin and confirmed in 1888, providing that the area between the 10th parallel of latitude and the latitude of the confluence of the Volta and the Daka (approximately 8° 6′) and between 1° 7′ W and 0° 33′ E should be a neutral zone, in which both countries should refrain from annexations. This provisional arrangement was terminated by an agreement in 1899 under which the neutral zone was divided between the two countries, and the frontiers of the Gold Coast and its dependencies thus were fixed until 1914. The frontiers thus drawn were determined without reference to African wishes, and both on the east and on the west African political units were divided by an arbitrary frontier line. The western boundary left the greater part of the Gyaman state, including its capital and all but one of its principal divisional chiefs, to France. The one chief left on the British side of the line was created an artificial sort of paramount chief of British Gyaman. The national unity is, however, still remembered, and it would be well if the frontier could be realigned so as to reunite the divided state. A similar condition of affairs exists with regard to the Dagomba, where the capital of the state, Yendi, was handed over to Togoland, and a considerable part of the territory remained British.

During the war of 1914, the Gold Coast Regiment served with distinction outside the Gold Coast. Its first duty was to assist in the Togoland campaign, and then it served similarly in the conquest of the Cameroons. After a short rest it then went overseas and served through the East African campaign. It was the first West African contingent to arrive in East Africa and the last to leave.

The peacetime strength of the regiment is a battalion of infantry and a battery of light guns; but during the war the regiment was greatly expanded, and during the last months of the war the authorities were thinking of raising it to the strength of a full brigade.[5] After the war, a strip of Togoland was attached to the Gold Coast to be held by Britain on a mandate from the League of Nations.

[5] The history of the Gold Coast Regiment during the war is told in Sir Hugh Clifford's book, *The Gold Coast Regiment in the East African Campaign*. It cannot be followed without a grasp of the whole campaign, and therefore I regretfully omit it from this book. The regiment distinguished itself again in East Africa and Burma in the war 1939-45.

PLATE XI   One of the buildings of the Kumasi Technical College   (photo: C.O.I.)

PLATE XII   The bridge over the Volta   (*Crown copyright*)

The history of the Gold Coast since 1919 has been full of political activity; but the questions which have aroused political feeling have been at bottom questions of the constitutional relationship between the Crown and the Gold Coast people. They are, therefore, better postponed to a separate chapter dealing with the constitutional issues involved.

CHAPTER XIV

TOWARDS INDEPENDENCE

WHILE the Gold Coast was under British rule, its form of government was developed, by a series of Letters Patent and Royal Instructions, along the usual line of colonial evolution. Power was at first in the hands of the Governor and his officials, and development lay in increasing, first unofficial, then African, and lastly elected representation.

Until 1951 the Governor was assisted by an Executive Council and by a Legislative Council. The Executive Council in 1897 consisted of four senior officials: the Colonial Secretary, the Attorney General, the Treasurer, and the Inspector General of the military forces. Six years later we find that the Inspector General is replaced by the Director of Public Works, a change significant of the fact that the *pax Britannica* has arrived and a period of rapid economic development is beginning. From that time until 1943 the Executive Council consisted of five officials: the Colonial Secretary, Attorney General and Treasurer remained, and the other two places were filled by the Director of Medical Services and the Secretary for Native Affairs. In 1943 this Council was strengthened by the appointment of two unofficial African members, one a distinguished barrister and the other a paramount chief. Both had been members of the Legislative Council. The Governor was not bound to follow the advice of his executive council, even if unanimous; though no doubt any Governor would need to be very sure of himself before acting contrary to the advice of seven such men.

The Legislative Council in 1897 consisted of the four members of the Executive Council, with the Chief Justice and three unofficial members. Six years later there were the same five officials, but with four unofficial members instead of three; in 1916 there were eleven official and ten unofficial members. This formula of an official majority of one member was maintained in the constitution of 1925, which provided fifteen official and fourteen unofficial members.

Under the constitution of 1925, six of the fourteen unofficial members were African provincial members, representing the Western, Central and Eastern provinces of the Colony. In each province there was established a provincial council, consisting of all the paramount chiefs of the province. The Western and Central provincial councils formed each one undivided body, the Western provincial council returning one representative to the legislature and the Central provincial council two. The provincial council of the Eastern Province, the richest and most developed, and also the most mixed of the provinces from the ethnographical point of view, was divided into three sections, the Ga-Adangbe, Ewe and Akan sections, each returning one representative.

The Legislative Council of 1925 next contained three municipal members, one for each of the three towns of Accra, Cape Coast and Sekondi, elected by citizens occupying a house of the rateable value of £6.[1] The provincial and municipal members thus totalled nine; the provincial members had to be members of their provincial councils, and were bound, therefore, to be Africans, the municipal members were not bound to be Africans, but in practice always were.

The remainder of the fourteen unofficial members consisted of five Europeans, one representing the chamber of commerce, another representing the mining industry, and three being nominated by the Governor.

The Council thus consisted of fifteen official and fourteen unofficial members, nine of the latter being Africans. As in other Crown colonies, the fifteen official members were compelled, whatever their private opinions, to vote in accordance with the declared policy of the Governor, and no measure affecting finance might be proposed "except by the direction or with the express sanction of the Governor". These two provisos gave the Governor complete control of legislation. He had in theory the power to force any measure through the Legislative Council by means of his official majority; and most measures of which he disapproved could somehow be shown to affect finance. In practice, however, this rigid control was not often exercised. It was seldom that the Government contemplated forcing a measure through in the face of opposition from a solid block of unofficial members; and seldom that it even relied on the support of the European unofficial members and forced a measure through against strong African opposi-

[1] A somewhat high qualification; the Accra electorate in 1931 was under 2,000 out of a population of 60,726.

tion. There have been cases of this last, such as the Forests Ordinance of 1926; but there are many cases of bills dropped in deference to African opposition; for example, the Land Bills of 1894 and 1897, and the various proposals for direct taxation culminating in the Native Administration Revenue Ordinances of 1932 and 1934.

In 1946, after twenty years of great economic and educational progress, the constitution of 1925 was replaced by a new constitution, which took the decisive step of abandoning altogether the idea of an official majority and handing over political power to the elected members. The new Legislative Council consisted of a President (the Governor or his representative), six ex-officio and six nominated members, and eighteen elected members. The ex-officio members were the Colonial Secretary, the three Chief Commissioners of the Colony, Ashanti and the Northern Territories, the Attorney-General and the Financial Secretary. The eighteen elected members comprised nine provincial members from the Colony, four Ashanti and five municipal members. Ashanti was represented for the first time.

The municipal members represented the three old constituencies of Accra (two members), Cape Coast and Sekondi-Takoradi, with the new constituency of Kumasi. The provincial members were elected as before by the provincial councils, which were reduced in number from three to two, the Central Province disappearing; the Eastern Province had five members, the Western Province four. A provincial member was required to be either a paramount chief, or the subject of a paramount chief, of the province for which he sat. The four Ashanti members were similarly elected by the Ashanti Confederacy Council.

The elected members were thus in a decisive majority over the ex-officio and nominated members together: eighteen against twelve, a stage of political advance which no other colonial territory in Africa had hitherto reached. The constitution nevertheless did not confer full responsible self-government. The executive power still lay in the hands of permanent officials, who were appointed by the Governor on the nomination of the Secretary of State. The highest posts in the official hierarchy were in theory open to Africans, and a far-sighted Governor, Sir Gordon Guggisberg, had indeed formulated a scheme twenty years earlier for training Africans to fill senior posts; but his scheme had not been carried into effect, and in 1946 all the senior Government posts were held by officers from the United Kingdom. The constitution did not provide each Government department with a responsible Minister who was a member of the Council and could be compelled to resign his position by an adverse vote. The permanent official was responsible to the Governor, not to the Council. He was a professional man, with an assured position and prospects in his service; he advised the Governor on policy, and could not be expected to modify his professional advice in response to criticism from the Council.

The 1946 constitution was devised by the Governor, Sir Alan Burns, and the Secretary of State in consultation with African leaders. It was a bold and imaginative advance, and was greeted as such by African public opinion. It would be wrong to criticise it as unduly cautious. But it is important to bear in mind that although the Executive Council included African members, the Burns constitution of 1946 did not require these African members to be members also of the Legislative Council, and they, like their European colleagues, were responsible to the Governor, not to the legislature.

The African members of the Legislative Council thus had no responsibility for making Government policy, only for criticizing the policy which the officials laid before them. The elected members had of course the power of the purse, and in the last resort they could, in theory, refuse to vote the estimates. In fact, however, their powers of this nature were limited by the powers which the Burns constitution reserved to the Governor. As in the 1925 constitution, the Council might not discuss financial matters without the Governor's approval. Moreover, in addition to his usual powers of disallowing a Bill, the Governor had power in certain circumstances to declare that a Bill or a Motion introduced in the Council should have effect as if it had been passed, even if the Council had refused to pass it. The Governor could use this power if he considered it expedient in the interests of public order, public faith, or good government; but if he used this power, he must forthwith report his reasons to the Secretary of State, and must also forward any written objection made by any member of the Legislative Council.

These are wide powers. In spite of their elected majority, the

African members appeared to have no power of initiating policy, and little power of enforcing their criticism on policy initiated by the Government. On paper it looked as if there might be a constant deadlock between a Council determined to assert its right to be master in its own house, and an obstinate Governor refusing to permit any discussion of business involving finance and claiming that this or that measure which the Council disapproved of must be passed. But clearly, such a reversion to the days of Grenville and Lord North was unthinkable. It had long been the regular routine for Legislative Councils in the Gold Coast and other colonies to go through the revenue and expenditure estimates in detail, and to use the budget debates for a general examination of Government policy. Sir Alan Burns was well aware that the history of the Gold Coast legislature gave no ground for fearing that it might be stampeded into irresponsible motions which were contrary to public faith or public order or good government, and which would thus call forth the Governor's dormant emergency powers. On the contrary, like anyone else who has had experience of Gold Coast Africans in discussion, whether in a chief's court, a town council, or a club committee, he was impressed by their dignity, sobriety and common sense. In framing the 1946 constitution, he and the Secretary of State were confident that they could count on this African maturity; and it was only reasonable to expect that the Governor's dormant emergency powers would rarely be awakened from their slumber until in the fullness of time the achievement of self-government should sweep them away.

The 1946 constitution was greeted in the Gold Coast with enthusiasm, and Sir Alan Burns's personal popularity was immense. There seemed every justification for the general hope that the new constitution would work smoothly and that the Gold Coast would advance steadily towards increasing prosperity and self-government. It was a time of hope. The war of 1939 was over. The charter of the United Nations had just been adopted at San Francisco, and the framers of the charter assumed that the victorious war-time alliance between Russia and the West would continue into a system of close partnership in the tasks of peace. In Britain, one of the last acts of the coalition Government which went out of office in 1945 had been to pass the Colonial Development and Welfare Act, which provided a sum of £120 million for helping colonies with their economic development and their social services. The "political experiment", as it was widely called, of giving an African colony an elected majority in its legislature was one of the earliest achievements of the new Socialist Government headed by Mr. Attlee. If, both in London and in the Gold Coast, there was a certain complacency, it is perhaps understandable.

The Burns constitution left the control of policy in the hands of the Governor and his permanent officials, and the most effective function of the enlarged legislature was still to criticise. It was an unpleasant surprise for the authorities to find the mood of the country change rapidly from praise and thanks for the new constitution to bitter criticism of the Government's economic policy.

There were two main grievances. The bigger of the two was a threat to the cocoa industry. The cocoa trees were smitten by a new disease called, from its most conspicuous symptom, swollen shoot. It was a virus disease, carried by an insect, the mealy bug, it was rapidly fatal, and it spread with alarming speed. The cocoa farmers of course were familiar with various pests and diseases. One insect had caused such devastation in the early days that they named it *Sankonuabe,* 'go back and grow oil-palm'. But no insects or fungoid diseases had ever been more than a nuisance, and the Government agricultural officers had been assiduous in spreading a knowledge of how to combat them. Swollen shoot was different; it killed the trees in thousands, and there was nothing that the individual farmer could do about it. The advice of the pathologists was that every infected tree must be cut down and burnt.

An English dairy farmer whose herd of pedigree Shorthorns has to be slaughtered for foot-and-mouth suffers a heavy blow; but he understands the necessity. A Gold Coast cocoa farmer who was ordered to cut down every tree of his farm had no such understanding. The disease was new, the idea of a virus was quite beyond the farmers, and when they were told that there was no cure for the disease, and that if unchecked it would utterly destroy the Gold Coast cocoa industry, they did not believe it. Cocoa was a poor man's crop; it was everybody's ambition to have a patch of cocoa farm, and take advantage of the high price that it fetched. What possible motive could the Government have for thus hitting at the poor man? The wildest rumours ran around. The Government wanted to cripple the Gold Coast cocoa industry so as to give

Nigeria and Trinidad a chance to compete. Having given the Gold Coast more political freedom, the British Government was determined to make its gift worthless by destroying the country's economic prosperity. Having wrecked the cocoa farms, the Government would achieve its old ambition, and buy up the derelict land for a song. And so on. The cocoa farmers were in an ugly mood; they refused to cut down their trees; and the swollen shoot spread abroad.

While the Government was thus suspected of desiring to rob the farmers of their land and their livelihood, it got into difficulties also with the townsfolk. The Gold Coast had become accustomed to living on an export-import basis, exporting its cocoa and minerals and timber, and importing vast quantities not only of textiles and bicycles and general consumer goods, but of food. During the war, prices had risen and supplies had been curtailed, and in the Gold Coast, as elsewhere, the end of the war did not mean a sudden drop in prices and a return to pre-war plenty. In the first few years after the war, the Gold Coast went through a time of great inflation. The price of cocoa was high, and there was plenty of money in the country, but there was little to spend it on. Prices rose, the black market flourished, and bitterly did the people complain. And here too the Government came under suspicion. It was felt that the big European firms were deliberately keeping prices high so as to recompense themselves for the high price they had to pay for Gold Coast cocoa; and there were dark suspicions that the European Government was in some way acting in collusion with the European firms. Suspicions of this sort were perhaps natural among a people ignorant of economics. But they show very plainly how utterly the Government was out of touch with public opinion. However amiable and popular individual Governors or British officials might be, the European Government in the Gold Coast remained to the end of its days a foreign Government, aloof, ill-informed, uncomprehending, incalculable.

There was perhaps little the Government could do about high prices. Price control regulations strengthen the black market, and it would of course have been unreasonable to expect the unsophisticated mass of the Gold Coast people to abstain from black-marketing. If high prices were the result of scarcity, the only way of bringing down prices would be to replace scarcity by plenty; and this was quite beyond the power of any Government. Until 1939 the Government had had nothing whatever in the form of a public relations department, and the two simultaneous tasks of convincing the farmers that they must cut down their cocoa and convincing the townsfolk that they must go on paying high prices would be beyond the capacity of the best of public relations departments.

There are always smaller grievances which can be used to swell the murmurs of discontent; notably, on this occasion, grievances felt by Gold Coast soldiers who were returning home and being demobolised after serving gallantly in Abyssinia and Burma, and who felt it hard to slip back into humble positions. They had broadened their horizon and measured themselves against men of other countries: their comrades the British and their enemies the Italians and Japanese. The problem of readjustment to civilian life which faces every returning soldier was harder for the African, who was coming back to live under a foreign Government, than for the Englishman returning to his London office or Bradford mill.

These grievances over demobilisation, the compulsory cutting-out of cocoa, and the high cost of living, were all genuine enough; and this made them the more dangerous in the hands of anyone who wanted to use them against the Government. The chief opposition party at this time was the Gold Coast Convention, led by the veteran Dr. J. B. Danquah. Dr. Danquah was a barrister and newspaper editor, but politics had of recent years come to occupy more and more of his attention. He was a younger brother of Sir Ofori Atta, the paramount chief of Akim Abuakwa, who had been a member of the legislative council for many years and in 1943 had become a member of the executive council. In politics, the two brothers were on opposite sides. As his record shows, Sir Ofori Atta, though he could be an outspoken critic of Government policy, found himself able to co-operate with successive British Governors and senior officials in working for a gradual broadening of the constitution. Dr. Danquah could never trust the Government, and was permanently in opposition.

Under Dr. Danquah's leadership, the Gold Coast Convention set itself to use the grievances to turn the country as a whole against the Government: an easy task.

The problem of high prices was the most serious of the Government's difficulties. Most of the big European importing firms had organized themselves into an association called the Association of West African Merchants, and such an organization was naturally regarded with suspicion. It was taken for granted that the merchants' object was to buy cocoa as cheaply as possible and to sell bicycles and Manchester textiles as dear as possible. In 1945 the Government and the Association agreed that imported textiles should be sold at a profit of not more than 75 per cent above the landed cost. In December 1946, the Joint Provincial Council of Chiefs of the Colony met the Chamber of Commerce in a conference under Government chairmanship, and complained of the high prices and of the consequent black market. Later that same month, the Government assured the Provincial Council that it had worked out a tentative scheme of price control. But no scheme was put into operation, and for more than a year there was no visible sign[2] that the Government was doing anything. The Government, knowing that the problem of scarcity and high prices was worldwide, felt that there was little or nothing which it could do in the Gold Coast to solve it. When supplies improved, prices would fall; and the public must wait for that to happen. It considered the problem of scarcity and high prices to be a purely commercial problem, concerning the shopkeeper and his customers only. It did not see how dangerous its own position was. Many people assumed that, as a foreign Government, it must of necessity be in league with the foreign merchants. Even its friends thought that it ought to take as much trouble to protect the citizen from foreign merchants who made him pay too much for their goods as it had long been taking to protect him from foreign mining and timber companies who wanted to pay him too low a rent for his land. In the view of the Gold Coast public, the Government could not be neutral in the dispute; by doing nothing it favoured the wealthy and well-organized foreign merchants against the public.[3]

[2] For my narrative of these critical events I am relying mainly on the report of the Watson Commission (Colonial No. 231) and the British Government's Statement thereon (Colonial No. 232). The Commission says roundly that the Gold Coast Government took no action for a year, that is till 11th February, 1948. The Government Statement is pained at this accusation; it pleads that during 1947 the Government imposed price control on the cheaper grades of cloth, and had in fact given a great deal of thought to the whole question. Moreover during the first three weeks of the boycott "the Government had been in touch with all parties in order to bring them together".
[3] This is also the view of the Watson Commission (para. 171): "We cannot emphasize too strongly our view that every economic aspect of life in a colony,

And so the people tried against the Association the weapon which they had so successfully used against the so-called Cocoa Pool ten years before.[4] One of the chiefs of Accra, Nii Kwabena Bonne III, put himself at the head of a movement to boycott all European imports. The movement was immediately successful; it spread all over the country, and was enforced by the chiefs and their councils. There was a good deal of intimidation used against people who wanted to ignore the boycott, and many offenders were fined—quite illegally—by native courts for breaking the native authority orders enforcing it. The boycott began on 26th January, 1948; on 11th February, Nii Bonne and some of his colleagues met the Chamber of Commerce representatives under Government chairmanship. At this meeting, it was agreed that the seventy-five per cent profit margin on imported textiles should be reduced to fifty per cent for a trial period of three months. On this assurance the boycott was called off.

The country was still in an excited and uneasy state. A few days later, the representatives of an ex-servicemen's association applied for permission to hold a public meeting in Accra and to march in procession to the Governor's official residence in order to present a petition concerning ex-servicemen's grievances. They were told that permission could not be given for a large body of men to march to the Castle; but their petition would be transmitted to the Governor, and if they wished to draw public attention to their grievances they might hold a public meeting and afterwards march through the streets of Accra. They were given a prescribed route which would take them through the main shopping district of the city and would keep them more than a mile from the Castle. The organizers handed in their petition to be transmitted, and made no difficulty about accepting the conditions laid down.

On 28th February the meeting was held, and the march began. Very soon the marching column was joined by large numbers of people who were not ex-servicemen, and very soon it left the prescribed route and went off in the opposite direction to demand an interview with the Governor in the Castle. A few hundred yards from the Castle, the column was halted by a small force of armed

affecting the welfare of the indigenous population, is a concern of the highest priority to the tutelary Government of that colony."
[4] See pages 399, 400.

police under the command of a British officer, Superintendent Imray. The crowd had by this time lost its discipline, and was in an ugly mood; it took no heed of Imray's order to disperse and his warning that he would use force if necessary. Several police were injured by stones, and the police dared not advance for fear of exposing their flanks and being swallowed up in the crowd. Imray tried tear gas, but it was of poor quality and the wind was in the wrong direction; so he fired. Six shots were fired; the foremost of the ringleaders was killed on the spot, and the total casualties were two killed and five wounded. The crowd made no further attempt to advance, but it did not disperse until the police were reinforced by troops an hour later.

Meanwhile, rioting had broken out in the town. It was directed against the big European shops. The central prison was burst open and its inmates set free, and many of the biggest shops in Accra, both European and Syrian, were looted. The Government allowed the looting to continue for a time. In the temper of the crowd, it judged that the only way of stopping it quickly would be to bring in the troops and shoot rioters down, and loss of property was preferable to considerable loss of life. During the next few days there was similar rioting at Koforidua, Kumasi, and elsewhere; total casualties were 29 killed and 266 injured.

Dr. Danquah and his colleagues of the Gold Coast Convention thought that these events gave them their opportunity. They sent a long and luridly-worded telegram to the Secretary of State. They said that the civil administration had broken down, they represented the rioting and looting as the result of the horror caused by Imray's firing on the mob, and they urged that a constituent assembly should be summoned and that they themselves should be invited to form an interim Government, which they said they were quite willing to do.

The Government of the Gold Coast however proceeded to show that the civil administration had not broken down. It waited until the force of the riots had spent itself, and then it took the necessary action to restore order; and under emergency powers, it arrested Dr. Danquah and five of his close colleagues of the Convention, and removed them separately to distant parts of the country to keep them out of mischief. The Government in London appointed a Commission under the chairmanship of Mr. Aiken Watson, K.C., to enquire into the disturbances and their underlying causes, and to make recommendations. The Commission visited the Gold Coast to hold its enquiry, and submitted its report early in June.

On the events of February and March, the Commission was emphatic. In his extremely dangerous position, Superintendent Imray was entirely justified in opening fire on the mob, and his firm handling of the situation probably saved many lives. The Commission entirely approved also the Government's attitude in allowing considerable loss of property in the riots in order to save much bloodshed.

The Commission's discussion of the underlying causes of the disturbances amounts to a sustained criticism of the Gold Coast Government. The report lists sixteen causes, of which eight may be classed as specific grievances. They are: (i) discontent among ex-servicemen over pensions and resettlement and other grievances peculiar to them, (ii) political frustration among educated men who regarded the Burns constitution as inadequate, (iii) the concentration of economic power in European and Syrian hands, (iv) high prices, (v) unequal distribution of scarce consumer goods over the country, (vi) the cutting-out of diseased cocoa, (vii) undue centralization in the Cocoa Marketing Board, (viii) the housing shortage.

The other eight underlying causes can be regarded either as instances of the Government's remoteness from popular feeling, or of general—sometimes quite unjustified—popular suspicion of the Government's motives.[5] They were: (ix) the Government's failure to see that "the star of rule through the Chiefs was on the

---

[5] This suspicion is well described in the Watson Report (para. 17): "By far the most serious problem which the Administration has to face in the Gold Coast is the suspicion which surrounds Government activity of any sort. Its origin, apart from political propaganda, is disperse and often obscure. It does not attach to persons or individuals in Government service. That it exists we had evidence on all sides. That it must be overcome is the hard core of the problem of healthy relations between Government and governed."
I have had a striking example in my own experience of the way in which this suspicion exists without attaching to individuals. When I was in Ashanti studying traditional history, I was honoured with an invitation to witness a religious ceremony which no European, not even Rattray, had hitherto seen. As may be imagined, the invitation was not issued without anxious thought and debate, and there was a good deal of opposition to be overcome. When the opposition finally gave way, those who had made the proposal went further. They said, "Now that we have agreed that we can take a white man, why not let us also invite the District Commissioner? We all like him, and we know that he would give his ears to be invited." This D.C was very popular. He spoke the language well and

wane", (x) popular feeling that the Government, for all its talk of Africanizing the public service, did not mean business, (xi) the Government's failure to explain itself to the people, (xii) its neutrality in the price dispute, (xiii) the apparent absence of long-term plans for agricultural development, (xiv) the slowness of educational development, (xv) the ancient suspicion that the Government meant somehow to get hold of tribal lands, (xvi) the Government's tolerance of dangerously inflammatory speeches.

The Commission naturally made several recommendations. Apart from short-term measures to deal with the immediate situation, the main recommendations were: (i) that there should be further constitutional advances and a reorganization of local government, (ii) that the Government should establish an effective system of public relations, and (iii) that there should be a great speeding-up of educational advance.

The sixteen underlying causes of the disturbances which the Commission listed are not of equal importance. Some, such as the high prices, the cutting-out of cocoa, and the concentration of economic power in the hands of non-African firms, were burning topics of the day. Others, such as the suspicion over tribal lands and the Government's failure to explain itself to the people so as to be understood and believed, had been smouldering away for years like tree-stumps in a forest clearing, unlikely to start a fire unless fresh inflammable material were piled around them.

Of all the sixteen, one would have guessed that political frustration over the Burns constitution was the least important. As the Government in London pointed out in its Statement of commentary on the Watson Report:

"This constitution was framed in consultation with the representatives of the people of the Gold Coast; it was accepted

was interested in such matters. It was known that he was shortly to be transferred to another district, and no fewer than four villages had sent deputations to see me, begging me to use my influence to get him kept where he was. But the proposal to invite him to the ceremony was rejected. They said, "We will agree to take Ward; he is a teacher, and Achimota is not a Government school, so we feel safe with him. But although we know the D.C. so well and like him so much, he is after all a Government man; and you can never quite tell with the Government. Much better not have him." And they did not have him. I may perhaps add that when I attended the ceremony, the man who had led the opposition to my going constituted himself my guide and chaperone. Throughout the seven hours I was there he made it his business to see that I saw all there was to see, and a kinder or more efficient guide I could not have had.

with enthusiasm by the Press and the public and by the members of the old and new Legislative Councils; and it has been in force for two years only."

All that is true. The grievances of 1948 were economic, not political. Nevertheless, when the Commission recommended sweeping constitutional changes, its instinct was sound. The Gold Coast people had a Government which it could not move, could not understand, could not trust. The Commission was right in feeling that the events of February and March 1948 showed that the Gold Coast needed a Government which would be responsive to less forceful expressions of public feeling than a trade boycott.

To its honour, the Government in London fully accepted this conclusion. It demurred indeed to some of the Commission's criticisms of the Burns constitution, but it agreed with the principles underlying the Commission's proposals. The Olympian imperturbability of British Governments is often infuriating, but it sometimes inspires admiration. There are a few lines in the Government's Statement of which Burke need not have been ashamed:

"On future constitutional advance His Majesty's Government have indicated their views below in the comments on Chapter V of the Report. It need only be added that they see in the events of February and March no reason to be deflected from the course of ordered constitutional progress which is their declared policy."

The makers of the 1946 constitution had expected that Gold Coast freedom would broaden slowly down from precedent to precedent; but inflation, swollen shoot, and the riots had made this policy of gradualism unworkable. The grievances which had led to the trouble were economic, but to the man in the street the remedy for the grievances must be political. "*They* make us pay high prices, *They* make us cut down our cocoa trees; it is no use expecting anything else from *Them*. *We* must take over the Government; and then *We* will find a way of bringing down prices and of curing swollen shoot." Faced with this attitude among the people, the Government was wise in accepting the view of the Watson Commission that further constitutional changes were urgently needed. Another commission was clearly needed to advise on the details.

And here too the Government acted promptly and wisely. It

appointed an all-African committee, under the chairmanship of
Mr. Justice J. H. Coussey (now Sir Henley Coussey). The Government must have been tempted to stiffen the committee at least
with a senior British official as chairman, if not with one or two
official members; but it was magnanimous enough to resist the
temptation and to rely entirely on the political good sense of the
Gold Coast people.

The Coussey Committee was a body of thirty-six men, including
its chairman. The chairman and twenty-three of the members were
nominated by the Governor to represent all sections of the Gold
Coast community and all shades of political opinion.[6] Each of the
existing Councils (the Joint Provincial Council of the Colony, the
Ashanti Confederacy Council, and the Northern Territories
Council) elected four representatives to put forward the views of
the native authorities.

The Committee sat from January to August 1949. On 26th
October it produced its report, which made extensive proposals for
changing both the central and the local government systems. Its
proposals for local government are dealt with on pages 372 to 375.

As far as the central government was concerned, the chief task
of the Coussey Committee was to devise a system which would
place the responsibility for framing and executing policy squarely
on African shoulders, and to reduce British control enough to
satisfy African desires without frightening London.

The Committee's proposals for the legislature broke clean away
from the traditional type of colonial legislative council with its
careful adjustment of official, nominated, and elected members.
The Committee proposed a bi-cameral legislature, with an upper
house of thirty-eight members, of whom one should be nominated
by the Chamber of Commerce and another by the Chamber of
Mines, and the remaining thirty-six should be elected. The lower
house should have seventy-eight members, of whom not more than
three should be officials, the remainder being elected. The Committee, while preferring a legislature of two chambers, put forward
an alternative scheme for a legislature of only one. In this case,
one-third of the seats were to be filled by members elected by the

[6] Though Dr. Nkrumah criticises the Committee because it contained no representatives of "the workers—the farmers, the miners, the petty traders—and the
trades union movement". (*Ghana*, p. 87.)

territorial councils in Ashanti and the Northern Territories and by the states in the south; the two representatives of mines and commerce would sit, there would be not more than three officials, and the remainder, numbering two-thirds of the total minus five, would be elected.

The franchise should be given to every taxpayer or ratepayer aged twenty-five and over. Electors in the towns should vote directly for their candidates, rural electors should vote for membership of an electoral college which would subsequently elect the members of the legislature. In short, urban elections would be direct, rural indirect. If a bi-cameral legislature was accepted, the thirty-six elected members of the upper house would be elected in equal numbers from the four main regions: the Colony, Ashanti, the Northern Territories, and Trans-Volta.

The Coussey Committee recommended that the executive also should be changed beyond recognition. The Executive Council of the day was still the old traditional affair of five senior officials, together with the two African representatives who had been added in 1943. The Coussey Committee proposed to sweep this away and replace it by an executive council of twelve members. The Governor would continue to be chairman, and the remaining eleven members would include not more than three officials. The leader of the lower house, and at least five other members, should be designated Ministers, and should have departmental responsibilities. The Executive Council should be collectively responsible to the legislature, and should resign as a body if defeated on a division.

The Coussey Committee's recommendations on these matters would transform the Gold Coast's traditional colonial type of government into something much nearer to parliamentary and cabinet government on the British system. But not identical with it. Instead of a party Cabinet, there would be the executive council with His Excellency always in the chair: a sort of hybrid between the Cabinet and the privy council of Queen Anne's day. The Governor would still have reserved powers; he could refuse to agree to a law, and could certify that a law which did not commend itself to the legislature was vitally necessary.

The most serious difference between the British system and the system which the Coussey Committee recommended for the Gold

Coast was one which only time and natural development could remedy, not legislation. There could be no party ministry in the Gold Coast, for there were at that time no real parties. It was still felt to be the business of the foreign officials to lay down policy, the business of all African representatives to criticise it. It would take time for political parties among Africans to develop on the basis, not of personal feuds or of communal antagonisms, but of different views on policy.

The British Government felt this to be so important a difference between Gold Coast and United Kingdom politics that it would make the Coussey plan in its complete form unworkable. It accepted the plan, and announced its acceptance on the very day that the Coussey report was published. But as a temporary measure until a two-party system should develop, the Government announced three modifications which had the effect of considerably reducing the resemblance to British cabinet government. It kept the executive council still responsible to the Governor, not to the assembly. It rejected the system of collective responsibility; the assembly could dismiss individual Ministers, but not the executive council as a whole. And since in the Government's view the assembly could not very well elect its leader until a two-party system had developed to make a contested election possible, the Government rejected the recommendation that the elected leader of the assembly should as such be entitled to a seat in the executive council. Instead of this, it decided that the African members of the assembly who were appointed by the Governor to be members of this executive council should themselves elect one of themselves to be leader of the legislative assembly.

It should be stressed that these modifications of the Coussey recommendations were intended to be merely temporary, until a genuine two-party system should develop in Gold Coast politics. The Government fully accepted the Coussey proposals as the goal to be attained as soon as possible. It was of no special importance that the Government also announced that it favoured a legislative assembly of one house instead of the bi-cameral assembly which the Coussey Committee preferred.

It is always the British way in constitutional matters to soften the rigour of the law by constitutional usage. There would in practice no doubt be little difference between the pure Coussey proposal and the Government's modification in this last matter of the appointment of the leader of the assembly. In selecting the six members of the assembly to become members of the executive council, the Governor would in practice pick the leading men of the assembly, those who combined personal popularity with administrative ability. The Governor's choice would hardly ever differ from the assembly's own choice, and the man whom the six elected from among themselves would always be the man whom the whole assembly would have elected. Nevertheless, on paper the Government's modification looked substantial. It might have worked out all right; but it looked as if the Governor, like Queen Anne, was claiming the right to summon whom he pleased to be members of his Council; and what was to stop him from picking six yes-men and getting one of them elected leader of the assembly? It is easy for us to answer the question: the electorate was not likely to elect such candidates, and if the electorate did elect them and the Governor picked them, they would not be able to stand up to the majority of the assembly. But it was not so easy for the Gold Coast elector to see this in 1949.

In insisting on the development of a two-party system, London was perhaps mistaking the means for the end. It is hard to see why a man who had been elected leader of the assembly by seventy-four to four, or even unanimously, should have less authority, and be less entitled to a seat on the executive council, than one who had been elected by forty-five to thirty-three. It is possible that what London really desired was a disciplined assembly, and that it was so frightened of the prospect of an assembly divided into splinter parties that it overlooked the possibility that an assembly might be effectively disciplined by other means than a two-party system.

If this was in fact the mistake which the Government in London made, it soon discovered it. Gold Coast politics soon were brought under very effective discipline. And this is where the dynamic figure of Dr. Nkrumah enters the story.

Kwame Nkrumah was born in 1909—on a Saturday, as his name shows—in a small village near Axim. He spent four years at Achimota College training to be a teacher, and in 1937 he went to the United States for university education. He graduated in Lincoln University, Pennsylvania, majoring in economics and sociology, and then went to the University of Pennsylvania, where he studied theology and education, taking the degrees of M.A. and M.Sc. (His doctorate is an honorary degree awarded him by Lincoln University some years later.) He worked his way through college, American fashion, going to sea as an ordinary seaman and working in shipyards. He became president of the African Students' Association of North America, and naturally had his thoughts turned to politics. During the last year of the war he came to London, and worked with African student and political organizations there. At that time his thoughts were running in the direction of a pan-African movement; he attended a pan-African congress held in Manchester in November 1945, and became general secretary of the staff which was set up to follow up the conference.

In 1947, Dr. Danquah, casting about for a bright and energetic young man to take charge of the Gold Coast Convention party machine, appointed Dr. Nkrumah as the Convention's paid secretary. He had certainly found what he wanted, but the ally whom he had called in ruined him. Nkrumah was a first-class party organizer, and soon had cells of the party proliferating all over the country. He knew the value of a simple slogan which everybody could shout and at least think they understood, and he set on foot the phrase *Self-Government Now*. Perhaps most important, he had the personal charm, captivating eloquence, and gifts of leadership which made men follow him. In June 1949, while the Coussey Committee was in the midst of its deliberations, he left the Gold Coast Convention and set up his own party, the Convention People's Party; most of the members of the Gold Coast Convention joined him, and only a handful remained faithful to the party's original leaders. The unfortunate Dr. Danquah, his thunder stolen, resumed his role of opposition leader, but this time as leader of a small splinter party in opposition to the main body of African opinion.

Dr. Nkrumah and his Convention People's Party now had to make up their minds about the Coussey report and the Government's promised action on it. The Coussey proposals would have given the Gold Coast the essentials of *Self-Government Now*, but the Government in London was offering merely self-government—with luck—before long. The C.P.P. was not satisfied.

On January 9th, 1950, the C.P.P. called a general strike and a boycott of British goods. Influenced no doubt by the peaceful resistance tactics of Mahatma Gandhi in India, Dr. Nkrumah insisted that there was to be no violence; the Government was to be brought to a standstill by peaceful non-co-operation. But the Gold Coast was not used to such ideas, and in spite of the party's instructions, some rioting and disorder did break out, and two policemen were killed. Nkrumah and others were arrested, charged with sedition, found guilty, and sentenced: Nkrumah himself to twelve months, and the others to shorter periods of imprisonment.

Legally no doubt the sentences were inevitable. Politically, their only effect was to heighten Dr. Nkrumah's popularity. It was natural that the judicial sentences should be widely regarded as purely political. The mass of the people had never heard of the dogma that judiciary and executive are strictly separate, and to them it was only to be expected that the Government should imprison the heroes who had given it so much trouble. When in due course the prisoners were released, they adopted as a badge of distinction a round white cap with the letters P G, standing for 'prison graduate', embroidered on it. To have served a term in jail for such offences gave them the sort of standing which Siberian exile gave to a Bolshevik in 1917.

The Government might perhaps have been forgiven if the strike, the boycott, the riots, and the imprisonment of the leading politicians had caused it to falter in its purpose of developing Gold Coast self-government. As might have been expected, there were critics who urged it to go slowly, and to be chary of handing over power to 'agitators'. It is to the Government's credit that it did not falter. While Dr. Nkrumah was still in prison, the Government announced the terms of the Gold Coast's new constitution. They followed the recommendations of the Coussey Committee with the modifications of which the Government had already given warning. There was to be a legislative assembly of one house, containing seventy-five elected and nine nominated members. Of the seventy-five elected members, thirty-eight were to be elected by the voters, by direct election in the towns and indirect election in the country; thirty-seven were to be elected by the state councils of the native authorities in the Colony and Trans-Volta, and by the territorial councils of Ashanti and the Northern Territories. All this was in accordance with the Coussey recommendations (the Coussey report had made provision for an assembly of one house, although the Committee would have preferred two), save that in the new constitution one-half of the elected members were representatives of the native authorities instead of only one-third as the Coussey Committee had proposed.

The new executive council too followed the Coussey proposals as modified. The Governor was to be chairman, and the eleven members included three European officials and eight African members of the assembly. The members of the executive council were to have ministerial responsibilities, and the European departmental heads who had hitherto been responsible for policy were to become permanent secretaries to the new Ministries. This was the crux of the matter: departmental policy was no longer to be laid down by a permanent official who could be criticized but could not be dismissed, but was to be laid down by a Minister who would have to resign if defeated in the assembly.

Though a great step forward, the new constitution could not be regarded as full *Self-Government Now*; and the question was whether the Convention People's Party would accept the constitution and work it, or would feel bound to swing the country against the offer and prolong the time of troubles. Fortunately the Government's statesmanship in making the offer drew forth an equally statesmanlike response from the C.P.P. The party declared itself ready to work the new constitution and to take part in the elections for the new assembly, which were to be held in February 1951.

The elections were a triumph for the C.P.P., which won twenty-nine out of the thirty-three country seats and all five of the town seats; but they were also a triumph for the British and African officials of the public relations and other departments, who so successfully carried out their difficult task of explaining to a largely illiterate electorate how democratic elections of the Western type should be run. The new assembly contained thirty-four C.P.P. members, three from Dr. Danquah's Gold Coast Convention and one independent member, with thirty-seven elected representatives of the territorial and state councils, six nominated European members representing mining and commerce, and three ex-officio members. Dr. Nkrumah himself was elected in his absence; when the election results were known, the C.P.P. asked the Governor as an act of grace to release the prisoners; and Dr. Nkrumah and his colleagues came straight out of jail to take their seats on the executive council.

The new Government was by no means what the C.P.P. wanted. Nkrumah and his colleagues were party men and they wanted a party government; they could not be content to see the three Ministries of Defence and External Affairs, Finance, and Justice held by European officials who were not members of their party and were not responsible to the electorate. Moreover, they had made up their minds that as far as the central Government was concerned, the day for direct representation of the native authorities was past. The country had never altogether liked the 1925 arrangement under which paramount chiefs sat in the legislature to represent the provincial councils of chiefs. There had always been a feeling that in taking part in the discussions of national affairs these paramount chiefs were to some extent stretching their constitutional position.[7] But the C.P.P. had another reason for wanting to exclude the native authorities from the central legislature and to confine them to local government. On the whole, the native authorities represented the old order, whereas the C.P.P. represented the new. The chiefs and their elders were bound to think of libations and sacrifices and religious ritual, of precedence and ceremonial, of native customary law, of local interests and of the traditional and stately manner of doing things. It was their duty. And it was not easy for them to combine this essential duty with responsibilities to the nation as a whole. Moreover, there was an unfortunate cleavage between these members of the state councils and the younger educated men. The interests of educated men usually lay outside tribal affairs: in a career of Western type or in national politics. Conservative elders were reluctant to admit educated men to membership of the councils, and were especially distrustful of an educated chief. In 1945, out of 2,471 members of state councils in the Colony, only 614 were educated. To the C.P.P. the presence in the assembly of thirty-seven members representing this essentially conservative and traditional outlook could be nothing but a hindrance to its efforts to modernize the country.

The party's acceptance of the constitution, and the rapid progress that followed, were largely due to the happy understanding

[7] Compare the description of the traditional position of the chiefs on pp. 99-102.

that developed between Dr. Nkrumah and the Governor of the country, Sir Charles Arden-Clarke. The two men trusted each other; and while the Minister controlled his party, the Governor convinced Whitehall. The Gold Coast was fortunate in finding two men who could thus work together. Other Governors had been popular, especially Guggisberg more than twenty years earlier, who drew up a bold programme of training Africans to fill senior positions in the public service, and would gladly have carried out the transition from colonial status to self-government if the times had been ripe. But the times were not ripe; and above all, Guggisberg had no Nkrumah.

The programme of the new Government was studiously moderate, and only its new educational proposals, which the assembly approved in August 1951, revealed the new drive and determination which were possible to an African Minister with a strong party to back him, and could never have been possible to a foreign administrator.

In March 1952, the British Government took a further step forward. It announced that the leader of the assembly should be re-named Prime Minister and the executive council re-named the Cabinet. The Governor should 'present' to the assembly the name of a man to be elected Prime Minister, and if the assembly so elected him the Prime Minister should be responsible to the assembly, not to the Governor. The Prime Minister should advise the Governor whom to appoint as Ministers, and the assembly would be invited similarly to elect them to their posts. By constitutional usage it would of course be impossible for the Governor to 'present' to the assembly for election as Prime Minister anyone but the leader of the strongest party in the assembly.

The Governor accordingly presented to the assembly the name of Dr. Kwame Nkrumah, and on 21st March, 1952, the assembly elected him Prime Minister. When we bear in mind that thirty-four members of the assembly had been elected as members of the C.P.P., the voting is significant; forty-five voted for him, thirty-one against, and eight abstained. It is clear that the majority of the thirty-seven council representatives must have voted against Dr. Nkrumah—which would do nothing to reconcile Nkrumah to a constitution which established this block of council representatives in the assembly.

We leave to later chapters the discussion of the Nkrumah Government's achievements in education and local government, and its plans for economic expansion. For the moment we confine ourselves to the advance towards responsible self-government at the centre.

In this matter, Dr. Nkrumah clearly had two main objectives to gain if he was to be master in his own house. He must replace the three European ex-officio Ministers with Africans from his own party, and he must get rid of the block of thirty-seven members of the assembly elected to represent the traditional native authorities. He bided his time, but not for long; in 1953 he asked for the necessary changes in the constitution, and in April 1954, only just over two years since he had become Prime Minister and three since he had emerged from jail to take over power, he received them.

The constitution of 1954 provided for an assembly of a Speaker and 104 members, all elected on ordinary party lines, with no special or nominated members. No doubt in making this concession the Government was influenced by the far-reaching reforms in local government made by the Local Government Ordinance of 1951,[8] which gave the traditional native authorities ample scope for con-structive work in their own areas; they would be far too busy to have any time left for central politics. The assembly had seven municipal members (three for Accra, two for Kumasi, and one each for Cape Coast and for Sekondi-Takoradi), and ninety-seven rural members: thirty-nine for the Colony, thirteen for Trans-Volta and Southern Togoland, nineteen for Ashanti and twenty-six for the Northern Territories and Northern Togoland. The life of the assembly was to be four years at most.

The Cabinet was to consist of at least eight persons, all members of the assembly and collectively responsible to it, chosen on the advice of the Prime Minister. And so Dr. Nkrumah had obtained his all-African, all-party Cabinet at last; though theoretically there was nothing to stop a European or Syrian resident in the Gold Coast from being elected to the assembly and becoming a Minister.

The new constitution was still short of complete self-government. The Governor still had certain reserved powers, though the con-stitution was careful to define how they were to be used. More important, the two subjects of external affairs and defence (which

[8] See below, pp. 375-7.

included police) were not placed under Ministerial control but were reserved for the Governor. And although British Togoland continued to be administered as part of the Gold Coast as a trust territory under the United Nations Charter, though Togoland members sat in the assembly in Accra and African Ministers were responsible for policy in Togoland as well as in the Gold Coast, yet the Governor as the representative of the Administering Authority could not divest himself of a certain special responsibility for Togoland affairs.[9]

But these limitations clearly could be only temporary. In any case, the 1954 constitution gave the Gold Coast complete self-government in its internal affairs, and in 1955 it seemed as if full self-government could be only a few months distant. The Nkrumah Government was firmly in the saddle, and had dealt sharply with some party members who flirted with Communism and others who were convicted of corruption. It was making an energetic and promising start with its task of developing the country, and the C.P.P. party discipline was still holding together, in spite of the

[9] The position of Togoland was much bedevilled by local and international politics, and gave a great deal of trouble to the British, French and Gold Coast Governments, and to the United Nations. The German colony of Togoland had never been an ethnological or geographical unit. It had one useful port at Lome, but communications with the interior were made difficult by the steep range of the Togoland hills. The population of southern Togoland was mainly of Ewe stock, like that of French Dahomey to the east and south-eastern Gold Coast to the west; the population of northern Togoland was mainly of Dagomba and related tribes. The Germans administered the colony from 1899 (when its frontiers were fixed) to 1914, and after the 1914 war it was divided into two, the western strip being administered as part of the Gold Coast, the eastern as part of Dahomey. But the League of Nations, and later the United Nations, continued to regard Togoland as a unit. Various possibilities existed, each with its disadvantages; and neither the Governments concerned nor the United Nations, nor—more important—the Togolanders themselves, could agree on any one of them. Togoland might be reconstituted as a political unit. The existing division might be made permanent, subject possibly to slight rectifications of the frontier, so that Western Togoland should throw in its lot with the Gold Coast and Eastern Togoland with Dahomey. The territory might be divided afresh, the Dagomba and other northern tribes joining their brethren in the Gold Coast and the Ewe people of the south combining with their brethren in the Gold Coast and Dahomey to form a new Ewe-speaking state. Petitions and counter-petitions, proposals and counter-proposals went on continuously from the founding of the United Nations onwards, and were still going on in 1955. Eventually, in May 1956, a plebiscite was held in British Togoland under United Nations auspices. The alternatives placed before the voters were union with an independent Gold Coast, and a continuance of the existing trusteeship until something better could be devised. Out of 194,000 voters, 159,000 voted: 93,000 supporting union with the Gold Coast and 66,500 supporting continuance of the trusteeship. The Trusteeship Council and the General Assembly of the U.N. accepted the result of the vote, and British Togoland was duly united to Gold Coast in March 1957.

fact that no rival party had yet appeared to be a serious challenge to it in the assembly.

The official Opposition in the 1954 assembly was the Northern People's Party of fourteen members; the assembly contained six independents and five members belonging to four small parties. The C.P.P., with seventy-nine members in a house of 104, was thus in an overwhelmingly strong position. But soon after the elections a new party arose, calling itself the National Liberation Movement, and its strength began to grow in a way which caused the Government some alarm. The National Liberation Movement, in spite of its name, was mainly an Ashanti movement, and was openly supported by the Asantehene. Its leaders criticized the C.P.P. on various grounds, notably with accusations of corruption and of dictatorial tendencies; but the N.L.M. policy was to advocate a federal system of government. The N.L.M. drew its strength from various sources: from chiefs and other supporters of the traditional order who resented the loss of some of their authority, from cocoa farmers who were disappointed at the price the Government allowed them to receive for their cocoa, and of course from individuals and rival groups who found the C.P.P. uncongenial. But its only divergence in policy was its support for a federal constitution.

In Ashanti, the N.L.M. was strong. Some C.P.P. members broke away from their party and joined it. Many who were not party men sympathised with the N.L.M. when they said that the C.P.P. machine was altogether too powerful, that the day was not far off when nobody would be able to succeed in life unless he were a C.P.P. member, and that government by a party machine was not the self-government they had fought for. Feeling ran so high that it was not safe for Ministers to show themselves in Kumasi.

The N.L.M. and the Northern People's Party worked together. When the Government proposed to set up a Select Committee of the assembly to draw up the draft of a constitution, the Opposition objected that such business could not properly be undertaken by the assembly, but only by a specially convened constituent assembly. When it failed to persuade the Government, it walked out of the chamber, and refused to take part in further discussions on the subject.

This was serious, for it raised the possibility that the Government in London might consider the country not yet ripe for the final instalment of self-government. The British Government sent out Sir Frederick Bourne, a former Indian Governor, as a constitutional adviser to try and bring the two sides together over the question of regional devolution. The Opposition in the Gold Coast did not help the situation by refusing to have any official contact with him or to take 'part in any formal discussions. In due course, Sir Frederick Bourne produced his proposals, which fell distinctly short of federalism.[10] It was natural that the Gold Coast Government, irritated by the tactics of the Opposition and encouraged by Sir Frederick's concurrence, should at first be inclined to stand on its dignity as the duly elected Government of the country. The N.L.M. however was claiming that public opinion had swung so much away from the Government since the elections, that Dr. Nkrumah and his colleagues were no longer the people's representatives. It is to the credit of Dr. Nkrumah's statesmanship that he accepted this challenge, and dissolved the house in which he held such a strong majority. The British Government for its part promised that it would be "ready to accept a motion calling for independence within the Commonwealth passed by a reasonable majority in a newly elected Legislature". The elections were held in July 1956. The C.P.P. won all forty-four seats in the Colony, and eight out of thirteen in Trans-Volta Togoland. In Ashanti and the North the C.P.P. was in a minority; it won eight Ashanti seats to the N.L.M.'s twelve, and eleven Northern seats to the fifteen of the Northern People's Party, which was allied with the N.L.M. Three independent candidates and three small-party candidates were returned; one of the three Independents applied for and was granted the Government Whip. The C.P.P. thus had the support of seventy-two members in a house of 104.

Dr. Nkrumah naturally claimed this result as conclusive evidence that the National Liberation Movement was not really national at all, and that the country as a whole was with him; the Opposition naturally pointed out that Ashanti and the North were against him. The responsibility was thus on the British Government to say whether it considered that the election results gave Dr. Nkrumah the 'reasonable majority' which it had stipulated. A motion authorising the Government to request independence within the Commonwealth was duly passed in the Gold Coast legislative assembly

[10] Details are given in the chapter on local government; see pp. 384-6.

by seventy-two votes to nil; the Opposition did not attend the debate.

The independence debate in Accra was held on 3rd August; on 15th September, the Secretary of State conveyed the Government's decision. He wrote to the Governor that "the motion calling for independence within the Commonwealth has been passed in the newly elected legislative assembly by a majority which must clearly be regarded as reasonable", and undertook to introduce into the United Kingdom Parliament a Bill to give the Gold Coast independence under the name of Ghana; independence day was fixed for the 6th March, 1957, the anniversary of the Bond of 1844.

And so the British territory of the Gold Coast became the independent state of Ghana. The Gold Coast had known European rule since 1482. The Portuguese departed in 1642, the Danes in 1850, the Dutch in 1872; the British, the most enduring and the most effective of all the foreign rulers, departed in 1957, 326 years after building their first fort, and eighty-three years after proclaiming the Gold Coast a British colony.

I have set out earlier in this book the reasons which make me hesitate to agree that there is any historical continuity between the Akan people and the ancient kingdom of Ghana. In this sense, the true heirs of Ghana seem to me to be the Mandingo, not the Akan. But we must readily accept the symbolic appropriateness of Ghana as a name for the first independent West African state of modern times. The old Ghana so struck the imagination of Europe that to this day we call the whole of West Africa Guinea. Ghana was an African state with a civilization which owed little or nothing to Europe, and may indeed have been in some respects superior to the civilization of Western Europe in the age of Charlemagne. For nearly five hundred years, West Africa has looked to Europe for guidance and material equipment, while European historians, ignoring the history of the medieval Sudan, have repeatedly stated that Africa has produced no civilization of its own. It is natural that, as national feeling developed, Africans should have looked back to Ghana as the symbol of an Africa that was culturally as well as politically independent of Europe.

For some years the name Ghana was freely used in naming political groups, newspapers, schools; and all politically conscious citizens of the Gold Coast agreed in their affection for the name

Ghana. The name Gold Coast proclaims itself to be a name given by foreign seamen who came to the country to enrich themselves; the name Ghana should be an inspiration to a free African people to draw its spiritual and cultural strength from African sources.

CHAPTER XV

THE DEVELOPMENT OF LOCAL GOVERNMENT

FOR many years, the British authorities in the Gold Coast were unable to bring about a clear separation between local and central government. Local government institutions already existed; they were the traditional tribal authorities, the chiefs and their state councils. The central Government existed, with its agents, the administrative officers and their technical and professional colleagues. The idea of Indirect Rule had been introduced by Lord Lugard and others, and the Gold Coast Government was trying to adapt the Nigerian model of indirect rule to Gold Coast conditions. Lord Lugard intended the system to imply two types of effort. One was to maintain the traditional system and prevent it from being weakened by the disintegrating forces of Western life; the other was to educate the chiefs and their councils to carry out new functions. The Gold Coast Government made a valiant effort to maintain the traditional system, and met with a fair amount of success. But it made hardly any progress until its very last years in developing the tribal authorities into modern local government bodies.

From the beginnings of British rule until its last days, the question of the relationship between the traditional native authorities and the central Government was the most important and most difficult problem which Governors and Secretaries of State had to solve.

The Government regarded the rights of chiefs as derived from the Crown, and several Ordinances were passed by which the Government claimed to confer powers on the chiefs; though, as Lord Hailey points out, the Crown hesitated long before taking the position which it took in Nigeria and in Tanganyika, that a chief could exercise no legal powers before being formally recognized as native authority.

Many African leaders, on the other hand, claimed that the rights of the African chiefs, "our natural rulers", as they fondly called them, were inherent, and not derived from the Crown. They regarded the position of a Gold Coast chief as depending on a treaty freely negotiated between his state and the British Government. They were no doubt encouraged in this belief by the anxious care which the Government always took, whatever its theories on the matter, to do nothing which might weaken the position of the traditional native authorities.

There is a string of Ordinances, and another string of abortive draft Ordinances, regulating the position and the powers of the native authorities. The earliest such ordinance in the history of the Colony is the Native Jurisdiction Ordinance of 1878. This was replaced by a second ordinance with the same title five years later, and this N.J.O. of 1883, with certain amendments in 1910 and 1924, remained the basis of the law in this matter until 1927.

The N.J.O. provided that a head chief, with the assent of his councillors, might make by-laws on a list of prescribed subjects, the by-laws being, of course, subject to the Governor's approval. Head chiefs and minor chiefs alike were not merely empowered but enjoined to establish tribunals,[1] and the jurisdiction of these tribunals was laid down. They were declared competent to hear minor civil cases where the sum in dispute was not more than £25, testamentary cases up to a limit of £50, and all cases dealing with land tenure, native custom, and breaches of the state's by-laws. Every chief was given the powers of a conservator of the peace, with power to arrest offenders and send them, if outside the province of his own court, to the District Commissioner. The Governor was empowered to suspend or depose a chief, and the rights of the traditional native authority, the state council, to depose its chief were carefully safeguarded.

The aim of the N.J.O. was to preserve the existing organization of native tribunals, to reserve to those tribunals a sufficient body of work, and to maintain some at least of the chief's traditional executive and legislative powers. Its effect, however, was disappointing. In the first place, too much stress was laid on the establishment of a tribunal as the characteristic of chieftainship; and the result was that hosts of petty tribunals were established by small chiefs and headmen who would have had no right to establish them under the old order of things. The ordinance made no attempt to control the working of these petty courts; and as the court fees and

[1] Section 10: "The head chief of every division and the chiefs of sub-divisions or villages shall, with their respective councillors, authorized by native law, form native tribunals, having power and jurisdiction" as provided in the Ordinance.

the proceeds of fines were appropriated by the court, the right to hold a tribunal speedily became recognized as a profitable privilege. An appeal lay from a native tribunal to the D.C.'s court; but the D.C. had no right or duty of exercising a general scrutiny of all decisions other than those brought before him on appeal. It cannot be assumed that a litigant who does not appeal from a decision is satisfied with it. When the judge who pronounces sentence is also the local chief, it may often be better to submit to a decision rather than to make trouble for the chief and his councillors by appealing. The members of the court are the traditional councillors, and the small man, however dissatisfied he may be, can do little against the close ring of ruling elders who hold all political power in the village as well as judicial power.

The N.J.O. did not limit its attention to the working of the traditional judicial organization. It intended also to increase the legislative authority of the chiefs and their councils. In this respect, however, the ordinance was a failure. The chiefs and their councils were empowered to make by-laws; but on matters which did not interest them they did not make by-laws, or did not enforce them. In such urgent matters as the control of cocoa pests and the creation of forest reserves the Government, after waiting for years in vain for the native authorities to act, was forced to take action itself. This meant that there was a system of indirect rule in trivial matters and in matters which particularly interested the village folk, whereas in major affairs, what may be called national as opposed to village affairs, the Gold Coast was ruled directly. This, of course, led to a decline in the reputation of the chiefs, and this decline was helped by the constant trouble that arose because without authority from their councils the chiefs alienated stool lands for mining or cocoa or timber concessions. Many destoolments were carried out because a chief had granted lands to European concessionaires or to African farmers from another tribe, and it was alleged either that he had done so without the authority of his council, or else that in doing so he had dispossessed some family of its land or had misappropriated part or the whole of the consideration received. There was in most places no system of accounting whatever, and no means, other than the memory of the witnesses, of finding out how much had been received, and what had happened to it.

M

The Government's main attention, however, was given to improving the judicial work of the tribunals; and several ordinances were drafted to amend the N.J.O. in this respect. Most of these, however, were opposed by the chiefs and their advisers on the ground that they infringed the chiefs' traditional rights; and the Government did not press them. By the Chiefs' Ordinance of 1904, however, the Governor was empowered to confirm the election and installation of a chief, the N.J.O. having already given him the right of suspending or deposing a chief. Nothing was said to imply that a chief could not legally act until he had been confirmed by the Governor.

The N.J.O. was amended in 1927 by the Native Administration Ordinance; the change of title is significant of a change of emphasis. But before that happened, feeling had been embittered by the events of 1894 and 1897.

In 1894 the Government, anxious to prevent the wholesale alienation of land to timber and mining companies, proposed an ordinance vesting all waste lands, forests and minerals in the Crown. This, of course, roused intense opposition, for all classes in the African community declared that there was no such thing as waste land, if by waste was meant unoccupied land. All land was, and still is, just as much the subject of possession as land in England. Even if not in use for farming or any other purpose, the land is the property of some stool, that is to say, some tribe. The practice of shifting cultivation means that land lies fallow for several years to recover its strength, and land which is lying fallow at the moment will be needed in the future. The conception of land tenure in the Gold Coast is similar to what it was in sixth-century England. Land is the property of families or of the tribe, be it Akim Abuakwa or the East Saxons. The tribe has a chief, who is the trustee or the manager of the tribal land; and he with his councillors can make grants out of it to new arrivals, and must settle all disputes between families over boundaries and such. In England, as the kingship rose to greater power, the idea of the chief or the king as the manager of the tribal land gradually hardened into the theory that all land was held from the king; this theory was worked out by the feudal lawyers, and the modern idea of free-hold land was reached as the result of an agreement by which the Stuart kings surrendered their feudal rights over the land in return for cash. In the Gold Coast the development has not gone so far. There is a tendency for the chief to assume more powers of control over the land than his people are inclined to allow him, and folk-land is being more and more transformed into book-land (to use the Saxon terms) by the alienation of stool or tribal lands and the drawing up of title deeds. But the feeling that all land is family land or tribal land is immensely strong.

The Government, with its plan of vesting in the Crown all tribal land not actually in visible use, provoked such a storm that it did not venture to press the matter. Three years later, in 1897, it tried again, and introduced a measure called the Lands Bill. This was "An ordinance to regulate the administration of public land and to define certain interests therein, and to constitute a Concessions Court."[2] The preamble declared, "Whereas from time to time various instruments purporting to create interests and rights over land in the Gold Coast Colony, especially in regard to mining and timber felling, have been executed by natives purporting to be Chiefs . . . and whereas it is expedient to provide for the proper exercise of their powers by those entrusted with the disposal of public land . . . and to facilitate the acquisition of public land by private persons . . . " and the Bill proceeded to define public land and the powers and rights that existed in respect of it, and to lay down procedure for administering and alienating such land.

The first step was to define 'public land'. This was described as follows: " 'Public land' means land over which there has not been acquired one of the inferior rights mentioned in section 13 hereof and which has not been or may not hereafter be acquired or reserved for or dedicated to any public purpose." Section 13 describes the inferior rights referred to, and also the superior rights which are contrasted with them. By 'superior rights' the bill meant (a) rights exercisable by the Governor under the bill and (b) the customary rights of a native chief in respect of land appurtenant to his stool. The inferior rights, on the other hand, were rights acquired by the Government for public purposes or rights created by certificates and previous grants. The effect of the definition of public land, therefore, was to class as public land all land, not already alienated by concessions or deeds, which was not already

[2] I quote from the bill as amended for the second reading; the text and a verbatim record of the debate are printed in the *Gold Coast Gazette* for 1897, pp. 83-9.

occupied by the Government for roads, railways, public buildings, etc. and which could not be shown to be stool land. The implication is obvious. The Government believed that in between villages there were areas of no man's land. It would recognize an area round a village in which the village farms lay as village land, but virgin forest and bush in between would not be recognized as stool land and would be thrown into the pool of public land. The sting of this lay in section 4 of the bill, which provided that all public land in the colony might be administered by the Government of the colony under certain provisos set forth in the bill.

The main purpose of the bill was twofold: to control and regulate alienation of tribal land by chiefs, and to encourage permanent settlement as distinct from shifting cultivation by individual tribesmen, by giving the permanent occupier security against his chief. In his address to the Legislative Council when introducing the Bill the Governor (Sir William Maxwell) said:

" . . . The Bill . . . while preserving to the natives of the Colony their right to use public land for shifting cultivation in the manner to which they are accustomed, encourages them to settle permanently on cultivated land by assuring to them the right of proprietorship (a 'settler's right'), if occupation is continuous. The mere fact of periodically resorting to the same land for shifting cultivation does not give to a native any right to the land itself. His right is to the crop alone, and it is in respect of the crop only that he will be compensated if the land happens to be dealt with at any time as public land. . . . "

But the idea of public land raised a storm of opposition. At the second reading of the bill objections were heard, and a short extract from the speech of Mr. J. M. Sarbah, counsel for some of the objectors, sums up the main grounds of their objection.[3]

"Another point which we have endeavoured to bring before this Council is the definition of what is called public land. In going through the Bill we have endeavoured to understand the meaning of each clause and the meaning of the words in it. Looking at the definition of public land, our instructions are that the Bill seems to fall into the error that every piece of land in this country except those enumerated in section 13

---

[3] Mr. Sarbah afterwards became a member of the Legislative Council, and a C.M.G.

of the Bill is public land; as to this we most respectfully refer Your Excellency and the Hon. Members to the reports of various persons included in the report on land tenure in the Gold Coast, by which it is affirmed that every piece of land and every plot of land in the Gold Coast has an owner whether such piece or plot be waste land or forest land. . . . When it is said Chiefs own lands, it is erroneously supposed or presumed that because a Chief happens to be the ruler of the village, he is the owner of the lands of the village community. No, as a member of his own family such a person may have certain lands which he holds with the other members of his family, and over which the villagers have no control at all. With the village elders and headmen, the Chief looks after the common land. Plots of land under cultivation by or in the possession of a family are the property of such family, and it has always been decided by Her Majesty's judges in the law courts that the successor of the owner of such land is entitled to it. It is only on failure of successors that such land falls back into the common land of the village. . . . "

The Government so far yielded to the protests as to refer the Bill to the Secretary of State. The opposition also appealed to the Secretary of State. A society was formed with the name of the Gold Coast Aborigines' Rights Protection Society, numbering among its members very many chiefs; and the Society[4] sent a deputation of three of its officials to England to plead its case. The deputation succeeded in convincing Mr. Joseph Chamberlain, then Secretary of State for the Colonies, and the obnoxious Bill was withdrawn. The Government limited itself to passing a Concessions Ordinance in 1900, which provided that all proposed concessions were to be reviewed by the Supreme Court of the colony, which was empowered to modify the terms if it considered them unreasonable. The Concessions Ordinance provided also that concessions must not exceed five square miles for mining and twenty square miles for timber, and that existing rights such as hunting, shifting cultivation, and firewood gathering must be safeguarded. The Government no doubt hoped that by handing over the revision of concessions to the judiciary it would be acquitted of any suspicion

[4] The society is still active, and is commonly called the Aborigines' Society for short.

of trying to get administrative control over them. But the dogma
of the separation of the judiciary from the executive had not sunk
as deep in the mind of the Gold Coast man in the street as it had
done in England; he often felt that a Government judge was as
much a Government official as a Government administrative officer.

The Lands Bill was dead, but it was not forgotten; and its effect
on public opinion was disastrous. For the rest of its days, the
British Government in the Gold Coast had to live under the constant suspicion of wishing to filch the people's land, and its best-
meant actions were misrepresented in the light of that suspicion.

In 1927 the Government tackled the question of Native Administration. The moment was not very propitious. Much opposition
had been aroused in 1925 by the establishment of provincial councils: more in 1926 by a Forests Ordinance, which empowered the
Government to set up forest reserves. Although the forest reserves
were to remain stool property and be administered under stool
by-laws, it was alleged that the Government's motive was to obtain
control of stool land; and the provincial councils of chiefs were
represented as a device to detach the chiefs from their people and
erect them into autocrats. Indirect rule was described by the
Government's African opponents as a system whereby an autocratic 'emir' was able to oppress the people at his pleasure as long
as he obeyed the Government's will. The Gold Coast Government
was accused of conspiring to transform the constitutional Gold
Coast chieftainship into this 'Nigerian' autocracy. The Government as usual made no effective attempt to counteract this propaganda, so that this travesty of the system of indirect rule became
widely known.

The long and important Native Administration Ordinance of
1927 is divided into 129 sections. It makes a great advance on the
N.J.O. in recognizing much more explicitly the state council of a
stool, and in laying responsibility upon it. The state council is to
consider all problems of disputed elections and destoolments, and
of the wrongful detention of stool property. The relative positions
of paramount chiefs, divisional chiefs, chiefs and headmen (the
four terms used in this ordinance) were defined; and the procedure
in election and destoolment was laid down. Elections and destoolments were to be reported to the Government. It was made an
offence, punishable by heavy penalties, to undermine the position

or authority of a chief of any rank; complaints against a chief were to be brought before the state council in the customary way. A divisional chief defying the authority of a paramount chief was liable to especially heavy penalties, including deportation; and it was an offence also for the divisional chief, once his subordinate position was recognized by the Government, to claim independence or to withdraw his allegiance. Chiefs and councils were empowered to make by-laws. A right of appeal was created from a subordinate tribunal to the tribunal of the paramount chief, and the powers of the tribunals were extended. Their jurisdiction covered civil cases under native customary law on the subjects of marriage, divorce, land and succession, to a limit of £100 in the case of a paramount chief's court and £25 in that of a division chief. In criminal cases, such as assault, oaths, abuse and slander, seduction, disobedience to customary duty, similar limits were laid down.[5] The beginnings of a system were laid down whereby the Government could supervise the working of the native tribunals; the Provincial Commissioner was empowered to issue a writ removing a case from a native tribunal and transferring it to a higher court. This writ could be issued by the Provincial Commissioner either at his own instance or on the application of one of the parties in the case.[6] There was, however, no supervision or control of tribunals beyond this provision. A state council was empowered to make a formal statement of what it conceived to be the existing native customary law in its division, and this statement, when accepted by the Governor, was to become an authoritative declaration of which all courts were bound to take cognizance. Lastly, the Provincial Councils, which had been established two years earlier, were made into tribunals to determine disputes on matters of native customary law, such as land, between two paramount chiefs or between divisional chiefs who were subjects of different paramount chiefs.

[5] In the original list of criminal offences coming within the cognizance of a divisional chief's court appears the following: "(The practice of witchcraft, or) the possession of any poisonous noxious or offensive thing with intent to use such thing to endanger or destroy human life or to hurt aggrieve or annoy any person." This definition was afterwards amended by the omission of the words in brackets.
[6] This reminiscence of Henry II's writ *Praecipe*, which so annoyed the barons of Magna Carta, strengthens the general resemblance between Gold Coast native customary law and the law of feudal England.

The Native Administration Ordinance was described in its title as "An ordinance to define and to regulate the exercise of certain powers and jurisdictions by native authorities, and to assign certain functions to the Provincial Councils, and for purposes connected therewith." It aimed at defining and regulating powers and jurisdictions that already existed. Its only deliberate innovation was the assignment of this new function to the Provincial Councils, and it made no attempt at all, beyond the step of empowering the Provincial Commissioner to transfer a case from a native tribunal to a higher court, to define the relationship between the Government and the native authorities. Moreover, in spite of its title, the ordinance did not concern itself with administration, but with the constitutional relationships of different native authorities with each other, and with their judicial powers. As Lord Hailey says, "On the judicial side, it did not give the Governor power to vary the schedule of chiefs empowered to hold tribunals, except to include a chief who had proved his claim to be included, nor did it categorically lay down that the power to exercise jurisdiction depended on recognition of the chief by Government, or provide for administrative supervision and control over tribunals. On the executive side it made no provision for the introduction of the native treasury system which, as experience has shown, is the most essential feature in indirect rule." [7]

The gist of these criticisms is that the Native Administration Ordinance was too timid; assuming that the Government was desirous of developing a system of indirect rule, it shrank from taking the essential steps—the organization of native administration treasuries and the settlement of the relationship between the native authorities and the Government—which must be taken if indirect rule is to become a reality. African criticism, however, was on quite opposite lines. The ordinance was based on suggestions made to the Government by a number of chiefs; and African critics accused the Government of fostering the power of the paramount chiefs in order that it might afterwards use them as instruments in a 'Nigerian' system of autocratic Government rule. The provision for increasing the powers of the Provincial Councils was very unpopular. The Provincial Councils themselves were unpopular, and the whole idea of bringing paramount chiefs to sit in the

[7] *An African Survey*, 471.

Legislative Council was bitterly opposed: on the ground, in both cases, that by the traditional Gold Coast constitution it was impossible to expect a chief to give an opinion of his own, since he must of necessity be given time to discuss with his people, and must voice not his own opinion but theirs. This criticism was a fair one, but it could easily be met by arranging business in the Provincial and Legislative Councils so that members might have time to consult their counsellors as tradition required. As for the more general criticism of the N.A.O., namely that it fostered the power of paramount chiefs unduly, it would be more accurate to say that the ordinance fostered the power of a superior chief of any grade against the chiefs subordinate to him. The traditional feudal right of defying a superior and casting off your allegiance if he has wronged you was greatly restricted by the ordinance, and in fact rendered almost impossible. But as there were already over sixty paramount chiefs in the Colony alone, a country half the size of England, this right of defiance and secession had gone far enough.

Experience showed the force of the criticism that the N.A.O. was unduly timid, particularly in refraining from developing native administration treasuries. In 1930 and 1931 the Gold Coast suffered from the world-wide slump in trade, and the Government was hard put to it to raise enough revenue to maintain its commitments. Attempts were made to introduce some form of direct taxation to supplement the indirect taxation on which the country had hitherto relied exclusively. One proposal was to levy a direct tax of sixpence in the pound on incomes of £40 a year and upwards,[8] and an alternative to this was a tax to be levied by native authorities, and to be shared between stool treasuries and the central Government. Both proposals, however, raised the usual storm of protest, on the usual grounds that the Government had no right to levy a direct tax without the express consent of the people, given by a truly representative assembly.[9] In 1934 the Government tried

[8] The commencing salary of a junior Government clerk and of a Government primary school teacher was £48. The tax would reach all clerks and teachers and skilled artisans; unskilled workmen and nearly all domestic servants would be outside its scope. It would be difficult to assess and levy the tax on illiterate farmers and fishermen, some of whom might well be liable to pay.

[9] The Legislative Council of the day was not, of course, regarded as a representative assembly. It is hard to see why indirect taxation should be permissible if direct taxation is not; however indirect a tax may be, it is still a tax.

again, and hoped that by giving up all claim to a share in the proceeds it would be able to induce the people to agree to the establishment of native administration treasuries. But the opposition was implacable, and this proposal, like the others, was abandoned. It was not till 1943, in the middle of the war, that the Government again introduced a scheme for a centrally collected income tax. The income tax then adopted was a graduated tax with a system of rebates on the English model.

The Government, however, had set its heart on establishing a system of native administration treasuries. In 1936 an amending ordinance was passed empowering paramount chiefs to levy taxes on their people under certain conditions, but the power was not used. A few chiefs set up stool treasuries, and one stool had a treasury system imposed upon it by a special ordinance.[10] But in 1939 the Government grasped the nettle firmly by passing the Native Administration Treasuries Ordinance. This ordinance provided that a state council may, and if required, shall establish a state treasury; and if it failed to comply within three months with the written order of the Provincial Commissioner, the Governor might establish a treasury for it. The treasury was to be managed by an *ad hoc* finance board appointed by and responsible to the state council; its accounts were to be properly prepared and inspected, and proper estimates of revenue and expenditure were to be drawn up. A native authority with a properly constituted treasury might (with the Governor's approval) levy a tax on its people.

The Native Administration Treasuries Ordinance was a most important step forward. It gave the native authority work to do beyond the traditional routine of hearing land cases and disputes over oaths. It brought into the service of the native authority clerks, accountants and technical workers of all kinds, who had hitherto tended to stand aloof and to look for careers to European commercial firms or the central Government. Lastly, a properly run treasury whose revenue and expenditure were all plainly

[10] Asamankese, an old Akwamu division now serving Akim Abuakwa. It had a considerable revenu from diamond royalties, but spent all its energies, and presumably all its money, in litigation. The paramount stool claimed a share of the diamond royalties, and Asamankese carried the case to the Privy Council, being defeated at every stage. The town of Asamankese meanwhile was in a pitiable condition, and after the Privy Council's decision the Government took matters into its own hands.

accounted for would kill the old suspicion that chiefs and councillors were feathering their nests at their people's expense.

The second great question left unanswered by the Native Administration Ordinance of 1927, that of the relationship of the Government to the native authorities, was resolutely tackled by a pair of ordinances passed in 1944, the Native Authority Ordinance and the Native Courts Ordinance. Both applied to the Colony only.

The Native Authority Ordinance set out to remodel the entire system of native administration; it repealed the N.A.O. completely and proceeded to re-enact such parts of it as were found useful. The ordinance abandoned the old conception of the central Government and the native authorities as two separate powers, which might co-operate but need not. It replaced this by a new conception: both central Government and native authorities were parts of one unified Governmental system.

This new conception gives rise to several radical changes. It is laid down that the Native Authorities are to be appointed by the Governor, and the only restriction on his choice is that the person or persons appointed must be natives of the areas concerned. A Native Authority may legally act as such only "if and so long as he is recognized by the Governor"; and the Governor may revoke the appointment of any person as a Native Authority, whereupon "such person shall cease to be such Native Authority". The Native Authority is granted wide powers of local government, and is explicitly invested with the duty of using them. But if it neglects to make an order which the Provincial Commissioner thinks it should make, the Provincial Commissioner may direct it to make the order, and in default may make it himself; while if it makes an order which he thinks it should not have made, the Provincial Commissioner similarly may direct the Native Authority to revoke the order, and if necessary he may revoke it himself.

These clauses lay it down quite plainly that the Native Authority's power to exercise jurisdiction depends on the recognition of the Authority by the Government, and that its jurisdiction must be exercised in accordance with Government policy.

In its provisions regarding the functions of the state council in matters of constitutional procedure and native customary law, the Native Authority Ordinance resembles the N.A.O. of 1927; but there is a significant proviso that if the Provincial Commissioner considers it inadvisable to entrust the state council concerned with an enquiry into such matters he is empowered to appoint an *ad hoc* committee of enquiry with the powers of the Supreme Court in obtaining evidence. An appeal lies from the state council's decision to the Provincial Commissioner in his administrative capacity.

The judicial powers of Native Authorities were brought under similar control by the Native Courts Ordinance. Native Courts are to be established by the Governor, and the Governor is to appoint the members of the Court; while nobody is to sit as member of a Native Court unless so appointed. Native Courts are divided into four grades, the powers of jurisdiction of each being defined, while careful provisions are made as to fees, evidence, procedure, and appeals. Supervision over the working of Native Courts is secured by Parts 9 and 10 of the Ordinance. Part 9 empowers a magistrate to transfer a case from a Native Court to another Native Court, to his own court, or to the divisional or land court. Part 10 provides for the routine supervision of all Native Court records by the District Commissioner, and establishes an officer called the Judicial Adviser, whose duty is to review the judgments of Native Courts and see that justice is properly done. The Judicial Adviser has powers to order a retrial, to disallow a court order and make a fresh order, to disallow or reduce costs, or "to make such order or pass such sentence . . . as the Native Court itself could have made or passed or (to) make such further order as may be necessary as the justice of the case requires". The duties of the Judicial Adviser of 1944 were identical with those of Maclean a century ago as Judicial Assessor: but he had at his disposal far greater means of fulfilling them.

These two ordinances, together with the Native Administration Treasuries Ordinance, gave the Government complete control over the working of the native authorities, and provided a complete answer to Lord Hailey's criticisms of the N.A.O. of 1927. The Governor now had power to decide who might and who might not hold a tribunal, and to supervise and control the working of the tribunals; it was categorically laid down that the jurisdiction of a native authority depended on its recognition by the Government; and the financial administration of native authorities was amply established and secured.

Thus, by 1944 the old distinction between direct and indirect rule was becoming meaningless. To talk of direct or indirect rule implies that Government, native authority, and people are three distinct entities. The result of the legislation of 1939 and 1944 was to combine the central Government and the native authority into one body; and provided that the native authority continued to command popular support, the old harmful division between rulers and ruled would vanish. This was the solution which the British Government in the Gold Coast finally proposed for the old problem of the place of the native authorities in relation to the central Government, which had exercised it for over sixty years of British rule, and which indeed was the basis of much of its perplexities in the days of the old 'Protectorate'.

We have so far been discussing the political or constitutional evolution of the Colony. Ashanti and the Northern Territories are in a different position.

The constitutional position of Ashanti in 1902 was one of considerable confusion. Ashanti had been annexed as a colony, and the Asantehene and many of his subordinate chiefs had been deported to the Seychelles or removed from their positions. Ashanti as a political unit had thus ceased to exist, and the important chiefs who had been immediately below the Asantehene had become completely independent. Many divisional stools were vacant, and the vacancies were filled by the Government with men on whose loyalty the Government could rely; they were elected by their people from the stool families, but naturally did not command the same respect among their people as the deposed chiefs.

In 1924 the Government allowed the former Asantehene, Prempeh, to return to Ashanti, and he was once again installed as chief of the Kumasi division. His title, however, was restricted to Kumasihene; the Government would not yet agree to the restoration of the confederacy. The Kumasi division had been without a head while Prempeh had been away, so that his restoration filled a serious gap. As time went on, however, it became perfectly clear that the Kumasihene was being regarded as Asantehene by everybody in Ashanti, and whether the Government recognized him as Asantehene or not he was Asantehene in the eyes of his people. In January 1935, after Nana[11] Prempeh's death, his successor, Nana

[11] The Akan word *nana*, meaning 'grandfather' (on the mother's side) is used as a title of respect for a chief.

Osei Agyeman Prempeh II, was accepted and installed by the Government as Asantehene, not merely Kumasihene; and the Ashanti state was thus reconstituted.

A Native Jurisdiction Ordinance for Ashanti was made in 1924, and stool treasuries began to be established from that time onwards. When the Ashanti state was reconstituted in 1935 legislation was passed restoring the Asantehene to his old position as at the same time paramount chief of the Kumasi division and paramount over the whole of Ashanti. In his first capacity he is assisted by the Kumasi council of chiefs; in his second capacity of Asantehene he is assisted by the confederacy council, composed of the head chiefs of the old divisional states, Mampon, Juaben, Bekwai and the others. Both these councils have judicial powers, the latter, of course, acting as a court of appeal for the whole of Ashanti. As a temporary measure, a court of privileges was established in 1935 to review the constitutional position of the Ashanti chiefs, many of whom were not chiefs that the Asantehene could recognize according to Ashanti tradition, and many again had assumed privileges to which tradition did not entitle them. With remarkably little difficulty the court was able to sift the many conflicting claims; chiefs who had been acting independently for thirty years acknowledged themselves to be subordinates, and others who had been regarded by the British authorities as unimportant were restored to the traditional position they had held in the old Ashanti.

In 1943, "in recognition of the loyalty of the Asantehene and people of Ashanti", the Government ceded to the Asantehene, "for the support and dignity of the Golden Stool of Ashanti and the benefit of the Kumasi division", all the lands in Kumasi which had been declared Crown land when Ashanti was annexed.

A somewhat similar development took place in the Northern Territories. At first sight the prospects seemed gloomy. The great states, Gonja, Dagomba, Mamprusi and so forth, were military states which had established themselves as ruling aristocracies above the old order of the *ten'dama* with their priestly authority over the primitive totemic clans. When their opportunities of fighting ended, the military aristocracies tended to lose their grip. Their authority was further weakened by the fact that the colonial boundaries cut through the native states. Dagomba was divided between Britain and Germany, Moshi between Britain and France.

It seemed that the social organization of the north would crumble into a chaos of tiny family groups.

Investigations that were carried out from 1928 onwards, however, revealed that under this superficial confusion, as had been the case in Ashanti, the ancient political organization still persisted in the minds of the people. In 1932 and 1935 legislation was passed establishing a system of native authorities with tribunals and treasuries; and in 1936 direct taxation was introduced. The people were traditionally bound to pay a tribute to the chiefs, and the new tax was designed to replace the old tribute, and was called a tribute tax to make this clear. There was no trouble over the introduction of the tax, and the native authorities collect it with little difficulty since it is paid entire and directly into the native administration treasuries. The revenue of the native authorities increased from £860 in 1933 to nearly £40,000 in 1937.[12] A Northern Territories territorial council of chiefs was established as a consultative body in December 1946.

Right up to the very end of the second World War, the Government clung to its policy of developing what it called Native Authorities into efficient organs of modern local government. But there were widespread doubts whether the policy was workable. The most obvious weakness of the native authorities for modern functions was that their members were mainly uneducated. In 1945, out of 2,471 members of the native authorities in the Colony, only 614 were educated. This criticism was often made, and from time to time the matter was discussed at provincial councils, but little progress was made. The reason was natural and human enough. Most elders of the old school did not want to be hustled and guided along unfamiliar paths by youngsters; they did not regard a Western-type education as an adequate equivalent of grey hairs. The young men on the other hand wanted a wider scope for their energies, and were unwilling to spend their time in discussing local affairs along with old men who lived in the past and who regarded them as intruders.

The native authorities had other defects. Most of their members held their places *ex officio*, and thus, quite apart from any question of education, naturally tended to hold themselves apart from the few members who were nominated to represent interests outside

[12] Hailey, *An African Survey*, 476, 477, 585, 586.

the official or traditional hierarchy. Most of the councils were large, and as most members were illiterate, their procedure was slow and cumbrous. Lastly, such councils could not attract an adequate staff; a career in local government service could not compare in attraction with a career in the Government civil service.[13]

These defects were realized by many people: by many District Commissioners and by many chiefs, as well as among the politically conscious public. No doubt they could be remedied with time; but how much time would be needed? And here again the Government came under suspicion: did it regard the problem as one of urgency, or would it be content to wait indefinitely?

The matter was brought to a head by the disturbances of 1948 and the Report of the Watson Commission. In its Report, the Commission suggested that one means of lessening the remoteness of the Government from the people would be a measure of devolution. It suggested the establishment of regional councils for the Colony, Ashanti, and the Northern Territories, with executive functions and the power to make by-laws; and it suggested also that the development of modern local government bodies should be speeded up. Though the Commission did not attempt to work out a detailed scheme of local government, it is clear that it thought efficiency more important than traditionalism.[14]

This section of the Report drew on itself some unfavourable comment from the Government in London. In its Statement on the Watson Report, the Government suggests that if the Commission had listened rather less to the keen politicians in the towns, and rather more to the solid good sense of the countryman, it would have realized that the Gold Coast people as a whole were attached to the chiefs and the system of native authorities, and would be unwilling to see the system drastically modernized.[15] It accepted the idea of regional councils, though it could not accept

[13] These criticisms are well summarized in the Coussey Report, paras, 70-75.
[14] In rural areas, the Commission recommended the establishment of local authorities, which should be the existing native authorities augmented with greater popular representation. In towns with an elected town council, the 'anomaly' of a native authority should disappear, and the town council should be the sole authority. (Para. 122.)
[15] "Their comments on chiefs do substantially less than justice to the strength of the tradition and custom which a large part of the country still regards as essential to an ordered society. (page 3) . . . They refer at some length to the views of Africans with a modern political outlook. In the very short time available to them in the Gold Coast the Commission were not, it is understood,

the Commission's proposal that they should levy rates and make grants out of their rates to subordinate local authorities. However, the task of working out a detailed scheme of local government would be better entrusted to a committee in the Gold Coast: that is, to the Coussey Committee.

The Watson Commission had thus made one appreciation of the state of local government in the Gold Coast and of the state of public opinion on the subject; the British Government had made a different appreciation. They were agreed that local government in the Gold Coast must develop out of the existing system of native authorities; they differed over the speed and method of the development. The Commission was for speedy and radical reform, and thought that the Gold Coast people would welcome it. The Government was cautious and conservative, and thought that the people would prefer to go carefully. It would be for the Coussey Committee to express a preference.

The opinion of the Coussey Committee is quite clear. On the whole it agreed with the view of the Watson Commission; it demurred on one point only, the status of the chiefs in a modern system of local government. The Coussey Committee's comments on this point are these:

> "The Native Authorities, through which local government is at present carried on, are virtually the old state councils vested with modern administrative powers. Their deficiencies include the restricted basis of their membership, their old-fashioned procedure, and their inadequate finance and staff.
>
> "These deficiencies, despite the gallant efforts which have been made by the Native Authorities, efforts which have resulted in definite progress and solid achievement, have in general hampered their effectiveness as agencies of local administration, have made them unequal to the demands

able to travel extensively in the rural areas, and they can therefore have had less opportunity of hearing evidence from representatives of the rural communities which form the great bulk of the population of the Gold Coast. His Majesty's Government therefore feel it necessary to state that, while they attach the greatest importance to modernizing the Native Authorities and making them fully representative of the people, they regard the Chiefs as having an essential part to play. In general the Chiefs in the Gold Coast are the traditional leaders of the people. Their functions in regard to local administration are based on popular support; and the transfer or delegation of any of their functions would require popular sanction, since the position of the Chiefs affects the whole system of relationships on which community life is traditionally based" (pp. 6, 7).

being made on them, and have prevented them from reaching the standard of efficiency required of modern local authorities.

"The complexity and stress of modern life, the desire for change and the progressive outlook, which are now pervading even the remote villages, call for more efficient organs of local administration. We therefore recommend entirely new councils, more democratic in composition, which should prove more efficient and effective in the discharge of greater responsibilities for the social welfare and wellbeing of their local communities.

"The accumulated experience and wisdom of the old councils, based as they are on deep-rooted social forces in the country, are not jettisoned by our proposals, as the new councils will draw upon the old for some of their members . . .

"The whole institution of chieftaincy is so closely bound up with the life of our communities that its disappearance would spell disaster. Chiefs and what they symbolize in our society are so vital that the subject of their future must be approached with the greatest caution. No African of the Gold Coast is without some admiration for the best aspects of chieftaincy, and all would be loath to do violence to it any more than to the social values embodied in the institution itself. Criticisms there have been, but none coming from responsible people whom we have known or met is directed towards the complete effacement of chiefs. We cannot, therefore, accept the status which the Watson Report would assign to them."[16]

The Government was very likely right in its conjecture that the Watson Commission formed its deepest impression of the need for local government reform from the anomalies which it found existing in the towns.

Town Councils were established at Accra in 1896, Sekondi in 1904, and Cape Coast in 1905. The council in each town consisted of five nominated and five elected members. In 1925 provision was made for the local government of Kumasi by the creation of the Kumasi Public Health Board, consisting of five official members, two representatives of the Kumasi council of chiefs, two commercial members, and a non-Ashanti African representative. The Board was replaced in 1943 by a Kumasi Town Council of six

[16] Coussey Report, paras. 32, 33, 34, 36.

nominated and six elected members, two of the nominated members representing the Asantehene and the divisional council of the Kumasi division, and one representing the local chamber of commerce.

In 1924 a Municipal Corporations Ordinance was introduced by the Government with the aim of extending the powers of the Town Councils, and of bridging the gap between the old tribal institutions and the new European type of local government body. It was proposed to revise the rating system, to tap new sources of local revenue, to give the Councils an elected majority, and to give the head chief in each town the right of membership of the Council. But the proposal was contested: it was felt by many that an elected mayor would be a dangerous rival to the head chief, and that relationships between the Town Council and the tribal authorities would be very complicated and difficult. The Government dropped its proposal, and for twenty years more made no attempt to tackle the problem of the relationship between the Town Councils and the tribal authorities.

In 1943, 1944 and 1945 a series of four Ordinances re-modelled the Town Councils to provide for an African majority. Each Council henceforth consisted of three official members appointed by the Governor, two unofficial members nominated by the state council[17] and one nominated by the chamber of commerce, and a number of elected members, six in Kumasi and seven in each of the other three Councils. For electoral purposes the towns were divided into wards, one member sitting for each ward. The Town Councils had power to levy rates, and they also received grants from the central revenue. They ran bus services, maintained their

[17] That is, the state council of the tribal authority: the chief and his councillors. From 1944 onwards the Government used the phrase 'native authority'; unfortunately, as the Coussey Report points out (para. 83) this term is disliked by most Africans, and there is no convenient synonym for it. The phrases 'state' and 'state council' are often used, but there is a risk of ambiguity when there are many small states inside one large one. Ambiguity is sometimes avoided by the use of an African word; thus we read of an 'oman council', and especially of the 'Asanteman Council', oman being the Akan word for 'nation', and Asanteman meaning the Ashanti nation. I avoid the term 'native authority' as much as I can, but it is sometimes unavoidable in a historical context. It should be added that 'native authority' and 'state council' do not mean exactly the same thing. The native authority was the state council with a few additional nominated non-traditional members, but the distinction between the two, as the Coussey Committee observed (para. 60), was "largely obscured by the practically identical membership of the two councils".

roads, and had responsibilities for town planning and the control of building. They had their medical officers of health, who supervised markets, food supply and sewage disposal. They did not, however, control their own police, or education, or water supply, and only one of the four ran its own electricity supply.

The Watson Commission thus found local government in these four urban areas in a transitional stage. On the one hand there was the regular traditional hierarchy of chiefs and their state councils, holding courts and carrying on the traditional system of government as if they were completely unaffected by the development of their native place from a small fishing or farming village to a large modern town. On the other hand there was a small Town Council, composed partly of Europeans and partly of African nominated and elected members, carrying on many of the functions of an up-to-date municipal body. The link between the two was the presence on the Town Council of two members nominated by the state council. The position was further complicated by the fact that the authority of the Town Council was territorial, whereas that of the chief and the state council was personal; that is to say, by occupying a house or pushing a hand-cart within the limits of the town of Accra you automatically came under the jurisdiction of the Accra Town Council, but you did not automatically come under the jurisdiction of the Ga Mantse, the head chief of Accra. You only came under his jurisdiction by being born a member of the Ga tribe of which he is chief.

Like the Watson Commission, the Coussey Committee was well aware of the inadequacies and the anomalies of such a system. It commented:

> "The Municipalities while not sharing the same defects as the Native Authorities are not responsible for all those services which should belong to a municipal authority, and are kept in leading strings by the Central Government. But this fact may be the result of their undue financial dependence on the Central Government."[18]

Having thus pointed out the weaknesses of local government both in urban and rural areas, and reaffirmed that in any soundly-conceived system of local government, the chiefs and state councils

---

[18] Para. 75. Native authorities were large, narrowly traditional, mainly illiterate; town councils were small, largely elected, well educated.

had an essential part to play, the Coussey Committee made its proposals for reorganization.

The Committee accepted the Watson recommendation that the country should be divided into regions, but recommended four regions instead of the Watson three: the Colony, Ashanti, the North, and Trans-Volta Togoland. This last region was to include the small part of the Colony which lay east of the Volta, and the southern half of Togoland, lying adjacent to the Colony and Ashanti. The northern part of Togoland should fall within the Northern region, so that the states of Dagomba and Mamprusi should not be administratively divided.[19]

The regions, as the Committee noted, could have no power except what the central Government might see fit to delegate to them, and they must be agents of the central Government and carry out its policy. There was no thought of a federal system of Government. The Committee recommended, however, that the central Government should devolve as much of its powers as possible on the regional administrations, especially in matters of health, education, public works, and social services. The regions should be financed by grants from the central revenues. In each region there should be a regional council, two-thirds of which should be elected and one-third should be chiefs. Regional administrations should supervise the work of the local authorities within their area. Their estimates of revenue and expenditure should be subject to the control of the central Government.

The Coussey Committee recommended the establishment of three classes of local authorities, which it called 'A', 'B', and 'C', graded according to size and wealth. Class 'A' councils should normally have a population of 100,000 to 200,000, with an upper limit of 400,000. The four existing municipalities should be Class 'A' local authorities, and in rural areas, Class 'A' authorities should consist of single states or of groups of smaller states. Class 'B' authorities should be smaller towns, or states which were grouped with others to form a Class 'A' authority. Class 'C' authorities, which the Committee hoped would be few in number, would be the smallest units which had a real life and cohesion of their own. The Committee suggested that Class 'A' authorities

[19] For historical reasons, one small area east of the Volta was kept in the Colony, and one small area west of the river became part of the Trans-Volta region.

should control all types of local administration, including such important affairs as major water supply schemes, small hospitals, fire services, primary education, transport services, and district feeder roads. The smaller authorities naturally should have lesser powers.

All local councils should have one-third of their members appointed by the traditional councils, and two-thirds popularly elected. Class 'C' councils should not exceed nine members, Class 'B' eighteen, Class 'A' twenty-seven.

In making these recommendations, the Committee was frankly balancing opposing arguments. On one hand, everybody in the country wanted to retain the authority of the chiefs, "and they in fact vie with each other in asserting their loyalty to the rule of chiefs".[20] Some chiefs said that this should be good enough, and that they were the people's representatives by virtue of their election. On the other hand, there was a general demand for larger representation on local authority councils and for popular elections to the councils. Ratepayers wanted a larger say in the spending of the rates, and if local authorities had an elected majority, "the elected members cannot evade responsibility for actions of the Council, and . . . the frequent attacks, not always justifiable, on traditional authorities will lose their force".[21]

Generally speaking, only Class 'A' authorities should be empowered to levy rates, though a few Class 'B' authorities should have this power for special reasons. Minor authorities should issue requisitions to their Class 'A' authority for the revenue they need. In addition to rates and miscellaneous revenue arising within the area such as profits from public undertakings, local authorities should derive revenue from the regional administration, and from the state councils in their area. The regional administration would make grants in respect of such services as education and maintenance of roads, grants towards equalization of rates, and reimbursements for services which the local authority rendered as agent of the regional administration. State councils would pay over to the local authority an agreed proportion of their traditional revenues.[22]

[20] Para. 136.
[21] Para. 141.
[22] Paras. 207, 209, 211.

Summarized, these proposals of the Coussey Committee for local government would give the country a system closely resembling that of England and Wales with its county or county borough councils and its urban or rural district councils and its parish councils. But there would be some important differences. In England and Wales, rates are levied by the urban and rural district councils, the larger units issuing precepts to the rating authorities. Under the Coussey proposals, it would be the Gold Coast equivalent of the county or county borough council that would levy rates, and the subordinate councils would issue requisitions to it. A second difference is that one-third of the members of all local authorities in the Gold Coast would be representatives of the traditional authorities, a provision to which there is no counterpart in Britain.[23] A third difference is that in the Gold Coast there was to be a regional organization, to which as much as possible of the functions of the central Government was to be devolved: as if there were local Parliaments in Edinburgh and Cardiff just as in Belfast.

One of the first pieces of legislation carried through by the Nkrumah Government was the Local Government Ordinance of 1951, which was based upon the Coussey proposals. The Class 'A' authority of the Coussey Report was named the district council, and the country was divided into thirty-seven districts: ten in Ashanti, fourteen in the Colony, nine in the Northern Territories, and four in Trans-Volta.[24] Within the area of the district council, the Ordinance established (as the equivalent of the Coussey Class 'B' councils) urban and local councils, a local council being the equivalent of the English rural district council. There were to be fourteen urban councils and 229 local councils in the whole country. One-third of the members of all councils were to be nominated by the traditional authorities, the other two-thirds being elected. Local government elections were to be held at the level of the urban and local councils, and these councils would form district councils by electing certain of their members to represent them on the district council. The local government

---

[23] The Coussey Committee also proposed a system of elected 'elders', who it specifically states were to be the equivalent of the aldermen in England (para. 154).
[24] The districts were not established by the Ordinance itself, but by instruments made by the Minister of Local Government under the provisions of the Ordinance. So were the urban and local councils.

franchise was given to all men and women who were at least twenty-one years old, owned land or a house in the area or had lived in the area for six months during the year before an election, and had paid rates. Some of the councils were to include members representing special interests, such as the mining interest at Obuasi, the centre of the gold mining industry. All this was in agreement with the Coussey proposals, except that the Coussey Committee had contemplated that only some, and not all, of the members of the district councils, its Class 'A' authorities, should be elected by the subordinate councils.

But there were some divergencies from the Coussey proposals. In the first place, the Ordinance made the urban and local councils the rating authority, not the district council. In the second place, the Ordinance did not establish regional councils and regional administrations after the Coussey model. The Chief Regional Officers in Ashanti and the North were responsible to the Ministry of Local Government, as their predecessors the Chief Commissioners had been to the Governor; there was no regional council to which they owed any responsibility. It was the view of the Nkrumah Government that the country would have enough to do for some time to come in getting the machinery of district and of urban and local councils into working order. Meanwhile, the existing councils of chiefs, the Joint Provincial Council of the Colony, the Ashanti Confederacy Council, and the Northern Territories Territorial Council, would serve to represent regional feeling.

In thus deferring the devolution of power to regional administrations, the Government was very likely acting wisely. Every new administrative organization meant a new staff, and qualified men were desperately scarce. Otherwise, the Ordinance followed so closely the Coussey proposals, that it might have been expected to receive general approval. But a great change had come over the political scene since the Coussey Report, and Dr. Kwame Nkrumah was the man responsible. The Convention People's Party welcomed the chance of setting up its organization to control local government elections to the central Legislature; its opponents saw that an elected majority on local councils was going to mean in practice a C.P.P. majority. Many chiefs and state councillors suspected that Dr. Nkrumah himself, in spite of his protestations, was no friend to the traditional system and would prefer to see the chiefs restricted to purely religious and ceremonial functions. Their fears were intensified by a difference in emphasis between the Coussey proposals and the Ordinance in the matter of stool lands. The Coussey Report had proposed that state councils should pay to the local authorities an agreed proportion of the revenue from stool lands. The Ordinance proposed that stool lands should be managed by the local authorities, and that the authorities should pay part of the revenue[25] back to the stool to support its dignity. It seemed to the chiefs that the Ordinance would do much more than add a genuine popular element to the local government bodies; it would put them at the mercy of the C.P.P., that is to say, of the central Government itself. The whole tendency of the British administration to build up the chiefs and their councils into effective organs of local government would be reversed. Local government would be controlled from the party headquarters in Accra.

The Local Government Ordinance was therefore opposed in the legislature, not only by the few elected opposition members, but by the great mass of the territorial representatives, the provision concerning the control of stool lands being particularly bitterly fought. The opposition, however, gained only unimportant concessions; the Ordinance was passed substantially as drafted, and the rift between the C.P.P. and the chiefs and their councillors widened. It is significant that when in March 1952 the assembly elected Dr. Nkrumah as Prime Minister, there were thirty-one hostile votes, although he commanded thirty-four out of the thirty-eight elected seats.[26]

This disagreement between the C.P.P. and the general body of traditional opinion was one of the main causes of the National Liberation Movement. The Government was sure of carrying the country with it when it was engaged in the struggle for independence, or in planning educational or economic expansion. But in reorganizing local government and the functions of state councils it was touching a sensitive nerve. Many people feared that the

[25] Coussey Report, para. 207, Ordinance, section 74.
[26] There is no division list, as the voting was by secret ballot. I would guess that the three ex-officio members would vote for Dr. Nkrumah as the Governor's nominee, and that the six nominated European members would abstain. If so, the figures of 45 for Nkrumah, 31 against, and 8 abstentions would be made up thus: *For,* 34 C.P.P., 3 ex-officio, 8 territorial members; *Against,* 4 Opposition elected members, 27 territorial members; *Abstentions;* 6 nominated members and two territorial members. But this is pure guess-work.

C.P.P. was only biding its time to exclude state councils altogether from local government and restrict them to ceremonial functions. Some thought that the Prime Minister himself would not wish to go so far, but that certain members of his party would: and did the Prime Minister control his party, or did his party control him? Others quoted—out of its context—a phrase which the Prime Minister was alleged to have let fall in one of his speeches: if he had opposition from the chiefs, "he would make the chiefs run away and leave their sandals behind".[27] There were cases in which local party leaders treated chiefs and state councils with scant deference. The Wenchi case, in which Dr. Nkrumah was felt to be personally involved, was more serious.

Wenchi is a state in north-western Ashanti, on the border between Ashanti proper and the Brong country of Techiman and Ofinsu. There was a long-standing dispute between two families over the right to the Wenchi stool, and at this time the stool had been held for some years by the Busia family. This family, as it happened, was conspicuous in national, not merely in Wenchi politics. Kofi Abrefa Busia, when a small boy, had attracted the attention of a Methodist missionary who was stationed at Wenchi. The missionary sent him to school, and subsequently to Wesley College at Kumasi, where he was trained as a teacher. The Wesley College authorities were struck by his abilities and character, and sent him to Achimota, where he took an external London degree with honours in history. Achimota then gave him a scholarship to Oxford, where he read history for his degree and afterwards took a doctorate in sociology. Busia was one of the first two Africans in modern times[28] to be appointed to the administrative service; but he gave this up and appeared to throw himself into an academic career. He became head of the department of African studies at the newly-founded university college of the Gold Coast, he produced a sociological study of conditions in the seaport area of

[27] It should be remembered that it is taboo for a chief's bare foot to touch the ground; even when he is sacrificing and slips his feet out of his sandals like Moses before the burning bush, he stands on the sandals. The threat therefore was more than a vivid description of panic; it contained an insult. Whether Dr. Nkrumah really said this, or in what context, is unimportant for our purposes; the point is that it was widely quoted, and held against him. It was quoted against him, for example, in the Legislative Assembly on 4th April, 1951, by Ofori Atta II, chief of Akim Abuakwa.
[28] Though there had been several African district commissioners in the last century.

Sekondi-Takoradi, and he held various visiting professorships in sociology at universities in the United States and Europe.

Dr. Busia was not attracted to politics, but he went into it because he felt strongly that the country needed an alternative to the demagoguery of the C.P.P. He helped to found a new opposition party, the Ghana Congress Party, and became the party's chairman, though his position was an uneasy one. He was defeated at the 1951 elections, but was returned to the assembly by the Ashanti Confederacy Council as one of its nominees. In the 1954 election Dr. Busia was the only member of his Ghana Congress Party to win a seat, and in the 1956 election, standing for the N.L.M., he was returned for the constituency of Wenchi West, beating his C.P.P. opponent by 4,884 votes to 3,125.

Wenchi is a borderline state between Ashanti proper and the Brong states. Its Brong neighbours tried to get Wenchi to join them in breaking away from the Ashanti Confederacy, and when Wenchi preferred to remain loyal to Ashanti, relations were strained. The chief of Wenchi was Dr. Busia's brother, and he and his adherents supported the Ghana Congress Party. Their rivals supported the C.P.P., and so family feuds and personal rivalries were intensified by national party politics. Party feeling in Wenchi ran so high that when Dr. Nkrumah visited the town as Prime Minister to make a public speech, he was booed and stoned.

For many years there had been complaints, in Wenchi as in many other states, that stool funds were mismanaged. In 1951 some of the 'youngmen'[29] petitioned for an enquiry into the stool finances. An enquiry was held, and serious irregularities were discovered; the whole finance committee of the Wenchi native authority was dissolved, but no recommendation was made that the chief should be destooled. This did not satisfy the petitioners. They held that the chief himself was so deeply involved as to merit destoolment, and they secured the help of one or two elders in bringing formal destoolment proceedings. The chief and the state council prosecuted them for rebellion. Five of the leaders were

[29] This term 'youngmen'—run into one word—is a convenient and commonly used Gold Coast term. It does not mean the young men, but the commoners, those who do not hold traditional or customary office in a state and are not members of the state council. The Wenchi incident is reported at length in the *Report of the Commission of Enquiry into Wenchi Affairs*, Accra 1952. The Commissioner was a judge with thirty-one years of West African service, fourteen of which he had spent as a district officer in Nigeria.

tried by the Ashanti Confederacy Council and fined; and on the strength of this victory the Wenchi state council proceeded to levy fines, or 'pacification fees' right and left on C.P.P. members in Wenchi, identifying membership of the C.P.P. with disloyalty to the Wenchi state.

The Government could hardly submit to this. For the Wenchi authorities to make membership of the Government party a criminal offence within the limits of their jurisdiction was carrying the principle of *Cujus regio ejus religio* too far. The Government replied by dissolving the Wenchi native authority and native court, and placing Wenchi under direct administration for the few months that remained until the Local Government Ordinance should come into effect. And since the Ashanti Confederacy Council had supported the Wenchi authorities—though it was of course not responsible for their subsequent excesses—the C.P.P. and the Ashanti Confederacy Council found themselves in direct conflict.

It is clear that there was much in Wenchi which needed reform. But it is natural that the Wenchi state council should blame the C.P.P. for what had happened. For nearly thirty years there had been complaints about Wenchi finances; the British authorities had reported unfavourably about Wenchi administration, and had given the state council several warnings. But that was all. This time, however, things are very different. The malcontent 'young-men' join the C.P.P.; the chief and the state council take steps to deal with them on traditional lines;[30] and in the moment of their triumph, the C.P.P. Government swoops down on them and they are ruined.

Here then is one root of the National Liberation Movement: the fear felt by supporters of the traditional authorities that they were to be ridden over roughshod by a party which cared nothing for their traditions. It is true that at the 1956 election the C.P.P. captured every seat in the Colony, and has received a good deal of support from the Colony's Joint Provincial Council of chiefs. But there were four constituencies in which the N.L.M. put up a strong fight, and they were all constituencies in which there was a strong tradition of loyalty to the state. They were:

[30] More or less traditional lines: the Commissioner shows that some of the state council's proceedings were of dubious legality from the traditional point of view, quite apart from any question of equity or British justice.

AKIM ABUAKWA WEST	...	...	C.P.P.	4,544
			N.L.M.	3,897
AKIM ABUAKWA CENTRAL	...	...	C.P.P.	6,052
			N.L.M.	4,661
AKIM ABUAKWA NORTH	...	...	C.P.P.	4,679
			N.L.M.	4,122
NEW JUABEN ...	...	...	C.P.P.	1,925
			N.L.M.	1,186
			Ind.	916

Even in the Colony, the C.P.P. could not afford to relax its
vigilance.

The second root of the National Liberation Movement, and of
its ally the Northern People's Party, is national or regional feeling
in Ashanti and the North. It would be interesting, but profitless,
to speculate whether this feeling would have been contented, had
the Government included in the Local Government Ordinance
provision for strong regional councils and administration after the
Coussey model. When the Northern People's Party first appeared
as a substantial opposition group in the 1954 legislative assembly,
the Government made a tactical error in denying its claim to be
regarded as Her Majesty's Opposition. Only national parties, said
Dr. Nkrumah, were entitled to be so regarded, and this party's very
title proclaimed that it was not national but regional. The Speaker
of the House however ruled that the N.P.P., being the largest
minority party in the House and declaring itself ready to assume
office if the Government were defeated, was to be regarded as the
official Opposition.[31]

Traditionalism and separatism were given additional strength in
1954 when the Government fixed the price of cocoa at 72s. a load.
The Cocoa Marketing Board would buy cocoa from the farmer at
that price, and would sell it on the world market at current prices.
The world price at the moment was over 200s. a load,[32] and the
balance would go to swell the Marketing Board's reserves, and

[31] Legislative Assembly Debates, 4th August and 11th August, 1954, cols. 122, 271.
[32] Cocoa prices are reckoned by the farmers at so many shillings per head-load
of sixty pounds. The price of 72s. a load was the same as the previous year's.
But in that year the world price had been 127s. a load, and it had now jumped to
212s. The farmers naturally had been hoping for a corresponding rise in the price
they received. For the Cocoa Marketing Board and the cocoa industry generally,
see chapter XVI.

could be used to finance the country's capital development. The price of 72s. was bitterly resented. The reserves of the Marketing Board were already enormous, and the farmers felt that it was time that they received a larger share of the value of their cocoa. They would rather spend the money themselves than see it spent by the Government on public needs. This brought into the National Liberation Movement large numbers of plain men who were not interested in regional feeling or in the grievances of the chiefs, but who raised the familiar cry, "Why should the Government take nearly two-thirds of my money to spend for me?"

The National Liberation Movement was thus a party made up of people who opposed the Nkrumah Government for different reasons. But a party must have a policy; and the N.L.M. and its allies adopted a policy of federalism.

The N.L.M. was launched in September 1954. In October, the Asantehene and fifty Ashanti chiefs joined in a resolution which asked the Queen to appoint a commission to enquire into a federal form of government for the Gold Coast. In December, Dr. Nkrumah invited the N.L.M. and the Ashanti Council to confer on the question, but they refused. Dr. Nkrumah's view was that the Gold Coast was too small for a federal government; and he pointed out that the idea of federalism was new. The 1954 constitution, he said, had been worked out in consultation with the Joint Provincial Council of chiefs in the Colony, the Ashanti Council, the Northern Territories Council, the chiefs in the North, and the then Opposition party in the Assembly. Federalism was not mentioned in those discussions and no party included federalism in its programme at the 1954 election.[33] The Ashanti leaders refused the Government invitation because "bilateral discussion between the Government on the one hand and certain sections of the community on the other, on a specific problem (such as with us on a federal constitution and with the Joint Provincial Council on the bicameral legislature) is not the right approach". Constitution-making was "too serious to be left to private consultation between the Prime Minister and Territorial Councils and political parties individually". It should be done by a properly convened Constituent Assembly.

[33] Speech in the Legislative Assembly, 12th November, 1956; statement issued on behalf of the Ashanti (or Asanteman) Council, 3rd February, 1955.

In January 1955, the Secretary of State replied to the Ashanti resolution that he could not advise Her Majesty to grant the request for a commission of enquiry.

In April, the Government moved in the Legislative Assembly that a Select Committee should be appointed "to examine the question of a federal system of government for the Gold Coast and the question of a Second Chamber which have been raised in some quarters, and after consultation with responsible bodies or individuals, to make recommendations for the consideration of the Legislative Assembly". The Opposition put down an amendment, to the effect that the Select Committee should not itself examine these constitutional questions, but should merely make proposals for the summoning of a Constituent Assembly. The Opposition however did not move its amendment; it changed its mind, and after making a statement in the House, withdrew from the whole discussion.[34]

The statement made by Mr. S. D. Dombo, leader of the Northern People's Party, makes quite clear the Opposition's fear and distrust of the Government. After protesting that a special Constituent Assembly was the only proper body to discuss changes in the constitution, Mr. Dombo said:

> "We of the Opposition are convinced that the motion is an insidious attempt by the Government under the guise of democratic procedure to arrogate to itself power to force a constitution of its own liking and making on the people of this country. This House, by the very nature of the constitution, is not representative of all the national interests and states, and many of its members have, by events since the last general election, been rendered unrepresentative of their constituencies . . . "

In plain English, this means: You of the Convention People's Party will see to it that no constitutional changes are made which might limit the powers of your own party organization. You have already driven out of this House the members nominated by the councils of chiefs, simply because you could not control them, and you knew that most of them were opposed to you. Further, the N.L.M. has come into being since the election, and some of your own members have left you and joined it.

[34] Legislative Assembly Debates, 1955, cols, 1864-1898.

Having made its statement, the Opposition walked out of the House, and took no part in the discussion. The Select Committee was duly appointed, and receiving no proposals from the Opposition, naturally reported against a Second Chamber and against a federal form of government. Still hoping for help from London, the Opposition drew up an outline of its federal proposals and sent them to the Secretary of State in August 1955. The Gold Coast Government and the Secretary of State then adopted a suggestion, originally made by the Opposition, that a constitutional adviser should be sent out to the Gold Coast to work out a scheme acceptable to both parties. The adviser appointed was Sir Frederick Bourne, whose distinguished career in India had culminated in two successive provincial Governorships. Sir Frederick arrived in September, but the N.L.M. and its allies would not co-operate with him in any way.

This was an unexpected obstacle. Two reasons were given for the unfortunate decision. One was that the Constitutional Adviser's terms of reference were inadequate: he was sent to give advice on problems of regional devolution, whereas he should have been invited to take into account all points of difference on constitutional matters, such as federal government and a Second Chamber.[35] The other was that although Sir Frederick was given wide latitude in interpreting his terms of reference (and as a matter of fact did consider the question of federalism), the Government showed its obstinacy by choosing the very moment when he was beginning his work to carry through fresh legislation which removed from the regions to the centre certain constitutional powers which they already enjoyed, and thus rendered his mission futile.[36]

Sir Frederick was of course hampered by the Opposition's refusal to discuss its proposals with him. He pointed out however that the N.L.M. proposals for a federal government, which were a revolt against excessive centralization, were unnecessarily drastic.[37] Undue centralization, he said, "can surely be corrected by less

[35] Letter from Dr. J. B. Danquah to the *New Statesman and Nation*, 3rd September, 1955.
[36] Letter from Dr. K. A. Busia to *The Times*, 20th October, 1955; see also the opening paragraphs of Sir Frederick Bourne's report: Gold Coast, *Report of the Constitutional Adviser*, 1955.
[37] *Report*, introduction and paragraph V.

drastic administrative changes than those so far recommended by the N.L.M." He dismissed the idea of a Constituent Assembly: "Under the existing Constitution responsibility for the government of the country has been conferred on the Legislative Assembly and the Cabinet, under the general supervision of His Excellency the Governor, with reference, when occasion demands it, to the Secretary of State. This responsibility cannot be transferred to any other body nor do I see what authority a Constituent Assembly appointed in the manner suggested would have had."

Sir Frederick recommended that a regional assembly should be set up in any region in which a complete network of district councils existed, and in which a majority of the district councils desired it. A regional assembly should be composed of three classes of members: first, of all members of the Legislative Assembly elected from the region, except Ministers and Ministerial Secretaries; second, about the same number of members elected by district and municipal councils; third, co-opted members. Each regional assembly should be established by a separate law; "it would have to be made clear that the supreme legislative power remained at the centre, but that in order to carry out the objects stated in the previous clause[38] Government would transfer to regions the powers and functions necessary for the purpose. This is the reverse of the system recommended in the N.L.M.'s Federal Scheme, whereby the Centre's powers are to be prescribed and all residuary powers are to rest with the units. This extreme form of Federation would, I believe, slow down development and introduce an intolerable handicap to the administration of the country." Sir Frederick went on to recommend a very thorough measure of devolution, and to propose that, in order to prevent the regional assembly and the Legislative Assembly from "working in watertight compartments", all Ministers should have a right to address the regional assembly and be questioned on their departmental affairs.

Sir Frederick was not asked to comment on the proposal for a Second Chamber. But the chiefs and state councils were so important that he had to make proposals for safeguarding their position. He proposed that matters affecting the traditional functions or

[38] The previous clause (para. IV) of Sir Frederick Bourne's report, suggested three purposes for regional assemblies: (i) to avoid over-centralization, (ii) to obtain local opinion on matters of national importance, (iii) to adapt legislation and Government activity to regional needs.

N

privileges of chiefs should be introduced in the Legislative Assembly only after consultation with the chiefs concerned; and the views of the chiefs should be circulated to all members of the House and should be debated and decided by a free vote without party whips. Further, any recognized Council of Chiefs should have the right of giving advice to its regional assembly.

The proposals of the Constitutional Adviser naturally did not satisfy the Opposition. Since its main strength was in Ashanti and the North, no constitution would satisfy the Opposition which did not give Ashanti and the North complete security against any strengthening of the political dominance of the Colony.[39]

The Constitutional Adviser's report was published in December 1955. In February 1956, the Government made another effort to reach agreement with the Opposition. It summoned a conference to meet at Achimota, to discuss the Bourne recommendations and to work out the details. The N.L.M. and the N.P.P., the Ashanti Council of Chiefs, and the Northern Territories Council all refused to attend or to submit their views. The conference was attended by eight delegations, representing the C.P.P., the Brong council of chiefs,[40] the ex-servicemen's union, the Muslim Council, the Trades Union Congress, the Joint Provincial Council of the chiefs in the Colony, local government councils in the North, and the Trans-Volta Togoland Council, Sir Frederick Bourne was present to advise the conference.

The Achimota Conference met on 16th February, and in response to an urgent appeal from the Joint Provincial Council, adjourned for ten days to enable the Council to make a desperate effort to secure the attendance of the N.L.M., the N.P.P., and the Ashanti chiefs. All three Opposition bodies remained silent. Eventually, on 8th March, a deputation consisting of two paramount chiefs from the Colony went by invitation to Kumasi, and on the 12th they returned to report the complete failure of their mission. The Conference decided that it could wait no longer, and on 16th March its report was signed.

---

[39] The Colony was dominant in the Legislative Assembly; out of 104 members, 44 represented the Colony, 21 Ashanti, 26 the North, and 13 Trans-Volta Togoland. Moreover, the Colony was solid for the C.P.P.
[40] It will be remembered that there was tension between the Brong and the Ashanti; the Wenchi case is an illustration of this. Since the Ashanti boycotted the conference, it was to be expected that the Brong would attend it.

One of the two chiefs who went to Kumasi was so unhappy at this decision that he withdrew from the conference. He explained: "The Asanteman Council, the Northern Territories Council and the other groups made it quite clear that to continue and conclude this Conference without them would mean closing the door to further association . . . We are faced with possible secession of the two regions." He felt that this created a new situation, which should be discussed afresh by the Joint Provincial Council whose delegate he was. To such intransigence had the Opposition been driven by its fear and distrust of the Government.

The recommendations of the Achimota Conference were broadly in line with those of the Constitutional Adviser. The Conference abandoned Sir Frederick's stipulation that a complete network of district councils must exist in a region before a regional assembly can be established, pointing out that so far there were only two district councils in the whole of the Colony—an interesting side-light on the difficulty of putting the Local Government Ordinance into effect. It disapproved of the proposal that all members of the Legislative Assembly should be ex-officio members of their regional assembly, but was prepared to see them elected by local government councils. It accepted Sir Frederick's recommendations on the place of chiefs, and worked them out in considerable detail. In each region there would be a House of Chiefs, with the responsibility for advising the Government on all proposed legislation affecting traditional affairs. A House of Chiefs might advise the Government to refer a Bill to a Select Committee, and there should be a convention whereby the Government should hold itself bound to refer a Bill to a Select Committee if advised to do so by two regional Houses of Chiefs.

In April 1956 the Government issued its constitutional proposals, which were generally in line with the recommendations of the Achimota conference. They were debated in the Legislative Assembly and unanimously adopted with minor amendments. The Opposition again took no part in the proceedings.

In July the elections were held, and Dr. Nkrumah's Government was again returned to power by a majority only slightly reduced: seventy-two to thirty-two instead of seventy-nine to twenty-five. The Opposition took no part in the debate on 3rd August which authorized the Government to request the grant of independence.

When the Secretary of State accepted the result of the independence debate and undertook to introduce the Ghana Independence Bill into Parliament, the Opposition had six months in which to reach agreement with the victorious Dr. Nkrumah, or to persuade the politicians at Westminster to insert some acceptable safeguards into the Bill, or to proclaim Ashanti and the North as a separate state, or to submit.

There were three main points of disagreement. The first was the powers to be possessed by the regions. The second was the Second Chamber. The third was a Council of State.

The Joint Provincial Council of Colony Chiefs, the Northern Territories Council, and the Trans-Volta Togoland Council came to agree with the Government that regional Governments "should have powers similar to those of the London County Council, but these powers should come into operation by a gradual process". The Opposition and the Asanteman Council insisted that the regional Governments should have powers similar to those of the Government of Northern Ireland.

The Opposition insisted on a Second Chamber. The Joint Provincial Council and the Asanteman Council wanted it to be composed entirely of chiefs; the Opposition was prepared to see it include 'elder statesmen', and even an elected element; the Northern Territories Council wanted a Second Chamber but made no suggestions as to its composition. The Government offered to accept a Second Chamber instead of the proposed regional Houses of Chiefs, but this offer was not accepted; the Opposition wanted both.

The Opposition wanted a Council of State, to consist of the Governor-General, the four 'Heads' of the four traditional regions,[41] the Prime Minister, the Leader of the Opposition, and the Attorney-General. The main purpose of the Council was to advise the Governor-General on the exercise of the Crown's prerogative powers, in order that he might be kept out of party politics. There was some difference over the powers and duties of the Council of

---

[41] Sir Frederick Bourne had contemplated that each regional assembly should have a formal President (Report, para. VI). The Achimota Conference agreed (para. 47) that there should be such a President, who should be ex-officio the President of the House of Chiefs in the region. The Government accepted the recommendation. The 'Head' of a region would thus be the chief who, having been elected to preside over the regional House of Chiefs, became automatically the formal President—not the chairman for business purposes—of the regional assembly.

State; Ashanti wanted them to be very wide, the others were more modest. The Government said that this whole proposal was unworkable, and would have none of it.

The real difficulty was that the Opposition, and especially the Ashanti, did not trust the C.P.P. On the crucial question of regional devolution, there was not much difference between the regional powers which the Opposition demanded and those which the Government was willing to grant. The great difference was that the Opposition demanded that those powers should be entrenched by an Act of the Parliament at Westminster in a Constitution difficult to amend; the Government declared its intention of granting powers by simple legislation after independence. The C.P.P. already held more than two-thirds of the seats in the Legislative Assembly, and the Opposition feared that it would use any means—trickery, intimidation, and if necessary force—to retain its political power. The Government proposed, as a safeguard to the powers of a regional assembly, that no bill abolishing or suspending a regional assembly could be passed save by a two-thirds majority of the members of the National Assembly present and voting. What was this safeguard worth in the hands of a Government which already had its two-thirds majority? It could set up a regional assembly today and abolish it tomorrow.

The British Government was in a difficult position. Whether or not it considered the apprehensions reasonable which the Opposition leaders in the Gold Coast expressed to it in resolutions, telegrams, delegations, and letters to *The Times*, it would be impossible for it to overrule the wishes of the Gold Coast Government, especially when the feeling of the Gold Coast electorate had so recently been expressed in a specially held general election. In the Gold Coast, although the talks which the Government and Opposition delegations held in October had brought about a slight approach towards agreement, the gap was still wide. In December the Ashanti threat of secession was made explicit enough to draw from the Secretary of State a telegram announcing that Britain could not entertain the idea. In reply, the Asanteman Council sent a letter repeating that "Much as Ashanti would wish to be associated with the other territories in this country at independence, we wish to emphasize that secession is an inherent right to which recourse may be had as a last resort by any nation whose liberties are at stake." The Council asked the Secretary of State either to come to the Gold Coast himself or to appoint a commission to try and resolve the differences.

The matter was urgent, for the Ghana Independence Bill had already been introduced into Parliament. The Secretary of State, Mr. Alan Lennox-Boyd, visited the Gold Coast at the end of January. His mediation was successful. On his return to London, the Government issued a White Paper[42] containing its proposed constitution for Ghana, and the leaders of both parties in the Gold Coast declared themselves ready to accept it.

The constitutional proposals were, inevitably, a compromise. There was to be no Second Chamber, and no Council of State; and the powers of regional assemblies were not to be entrenched in the Constitution. On the other hand, Dr. Nkrumah made some concessions. A regional constitutional commission, fifteen members of which were to represent regional interests and not more than six to be nominated by the Government, was to sit under an independent chairman to make recommendations on "the composition, authority, functions and powers of the regional assemblies, the funds they will require, and the means by which these funds shall be provided". The commission's report was to be presented to the Parliament of Ghana within nine months of independence, and "as soon thereafter as may be", a Bill was to be introduced to give effect to the commission's recommendations.

There were further important concessions to the Opposition. Amendments to the Constitution could be made only by a two-thirds majority of the whole number of members of the assembly: not a two-thirds majority of those present and voting, as the Nkrumah Government had proposed. On certain fundamental subjects, amendment of the Constitution was still more difficult. On those subjects, an amending Bill must be referred to all the regional assemblies and the Houses of Chiefs, and it could not receive its third reading in the Assembly until two-thirds of the regions had expressed their approval. Further safeguards were provided when it was a case of abolishing or suspending a regional assembly or of altering the boundaries of a region. A less spectacular, but still important concession to the Opposition dealt with the Public Service Commission, which was already in existence to

[42] The Proposed Constitution of Ghana, Cmd. 71, February 1957.

advise the Governor on matters concerning the civil service. Dr. Nkrumah undertook that before giving the Governor-General his advice on appointments to membership of the Public Service Commission, he would consult the Leader of the Opposition; and he hoped that this convention would be followed by his successors. This removed any fear that the Public Service Commission might be packed by the party in power and that in consequence the public service itself might be controlled by party politics.

Mr. Lennox-Boyd's diplomacy had been brilliantly successful, and it is no disparagement of his skill and patience to observe that the function of a mediator is more important and familiar in the Gold Coast than it is in Britain. It is common for disputants in the Gold Coast to invite a third party to mediate between them. Their views are irreconcilable, each makes some small concession and then declares he cannot move another inch. The mediator proposes a compromise, and it is at once accepted; each is ready to concede to the mediator what he would never concede to his opponent. Why Mr. Lennox-Boyd succeeded in January 1957, whereas Sir Frederick Bourne failed in September 1955 we do not yet know. It may be simply that in September 1955, independence day was still eighteen months away, the Ghana Independence Bill had not yet been drafted, and the Opposition leaders in the Gold Coast felt that they still had time for manœuvre and hope of concessions. In January 1957, independence was near, the Bill already through the Commons and in the Lords, the Gold Coast Government immovable, and time was against them. Whatever the reason, it is a cause for thankfulness that the statesmanship, not only of the Secretary of State but of the Government and the Opposition leaders in the Gold Coast, enabled an agreed solution to be reached before independence day.

The Ghana Independence Act received the Royal Assent on 7th February, 1957. An Order in Council was issued laying down the constitution of Ghana on the lines of the White Paper; and independence was safely reached on 6th March, 1957: not only independence, but independence with the prospect of an acceptable and efficient system of regional government. This question of local government, and especially of regional government, had been the most controversial question in Gold Coast politics for years; it came to a head with the Coussey Report and the Local Government Ordinance, and ever since the foundation of the N.L.M. in 1954 it had threatened to postpone the grant of independence and to disrupt the country. That question being thus settled, Ghana was able to make a successful start to its independent life.

CHAPTER XVI

SOCIAL AND ECONOMIC HISTORY

THE most important economic result of the war of 1874 was the abolition of slavery. The export slave trade had, of course, been abolished long before, but the institution of domestic slavery still existed in the new colony. Gold Coast slavery was of a very mild type. There was no plantation slavery whatever, though we may conjecture that if slavery had existed in modern times, a form of plantation slavery might well have developed in connection with the cocoa industry. However, slavery was abolished before cocoa was introduced. The domestic slave of the Gold Coast was well treated.

"Slavery in West Africa has been aptly described by Mary Kingsley as 'a state of servitude guarded by rights'. There were so many apparent serious disabilities attaching to the status of a slave, that the numerous and sometimes striking rights he enjoyed may easily be overlooked. . . . A slave might marry; own property; himself own a slave; swear an oath; be a competent witness; and ultimately become heir to his master. . . . Such briefly were the rights of an Ashanti slave. They seemed in many instances practically the ordinary privileges of an Ashanti free man, with whom, in these respects, his position did not seem to compare so unfavourably. The chief danger in which his peculiar status placed him appears to me to lie in the fact that the slave was generally a solitary creature more or less at the mercy of a single individual. . . . It seems probable that circumstances generally would have tended towards his kind treatment. An Ashanti slave, in nine cases out of ten, possibly became an adopted member of the family, and in time his descendants so merged and intermarried with the owner's kinsmen that only a few would know their origin. One outstanding fact, however, remained, that the status of a slave . . . could never be lost, and, when necessity arose, or the terrible practice of human sacrifice became the vogue, an otherwise kind and considerate master would turn instinctively to the man who had no friend in the world, to satisfy the need for money or for a victim. The liability to be sacrificed at funeral customs may have been an ever-present fear in the mind of a West African slave. . . . "[1]

There was also an intermediate status, that of a pawn. A pawn was a human being pledged as security for money, redeemable when the debt was paid. It was common for a person to be pawned by his family to raise money for some special occasion, and as far as possible a woman was chosen to be pawned to her husband or a child to his father. In this case the debt bore no interest, the pawn's services during the period of his servitude being counted as interest on the debt.[2] Rattray considers that this Akan institution, like some others, suffered by being brought into contact with coast conditions: originally mainly a family affair, it would be far less lenient when pawning went outside the family and carried its subject among utter strangers far away from home. This may be the reason why European observers on the coast felt it to be a specially objectionable form of slavery, whereas it might have been expected to be a specially lenient and tolerable form.

In November 1874 the Governor, Captain Strahan, consulted the chiefs of the western and central provinces at Cape Coast, and those of the eastern province at Accra, and explained to them two ordinances which had been drawn up and approved by the Secretary of State. The first prohibited slave dealing, and the second emancipated all existing slaves and declared that all children born after 5th November, 1874, were born free. The Governor was careful to point out that there was no intention of forcing slaves to leave their masters, and that if a pawn chose to leave his master, the debt for which he was pledged would remain recoverable in the courts. The chiefs were uneasy at the thought of losing their pawns, but declared that the Governor's explanation was satisfactory, and that they had no objection to the proposal. The laws were duly published, and few slaves chose to leave their masters and embark on the task of earning their own living. Most of them were content to stay where they were, even though legally free. The abolition of

---

[1] Rattray, *Ashanti Law and Constitution*, 38, 40.
[2] Rattray, *Ashanti Law and Constitution*, chaps. V and VI. The weakness of the pawn system seems to have been that the pawn had no hope of ever working off the debt by faithful service, but was entirely at the mercy of his family, who might or might not redeem him.

slavery, however, did have an indirect effect on the trade of the colony. The trains of carriers that came down to the coast from the interior and returned with European goods were mainly composed of slaves. The possibility of having to pay wages to the carriers to keep them from deserting when they entered British territory was a deterrent to their owners, and they tended to divert their trade to coast districts not under British authority. The life of a slave-carrier, marching in a semi-disciplined formation fifteen miles a day with a sixty-pound load on his head, is not as quiet and attractive as that of the ordinary domestic slave. The domestic slave might be content to stay where he was, but the owner of the carrier-slave could not expect that all his carriers should feel the same.[3]

The internal trade of the Gold Coast, however, was greatly hindered in any case by the uncertainy on the northern frontier from 1874 till the annexation of Ashanti.

In 1877 the first steps were taken to develop the gold mines with European capital. A French company, in which the indefatigable M. Bonnat[4] was interested, took up a concession at Tarkwa and was soon followed by other companies. During the next five years mining began at Abosso and Abontiakoon, and concessions were freely granted all over the Wassaw district. In those early days little care was taken to keep different concessions from conflicting; for the usual practice was to grant mining rights over a given radius from a fixed point. Few of these mines made much profit, in spite of the richness of the ore, owing to the difficulty and cost of transporting machinery from Axim. There was no road and no railway, and machinery had to be taken over the bush paths in pieces, the biggest of which had to be kept down to a four man load. The cost of transport was from £25 to £30 a ton, and although the companies were willing to pay a heavy toll if a road could be constructed to the mining area, the Government could not afford the £17,500 which the road would cost to construct. It is to be inferred that the companies were short of capital, for such a sum, one would have thought, should not have been beyond the joint resources of several

[3] Claridge, II, 177-86.
[4] M. Bonnat, the same man that had been captured by the Ashanti at Ho and had been in captivity with Messrs. Ramseyar and Kühne, had returned to Kumasi in 1875 and had ventured to take part in politics there as an agent for the Asantehene in negotiating with Juaben. But his diplomacy had not been success-ful, and he was lucky to escape with his life.

mining companies who were all going to use the road when it was made. These early companies, of course, were very different from the vast concerns of today. Gold mining was in other parts of the world an affair for the small man; and a few old timers did come from South Africa in the hope of making their fortunes with pick and shovel and basin. But they soon found that it was not a country for them.[5]

The gold-mining industry developed only slowly till the end of the century, and production did not exceed 18,000 fine ounces a year.[6] The rich reefs at Obuasi, which had been worked by the Denkyera in the seventeenth century, were opened to European mining in 1897 by the Ashanti Goldfields Corporation, and there were over fifty European miners at work there by 1900. In 1898 the Government began to build the railway from Sekondi to the interior, and the line reached Tarkwa in April 1901, a distance of thirty-nine miles, bringing the cost of transport down with a run from £25 a ton to about £2. The result was a boom in the mining industry, marked by the usual over-speculation and followed by a slump. The production of gold nevertheless went on rising, although many of the new companies that were floated soon went out of business. The Ashanti Goldfields Corporation, and the companies at Tarkwa and Prestea and a few other places, were so well established and the reefs they worked were so rich that the speculation did them no harm. Production in the present century has varied largely according to the available supply of labour. The labourers are mostly from the Northern Territories and from the French country farther north still. The supply is not unlimited, and when cocoa is fetching a high price on the market, many of the labourers are attracted to carrying cocoa at piece rates. This was specially marked during the cocoa boom of the early twenties.[7] The Concessions Ordinance of 1939 required concession holders to pay five per cent of their profits to the Government, and subsequent legislation has increased the mining industry's direct contributions to the revenue.

Cocoa was introduced into the Gold Coast in the year 1879 by an Accra man, one Tete Kwashi, who brought it from the islands of Fernando Po and San Thomé. The first export of eighty pounds

[5] Claridge, II, 246-9.
[6] Hailey, *An African Survey*, 1502.
[7] *Gold Coast Handbook* 1927, pp. 77-8.

of cocoa beans was made in 1891; ten years later this had risen to 536 tons, and the export of cocoa rapidly increased. The cocoa industry is remarkable for being almost entirely a peasant industry; the average cocoa farm is only from two and a half to six and a half acres. The crop proved immensely popular, and it was extremely profitable. By 1935 the Gold Coast was supplying half the world's consumption of cocoa. The industry was run by the farmers only partly with the help of their own families; there was so much money available that they developed a sort of plantation system, importing labourers from the north in large numbers to tend the farms and carry the cocoa to the market.

By 1935 the area under cocoa was estimated at 950,000 acres.[8] This huge acreage had been obtained by far-reaching modifications in the old African environment and ways of living. The old traditional food crop farming had been largely abandoned in order to concentrate on export production, and the Gold Coast had become a large importer of foreign food, especially of rice and of tinned meat and fish. The cocoa clearings had involved great destruction of forest. Perhaps most important of all, land had been placed under a semi-permanent crop, and a new vested interest in land had been created. Unfortunately the African farmers kept to their traditional happy-go-lucky methods of agriculture, and turned a deaf ear to Government officials who besought them to weed and manure their farms, to provide shade trees, and to make war on cocoa pests. In course of time the early cocoa farms, especially in Akwapim, began to die out, and the whole of the forest country was filled with energetic Akwapim and Krobo cocoa farmers seeking for concessions to grow cocoa on virgin forest soil. Land acquired a market value, and chiefs and state councils were under increased temptation to make money by granting concessions. Since money which was made for the state was never completely brought to account, some of it inevitably finding its way into private pockets, this led to increased suspicion on the part of the 'youngmen', and the growth of a feeling that stool lands should not be exclusively controlled by the state council—a feeling which found expression in the Local Government Ordinance.

The social importance of cocoa is that it is the industry which affects the poor man's purse. Gold is for the big European com-

[8] Hailey, 907-8.

panies, but cocoa is the affair of the small African farmer. A high price of cocoa means money in his pocket and general prosperity; a low price means that he has to go without necessary luxuries, and is miserable and surly. The Nowell Commission[9] quotes a typical example from Akim in which a village of 1,181 inhabitants produced and sold 5,451 loads of cocoa in a season, which at the current prices would bring in a cash income of about £5 16s. a head.

On the other hand, though the average size of cocoa farms was so small, the simple conception of a small family farm run entirely by the family's own labour ceased to be generally true. As time went on, all but the poorest families came to hire labour. Many ceased to reside on their farms and relied entirely on hired labour. Some accumulated farms and became wealthy; the Nowell Commission mentions one farmer who owned, or enjoyed the produce of, no fewer than seventy-nine scattered farms. This shows how primitive systems of land tenure were adapting themselves to new conditions.

In the years between the wars, the cocoa was marketed through an intricate system of brokers and sub-brokers, who acted as intermediaries between the farmer and the wholesale buyer. No doubt many farmers were also brokers, selling other farmers' cocoa as well as their own. The wholesale exporting firms were European; thirteen firms handled ninety-eight per cent of the trade in 1937. The brokers were Africans. The European firms sent their agents up country to buy cocoa from the brokers, who were prepared to buy forward where necessary. The brokers thus acted as suppliers of credit to the farmers, and there were naturally cases in which they acquired mortgages and other liens on the farmer's produce and livelihood.

As time went on, many of the European firms amalgamated, and in 1929 the United Africa Company came into being in this way, and became the largest firm trading in West Africa. Like many other firms on the Coast, the U.A.C. was both an export and an important trading concern, and this movement was watched with a good deal of suspicion by the African farmers, who feared that the U.A.C. and similar big firms might be able to manipulate

---

[9] See below, pp. 400-401. The report of the Nowell Commission, *Report of the Commission on the Marketing of West African Cocoa*, Cmd. 5845, 1938, describes the organization of the cocoa industry in great detail.

prices entirely in their own favour, depressing the price at which they bought African produce and inflating the price at which they sold European goods. On various occasions before and after the first World War, there were temporary agreements between the European buying firms to eliminate competition, and in 1930-31 the cocoa farmers responded by holding up supplies, though their boycott was not fully effective, and collapsed.

In 1937, nearly all the large European firms entered into another agreement to restrict competition. In that year the export of cocoa was some 236,000 tons, valued at nearly ten million pounds. Next year's crop, it could be seen, would be greater, and it actually rose by over ten per cent to 263,000 tons. The value, on the other hand, went down to four and a half millions, a drop of over fifty per cent. The firms saw this coming, and proposed to keep the local price of cocoa from rising above the world market price. Their agreement had two main features: (i) each member was allotted a quota of the total crop, based on the firm's past performance; and (ii) all members agreed on the price they would pay, which was to be based on the world market price less an agreed amount to cover costs and profit.

The agreement was drawn up in England. The firms did not consult the Gold Coast Government, and although they explained their position and their intentions to the Colonial Office, it does not seem to have occurred to them that they should undertake any publicity on their own behalf among their African clients. They did however ask that the Secretary of State should explain the agreement to the Gold Coast Government, in order that district commissioners and other officials might be briefed to answer African criticisms.

The Gold Coast Government disliked the whole affair, and advised the firms to drop the agreement altogether. African criticism was soon forthcoming. The agreement came into effect at the beginning of October, and by the middle of November there was a nearly complete hold-up of cocoa and a boycott of European imported goods all over the cocoa-growing region, stiffened by the support of the chiefs and state councils. The firms refused to drop the agreement at the suggestion of the Gold Coast Government, and they refused to publish it at the suggestion of the Secretary of State. Both parties in the dispute appealed to the Government. The

Africans urged the Government to "come to the rescue of the defenceless farmer"; the European firms urged the Government to "give a definite lead" in favour of the agreement by stating that the agreement contained nothing harmful to the farmers, that the European firms were offering as high a price as the world market permitted, and that the Government itself would keep an eye on the working of the agreement.

The Gold Coast Government was in a difficult position. It had not been consulted before the agreement was made, and if it had been consulted it would have advised the firms to drop the idea. It thus could hardly urge the farmers to accept the agreement, and if it had felt able to do so, it would have lost the confidence, not only of the cocoa farmers, but of the chiefs and other leaders of African opinion. On the other hand, though it disliked the agreement it could not but admit that the fluctuations of the world market were making things difficult for the exporting firms. The Government therefore remained neutral in the dispute, and confined itself to giving publicity to the Secretary of State's view that the buying agreement would not materially affect the world price for cocoa: nor would a holdup: that the agreement would give producers a price nearer the world price than before: and that in consequence the best thing to do would be to give the agreement a trial.

This sort of neutrality was not neutral enough to satisfy the farmers, or the chiefs; and the Government incurred a good deal of resentment because it was regarded as taking sides with the exporting firms. The hold-up continued without a break throughout January, February, and March. In February, the Secretary of State appointed a Commission, under the chairmanship of Mr. William Nowell, to look into the whole matter of the West African cocoa trade and submit recommendations. The Commission arrived in the Gold Coast towards the end of March, a truce in the dispute was arranged to come into effect at the end of April, and the sale of cocoa began once more.

The Nowell Commission reported at the beginning of September 1938. It recommended that the cocoa buying agreements should be withdrawn. At the same time, the Commission thought that the existing system of cocoa marketing needed radical reform. There was intense competition among the exporting firms to secure the maximum tonnage of cocoa. They worked through an intricate and very loosely organized system of brokers and sub-brokers, and there was unlimited opportunity for brokers, working with large credits supplied by the firms and often beyond the reach of telegraph and telephone, to manipulate the market by speculative purchases or false declaration of the stocks they held. Some alternative system must be found; and the Commission recommended the establishment of a statutory marketing board. All cocoa farmers should become members of an association, whose main function would be to assemble and sell, on behalf of its members, the entire cocoa crop of the Gold Coast. Normally, the association would sell its cocoa to firms or individuals on a competitive basis, but it should be free to ship direct to world markets if it chose. The association should be organized in six to ten regions and some 500 local groups, with local group committees and regional committees; the central Board should include African representatives, official representatives, and perhaps independent co-opted members. Groups would be paid for their cocoa on the basis of an average price, obtained by pooling the proceeds of all cocoa sales and deducting a levy for operating and other necessary expenses. The association should arrange for grading cocoa, developing agricultural credit, preparing crop estimates, and generally educating its members in agriculture and economics.

There is no point in trying to allocate the blame for this unhappy story of the cocoa hold-up. All parties—the exporters, the brokers, and the farmers — had reason for dissatisfaction with the organization of the cocoa trade. I have criticized the Gold Coast Government for its aloofness from African opinion, but it is only fair to say that in this episode the Government showed itself in much closer touch with African opinion than the exporting firms. The situation may be summed up in two isolated quotations from the Nowell Report. The Commission says:

"If harmonious relations are to exist between the African community and the trading firms, it is vital not only that the African should get a square deal, but that his present suspicions that he does not should be allayed."

And elsewhere it comments that the dispute could not be cleared up by the normal means of arbitration, explanation, and compromise, for the necessary goodwill was lacking:

"Such goodwill does not exist. Instead, we have an attitude

of intense suspicion on one side, and of injured integrity on the other. We detected no disposition to compromise."[10]

Cocoa sales began again in April 1938 under the terms of the truce. The Government was anxious that the accumulated stocks of cocoa should not be so suddenly thrown on the market as to knock the bottom out of the world price. It therefore imposed a temporary system of export quotas, based largely on the exporting firms' past performance. It is understandable that the African chiefs and cocoa farmers found it difficult to distinguish this Government-enforced quota system from the quota system which the exporters had imposed on themselves by their hated agreement; and the Government's reputation for impartiality was in no way enhanced.

Before the Nowell recommendations could be put into effect, the war came. In November 1939, the British Government announced that it would buy all West African cocoa. The official monopoly was exercised first through the Cocoa Control of the Ministry of Food, then through the West African Cocoa Control Board, and lastly through the West African Produce Control Board, which continued to handle all Gold Coast cocoa until 1947. From 1939 to 1942, the exporting firms bought and shipped cocoa as agents for the Government; after 1942 they were buying agents only, and the Produce Control Board itself became the shipper. The quota system was maintained.[11]

In 1947, the handling of Gold Coast cocoa was transferred from the West African Produce Control Board to the newly-established Gold Coast Cocoa Marketing Board. The objects of the Board were defined by the ordinance which established it as being

"To secure the most favourable arrangements for the purchase, grading, export and selling of Gold Coast cocoa, and to assist in the development by all possible means of the cocoa industry of the Gold Coast for the benefit and prosperity of the producers."

The Ordinance[12] empowered the Board to control and fix the price to be paid to the farmer, to buy cocoa, to appoint buying agents to act for it, and to license them on any conditions it

[10] Nowell Report, paras. 395, 488.
[11] P. T. Bauer, *West African Trade*, pp. 249, 250.
[12] Ordinance, Sections 6 and 8.

thought fit. The Ordinance forbade the purchase of cocoa except by the Board or its agent, and forbade the export of cocoa which was not the Board's property or which the Board had not authorized for export.

The idea behind this monopoly was that the farmers should be cushioned against such wide fluctuations of price as had occurred in 1937 and 1938. The Board would buy cocoa at much less than the world price when that price soared, and at much more when it dropped; in a fat year it would accumulate a surplus, and in a lean year it would pay the farmers out of its surplus.[13]

In practice, things did not work out that way. The price of cocoa remained high, and the Board's surpluses piled up and up, reaching tens of millions of pounds. It is not surprising that the argument began to be heard that such large reserves were not needed to stabilize prices, and that they could be divided into a 'stabilization reserve', earmarked for that purpose, and general reserves which might be used for any other purpose likely to be "for the benefit and prosperity of the producers". The Board made a large grant, for example, towards the establishment of a faculty of agriculture at the university college of the Gold Coast.

We need not follow the fortunes of the Board, or of the cocoa farmers, in detail. The existence of these large cocoa reserves was a source of great strength to the Government of Dr. Nkrumah in its early days. Although at first the Board continued to use exporting firms as its buying agents, and bought no cocoa itself, the Nkrumah Government established a Cocoa Purchasing Company, which soon fell under suspicion of being too intimately connected with the C.P.P. party organization. The N.L.M. made political capital by accusing the C.P.P. and the Cocoa Purchasing Company of corruption, and by urging the Marketing Board to pay the poor farmers a larger share of the proceeds of their cocoa, instead of using the money for general national development. In 1956 the Government appointed a Commission of Enquiry into the working of the Company, which brought to light considerable irregularities, notably those which arose from the Company's buying cocoa with one hand and making loans to farmers with the other, and getting its

[13] The policy and operations of the Cocoa Marketing Board, and of other West African boards of a similar nature, are described in detail, and severely—though not always entirely convincingly—criticized by P. T. Bauer in his *West African Trade*, pp. 276ff.

accounts mixed. The Company was short of qualified staff, and there had been a good deal of carelessness and inefficiency, and some corruption. As a result of the report, the Government announced that it proposed to overhaul and reform the whole system; and a few weeks after Independence it went further and abolished the Cocoa Purchasing Company altogether.

In spite of the gold which gave the country its name, in spite of the manganese, diamonds, bauxite, timber and citrus produce, cocoa is still the country's main source of wealth. Cocoa exports first passed 100,000 tons in 1919; in that year the export was 176,000 tons, worth £8,279,000. The Gold Coast has always suffered from being exclusively a primary producer. The cocoa figures for the four years 1918 to 1921 are a good illustration of the financial uncertainty which has always hampered the country's development:

	Thousands of tons	Millions of pounds
1918	66	1.797
1919	176	8.279
1920	125	10.056
1921	133	4.764

Cocoa production rose to a peak of 311,000 tons in 1936, with a value of £7,660,000. Tonnage has never since touched 300,000, but has fluctuated round 200,000, with a maximum (1950) of 267,000 and a minimum (1942) of 124,000 tons. The value of the cocoa exports has of course increased enormously since the war, greatly to the advantage, not only of the country as a whole, but of the young African Government working for independence:

	Thousands of tons	Millions of pounds
1949	263	34.018
1950	267	54.604
1951	230	60.101
1952	212	52.533
1953	237	56.143
1954	214	84.599

But on the eve of independence in 1957 a chilly breeze of apprehension was felt; cocoa prices were falling.

The supreme importance of cocoa is illustrated by the value of the country's chief exports in 1951; roughly speaking, the figures, in millions of pounds, were:

Cocoa	...	...	...	...	60
Gold ...	...	...	...	...	8.5
Manganese ...	...	...	...	...	7
Diamonds	...	...	...	...	6
Timber	...	...	...	...	5

There has of course been a great deal of economic development in the last thirty years. If we take the 1925 figures as standard, the exports of the four main products, other than cocoa, have grown thus:

| | GOLD | | MANGANESE | | DIAMONDS | | TIMBER | |
	volume	value	volume	value	volume	value	volume	value
1925 ...	100	100	100	100	100	100	100	100
1937 ...	256	465	156	151	2,040	656	57	51
1951 ...	317	1,019	238	1,060	2,290	6,058	489	1,939
1956 ...	275	891	188	1,034	2,148	7,451	—	3,655

EDUCATION

We have seen in Chapter IX the beginnings of educational and mission work in the Gold Coast under the Methodist and S.P.G. missions from Britain and of the Basel and Bremen missions from Germany and Switzerland. The first Roman Catholic missionaries to work in the Gold Coast since the departure of the Portuguese arrived in 1881, during the excitement of the Owusu Tasiamandi episode. They, like the Protestant missionaries, worked largely through schools; and education began to progress rapidly.

In the following year, 1882, the first Education Ordinance was passed. It provided that a General Board of Education should be established, and that Local Boards also should be set up to inspect schools, certify the competence of teachers, and generally act as the agents of the General Board, to which they were responsible. Schools were to receive a Government grant if they satisfied the authorities that they were efficient; and the Government itself was to provide schools. The curriculum was always to include reading, writing and arithmetic, with needlework for girls; history, geography and English grammar were extra subjects to be added at the option of the teacher or the local board. The conditions for the Government grant were complicated. There was to be a grant in respect of buildings and equipment, and a separate grant in respect of salaries. The salary grant was to be reckoned as a grant for good organization and discipline, plus a capitation grant for attendance, plus a capitation grant for a pass in each compulsory subject. The Government appointed one inspector of schools, who was to divide his time between the Gold Coast and Lagos.

The 1882 Education Ordinance was not a success. The missions found it difficult to recast their systems so as to come into line with the Government requirements. The first inspector, the Rev. M. Sunter, considered the ordinance unworkable. He wrote in one of his annual reports:

"I cannot too strongly express my regret that no proper ordinance has yet been passed; after the lapse of nearly four years an unworkable and ridiculously complicated ordinance remains a dead letter."

It seems that the General Board was never completely filled; the local boards were not appointed at all; the inspector was burdened with his mission work, which he regarded as having first claim on his attention, especially as the Government did not provide its inspector with a salary; and the school attendance began to decline.

A new Education Ordinance was passed in 1887, which formed the basis of the educational system until 1925. The local boards were abolished, and in their place the system of managerial control was set up. The local governing body of a mission society was constituted the managerial board of its schools, responsible to the Government for their efficiency. The managing body appointed local managers, usually the minister in charge of the church, to control each school and to be responsible to the central managing body in Accra or Cape Coast. The general Board of Education was reconstituted to consist of the members of the Legislative Council and eight other nominated members, with the Governor in the chair.

The first Director of Education was appointed in 1890, and in 1898 the European staff of the department consisted of the Director, one Inspector and one Headmaster. From this time onward, progress depended largely on the amount of money available. In 1909 the Government established a Training College for teachers, and a Technical School, both at Accra. Other training colleges for teachers were established by the missions: the Basel mission settled at Akropong, the Methodists built Wesley College, Kumasi, the Bremen mission had a small theological seminary at Ho in Togo-

land, and the Roman Catholics had colleges at Bla in Togoland
and at Amisano near Cape Coast. During the war of 1914-18 the
work of the Basel and Bremen missionaries was taken over by the
missionaries of the Church of Scotland, and the Scottish missionaries organized the churches into independent Presbyterian
churches. When the Basel and Bremen missionaries began to
return after the war, they worked side by side with their Scottish
colleagues.[14]

A new Education Ordinance was passed in 1925. The Board
of Education under this ordinance consisted of the Governor, the
Colonial Secretary, three nominated officials, the Director of
Education and the Principal of Achimota College, four nominated
mission representatives, and four nominated African members, one
of which was to be a head chief. All teachers were to be registered,
and nobody was to teach unless he was a registered teacher;
registered teachers were not to be paid at a lower rate than should
be prescribed by the Board;[15] and the Board was empowered to
make detailed rules, subject to the approval of the Legislative
Council, for the control of education. The rules laid down by the
Board provide that all schools, assisted or non-assisted, shall be
open to inspection by the officers of the Education Department.
Schedules of curriculum, certificates of teachers, minimum standards of attendance, classroom space and so forth are provided.

The Ordinance of 1925 made it possible for any school to
qualify for a grant by attaining certain standards of efficiency; the
purpose of the Ordinance was to multiply as rapidly as possible the
schools classed as efficient. This aim was achieved, and the number
of schools on the assisted list rose year by year. Grants were paid on
the basis of the salary bill, on a scale determined by the school's
efficiency; and thus the Government expenditure on grants-in-aid
rose steadily. In 1933 it was felt that a halt must be called to this
infinite climb, and a system of block grants was instituted. A
mission or other educational body received a grant for a period of
three years, and could apply the money more or less at its discretion, instead of having to spend all the grant earned by a school

[14] This brief summary of educational history is largely based on the historical
section of the Report of the Educationists Committee appointed on 5th March,
1920.
[15] The salary scales were laid down by the Education Rules; but no minimum was
prescribed for teachers in non-assisted schools.

on that school. This block grant system had two advantages: from the Government's point of view it enabled the amount of grant to be controlled, instead of rising automatically year by year; from the point of view of the mission (or Primary Educational Unit, to use the official phrase) it enabled a young and struggling school to be helped out of the grant earned by the schools that were prosperous and well-established. The change did not have the effect, which might have been feared, of stopping the establishment of new schools.

From 1937 to 1941 a local committee sat to overhaul the country's educational system. It recommended among other changes the establishment of a new Central Advisory Committee and of district education committees. The Central Advisory Committee was duly established, and met for the first time in 1942. It is composed of the Director of Education and the Principal of Achimota, three representatives of missions and other educational bodies, one for female education, and four Africans; of whom one must be a paramount chief, one a teacher, and one an Ashanti representative. The first experimental district education committee met soon afterwards, and by the end of 1945 fourteen committees had been established. The district committees included representatives of the Government, of the native authorities, the educational agencies, and the teachers. People were always willing to contribute money for education, and local expenditure on education rose rapidly; in Ashanti for example it jumped from just under six thousand pounds in 1945 to over sixty thousand three years later. As the 1951 Local Government Ordinance comes into full effect, the district education committees are becoming absorbed into the new structure of local government very much on United Kingdom lines.

Until 1935 there was no spectacular increase in the number of children attending primary school. The figure increased gradually from about 15,000 in 1902 to about 50,000 in 1924, and there it levelled off. The educational policy, and especially the system of grants, then in force encouraged an increase in efficiency rather than an increase in enrolment; but there was not yet an overwhelming pressure of public demand for education. After 1935 however, such a demand began to grow, and during the war years the pressure became heavier and heavier. Hundreds of unassisted schools sprang up, most of them ill-housed, ill-equipped, staffed with untrained teachers, and unregistered. During the immediate post-war years, the understaffed Education Department grappled with the problem as best it could, concentrating its efforts largely on increasing the supply of trained teachers.

One of the first actions of the Nkrumah Government in 1951 was to introduce an accelerated development plan for education. The plan aimed at providing as soon as possible a basic six-year primary course for all children. The plan began to come into effect in January 1952 with the beginning of the new school year. Extensive schemes of emergency teacher training naturally were involved. Primary school enrolment increased thus:

1935	...	...	...	...	63,000
1945	...	...	...	...	185,000
1951	...	...	...	...	301,000
1957	...	...	...	...	456,000

With such an increase, no administration in the world could have prevented a temporary drop in efficiency. One of the main efforts of the Government for some time to come must be to provide more trained teachers. In 1955 there were 29 teacher training colleges, with nearly 3,500 teachers in training.

For a long time, secondary education lagged far behind primary. The Government took the view that its first business was to provide primary education for all; and that until this is done, its expenditure on secondary education must be limited.[16] In 1924, however, it founded Achimota College, a co-educational institution which for some years provided education from kindergarten to university grade. The entire capital outlay of well over half a million pounds was provided by the Government, and the Government at first financed the school's recurrent expenditure. In 1930, however, Achimota was transferred to the control of a council of governors, the Government nominating three representatives out of fifteen. It thus became independent of Government control, but continued to enjoy Government financial support, its annual grant being fixed

[16]The Government's policy on this matter is open to criticism. It is wasteful to provide large numbers of children with primary education but to provide very little opportunity of secondary education. Education once begun must be continued, and though good secondary education is costly, the Government should have expanded it in step with the expansion of primary. Guggisberg's successors should have continued his policy, and aimed at a 1938 enrolment in Government and assisted secondary schools of some 4,000 instead of 919. Much trouble would have been saved, and Ghana today would have been better equipped.

at £68,000, later reduced to £48,000, at which figure it remained for several years. It is not surprising that with this large annual expenditure on secondary education[17] the Government was disinclined to spend large sums in grants to other secondary schools; but it was natural also that other secondary schools should feel that they deserved a share of the Government's bounty. Achimota took over in 1927 the Government Training College.

The educational experiment of Achimota was founded by the Governor, Sir Gordon Guggisberg, as a result of the Phelps-Stokes educational commission, which toured Africa in 1920. It was originally planned as a pair of secondary schools, one for boys and the other for girls; but the whole scheme was revolutionized by the first principal, the Rev. A. G. Fraser, and his African right-hand man Dr. Aggrey. The combination of Fraser, with his experience, energy and enthusiasm, and Aggrey, with his genius for friendship, his slogan "Only the best is good enough for Africa", and his preference (to use his own homely metaphor) for catching flies with molasses rather than with vinegar, was irresistible. It was these two men who set before Achimota the high ideal of providing an education European in thoroughness but African as well as European in content. The future of Ghana will depend very much on its success in achieving this educational aim.

In 1902 there were sixty-five pupils in secondary schools. In 1938 there were 919 pupils in the four assisted secondary schools (including Achimota) with over 2,000 others in unassisted schools, many of which were of dubious value. By the end of 1948 there were ten assisted schools with 2,225 pupils, and the unassisted schools had almost as many again. In 1955 there were thirty-one Government and assisted secondary schools with 7,711 pupils; the staff of these schools had 238 graduates and 265 non-graduates.

When Sir Gordon Guggisberg founded Achimota College, he expressed the hope that it would one day develop into a university college for the whole of British West Africa. This hope soon became a national aspiration of the Gold Coast, and as Achimota developed its post-secondary classes the Gold Coast felt that its aspirations were near fulfilment. In 1943 the Secretary of State appointed a Commission to investigate the whole question of

[17] Not all this money was spent by Achimota on secondary work; some of it went on post-secondary work, as well as on teacher-training.

higher education in British West Africa. The Commission, under the chairmanship of Colonel Walter Elliot, visited West Africa in 1944 and reported in the following year. While agreeing in their analysis of the problem and in most of their recommendations, the members of the Commission were unable to agree on the immediate steps to be taken, the majority recommending the establishment of three university colleges, one for each of the major territories; and the minority regarding this as not immediately practicable, and preferring the establishment of one university college and a number of feeder institutions.

For the Gold Coast public, the immediate interest of the question was the future of Achimota; the arguments between the majority and the minority of the Elliot Commission meant little to the Gold Coast as long as its aspirations on behalf of its national institution were fulfilled. The new Secretary of State had been a member of the Elliot Commission and had signed the minority report. It soon appeared that the British Government was inclined to favour the minority recommendations and to establish a new university college in Nigeria with the aid of a large grant from Imperial funds, Achimota being left to its own devices and urged to content itself with the modest function of a feeder college to the Nigerian university-to-be. This roused Gold Coast national feeling. A strong local committee reported unanimously in favour of developing Achimota College towards full university status. The British Government bowed to the storm, and in 1947 it was announced that university colleges would be established both in Nigeria and in the Gold Coast. The University College of the Gold Coast was established on a site close to Achimota, and in 1951 a College of Technology was established at Kumasi. Both these institutions, and other developments in education and other social services, were made possible by grants made from United Kingdom funds under the Colonial Development and Welfare Acts of 1945 and later years.

COMMUNICATIONS

The first telegraph in the Gold Coast was the field telegraph used by the British in the 1874 war, in imitation of which the Ashanti ran a long string from tree to tree twenty years later, thinking it had magic powers to win battles. The first permanent telegraph was a line two and a half miles long from Accra to Christiansborg, erected in 1882; and three years later Aburi, twenty-five miles from Accra, was connected by telegraph. Telegraph and telephone communication has been greatly extended since 1920, and in 1939 there were five thousand miles of telegraphs and nearly ten thousand miles of trunk telephones. The length of motorable roads, which was 1,200 miles in 1918, increased to 3,150 miles in 1922, and 6,350 miles in 1937. There have been great developments since 1945.

The Sagrenti war was responsible for introducing to the Gold Coast not only the first telegraph but also, if not the first railway, at least the first consignment of railway material. Material for a line from Cape Coast to Prasu was actually landed, and a number of steam traction engines for road work. Neither road nor railway engines were any use; there was no road suitable for the traction engines, and Sir Garnet Wolseley's timetable would not allow the construction of a railway line through 100 miles of unsurveyed forest. One of the Ashanti messengers, when being dispatched to Kumasi with a letter, was given a short ride out of Cape Coast on one of the traction engines, with a view to impressing on him the might of the British. The experiment was not a success, for the engine broke down just outside the town, and he had to get down and walk; while it was impossible to tell from his impassive countenance what he thought of the whole affair.[18]

The first railway construction began in 1898, and in 1903 the line from Sekondi reached Kumasi. A line from Accra to Kumasi was begun in 1909, but construction was delayed through the war, and the first through train did not run till 1923. A Central Province line from Huni Valley on the Sekondi-Kumasi line to Kade was completed in 1927. In 1956, the Central Province line was linked with the line from Accra to Kumasi.

Ghana has no natural harbours. Sir Gordon Guggisberg, who planned Achimota and the 1925 Education Ordinance, set on foot the first drive for a better road system, established provincial councils, built the country its first big up-to-date hospital, and devised a scheme for training Africans for responsible posts in Government service, began the building of an artificial harbour at

[18] Claridge, II, 47, 81.

Takoradi, opened in 1928 and greatly extended in 1956. A new harbour, even bigger, is being built at Tema, east of Accra.

The most spectacular development of all will be the Volta River Project. The Volta, hitherto untamed, was bridged for the first time in 1956, but that is only the beginning of its servitude. The project is to throw a dam across the Volta gorge and generate electricity. The electricity would be used to work a bauxite quarry at present uneconomic, and to smelt the ore into crude ingots. Power and irrigation water would be available for light industry in the Accra plains. In addition, the Volta and the Afram would back up and form two long narrow lakes, on which water transport would become possible. By Independence Day, a good deal of preliminary surveying had been carried out, but no decision had been taken. The enormous capital outlay was to be provided partly from United Kingdom and partly from Ghana public funds, but partly also from British and Canadian aluminium firms; and the future of the project depended largely on whether Volta-produced aluminium would be able to compete with aluminium from other sources.

Ghana is a land of immense possibilities; its people achieved a high degree of unity and discipline in their struggle for self-government; and it sets out on its independent career with high hopes. Of course it has its difficulties. It has still much to do in economic development, it is very short of qualified men and women, and it may find, as other nations have found, that unity and discipline are easier to maintain during the struggle than during the enjoyment of victory. Nevertheless, Ghana has great advantages. Its people have the Englishman's practical common sense with the American's confidence. It has a nucleus of well-educated and devoted leaders. It has universal primary education, with some excellent secondary schools, a widespread system of adult education, and a pair of first-class higher institutions. Its society is broadly based on a land-holding peasantry with unbroken social traditions. African music, art and general culture are very much alive, and its people take a pride in their cultural heritage. If Ghana can continue thus to combine old traditions with new knowledge, it will show us a type of civilization which the world has not hitherto seen.

THE EUROPEAN FORTS ON THE GOLD COAST

Arranged in order from east to west; see map, page 92

1. Prinzenstein at Keta. Built by Danes 1784; besieged by the Anlo 1844, and rescued from starvation by the French warship *Abeille*. Bought by the British 1850.
2. Konigstein at Ada. Built by Danes 1784, bought by British 1850.
3. Friedensborg at Ningo. Built by Danes 1734, bought by British 1850.
4. Vernon at Prampram. Built by British about 1787, but soon abandoned.
5. Augustaborg at Teshi. Built by Danes 1787, bought by British 1850.
6. A small Portuguese fort stood near Accra during the first half of the sixteenth century; in 1578 it was taken and destroyed by the Accra.
7. Christiansborg at Osu near Accra. The site may have been occupied by the Portuguese from 1578 (after the loss of No. 6) till 1645. Castle built by Swedes 1657 and taken by Danes 1659. Sold to the Portuguese by the Danish second in command in 1679, and bought back from the Portuguese by the Danes three years later. Taken by Asameni and the Akwamu in 1693 and resold to the Danes next year. Bought by British 1850.
8. Crèvecœur at Accra. Built by Dutch 1650, taken by British in 1782, and restored to the Dutch three years later. The Dutch abandoned it for a short time in 1818, but afterwards reoccupied it. Ceded to the British in 1867, and renamed Ussher Fort.
9. James at Accra. Built by English in 1673; history uneventful.
10. For some time during the seventeenth century there was an English fort at Shido, but it was abandoned before 1700.
11. The Dutch built a fort at Beraku in 1667; it was taken by the

British in 1782 and restored to the Dutch in 1785, and later abandoned.

12. The British built a fort at Winneba in the seventeenth century. It was twice taken by the neighbouring people, the Agona, in 1663 and 1679, but restored. It was rebuilt and strengthened in 1694; in 1813 it was abandoned, but reoccupied two years later. For some years after 1812 it was customary for every British ship passing by Winneba to pour in a broadside from its guns into the town in revenge for the murder of the commandant of Winneba fort in that year.

13. Leydsamheid at Apam. Its name of Fort Patience was given it because the local people stubbornly opposed its construction by the Dutch, and the patient Dutch builders, who began it in 1697, did not finish it till 1702. Taken by British in 1782 and restored in 1785; taken and destroyed by Atta Wusu of Akim in 1811.

14. The British built a fort at Tantamkweri some time before 1726, and abandoned it in 1820.

15. Amsterdam at Kormantine. This spectacularly situated castle on a high ridge overlooking town and sea was built by the English in 1631, and taken by the Dutch under de Ruyter in 1665. Captain Shirley, R.N. took it in 1782 and it was restored to the Dutch three years later. The Ashanti occupied it in 1807; on their departure it was reoccupied by the Dutch and finally ceded to the British in 1867.

16. A small fortified house or 'lodge' at Egya was built by the English in 1663, and at once taken by the Dutch; retaken by Holmes in 1664, and when threatened by de Ruyter next year, evacuated and destroyed by the garrison.

17. William at Anomabu. Built by the English some time after 1673, presumably in the reign of William III. There was previously a Swedish fort at Anomabu, taken and destroyed by the Danes in 1659. Besieged by the Ashanti in 1807.

18. A small Portuguese fort at Anashan, occupied for a short time and abandoned soon after 1683.

19. A small 'lodge' built at Anashan by the English about 1660; taken by the Dutch in 1665 and subsequently abandoned.

20. Nassau at Mori. The Dutch established a post here in 1598, and built the castle in 1624. Taken by Holmes in 1664

and retaken by de Ruyter in 1665; taken again by Captain Shirley in 1782 and restored to the Dutch in 1785. Finally ceded to the British in 1867.

21. There was for a short time a small Dutch fort at Queen Anne's Point near Cape Coast, abandoned before 1662.

22. Fort Royal at Amanfur. Built by the Danes in 1658 and bought by the English in 1685.

23. Cape Coast Castle. Built by the Swedes in 1652, taken by the Danes in 1659, by the local people, the Fetu, in 1660, possibly by the Dutch in 1661, and by the English in 1662. Taken by the Dutch in 1663, but retaken by Holmes in 1664, and (alone among the English possessions) held against de Ruyter in the following year. Subsequent history uneventful.

24. St. George at Elmina. Built by the Portuguese in 1482, probably *not* on the site of earlier French work. Taken by the Dutch in 1637, greatly strengthened, and provided with satellite redoubts. Bought by the British in 1872.

25. Vredenburg at Kommenda. Built by the Dutch in 1688; unsuccessfully attacked by the Kommenda people seven years later. Taken and destroyed by the British in 1782.

26. In 1798 a local chief named John Kabes built a small fort at Kommenda, armed with guns bought from the British; but it was soon abandoned.

27. The English built a fort at Kommenda about 1670; they later abandoned it, but rebuilt it in 1695. It was ceded to the Dutch in 1867 and abandoned.

28. There was at one time a small French post at Kommenda, taken and destroyed by the local people in 1688.

29. St. Sebastian at Shama. Built by the Portuguese; taken and enlarged by the Dutch in 1640. Taken by Holmes and retaken by de Ruyter, 1664 and 1665; bought by the British in 1872.

30. Orange at Sekondi. Built by the Dutch about 1670; taken and destroyed by the Ahanta in 1694. The Dutch rebuilt it, and it was finally bought by the British in 1872.

31. The English built a fort at Sekondi about 1680. This fort, like the Dutch fort, was taken by the Ahanta in 1698, four years after the capture of Fort Orange. The English rebuilt it, and it was again taken, this time by the French, in 1779.

Ceded to the Dutch in 1867 and bought back by the British in 1872.

32. Witsen at Takoradi. Built by the Swedes about 1652, possibly (but improbably) on the site of an old French post. Taken by the Danes in 1657 and very soon afterwards by the Dutch; again taken and retaken by Holmes and de Ruyter in 1664 and 1665. Destroyed and abandoned by the Dutch, though the site was subsequently reoccupied by a smaller building.

33. Batenstein at Butri. The Dutch established a post here in 1598, and built the castle in 1640. The usual vicissitudes in 1664 and 1665; bought by the British in 1872.

34. Metal Cross at Dixcove. Built by the English in 1691; attacked by the Dixcove people in 1697, the siege being raised after a negotiated agreement which gave more favourable trading terms to the African traders. Ceded to the Dutch in 1867 and bought back by the British in 1872.

35. Apollonia at Beyin. Built by the British in 1750, ceded to the Dutch in 1867, and abandoned.

36. Dorothea at Akwida. Built by the Brandenburgers in 1685; taken by the local people in 1690 but restored in 1698; abandoned about 1709.

37. A small fort was built by the Brandenburgers at Takrama in 1694, but abandoned in 1708 or 1709.

38. Gross Friedrichsburg, between Axim and Cape Three Points, built by the Brandenburgers in 1685; abandoned with the rest of the Brandenburg possessions in 1708 or 1709. The castle was intermittently occupied by the local chieftain from then until 1725, when the Dutch occupied the place to forestall other possible rivals. They never made effective use of it, however.

39. St. Anthony at Axim. Built by the Portuguese very early in their occupation, and greatly enlarged and strengthened in 1515. This was the last Portuguese fort to hold out against the Dutch, who did not take it till 1642. Holmes and de Ruyter took and retook it in 1664 and 1665, and the place was finally bought by the British in 1872.

40. Duma on the river Ankobra. Built by the Portuguese in 1623, and destroyed by an earthquake in 1636. The Portuguese

o

did not rebuild the fort, but it was later rebuilt by the Dutch soon after their occupation of the Portuguese possessions. They soon abandoned it, however.

41. Ruyghaver and
42. Elise Carthago, both on the river Ankobra, were built by the Dutch about 1640, but soon abandoned, Ruyghaver having been taken by the local people about 1680.

* * *

It may be convenient to summarize this catalogue. Until the Dutch settlements of 1598, the only posts held on the Gold Coast were the Portuguese forts at Axim, Shama, Elmina and Accra, with possibly in addition a 'lodge' at Cape Coast. From 1598 to 1640 these Portuguese settlements had to compete against the Dutch trading posts, not yet converted into forts, at Mori, Butri, Kormantine and Kommenda.

If we ignore the short-lived Swedish and Brandenburger ventures, what may be described as the regular eighteenth century establishment was as follows:

Dutch	British	Danish
Crèvecœur (Accra)	James (Accra)	Christiansborg (Osu)
Beraku	Winneba	
Apam	Anomabu	
Mori	Cape Coast	
Elmina	Kommenda	
Kormantine	Sekondi	
Kommenda (Vredenburg)	Dixcove	
Shama	Beyin	
Sekondi (Orange)		
Butri		
Axim		

There were, of course, minor fluctuations.

In the latter half of the eighteenth century the Danes expanded their holding from the one castle of Christiansborg to five: Keta, Ada, Ningo, Teshi and Christiansborg. All were bought by the British in 1850.

From the treaty of 1867 until the final departure of the Dutch in 1872, the list of forts was as follows:

Dutch	British
Elmina	Keta
Kommenda	Ada
Shama	Ningo
Sekondi (both)	Teshi
Butri	Christiansborg
Dixcove	Ussher Fort (Crèvecœur)
Axim	James Fort
Beyin	Apam
	Kormantine
	Anomabu
	Mori
	Cape Coast

Beraku, Winneba and other smaller places had by then been abandoned.

THE KINGS OF ASHANTI

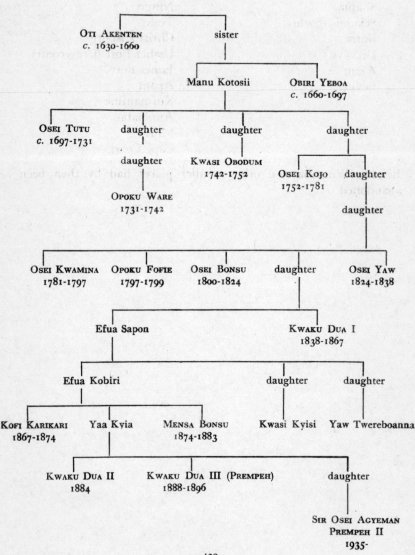

OTI AKENTEN
c. 1630-1660   sister

Manu Kotosii   OBIRI YEBOA
c. 1660-1697

OSEI TUTU
c. 1697-1731   daughter   daughter   daughter

daughter   KWASI OBODUM
1742-1752   OSEI KOJO
1752-1781   daughter

OPOKU WARE
1731-1742

daughter

OSEI KWAMINA
1781-1797   OPOKU FOFIE
1797-1799   OSEI BONSU
1800-1824   daughter   OSEI YAW
1824-1838

Efua Sapon   KWAKU DUA I
1838-1867

Efua Kobiri   daughter   daughter

KOFI KARIKARI
1867-1874   Yaa Kyia   MENSA BONSU
1874-1883   Kwasi Kyisi   Yaw Twereboanna

KWAKU DUA II
1884   KWAKU DUA III (PREMPEH)
1888-1896   daughter

SIR OSEI AGYEMAN
PREMPEH II
1935-

GENERAL INDEX

INDEX TO MAPS

GEORGE ALLEN & UNWIN LTD
London: 40 Museum Street, W.C.1

Auckland: 24 Wyndham Street
Bombay: 15 Graham Road, Ballard Estate, Bombay 1
Calcutta: 17 Chittaranjan Avenue, Calcutta 13
Cape Town: 109 Long Street
Karachi: Metherson's Estate, Wood Street, Karachi 2
New Delhi: 13-14 Ajmeri Gate Extension, New Delhi 1
São Paulo: Avenida 9 de Julho 1138-Ap. 51
Sydney, N.S.W.: Bradbury House, 55 York Street
Toronto: 91 Wellington Street West

KWAME NKRUMAH

BANKOLE TIMOTHY

Kwame Nkrumah, the first Prime Minister and outstanding personality in the Gold Coast, has hitherto been a shadowy figure; but his personal influence and the dynamism of the policies he has shaped have not hitherto been appreciated largely through lack of reliable knowledge.

Bankole Timothy's biography is, therefore, most timely. The author is well known both in his own country and in England as a shrewd and vivid reporter of the West African scene. He is personally acquainted with Dr. Nkrumah, though not blind to what he considers to be his shortcomings. Mr. Timothy traces Nkrumah's career from his childhood in the Gold Coast to America as a student, then to England, and finally back to the Gold Coast and the battle for independence that he led and won. It is a moving story of imprisonment followed by a phenomenal rise to power. His political strategy, his formidable struggles with the British Government and political opponents in the Gold Coast and his influence on the liberation movement in Africa are vividly portrayed.

Illustrated. Demy 8vo. 16s. net

FRENCH WEST AFRICA

VIRGINIA THOMPSON AND RICHARD ADLOFF

There have been a great many books on Africa since the war but astonishingly few in English that deal with the vast and important tropical areas under French Administration. As to the most extensive of these—French West Africa—the lack is particularly striking, contrasting as it does with the large number of works concerning adjacent Nigeria and Ghana. The few studies of French West Africa produced thus far by British and American writers have been mostly in specialized periodicals, and no work on the Federation as a whole has been available to the English-reading public.

The authors have provided a general and reliable survey of the main political, economic, social and cultural developments in the whole territory of French West Africa, supplemented by an analysis which takes into account both official and non-official French and African viewpoints. Some historical background is provided — especially where it is helpful to the understanding of current developments—but the book's emphasis is upon the rapid evolution of French West Africa, in many fields, since the end of the Second World War. While most welcome as a reference work for students, the book will also be read more widely for the light it casts on the role that the French West African group of territories may play in the future "Eurafrica".

Illustrated. Demy 8vo. About 45s. net

GEORGE ALLEN & UNWIN LTD